BETWEEN THE
betweoh
ROD AND THE
gyrd   *7*
ROOD
rod

BETWEEN THE ROD AND THE ROOD

betweoh
gyrd *7*
rod

Childhood and Monastic Formation in Late Anglo-Saxon and Norman England, c.950-1200.

cildhad *7* *mynsterlic* *on*
angel cynn *7* *norðmandisc* *engla lond*
gear-gerim

se writere
STEVEN G. HODGSON

First published in the United Kingdom by
Publishing Push Ltd,
2-4 Petworth Road, Haslemere, Surrey, England, GU27 2HR

Copyright © 2024 by Dr. Steven Hodgson

All rights reserved. No part of this book may be reproduced or used in any manner without written permission of the copyright owner except for the use of quotations in a book review.

First paperback edition 2024

Cover image of Anglo-Saxon "oblation" c.1031:
BL MS Stowe 944, fol. 7r.

Image permission from The British Library

978-1-80541-334-9 (paperback)
978-1-80541-335-6 (eBook)
978-1-80541-336-3 (hardcover)

CONTENTS

Acknowledgements   vii
Abbreviations   ix

INTRODUCTION: MONASTIC CHILDHOOD   1

CHAPTER ONE: DISCIPLINE AND BEHAVIOUR   42

Anglo-Saxon England:
   Infancy   43
   Boyhood   49
Anglo-Norman England: 68
   Infancy   69
   Boyhood   71
Communities of Religious Women:
   Infancy   92
   Girlhood   96

CHAPTER TWO: LITURGICAL FORMATION   111

Anglo-Saxon England:
   Infancy   112
   Boyhood   113
Anglo-Norman England:
   Infancy   126
   Boyhood   127
Communities of Religious Women:
   Infancy   138
   Girlhood   140

CHAPTER THREE: EDUCATION AND LITERACY   148

Anglo-Saxon England:
  Boyhood   150
Anglo-Norman England:
  Boyhood   173
Communities of Religious Women:
  Infancy   182
  Girlhood   183

CHAPTER FOUR: ADOLESCENCE AND ADULTHOOD   192

Anglo-Saxon England:
  The end(s) of boyhood   193
Anglo-Norman England:
  The end(s) of boyhood   203
Communities of Religious Women:
  The end(s) of girlhood   218

EVIDENCE OF CHILDREN'S "VOICES"   226

CONCLUSIONS   236

Infancy   239
Childhood   240
Adolescence   247

Bibliography   255

ACKNOWLEDGEMENTS

The manuscript behind this work has been in development for several years, originating in my D.Phil thesis at Lady Margaret Hall, The University of Oxford. As someone who attended a comprehensive school on free-school meals, I would first like to acknowledge the many teachers whose instruction and advice guided me onto this path. I would also like to acknowledge and thank the very generous support of the Wolfson Foundation, without whose financial backing between 2013 and 2016 I could never have undertaken the research which is present in this volume. I also owe a very significant debt of gratitude to my doctoral supervisor, Rev. and Regius Professor of Ecclesiastical History at Christ Church College, Sarah Foot; her guidance, patience, and encouragement were invaluable, and I shall forever treasure the opportunity I enjoyed to study and write under her guidance.

I would also like to extend my everlasting thanks to Dr. Maroula Perisanidi, who first expressed and fostered a belief in my abilities:

Για σένανε, αυτό το βιβλίο, είναι γραμμένο.

Moreover, I would like to thank my friend and proofreader Dr. Jason Dungca. In spurring me on to publication, I give my very deepest and heartfelt thanks to Jack Ryan-Phillips, who has been the most supportive, and thoughtful source of advice and expertise for many years, and I also thank Catherine Cockfield, who has been a constant and helpful source of encouragement in undertaking this endeavour. Of my family, I acknowledge the help given me by my father, Phillip, who provided vital financial support when I needed it most. I owe a great debt also to my mum, Teresa Hodgson (née Boyce), who, despite finishing her own education at fifteen, and having no interest in history, has given me every measure of support that has been within her power to give. I can hardly do justice to the value of the support she has given, but it should suffice to say that I simply could not have set these words to this paper without her. Any errors that remain are, of course, entirely my own.

The *Regularis Concordia:* showing Bishop Æthelwold, King Eadgar, and Archbishop Dunstan seated. By permission of the British Library (BL, Cotton, Tiberius A III, f. 2v)

ABBREVIATIONS

ÆlfBColl   Ælfric Bata, *Colloquia*, ed. and trans. Scott Gwara and David Porter, *Anglo-Saxon Conversations: The Colloquies of Ælfric Bata* (Woodbridge: Boydell Press, 1997).

ÆlfCHom I   Ælfric's Catholic Homilies: The First Series: Text, EETS s.s. 17 (Oxford: University Press, 1997).

ÆlfColl   Ælfric of Eynsham, *Colloquium*, ed. George N. Garmonsway, *Ælfric's Colloquy* (London: Methuen, 1939), rev. ed. Exeter: University Press, 1991.

ASE   *Anglo-Saxon England* (Journal)

BL   British Library

BT   Bosworth-Toller Dictionary of Old English: http://bosworth.ff.cuni.cz/. Last updated c. 2013.

CCCC   Cambridge, Corpus Christi College

CCCM   *Corpus Christianorum Continuatio Mediaevalis*

CCSL   *Corpus Christianorum*, Series Latina (Turnhout: Brepols, 1952-).

CCM   *Corpus Consuetudinum Monasticarum*, ed. Kassius Hallinger (Siegburg: Franciscum Schmitt, 1963-).

C&S   *Councils and Synods, with other documents relating to the English Church AD. 871-1204*, ed. Dorothy Whitelock, Martin Brett, Christopher N. L. Brooke and Frederick M. Powicke (Oxford: Clarendon Press, 1981), 2 vols.

Constitutiones   Lanfranc of Canterbury, *Constitutiones*, ed. and trans. David Knowles and Christopher N. L. Brooke, *The Monastic Constitutions of Lanfranc*, OMT (Oxford: Clarendon Press, 2002).

CSEL   *Corpus Scriptorum Ecclesiasticorum Latinorum*

DOE   *Dictionary of Old English Web Corpus: A to H online*, Dictionary of Old English Project, ed. A. Cameron, A.

	C. Amos, A. Healey et al (Toronto, 2016): http://tapor.library.utoronto.ca/doe/?E04749.
DOEWC	*Dictionary of Old English Web Corpus*, ed. Antonette diPaolo Healey with John Price Wilkin and Xin Xiang. (Toronto: Dictionary of Old English Project, 2009): http://tapor.library.utoronto.ca/doecorpus/.
DRV	Douay-Rheims Latin Vulgate: http:www.drbo.org/lvb.
EETS	Early English Text Society
o.s.	Ordinary Series
s.s.	Supplementary Series
EGA	Ælfric of Eynsham, *Excerptiones de arte grammatica anglice*, ed. Julius Zupitza., *Ælfrics Grammatik und Glossar: Text und Varienten*, Sammlung englischer Denkmäler in kritischen Ausgaben (Berlin: Weidmann, 1880); repr. with introduction by Helmut Gneuss, Hildesheim: Weidmann, 2003.
EME	Ælfric of Eysnham, *Epistula ad monachos Egneshamnenses directa*, ed. and trans. Christopher Jones, *Letter to the Monks of Eynsham*, Cambridge studies in Anglo Saxon England 24 (Cambridge: University Press, 1998).
Gneuss, *Handlist*	Helmut Gneuss (ed.), *Handlist of Anglo-Saxon Manuscripts: a list of manuscripts and manuscript fragments written or owned in England up to 1100*, (Tempe, Arizona: Center (sic) for Medieval and Renaissance Studies, 2001).
HBS	Henry Bradshaw Society
MGH	Monumenta Germaniae Historica
Auct. ant.	Auctores antiquissimi
Capit.	Leges, Capitularia regum Francorum, 2 vols.
Capit. Episc.	Capitula Episcoporum
Conc.	Concilia, Concilia aevi Karolini (742-842), 2 vols
Script. supp. tom.	Scriptores, Supplementa Tomorum
MS	Manuscript
OERB	*The Old English Rule of Saint Benedict*, ed. Arnold Schröer, *Die Angelsächsischen Prosabearbeitungen der Benediktinerregel*, Bibliothek der angelsächsischen Prosa 2 (Kassel: G.H. Wigand, 1885-88); repr. with introduction

	by Helmut Gneuss, Darmstadt: Wissenschaftliche Buchgesellschaft, 1964.
OMT	Oxford Medieval Texts
PG	*Patrologia cursus completus series: Graeca*, ed. Jacques-Paul Migne (Paris: Garnier fratres, 1857-66), 161 vols.
PL	*Patrologia cursus completus series: Latina*, ed. Jacques-Paul Migne (Paris: Garnier fratres, 1841-64), 221 vols.
RC	Æthelwold of Winchester, *Regularis Concordia*, ed. and trans. Thomas Symons, *Regularis Concordia Anglicae Nationis Monachorum Sanctimonialiumque. The Monastic Agreement of the Monks and Nuns of the English Nation*, Medieval Classics (New York: Oxford University Press, 1953).
RSB	*The Rule of Saint Benedict*, ed. and trans. Bruce Venarde, Dumbarton Oaks Medieval Library 6 (Cambridge Mass: Harvard University, 2011).

Note: All References to the Psalter and Bible will follow the *Douay-Rheims Vulgate* (see DRV above). My own translations are also marked as such in references.

Cover Images: Prefatory drawings in the *Liber Vitae* suggesting the oblation of a child into the Benedictine monastery of New Minster in Winchester, c.1031. MS written initially by Ælfsige, see British Library MS Stowe 944 fol.7r. By permission of the British Library.

Monastic Houses in England c.950-1100*

	Christ Church		Old Minster	Nunnaminster
[1]	St. Augustine's	[2]	New Minster	Hyde

* Watton Priory is a later foundation (1150) included in this study

** Religious Chapter of Regular Canons

INTRODUCTION: MONASTIC CHILDHOOD

Tibi gratias ago, summe Rex, qui [...] odelerium patrem meum aspirasti ut me sibi penitus abidi caret, et tibi omnimodis subiugaret. Rainaldo igitur monacho plorans plorantem me tradidit et pro amore tuo in exilium destinavit nec me umquam postea vidit. Paternis nempe votis tenellus puer obviare non presumpsi, sed in omnibus illi utro adquieri [...] A venerabili Mainerio abbate (c.1066-89) in monasterio uticensi undecimo aetatis meae anno ad monachatum susceptus sum, undecimaque kalendas octobris dominico clericali ritu tonsoratus sum. Nomen quoque 'Vitalis' pro anglico vocamine quod Normannis absonum censebatur michi impositum est. Idus Martii cum xvi essem annorum, iussu Serlonis electi Giselbertus, Luxoviensis presul (c.1077-1101), ordinavit me subdiaconum.[1]

This account of childhood memory, written by Orderic Vitalis (c.1075-1141) in the last year of his life, has long transfixed modern readers interested in the lives of medieval children. Orderic, a monastic historian of early twelfth-century Normandy, belonged to an influential group of

---

1 Orderic Vitalis, *Historia Ecclesiastica*, ed. and trans. Marjorie Chibnall, *The Ecclesiastical History of Orderic Vitalis*, OMT (Oxford, 1968-1980), VI, bk. 13, pp. 552-3, 554-5: 'I give thanks to you, supreme King, who [...] did inspire my father, Odelerius, to renounce me utterly and submit me in all things to your governance. Weeping, he gave me, a weeping child (*plorans*), into the care of the monk, Reginald, and sent me away into exile for love of You. He never saw me again. I, a mere boy, did not presume to oppose my father's wishes but in all things willingly obeyed him [...] I was accepted to be an oblate monk in the abbey of Saint-Evroult by the venerable Abbot Mainer in the eleventh year of my age and was given a clerical tonsure on Sunday the twenty-first of September 1085. In place of my English name, Orderic, which sounded harsh to the Normans, the name *Vitalis* (lit. 'lively') was given me, [and] on the fifteenth of March 1091, when I was just sixteen years old, Gilbert, Bishop of Lisieux ordained me as sub-deacon'.

men and women in medieval Europe of the Latin west who are now collectively described by scholars as 'oblates'. These individuals had been 'offered' (*offerare, oblatus*) by their parents to monasteries in childhood and were raised inside the cloister to become religious. Few of those who grew up in monasteries provided any account of their religious entry, however, and so Orderic's reflections here, have, over the intervening centuries, and with the emergence of an historiographical canon on monastic recruitment, come to dominate historians' views of oblation and represent the voices of oblates generally.[2] Orderic's recollection of his oblation, and the processes by which he entered a religious house in Normandy at the age of eleven, therefore provides a useful entry point for a book on this subject. His first-hand account provides us with a clear basis from which we can recognise that oblation had a life-long significance, encouraging him to adopt a monastic view of his life as part of a Divine Plan and to justify his father's decision to give him away.

Many hundreds if not thousands of children were given by their parents to religious houses across Europe in the early and high Middle Ages, however, and Orderic's account, useful though it has been to historical research on oblation, is rather singular. It is also rather slim, and represents only a handful of initial moments, centred on his entry into religion. His brief recollection tells us almost nothing of his monastic training between the age of eleven and the age of sixteen, when he was ordained, and, what memories of childhood he does provide also appear to have been deeply coloured by retrospection as an adult. If it is clear too that this portrait does not tell us much about the lives of other boys, who lived in other regions of Europe, who were born into different generations, and who encountered different customs and religious values in different houses after oblation, then it is clear that his words tell us even less about girls who entered religious communities of women in a similar period.

---

2 For example, Robert Bartlett, *England under the Norman and Angevin Kings: 1075-1225* (Oxford, 2000), p. 414: 'Traditional Benedictine monasticism presumed that large numbers would begin the monastic life as child oblates. A notable example was Orderic Vitalis . . .'. See also Conrad Leyser and Lesley Smith (eds.), *Motherhood, Religion, and Society in Medieval Europe, 400-1400: Essays Presented to Henrietta Leyser* (Farnham, 2011), p. 96.

INTRODUCTION: MONASTIC CHILDHOOD

We possess a large number of surviving documents which illuminate aspects of the lives of some of the many children who shared in Orderic's oblate status. The writings of contemporary religious authors throw light onto the different ways in which children entered religious communities and were cared for by those who raised them to become religious. Medieval school-texts, used by teachers to organise experiences of formal instruction, demonstrate that at least some monastic children were educated carefully. They indicate that contemporary religious recognised the importance of children, and went to extraordinary lengths to equip them with literary skills and forms of conceptual and socio-behavioural knowledge that would secure their communities for future generations. Monastic customaries, documents which were intended to organise the lives of monks and nuns, reveal more about the lives of children after oblation too, and show that they were initiated into the routines of the *Opus Dei*, learning cycles of monastic intercessory prayer framed by the hourly, daily, weekly, and yearly recital of Christian scripture.

Monastic histories also reveal that religious children were valued as conveyers of community memory. Indeed, several monastic historians active in Europe between the tenth and twelfth centuries appear to have begun their religious lives as oblates.[3] Historical writers even sought out the testimonies of religious men and women who had entered their communities as children and who were assumed to constitute particularly trustworthy witnesses to past events. We find one such example in the case of Eadmer, a monk of Christ Church, Canterbury (c.1060-1126), who sought out the senior monks who had entered Glastonbury as oblates before the Norman Conquest in order to confirm that Canterbury had acquired a collection of relics once held there.[4] Indeed, another oblate

---

3 Byrhtferth of Ramsey (c.970-1020), Eadmer of Canterbury (c.1060-1126), Orderic Vitalis (c.1075-1141), William of Malmesbury (c.1095-1143), Hugh Candidus (c.1095-1160), and probably Richard of Ely (fl.1170-90) being most prominent.
4 Eadmer of Canterbury, *Epistola ad Glastonienses*, in *Memorials of Saint Dunstan Archbishop of Canterbury*, ed. William Stubbs (London, 1874), pp. 412-22, at 421-2; trans. Richard Sharpe in *The Archaeology and History of Glastonbury Abbey: Essays in Honour of the Ninetieth Birthday of C. A. Raleigh Radford*, ed. Lesley Abrams, James P. Carley, and Courtenay A. R. Radford (Woodbridge, 1991), pp. 205-16: 'Puto superesse qui ante ista Normannorum tempora inibi nutriti in monachica religione fuerunt. Quaerite ab eis./I think that some survive [in your house] who were nurtured to become

author, Hugh Candidus of Peterborough, tells us that a 'little boy monk' (*puerulus monachus*) had even been trusted to decide who should become abbot of Whitby in c.1148, after his community had reached an empasse at a tied election.[5]

This wider body of evidence for oblate experience and for a contemporary appreciation of the importance of religious children within monastic communities has not, however, always found similar parallel in modern scholarship, much of which has either focussed on individual portraits, like Orderic's, or found a problematic origin in Philippe Ariès', *La Vie Familiale*.[6] This work was in fact fundamental to launching the entire field of childhood history. It played an important role in arguing for the historicity of childhood, demonstrating that childhood was a sociocultural construct, subject to change over time, and worthy of serious historical examination. But it also argued that childhood was a modern concept, and concluded, rather importantly for us, that there was no such thing as 'childhood' in the Middle Ages.[7]

Ariès' work has therefore provided one of the most puzzling of beginnings for research into religious childhood. While his research led to an explosion of interest in and publication on children's lives in a modern context, it also initially consigned medieval childhood to a kind of 'Dark Ages', confining scholarship to a rather narrow perspective which assumed that children lived in broadly the same manner throughout the medieval period; that children 'grew up' or took on adult roles relatively early, and that the lives of children were emotionally distressing, physically brutal, and subject to cultures where abuse was not only endemic, but normal.[8]

In this context, interest in Orderic Vitalis' emotional account appears less surprising. Many studies on medieval children which have emerged since the publication of Ariès' work have either followed or been affected

---

monks before these Norman times, please ask of them [what they remember]'.
5 W. T. Mellows (ed.), *The Chronicle of Hugh Candidus, a Monk of Peterborough* (London, 1949), p. 119.
6 Originally published in French and later translated into English, Philippe Ariès, *L'Enfant et la Vie Familiale sous l'Ancien Régime* (Paris, 1960); trans. Robert Baldick, *Centuries of Childhood* (London, 1962).
7 Ariès, *Centuries of Childhood*, trans. Baldick, p. 125: 'In medieval society the idea of childhood did not exist'.
8 Ariès, *Centuries of Childhood*, trans. Baldick, p. 129.

by his principles when approaching this kind of evidence, and have contributed further to an image of the difficult lives of medieval children. Lloyd DeMause's work on *Childhood in the Middle Ages*, for example, framed Ariès' picture of childhood in terms which emphasised the primitive nature of the Middle Ages, assuming that 'the further back in history one goes, the lower the level of child-care, and the more likely children are to be killed, abandoned, beaten, terrorized (sic) and sexually abused'.[9] DeMause characterised the Middle Ages as an embryonic stage in child-adult relations, and as little more than a starting point in a longer progression of parental attitudes which, beginning with 'Infanticide and Abandonment', led towards an enlightened and more child-friendly age of 'Socialising and Helping' in the twentieth century.[10]

David Herlihy's article on 'Medieval Children' contested parts of this picture, arguing that the process of Christianisation from Late Antiquity, and the adoption of ritual practices relating to baptism in particular, were positive for children. But his study also continued to frame childhood conditions in terms which assumed 'progress' over time, and only asserted instead that the Christian Church had been a primary motor for that development, and had humanised children in the eyes of adults, ensuring that previously widespread practices of infanticide became less acceptable.[11]

Linda Pollock's monograph, *Forgotten Children*, which focusses on the early modern period, is now considered to have played an important role in challenging some of the assumptions on which these studies depended. She argued, for example, that scholars working on the history of childhood not only tended to accept Ariès' thesis without question, but very often fell into a pattern of actively seeking out evidence of child neglect. This meant that scholars often ignored a far larger, if less sensational, corpus of evidence indicating that children were loved by their parents or guardians, and received the kinds of care which we could reasonably expect to find in any functional society, enabling children to

---

9 Lloyd DeMause, *The History of Childhood* (London, 1974), p. 10.
10 DeMause, *History of Childhood*, p. 10.
11 David Herlihy, 'Medieval Children', in *Essays on Medieval Civilization: The Walter Prescott Webb Memorial Lectures*, ed. Bede K. Lackner and Kenneth R. Philip (Austin Tex, 1978), pp. 109-41.

develop into socially and economically effective adults.[12]

It is the case of course that research on oblate monks predates the appearance of Ariès' thesis, and owes an origin to a period, long before the emergence of history and childhood history as academic fields, when the primary rationale for studying religious childhood was owed to the personal religious convictions of independent scholars. But these studies contributed little to our understanding of the lives of children beyond exploring the ritual by which they entered monasteries. Early studies of monastic oblation find a certain beginning in the works of religious historians who were writing in the early twentieth century, and perhaps chiefly in the works of M. P. Deroux and Dom Ursmer Berlière. But their researches primarily explored an early history of oblation as part of a wider church history, treating monastic childhood as an issue of recruitment, rather than as a kind of experience.[13]

Numerous studies which emerged later, in the 1970s and 1980s, were informed by early childhood studies, and began to integrate this history of oblation into currents of research that were more focussed on understanding childhood. Again, however, many of these framed experiences of oblation as symptomatic of medieval conditions and produced narratives which took a moralising approach, characterising oblation as just another, if more visible and more institutionalised, type of childhood mistreatment. John Boswell, in his *The Abandonment of Children*, identified oblation recruitment practices in this way, as a notionally more 'humane' alternative to otherwise prevailing practices of infanticide.[14] Joseph Lynch's study on *Simoniacal Entry into Religious Life* interpreted patchy evidence for the survival of oblation practices in the twelfth century in a similar way too, as an indication of the persistence of primitive attitudes and economic systems, and the result of an abiding attachment in the most socially and economically conservative areas of Europe to concepts

---

12 Linda A. Pollock, *Forgotten Children: Parent-Child relations from 1500 to 1900* (Cambridge, 1983), p. 8.
13 M. P. Deroux, *Les Origines de l'Oblature Bénédictine: Étude Historique* (Vienne, 1927); Ursmer Berlière, *Le Recrutement dans les Monastères Bénédictins aux XIIIe et XIVe Siècles* (Brussels, 1924).
14 John Boswell, *The Kindness of Strangers: The Abandonment of Children in Western Europe from Late Antiquity to the Renaissance* (New York, 1988).

of 'parental disposal'.[15]

Although this view of oblation continues to hold weight in some respects, the history of childhood has moved on from debates centred on Ariès, and ideas of the early medieval period as a time of pervasive neglect of children have undergone significant revision. Allison James and Alan Prout, who explicitly advanced a *New Sociology of Childhood* in the early 1990s, are perhaps emblematic of recent directions.[16] Their studies demonstrate a confluence which has emerged between scholars working in sociology and history and which has since contributed towards a shift in childhood history. This shift can be understood in terms of a process of theorisation, and in terms of an intellectual movement towards a more critical evaluation of how we represent childhood in narrative form and how, indeed, research methods determine our access to and understanding of childhood in historical contexts.[17]

This means that scholars now increasingly seek to understand and represent childhood on its own terms.[18] Scholars approach research on childhood in ways which recognise that 'childhood' refers to discrete experiences of gender, most readily associated with 'boyhood' and 'girlhood' in medieval texts (or 'boys' and 'girls'), and that the experience of childhood belonged to a wider continuum of experience – that it connected with and led into biologically and culturally determined 'adulthoods' – and that childhood was shaped by a wider historical context.[19] Sociologists also take more critical approaches to their understanding of 'child knowledge', pointing to the *acquired* nature of knowledge, and arguing for the need

---

15 Joseph Lynch, *Simoniacal Entry into Religious Life from 1000-1260: A Social, Economic and Legal Study* (Columbus Ohio, 1976), pp. 36-9.
16 Allison James and Alan Prout, *Constructing and Reconstructing Childhood: Contemporary Issues in the Sociological Study of Childhood* (New York, 1990), rev. ed., Washington DC, 1998.
17 For an evaluation of this 'Turn', see Sarah H. Matthews, 'A Window on the 'New' Sociology of Childhood', *Sociology Compass* 1 (2007), pp. 322-34.
18 For an example of this critique, see Judith Ennew, 'Time of Children or Time for Adults?', in *Childhood Matters: Social Theory, Practice, and Politics*, ed. Jens Qvortrup, Giovani Sgritta, and Helmut Wintersberger (Aldershot, 1994), passim, esp. p. 127.
19 Gisela Labouvie-Vief, Grühn Daniel, Manfred Diehl, and Mark Lumley, 'Developmental Trajectories or Ego-Development across the Adult Life-Span: Evidence from a 12-year Longitudinal Study', *International Journal of Psychology*, 43 (2008), p. 392.

to avoid projecting adult values, perspectives, and skills onto children.[20]

This shift now fundamentally shapes the direction of research in our field. These directions have provided particularly important road maps for historical researchers who might not otherwise sufficiently consider the significance of research questions or the way in which approaches to primary sources fundamentally determine our access to and understanding of children as historical subjects. They have also provided grounds from which we can better understand the role of children in the transmission of ideas, and, in the case of studies on religious childhood, ideas that were most important to monasteries, including religious identity and Christian doctrine. And they highlight a need to consciously represent perspectives which are often overlooked by virtue of the fact that researchers are adults – who tend not to value experiences most particular to children, such as growth, play, and ignorance.[21]

Yet while many areas of childhood history have responded to these currents, undergoing significant transformation and attracting renewed academic interest and publication, scholarship on monastic oblation has only partly responded.[22] Interest in the study of childhood in Anglo-Saxon England has been marked by the publication in 1999 of Sally Crawford's primarily archaeological study, *Childhood in Anglo-Saxon England*, by the publication of a number of studies interested in the education of children in medieval England, such as Nicholas Orme's *Medieval Schools*, and by studies of the representation of children in literary contexts, such as Susan Irvine's and Winfried Rudolf's edited collection on *Childhood and Adolescence in Anglo-Saxon Literary Culture*. But these either side-stepped advances between sociology and history, or did not seek to understand

---

20 See, Steven Pinker, *The Blank Slate: The Modern Denial of Human Nature* (New York, 2002); and also, Ian Butler, 'Children and the Sociology of Childhood', in *A Case of Neglect? Children's Experiences and the Sociology of Childhood*, ed. Ian Butler and Ian Shaw (Aldershot, 1996), pp. 1-18.
21 Paula Fass shows that all knowledge is acquired from childhood, see her 'The World is at Our Door: Why Historians of Children and Childhood Should Open Up', *Journal of the History of Childhood and Youth*, 1 (2008), p. 13.
22 These include, Ruth Karras, *From Boys to Men: Formation of Masculinity in Late Medieval Europe* (Philadelphia, 2002) and Merridee Bailey, *Socialising the Child in Late Medieval England, c.1400-1600* (Woodbridge, 2012).

monastic childhood as a discrete experience.²³

In fact, for the most part, the study of monastic oblation has remained firmly locked into a broader field of church history which has tended not to ask how children lived in their own terms, but what oblates and oblation tell us about the values of other adults and of the role of the Church in medieval society as a whole. Mayke de Jong's study on the oblation of boys in the Carolingian Empire, *In Samuel's Image*, characterises this state of affairs. Although published some decades ago, this study remains highly significant.²⁴ It demonstrated that the development of rituals of oblation for girls as well as boys in Europe was closely bound up with *do-ut-des* gifting pratices, and the growth in use of the *Regula Sancti Benedicti* (or 'Rule of Saint Benedict').²⁵ Although earlier customaries, including those of the Greek-speaking East, such as Saint Basil's greater and lesser *Asketikon* (Ἀσκητικῶν), had provided monastic houses with authorisation to receive children into their communities 'at any time and from the earliest age' (πάντα καιρὸν καὶ τόν τῆς πρώτης ἡλικίας),²⁶ she has argued that the *Regula Benedicti* was unique among monastic rules emerging in the sixth-century Latin west in that it contained the earliest-known prescription for a ritual which secured boys as permanent members of religious communities:

---

23 Sally Crawford, *Childhood in Anglo-Saxon England* (Stroud, 1999); Nicholas Orme, *Medieval Schools: From Roman Britain to Renaissance England* (New Haven, 2006); Susan Irvine and Winfried Rudolf (eds.), *Childhood and Adolescence in Anglo-Saxon Literary Culture* (Toronto, 2018).

24 Mayke de Jong's monograph is based on her Ph.D. thesis, 'Kind en Klooster in de Vroege Middeleeuwen: Aspecten van de Schenking van Kinderen aan Kloosters in het Frankische Rijk (500-900)', *Ph.D Dissertation, Amsterdam* (1986).

25 'I give so that you may give', refers to ideas of spiritual sacrifice in return for reward in transactions of the early medieval west. For more, seeMayke de Jong, *In Samuel's Image: Child Oblation in the Early Medieval West* (Leiden, 1996), pp. 56-99. For a more general study on the Frankish reforms see the 'Introduction' of Rosamond McKitterick, *The Frankish Church and the Carolingian Reforms, 789-895* (Cambridge, 1977). See also Matthew D. Ponesse, 'Smaragdus of St. Mihiel and the Carolingian Monastic Reform', *Revue Bénédictine* 116 (2006), esp. pp. 371-6.

26 *Asketikon*, ed. Migne, 'eiusdem regulae fusius tractatae', PG 31, cols. 890-1050, at cols. 952-8; see *Regula Basilii*, ed. and trans. Anna Silvas, *The Rule of St Basil in Latin and English: A Revised Critical Edition* (Collegeville Minn, 2013), c. vii, pp. 88-9: 'Any time from the earliest age is suitable to receive [children] for instruction and to lead them into the fear of the lord'.

[c. 59: *De Filiis Nobilium Aut Pauperum Qui Offeruntur*]
Si quis forte de nobilibus offerit filium suum Deo in monasterio, si ipse puer minor aetate est, parentes eius faciant petitionem quam supra diximus et cum oblationem ipsam petitionem et manum pueri involvebant in palla altaris, et sic eum offerant... in praesenti petitione promittant sub iure iurando quia numquam per se, numquam per suspectam personam nec quolibet modo ei aliquando aliquid dant aut tribuunt occasionem habendi [...] atque ita omnia obstruantur, ut nulla suspicio remaneat puero per quam deceptus perire possit... similiter autem et pauperiores faciant. Qui vero ex toto nihil habent, simpliciter petitionem faciant et cum oblationem offerant filium suum coram testibus.[27]

Mayke de Jong's study has shown that this ritual gained ground after a series of church reforms under Charlemagne (768-814), when the *Admonitio Generalis* of 789 and a complementary capitulary issued that year, known as the *Duplex Legationis Dictum*, called for the *Regula Benedicti* to serve the monasteries of the Carolingian Empire in preference to all others.[28] Canons such as the *Collectio Capitularis*, published by Benedict of Anniane (c.747-821) after later reform councils at Aachen between 817-819 under Emperor Louis the Pious (814-840), and an associated commentary known as the *Expositio in Regulam*, composed in c.820 by Abbot Smaragdus of Saint Mihiel (c.770-840), dealt with growing anxieties about the involuntary nature of child recruitment by insisting that oblations include the written permission of parents (using a *petitio* containing a statement that it was 'right to give back to the Creator

---

[27] RSB, c. 59, p. 193: 'If it happens that a nobleman offers his own son to the monastery, if the boy is young, his relatives should make the petition we discussed above, and they should tie together the petition and the boy's hand in an altar cloth, with the oblation, and offer him that way. Concerning his property, they should either promise under oath in this same petition that they will never give him anything themselves, nor through a third party [...] In this way, everything is closed off, so that the boy cannot harbour (sic) any hope by which, God forbid, he could be deceived and ruined [...] Let poorer people do likewise. Those who have no property at all should simply draw up the petition and offer their son before witnesses, with the oblation'.

[28] 'Duplex legationis edictum c.789', *Capitularia regum Francorum*, I MGH, c.23, no. 12, p. 63.

what we had produced').²⁹ It also allowed a mixed position, deciding that parents had a right to give away their children and that monasteries of the Carolingian Empire should consider oblations irrevocable, but requiring that boys should also confirm (*confirmare*) the terms of their religious status at a later 'age of understanding' (*tempus intelligibilis*).³⁰ De Jong's work made contributions to the history of childhood too. Her study moved historians of monasticism away from aspects of Ariès' thesis which had infiltrated scholarship on oblation, playing an important role in rejecting narratives that had viewed accounts of oblation, like those of Orderic, in overly emotional terms and as a form of 'abandonment'.³¹ De Jong's monograph was also innovative in its narrative focus on the oblation ritual, and so provided a close and sustained examination of a childhood experience.

This final contribution was perhaps achieved only incidentally, however. De Jong's monograph was more fundamentally an examination of the history of an institution and recruitment practice. Her study sought to replace narratives which had emerged from social history, including the studies of John Boswell and Patricia Quinn, which forwarded divergent views of oblation either as a form of child neglect or as an attempt to foster a microcosm of the ideal medieval society. De Jong adopted a position which was primarily aimed to support a view of oblation as a Christian ritual, sustained by aristocratic parents, enabled by the Church, and intended to save children's souls. She also adopted adult-centric methods, measuring the 'significance' of oblation practices in terms which represented the perspectives and assumptions of parents and priests first.

A little known study by Maria Lahaye-Geusen, *Das Opfer der Kinder* (The Oblation/Sacrifice of Children), moved the history of oblation towards a closer child-centric study of the experience of monastic childhood in early and high medieval Europe. She explored the nature of boys'

---

29   See, canon 17 of the Council of Achen c.817, Josef Semmler, 'Synodi secundae decreta authentica (a. 817): legislatio aquisgranensis', in Kassius Hallinger (ed.), Corpus Consuetudinum Monasticarum (Siegburg, 1963), vol. i, c.17, p. 477; D. Barry and J. Leclerqc (eds. and trans), *Smaragdus of Saint Mihiel: Commentary on the Rule of Saint Benedict* (Kalamazoo, 2007), p. 484.
30   *Collectio Capitularis*, CCM I, c. 48, 529; De Jong, *In Samuel's Image*, p. 234.
31   De Jong, *In Samuel's Image*, pp. 219-20.

lives through monastic customaries, asking whether and how far prescriptive documents surviving from dozens of male communities across Europe tell us how the boy oblate, as an 'Idealtyp', became a religious; what he learned, what form his education took, how he was supervised, how he was disciplined for misbehaviour, and how (and why) contemporaries sought to safeguard him from interactions with adult monks.[32]

Although this study was a work of theology, and had primarily sought to emphasise the religious significance of experiences in monastic boyhood, Lahaye-Geusen's study demonstrated the utility of prescriptive documents to the childhood historian, establishing how they can give us access to conditions which shaped boys' experiences in monastic contexts. Its greatest limitation lay in the fact that it did not extend to girls. Layahe-Geusen relied on customaries too, and did not give any space to exploring non-prescriptive sources which might have added useful nuance to her impressions of boys' conditions. It also ranged quite broadly across Europe, moving seamlessly between houses in Germany, Flanders, and France, and so it did not account for the ways in which childhood experiences likely depended on children's own communities, cultures, and emerging national polities.

This means that there is room for a study which explores the experiences of contemporary categories of 'boys' and 'girls' after they had entered religious houses, asking how far surviving sources enable our understanding of their development into adulthood. Indeed, there is space for a study which focuses on a particular area of Europe too, representing the ways in which childhood experiences intersected with religious communities and national cultures. It is with this in mind that this study asks how far surviving evidence gives us access to and allows us to understand the experience of religious boyhood and girlhood in the Benedictine monasteries of Anglo-Saxon and Anglo-Norman England. Beyond the fact that a closer regional and institutional focus could enable more meaningful explorations of identity, it recognises that England had become a relatively – and perhaps an unusually – coherent kingdom from the mid-tenth century.

---

32 Maria Lahaye-Geusen, *Das Opfer der Kinder: ein Beitrag zur Liturgie- und Sozialgeschichte des Mönchtums im Hohen Mittelalter* (Altenberge, 1991), esp. pp. 160-9.

It also recognises that monastic life in England was dominated by a close network of Benedictine communities from a similar period. The kingdom also supported a number of organised Benedictine communities which housed religious women in addition to those which housed men.[33] Many of these communities were stable, and, indeed, existed continuously until the dissolution of the monasteries under King Henry VIII (1509-1547). What is more, these institutions serve our material needs well. They produced and have left behind a rich and surprisingly large body of primary sources, and, indeed, they were the only institutions to produce the kinds of materials, revealing the gender terminology, conditions, and experiences of boys and girls, which make this study possible.

For this book, I have settled on a chronological focus starting in around 950, enabling me to use primary sources associated with a period of monastic history known to specialists as the 'monastic reform'. This phrase describes evidence for an extensive reorganisation of religious life across England in the mid tenth century which scholars, such as George Molyneux and John Blair, have argued had far reaching implications for the development of Anglo-Saxon cultural unity, urbanisation and nucleation of towns, the power of the monarchy, and the centralisation of governence in the emerging English state.[34]

---

33 For an excellent study which compares aristocratic foundations such as Barking, Shaftesbury, Wilton, Nunnaminster, Horton, Amesbury, and Romsey, organised in line with the Benedictine Monastic Reform with more ephemeral religious communities, see Sarah Foot, *Veiled Women I: The Disappearance of Nuns from Anglo-Saxon England 871-1066* (Aldershot, 2000), esp. ch. 4, pp. 85-110, 145-98, and ch. 7, pp. 199-208. For women's religious houses after the Conquest, see Sally Thompson, *Women Religious: The Founding of English Monasteries After the Norman Conquest* (Oxford, 1991), esp. pp. 83-93, 166-72, 174.

34 See, George Molyneux, *The Formation of the English Kingdom in the Tenth Century* (Oxford, 2015), esp. pp. 173-5, and 192: 'The proliferation of Benedictine monasteries during Eadgar's reign [...] had the effect of reducing royal dependence on the cooperation of lay magnates...[and] very probably boosted kings' ability to secure compliance with their will in certain localities', see also his position on the monastic influence on ideals of administrative uniformity, e.g. '[reformers] added to a general stock of Carolingian ideas about kingship, a belief that homogeneity was desireable in and of itself, since [they] not only called for the observance of a single monastic rule in The Regularis Concordia, but also appear to have cultivated standardised Old English spellings and vocabulary, with set translations of Latin words'; for John Blair, *Building Anglo-Saxon England* (Woodstock, 2018), p. 311: "George Molyneux...shifts the main

This reform owed an origin to a network of clerics – notably, Archbishop Oda of Canterbury (d.958), Bishop Ælfheah of Winchester (c.934-51), and Bishop Coenwald of Worcester (c.928-957) – shaped by the influence of Carolingian monasticism at the court of King Æthelstan (c.924-939).[35] It also describes a movement which emerged either at the Abbey of Glastonbury or the Abbey of Abingdon under the stewardship of a younger generation of clerics, namely Dunstan (Abbot of Glastonbury and later Archbishop of Canterbury, c.909-988) and Æthelwold (Abbot of Abingdon and later Bishop of Winchester, c.904-984). These figures appear to have played an important role in introducing into England monastic regulations related to the Carolingian reform councils which encouraged the widespread adoption of the *Regula Sancti Benedicti* as a universal guide for monastic life.[36] In addition, this period of monastic reform also gave rise to an Old English translation of the *Regula Benedicti* – meaning that the primary source base of England provides unusual insight into how monasteries in England sought to organise themselves and describe the childhoods of the boys and girls who joined them.[37]

My choice of end terminus for this study, set around 1200, bridges

---

institutional advances...several decades later...[so] the spotlight shifts from Alfred and the Vikings to Eadgar and the Monastic Reform'; and his 'Grid Planning in Anglo-Saxon Settlements: the Short-Perch and the Four-Perch Module', *ASSAH*, 18 (2013), pp.18-61, esp. 54 for his suggestion that monastic reformers may have been responsible for a transformative shift in building and town planning, using roman-style grid-plans around monastic centres.

35 David H. Farmer, 'The Progress of the Monastic Revival', in *Tenth Century Studies: Essays in Commemoration of the Millennium of the Council of Winchester and Regularis Concordia*, ed. David Parsons (London, 1975), pp. 10-19, at 10. For more on the role of Æthelstan's court, see Sarah Foot, *Æthelstan: The First King of England* (New Haven, 2011), pp. 107-9.

36 For more on the recension of the RSB known as the *textus receptus*, see Mechthild Gretsch, *The Intellectual Foundations of the English Benedictine Reform* (Cambridge, 1999), pp. 245-7. For an early hagiographic witness to Dunstan's introduction of the *Regula* at Glastonbury Abbey in the 940s, see 'B', *Vita Sancti Dunstani, in Early Lives of St Dunstan*, ed. and trans. Michael Winterbottom and Michael Lapidge, OMT (Oxford, 2012), pp. lvii, 51. Dunstan's leadership of this 'reform' has been disputed, and Æthelwold's expulsion of canons from the Old Minster in 963 is considered 'the start', see Nicola Robertson, 'Dunstan and Monastic Reform: Tenth-Century Fact or Twelfth-Century Fiction?', in *Anglo-Norman Studies XXVIII: Proceedings of the Battle Conference 2005*, ed. Christopher P. Lewis (Woodbridge, 2006), pp. 153-167.

37 See, OERB.

two important events in English and monastic history. First, it enables an examination of the lives of child oblates who grew up in either an Anglo-Saxon or Anglo-Norman context, providing a perspective useful to continued debates about the impact of the Norman invasion in 1066. Second, a terminus at the end of the twelfth century enables me to include primary sources composed in the late twelfth century and early thirteenth, ensuring that I support a revised picture of the decline and end of oblation practices in England after 1200. John Doran first challenged an assertion made by David Knowles in his *Monastic Order in England* that 'the last, or one of the last recorded cases of oblation was at Abingdon in 1150' before it was banned by the Lateran Council of 1215.[38] Nora Berend, exploring the evidence of canon law, has since shown that there were no prohibitions against oblation in either Gratian's *Decretum* (c.1140) or the Lateran Council, and showed that gradual changes in canon law allowed oblation practices to continue into the thirteenth century. Indeed, prohibitions which emerged in England after the Council of Oxford in 1222, and with Pope Gregory IX's (c.1228-1241) systematic collection of papal decretals known as the *Liber Extra* in 1234, only restricted abbeys from irrevocable oblations of children, allowing for oblations followed by later profession.[39] But despite these directions, a revised pattern for oblation practices has yet to find widespread acceptance.[40]

---

38 David Knowles, *The Monastic Order in England: A History of its Development from the Times of St. Dunstan to the Fourth Lateran Council, 940-1216* (rev. ed., Cambridge, 1963), p. 421; for a correction of Knowles' thesis, see John Doran, 'Oblation or Obligation? A Canonical Ambiguity', in *The Church and Childhood: Papers Read at the 1993 Summer Meeting and the Winter Meeting of the Ecclesiastical History Society*, ed. Diana Wood (Oxford, 1994), passim, esp. p. 141.

39 Nora Berend, 'La Subversion Invisible: La Disparition de l'Oblation Irrévocable des Enfants dans le Droit Canons', *Médiévales* 13 (1994), 123-36, esp. 125-6: 'Dans la littérature sur l'oblation, le rôle décisive dans la disparition canonique de l'oblation irrévocable est attribué soit à Gratien, soit à un des deux papes, Clément III (1187-1191) ou Célestin III (1191-1198) . . . je me propose de montrer que les textes de droit canon traitant de cette question présentment plus de complexité . . . il est possible d'avancer la thèse d'un changement lent et graduel'. See also E. Friedberg and E Ludwig (eds.), *Corpus Juris Canonici. Decretalium collectiones: decretales Gregorii P. IX* (Leipzig, 1879-1881), vol. ii, Bk iii, title xiv, c. i, p. 1050: 'si minor xiv annis ingreditur religionem in xv anno liber exit nisi ipso xv anno professionem fecerit vel habitum receperit'; also E. Friedberg (ed.), *Decretum Magistri Gratiani* (Leipzig, 1879).

40 Knowles' work continues to be cited, see for example Julia Barrow, *The Clergy in the*

For my study it will be important to set out how I organise chapters and handle sources in order to produce a meaningful picture of childhood experience in England's Benedictine houses. The first step in preparing this work has been to consider the process by which it should be undertaken and written: how (far) it should be supported by sociological frameworks, what shape it should take, in what order it should be arranged, and how far my study might be affected by and so must account for material and argumentative limitations. As such, this study adopts an analytical focus on evidence for child 'experience'.[41] In doing so, it follows the 'reflective and flexible' research methods outlined by Sheila Greene.[42] Her works recognise experience, or 'social action', as a central and consistent driver of all processes of psychological and sociological development during childhood. They suggest that a narrative on childhood experience should seek to represent a reality of childhood development in written form and, in a connected way, that research on childhood should aim to make visible any evidence of change in boys' and girls' conditions and contingent experiences over time.[43]

In order to represent a reality of experience of childhood over time, my planning, reading, writing, and revisions have therefore shadowed an expectation of biological growth. This has meant that I have sought out evidence according to the developmental stages of childhood, and organised each section of each chapter so that I can move through the life-cycle.[44] This study therefore benefits from a two-fold, diachronic and synchronic, form of organisation. By diachronic, I refer to the way in which the study

---

Medieval World: Secular Clerics, their Families and Careers in North-Western Europe, c.800-1200 (Cambridge, 2015), p. 194.

41 William James established that 'experience' must define the scope of development, William James, *The Principles of Psychology* (rev., ed. London, 1990), p. 361; Sheila Greene, 'Researching Children's Experience: Methods and Methodological Issues', in *Researching Children's Experience: Methods and Approaches*, ed. Sheila Greene and Diane Hogan (London, 2005), p. 2.

42 Greene, 'Researching Children's Experience', 8; see also, Shulamit Reinharz, 'Who am I, the need for a variety of selves in the field', in *Reflexivity and Voice*, ed. Rosanna Hertz (London, 1997), pp. 3-21.

43 Sheila Greene, *The Psychological Development of Girls and Women: Rethinking Change in Time* (rev. ed., London, 2015), pp. 137- 40.

44 Sheila Greene and Diane Hogan, *Researching Children's Experience: Methods and Approaches* (London, 2005), p. 8.

takes us through a period of historical time, from c.950 to c.1200, and by synchronic I refer to its longitudinal organisation by age and experience, unfolding within each main chapter. This organisation allows several modes of access to the reader. A primary point of access reproduces a conventional approach to a book, following a sequence of ordered chapters. Another, however, enables readers to adopt a more targeted approach to independent chapters and sections divided by age, and yet another divides each chapter according to gender, enabling a comparative reading of my approaches to the experiences of religious boyhood and girlhood.

Organising a book by experience and gender in this way does raise unique challenges. It has required me to work out how much space should be given to any chapter, age group, and gender. In a connected way, this has required me to decide whether 'reflective and flexible' methods mean that I can raise similar questions and impose similar forms of organisation upon each section – in a way which might seem rigid, but which would be most useful for the purposes of comparison – or should follow a more responsive method instead, allowing each chapter and section to behave independently – and in a way that would kaleidoscope evidence for childhood experiences and perhaps better represent variations in the nature of the available source base.

It is the case, however, that I have settled on a framework which adopts the first of these two sets of principles, one that uniformises, and which better meets the needs of a comparative study of childhood experience. This is not to say that the whole work follows this organisation. Of the four chapters which follow, only the three interior chapters, that is chapters one, two, and three, conform to these principles. Each focusses on specific areas of experience in monastic life, dividing into studies on discipline, liturgical training, and literary instruction. It will be important to note that these divisions and the sizes and order of each of these chapters should not be seen to represent any hierarchy of childhood experience. Any difference which readers may notice in their size, and I refer to the greater length of the first of these three, that is, of chapter one in particular, should be seen as the direct result of a desire to meet conventional academic expectations of style, and of a degree of 'front-loading' onto the first chapter which has been necessary in order to avoid repetition in succeeding chapters.

I have also arranged these chapters according to considerations of narrative convenience. This is particularly important to note in light of the works of both Mayke de Jong and Maria Lahaye-Geusen, however, since they have set a pattern in a historiography of approaches to church history which has tended to dismiss the value of studies, such as Patricia Quinn's *Better than the Sons of Kings*, which do not emphasise the religious dimension of monastic life.[45] That emphasis has become something of an *a priori* expectation in studies of religious childhood, and scholars could naturally assume that this present study might also give pre-eminence to a chapter on the liturgy, emphasising the centrality of the *Opus Dei*, the choir and the celebration of Mass around consecrated altars in the lives of religious children. But while that emphasis has many virtues, I do not adopt this approach here. There can be no question of the significance of religion in monastic life, and of the significance of religious thought and experience in the lives of monastic children by extension, but this point is now widely accepted, and would not seem very necessary to repeat. As we have seen above, in relation to sociological concerns about historical approaches to child knowledge, too unquestioning a focus on the sacred and on aspects of religious symbolism can undermine studies which aim

---

45 Patricia Quinn, *Better than the Sons of Kings: Boys and Monks in the Early Middle Ages* (New York, 1989). For scholarly criticism of Quinn's study, see de Jong, *In Samuel's Image*, pp. 5-6: 'Patricia Quinn's study of early medieval monastic education is apologetic rather than critical, depicting the monastery as a paradise for little oblates cherished by their loving masters [...] another problem with this book is that its author seems to have relied mostly on translated sources'. See also Lahaye-Geusen, *Das Opfer der Kinder*, p. 6, n. 14: 'Die kürzlich erschienene Arbeit von P. A. Quinn über *Better than the Sons of Kings* [...] ist das jüngste Beispiel für solch fehlgeleitete Interpretationen. Auf der Basis des Sankt Gallter Klosterplanes, des Utrecht-Psalters und einiger Bruchstücke aus Brauchtexten bemüht sich Quinn um eine psychohistorisch motivierte Darstellung des Lebens der *pueri oblati*, läßt aber die religiöse Dimension weitestgehend außer acht, was zwangsläufig zu Schlüssen fuhrt, da schließlich die Religion im Mittelalter *der* bestimmende psychologische Faktor *war*/Quinn's work is the most recent example of such misguided interpretations. On the basis of the *Saint Gall Plan*, the *Utrecht Psalter*, and some fragments from standard texts, Quinn strives for a psycho-historical-motivated portrayal of the life of oblates, but leaves the religious dimension largely ignored, which leads inevitably to false conclusions, since, after all, religion was *the* defining psychological factor in the Middle Ages', and see also on her treatment of the liturgy p. 137: 'behandelt die Liturgie überhaupt nicht und stellt den Alltag nur eklektizistich in oberflächlicher Weise dar, ohne seine religiösen Implikationen zu erfassen/([Patricia Quinn] does not treat the liturgy at all and merely presents everyday life in a superficial way, without grasping its religious implications' (my translation).

to understand and represent childhood experience. Ideas relating to the sacred are, after all, *acquired* forms of knowledge, and are necessarily most valued by informed adults. We cannot immediately assume or easily demonstrate they were significant to children, let alone to the youngest and least educated. While this book therefore accounts for the importance of religion in children's lives as they grew up, and insofar as I give space to considering the sources and significance of this acquisition in children's emerging world-views, I have arranged the following chapters in order to allow evidence for children's different areas of experience to sit equally side by side, in a way which is intended to improve our understanding of how those experiences intersected.

These chapters share similar approaches. Each divides into sections focussed on contemporaneously derived categories of boys and girls, each considers evidence of the most important dynamics of childhood experience in Anglo-Saxon and Anglo-Norman England, and each assesses prescriptive and non-prescriptive sources in sequence. I consider first the evidence of monastic prescriptions, asking how this source base gives us access to and allows us to understand children's experiences of religious discipline, the liturgy, and Latin instruction. I foreground each chapter with a brief survey of the contents of the *Regula Benedicti*, a rule which increasingly informed monastic practices in England from the mid-tenth century, and I then turn to examine a contemporary body of Anglo-Saxon and Anglo-Norman prescriptive texts, asking what these sources can tell us about how contemporaries shaped the lives of boys and girls instead.

There are no bespoke customaries surviving from Benedictine communities of women and girls before 1200, and this different set of documentary conditions means that I approach the opening of each of my three sections on girls' disciplinary, liturgical, and educational conditions with a view to weighing up evidence of potential conditions rather than to reaching certainties. Prescriptive sources continue to be useful, however. Since we know that the *Regula Benedicti* and other more contemporary customaries were adopted by religious women and men, my sections on the conditions of religious girls follow similar directions. Although this makes for a contingent approach, my sections on religious girlhood also draw attention to the evidence of adjustments made to prescriptions which were either made by women themselves or indicate how religious girls and women observed the prescriptive record.

Chapter one, on monastic discipline, asks how primary sources give us access to and allow us to understand how Anglo-Saxon and Anglo-Norman houses shaped children's behaviours. This area of my research has attracted some scholarly attention in the past and I build upon studies which have approached monastic prescriptions and emphasised the importance of supervision and corporal discipline in particular. This chapter also takes into account more recent directions of research, however, and seeks to integrate studies on child discipline on the European continent which have encouraged a wider view of behaviour and considered experiences of 'instruction' important to our understanding too.

This chapter therefore assesses conditions of 'discipline' from several angles, exploring evidence for children's entry into monastic routines as well as for their learning of behavioural norms and conditions of physical correction. The first of these *foci* allows me to ask how children might have adjusted into patterns of daily life and entered spaces and structures which signalled membership of a monastic community. The second allows me to ask what primary sources tell us about ideals of behaviour, and how, indeed, contemporaries expected children to adopt and express those ideals. The third of these also allows me to ask what the surviving record tells us about the place of violence in religious childhood, what forms violence might have taken, under what conditions it might have been imposed, what effect it might have been intended to have, and how those conditions might have differed between religious communities and changed over time.

Chapter two carries a similar approach to primary sources, asking how far evidence allows us to understand children's experiences of the liturgy in Anglo-Saxon and Anglo-Norman England. It asks what prescriptive sources tell us about how children integrated into a liturgical community after oblation and what they were expected to learn in the context of the monastic liturgy. Perhaps unsurprisingly, most studies concerned with the monastic liturgy have an origin in Christian theology and focus on aspects – on the sacramental and religious nature of the activities involved in the liturgy – which have often been wrapped up with a research focus on the significance of religious beliefs. As such, past scholarship has often neglected the child, treating children as incidental to liturgical activity, or as catalysts of development in liturgical dramas, and has tended to emphasise the role of children in the more significant history of the liturgy rather than to ask about the role of the liturgy in the history of childhood. This chapter is more concerned with recovering a picture of the conditions of children, however. It first considers what the contemporary prescriptive record tells us about children's earliest visible entry into liturgical communities, it then explores whether the liturgy was expected to shape all children similarly, in a way which might have been suitable to reinforcing a communal monastic identity, or whether it reveals a more nuanced reality of child experience, supporting a development useful to acquiring particular liturgical reputations too.

I carry similar questions about the liturgy into my section on girls, and consider whether contemporary prescriptions and non-prescriptive materials throw light onto differences with boys. This section assumes that some difference will have been necessary – and I recognise here in particular that girls and women were prohibited from roles belonging to the ordained orders of the priesthood, allowing men to monopolise areas of liturgical performance centred on the altar-space. But it also builds upon Maureen Miller's ground-breaking research, *Clothing the Clergy: Virtue and Power in Medieval Europe c.800-1200*, which has drawn attention to differences in women's use of craft-work in the liturgy.[46] This and similar studies have not yet been connected up with our understanding of religious girlhood, but this chapter gives space to explore that connection. In doing so, it analyses the documentary record to see whether girls were expected to develop skills in craft, and it asks whether such experiences might have informed their liturgical activities in ways which are not visible for boys.

Chapter three, the last of my three core chapters, focusses on experience relating to children's literary instruction in Anglo-Saxon and Anglo-Norman houses. This chapter builds upon a particularly extensive body of previous research which has been chiefly concerned with understanding the intellectual horizons of monastic authors who lived in England between the tenth and twelfth centuries. These studies have, at times, shown an interest in elementary areas of education, and so their directions provide important road maps for the organisation of a chapter on

---

46 Maureen Catherine Miller, *Clothing the Clergy: Virtue and Power in Medieval Europe, c. 800-1200* (New York, 2014).

childhood experience. These studies have tended to reinforce an impression that educational structures were 'curricular' and 'programmatic', and that they depended on an enclosed environment which scholars have often described as a 'classroom'.

This chapter adopts and problematises some of these directions. It approaches education in terms which focus on becoming 'literate' and follows a course of literary development which we can understand in terms of acquiring a discrete series of skill-sets and forms of knowledge, allowing children to read, understand, and compose Latin texts. Prescriptive materials again provide a framework within which I first explore the conditions of children's education. These are particularly useful in grounding our view of Latin literacy through the lens of liturgical performance, for example. But again, I turn away from prescriptive materials in order to explore evidence for children's wider experience of Latin texts. I ask what teachers expected children to learn over the course of their childhoods, and consider what role school-texts might have had in shaping students' worldviews, behaviours, and religious identities as their comprehension of Latin improved. This chapter also asks how successful children might have typically been in meeting adults' expectations. In doing so, I deliberately set out to challenge optimal views of educational development supported by studies on the contents of monastic libraries and school-texts. In order to do so, I explore areas of our documentary base which have potential to tell us about boys' struggles with Latin instruction, asking what impact such experiences might have had on their religious identities and on their intellectual trajectories and career prospects in a similar timeframe.

I carry similar questions and approaches into a study of girls' experiences of education, but there is a distinctive historiography on the literacy of religious women and so this section adopts some different directions. This section does not concern itself, for example, with establishing the now very well understood point that religious girls and women were educated in Latin. Monastic customaries indicate that the Latin liturgy was an essential feature of religious life, providing the same anchor for girls' experiences of Latin literacy. In order to retrieve a picture of girls' educational conditions and of girls' expected learning outcomes, this study explores female saints' lives and other writings composed by men who are known to have acted as teachers to religious girls. It asks how far this source base, which is dominated by portraits of women of a very privileged social background, should be considered representative of the experiences of less advantaged girls. This section builds on these questions by thinking about the nature of their participation in a broader pedagogic context before and after the Norman Conquest too, asking if the surviving corpus of Latin school-texts informed girls' experiences in parallel to boys.

Chapter four asks how monastic children became monastic adults. This chapter does not focus on exploring biological process of maturation, however. Instead, it understands monastic adulthood as an acquired status. It asks how children adopted it, and how, indeed, evidence for the most important dynamics of boys' and girls' experiences in those areas of discipline, liturgical training, and education which I examine beforehand, might have played a role in signposting children's acquisition of that status. Since this final chapter coincides with the study of more literate oblate religious, I also allow space here to examine evidence for children's own writings. It is argued that such texts, though neglected, have the greatest potential to reveal the life-trajectories of contemporary children, and not only offer us our most direct point of access onto their acquired-thoughts, values, and skill-sets, but offer a unique opportunity to confirm the significance of experiences explored in the preceding chapters too.

By choosing to do so here, I also consciously adopt an aim which finds an origin in the work of MacNaughton and Smith who have encouraged reconstruction of what they call children's 'Voice'.[47] For us, however, in a medieval context, 'Voice' takes on a wider significance than the direct speech of actual children – which, quite obviously, we cannot have. This requires us to make clear what exactly we mean by 'Voice' and how we might access and assess its significance in contemporary written sources. The significance of voice in written text is most obvious in the terms which I have mentioned above, and can be seen to take on a visible, accessible, and relatively unfiltered form in texts which we can be confident

---

47 I.e., Donaldson, Margaret, *Children's Minds* (London, 1978). See, Glenda MacNaughton, Kylie Smith, and Heather Lawrence (eds.), *Hearing Young Children's Voices* (Melbourne, 2003); Aspa Baroutsis, Glenda Mcgregor, and Martin Mills, 'Pedagogic Voice: Student Voice in Teaching and Engagement Pedagogies', *Pedagogy, Culture & Society* 24 (2016), pp. 123-40; Pam Alldred 'Ethnography and Discourse Analysis: Dilemmas in the Representation of the Voices of Children', in *Feminist Dilemmas in Qualitative Research: Public Knowledge and Private Lives*, ed. Jane C. Ribbens and Rosalind Edwards (London, 1998), pp. 147-70.

were composed by children themselves. But we can understand evidence of child 'Voice' more inductively too, in ways which recognise 'Voice' as a form and expression of 'Agency', allowing us to retrieve evidence of child voice through reported evidence of child behaviour and reported dialogue as well as through first-hand accounts written by children.

The feasibility of my research has depended on the survival and nature of our sources, and on documentary and prescriptive records which are often well-known to specialists, but which have attracted only moderate interest with a view to understanding monastic childhood in the past. As we shall see, some of these sources present greater difficulties than others. Some of these difficulties are also the product of our historiography, resulting from the fact that certain materials have attracted visible derision. As a result, my task here is not only to present an overview of the documentary base which is potentially most useful to us, but also to argue more forcefully for the significance of texts which have been characterised in various ways, to various extents, and for various reasons, as being unoriginal, ridiculously repetitive, and otherwise unrepresentative of the conditions of monastic childhood.

Prescriptive sources, in the form of customaries which organised daily life and liturgical routines, have tended to be dismissed as evidence of contemporary realities for example, and have often been considered as evidence only of adult aspirations and of borrowed ideals in the houses where they had been composed and/or to where they were eventually transmitted. This may be the case on one level, but it is not perhaps the limit of their usefulness. Prescriptions, like any written text, are more significant, and reveal more about their author and about the wider culture and community which produced, copied, and chose to read them, and on more levels than is often or immediately understood on a narrow genre-led basis of analysis alone. Maria Lahaye-Geusen has shown in a continental context that monastic rules tell us a good deal about local conditions for example, and might, in the case of more idiosyncratic and local customaries, even describe routines children typically followed.[48]

---

48 Maria Lahaye-Geusen, *Das Opfer der Kinder*, ch. 3 'Methodisches: die Evidenz der *Consuetudines*. Zur Problematik einer Monastischen Quellenart', pp. 29-41, esp. 13: 'In Bezug auf die *pueri oblati* geben die *consuetudines* Aufschluß über ihre Integration in Mönchsgemeinschaft und Klosterverband, ihre Erziehung und die grundsätzliche

INTRODUCTION: MONASTIC CHILDHOOD

We are fortunate in this regard that the monastic reform coincided with a renewed interest in and the production of several new prescriptive documents. As we have noted briefly above, Anglo-Saxons adopted the *Regula Benedicti* as their most fundamental source of monastic organisation, and, in addition to this code, the reform allowed for the emergence of an Old English translation composed by Æthelwold of Winchester, giving us useful insight into how Anglo-Saxon readers had understood the *Regula Benedicti*.[49] Arnold Schröer, author and compiler of the still critical edition of the *Old English Rule of Saint Benedict* recognised more than a century ago that the work was in fact 'not an accurate word for word translation but very often a work of enlargement and clarification', and, indeed, Nathan Ristuccia has shown this more recently too.[50] But it will perhaps be helpful to demonstrate this utility here, by considering briefly how Æthelwold's translation differed from the original Latin *Regula* and by showing how it gives us access to his views and to conditions which likely shaped the children whose lives were predicated upon them.

Einstellung der monastischen Gesetzgeber/Concerning the *pueri oblati*, the *consuetudines* provide information about their integration into the monastic community, their education and the fundamental attitude of the monastic legislators' (my translation). She recognises that descriptions of oblation contained in customaries like the *Constitutiones*, are 'nur ein Idealtyp' (p. 29), but argues that those ideals had real consequences for the children who encountered them.

49 All surviving late Anglo-Saxon copies of the Latin *Regula* conform to the Carolingian version known as the 'Textus Receptus', for more on this, see M. Gretsch, *Intellectual Foundations of the English Benedictine Reform* ASE 25 (Cambridge, 1999), pp. 245-247. Although Dunstan appears to have first introduced this version to England at his house of Glastonbury, Æthelwold appears to have been dissatisfied with how it was being interpreted, see E. John, *Reassessing Anglo-Saxon England* (Manchester, 1996), p. 114. For more on Bishop Æthelwold's authorship, see OERB, pp. xiii-xiv; Dorothy Whitelock, 'The Authorship of the Account of King Edgar's Establishment of Monasteries', in *Philological Essays: Studies in Old and Middle English Language and Literature in Honour of Herbert Dean Meritt*, ed. James L. Rosier (The Hague, 1970), pp. 125-36; Mechthild Gretsch, *Die Regula Sancti Benedicti in England und ihre Altenglische Übersetzung*, Texte und Untersuchungen zur Englischen Philologie 2 (Munich: Fink, 1973), pp. 9-11; Mechthild Gretsch, 'Æthelwold's Translation of the *Regula Sancti Benedicti* and its Latin Exemplar', *ASE* 3 (1974), pp. 125-51, at p. 125; Gretsch, *The Intellectual Foundations*, esp. pp. 226-33.

50 OERB, p. xxviii: 'Die Übertragung der *Regula* ist keine genaue wörtliche Übersetzung, sondern eine oft erweiternde, erläuternde Bearbeitung' (my translation). See also Nathan J. Ristuccia, 'Ideology and Corporal Punishment in Anglo-Saxon Monastic Education', *American Benedictine Review* 61 (2010), pp. 373-86.

We can do so with respect to unusual features occurring in its chapter 59, on the oblation ritual, for example.[51] Æthelwold's translation of chapter 59 of the *Regula Benedicti* is useful in that it would seem to disclose that Æthelwold had considered child oblations irrevocable. His translation largely followed the Latin *Regula*, and repeated terms stressing the permanence of the offering in similar positions and contexts. It opened much like the Latin text, requiring parents 'to offer' or indeed 'to sacrifice' (*geoffrian*) their child to a monastery, and it required kin 'to fasten' a child (*gefæstnian*) to the monastic life. It reminded them again that this involved a process of making 'an offering/sacrifice' (*offrung*). Æthelwold also mirrored requirements that parents submit a petition (*gewrit*) to testify to the child's 'fastening' (*his fæstnung*), and he required kin to promise again by word (*behaton*). But he did not replicate a legalistic reference in the Latin text, requiring parents to promise under law to keep to these terms. Instead, he added that they were 'to make firm with an oath' (*mid aþe*

---

51 OERB, c. 59, pp. 103-5: '"Be riccera and ðearfena bearna andfeng", gif hwylc rice mon and æþelboren his bearn Gode on mynstre geoffrian wile, gif þæt cild þæs angdites næbbe, þæt he sylf mæge oðþe cunne hine sylfne, gefæstnian hine þa magas mid ofrunge, þæt is, bewinde þæs cildes hand and þæt gewrit his fæstnunge on þæs altares weofodsceate and hine swa Gode geoffrien mid offrunge hlafes and wines. Behaten þa magas and mid aþe gefæstnian, þæt hi næfre syndrige æhta hyra mæge ne gesellan, ne þurh hy sylfe ne þurh nænne gespelian, ne hy næfre nænne incan ne secen, hu him to syndrigum æhtum gerymed sy. Gif hy þonne hwæt syllan willan, sellan hi þæt þære haligan stowe to rihtum gemænscipe, him to ecum edleane; And swa mid wegneste ham cyrren, gif hi þæs wilnien. Syn ealle þa æhta, þe þam cilde gebyrien, swa fordylegade and todæled, þæt him nan hyht beon ne þyrfe, þelæs þe he losige, gif he his hyht beset on syndrigum æhtum, þæt na ne geweord[þ]e; we forost onfundon, þæt mænig þurh þone hiht syndrigra æhta losode. Do handswagelice be hyra bearnum, þa þe unrice synd and hæfenlease þearfan. Gif hi nane æhta to sellenne næbben, offrigen hyra bearn anfealdlice on gewitnesse rihtgelyfedra manna'.

Compare: RSB c. 59, p. 193: '"De Filiis Nobilium Aut Pauperum Qui Offeruntur" Si quis forte de nobilibus offerit filium suum Deo in monasterio, si ipse puer minor aetate est, parentes eius faciant petitionem quam supra diximus et cum oblationem ipsam petitionem et manum pueri involvebant in palla altaris, et sic eum offerant. De rebus autem suis, aut in praesenti petitione promittant sub jure jurando quia numquam per se, numquam per suffectam personam nec quilibet modo ei aliquando aliquid dant aut tribuunt occasionem habendi, vel certe si hoc facere noluerint et aliquid offere volunt in elemosinam monasterio pro mercede sua, faciant ex rebus quas dare volunt monasterio donationem, reservato sibi, si ita nulla suspicio remaneat puero per quam deceptus perire possit, quod absit, quod experimento didicimus. Similiter autem et pauperiores faciant. Qui vero ex toto nihil habent, simpliciter petitionem faciant et cum obnlationem offerant filium suum coram testibus'.

gefæstnian) the disinheritance of their child.⁵²

It is possible that the contemporary written record allows us to confirm some of these features. Indeed, the monks of Ely appear to have kept copies of English petitions (*gewritas*) which parents and churchmen drew up to secure these oblations - including, in one case, two cousins, Wulfric and Æðelmær, the latter of whom was oblated as a penance for murder.⁵³ But Æthelwold's decision to invoke 'oaths' in his translation (*aða*) should strike us in particular. The term is easily overlooked perhaps, but it departs from original references to swearing under the law (*promittant sub iure iurando*) present in the *Regula Benedicti*. Although often treated as a universal reference for a pledge, modern scholarship on the vocabulary of sworn language in late Anglo-Saxon England has shown that the 'oath' was a culture-specific form of guarantee, and one of many forms of promise making which were recognised by contemporary religious thinkers (including 'swearing', for one, which was recognised by Æthelwold's student, Ælfric, in a description of juratives in a contemporary school-text on Latin grammar: '*Iuro per Deum, ic swerige ðurh God*', or 'I swear by God').⁵⁴ The presence of oaths in the *Old English Rule* suggests that Æthelwold avoided legalistic safeguards which depended on royal codes in order to commit parents to undertake what has been described as 'the most complex of all expressions of honesty'. Æthelwold's

---

52   OERB, 102-5; DOE: n. *fæstnung*: 'being firmly fixed, fixedness, stability', v. *behatan:* 'to promise, vow', and n. *ap*: 'oath, promise, declaration, pledge'; BT: v. [*ge-*]*offrian*: 'to offer, bring a sacrifice or gift in honour of another'.

53   The author of the *Liber Eliensis* tells us that these petitions took the form of *chirographia*, potentially tripartite assurances, which were written in Old English. None survive. Claiming to translate these texts into Latin, the author tells us that Æðelmær was a first-born son, and had been oblated by his father Leofwine as a punishment imposed by the Pope, to serve as penance for committing murder, see O. E. Blake, *Liber Eliensis* (London, 1962) pp. 131, 139, 143-4; trans. J.Fairweather, *Liber Eliensis, A history of the Isle of Ely from the seventh century to the twelfth* (Woodbridge, 2005), pp. 157-8, 166-7: 'de quo iniunctum est illi in penitentia suum primogenitum paupercule ecclesiae in monachatum...tradere/On which injunction, as a penance, he is to send his own first born son to a poor church to be raised as a monk'..

54   EGA, 227; Gregory Laing argues that there were three distinct categories of swearing in late Anglo-Saxon legal practice – the pledge, vow (*wed*) and oath, Gregory L. Laing, 'Bound by Words: The Motif of Oath-taking and Oath-Breaking in Medieval Iceland and Anglo-Saxon England', *Ph.D Dissertation, Western Michigan University* (2014), pp. 21-6.

translation could therefore be seen to have provided contemporaries with clearer committment from parents, using the strongest form of assurance available in England, not available 'through any other form of swearing'.[55]

What is more, the *Old English Rule* suggests that late Anglo-Saxon contemporaries expected a far wider source of donors and donated than just the biological parents and children apparently anticipated by the Latin *Regula*. Where the Latin text described parents (*parentes*) giving away their own son (*suus filius*), Æthelwold's translation instead referred to 'kin' (*þa magas*) standing as witnesses to the oblation ritual and agreeing to a 'child's' (*bearn*) disinheritance. By avoiding terminology which confined the ritual to a nuclear family and to sons (and boys) alone, Bishop Æthelwold's translation may reveal an intention to ensure acceptance of girls similarly to boys, and to receive them from a much wider variety of familial circumstances. Given we know that Carolingian clerics had also previously contested whether mothers could donate a child, it is equally possible that Æthelwold's translation connects us with a desire to ensure oblations across England conformed with Carolingian canon laws which had been transmitted through Abbot Smaragdus of Saint Mihiel's *Expositio*, insisting that, in the model of Hannah and Samuel, mothers could offer their children to monasteries alone.[56]

If this demonstrates that the Old English translation of the Latin *Regula* reveals conditions particular to England, this period also saw the emergence of new prescriptions which do so even more immediately. First among them appears to have been the *Regularis Concordia*, a Latin customary composed by Bishop Æthelwold of Winchester in c. 966x70 with the intention that it serve as a national customary in every Benedictine community and in addition to the *Regula Benedicti* and *Old English Rule*.[57] This document was not wholly original; Thomas Symons

---

55 Laing, *Bound by Words*, pp. 27-38.
56 D. Barry and J. Leclerqc (eds. and trans.), *Smaragdus of Saint Mihiel: Commentary on the Rule of Saint Benedict* (Kalamazoo, 2007), p. 484. The transmission of this work into England during the monastic reform is attested by the survival of two manuscript copies of early tenth-century date, possibly associated with Dunstan's house of Glastonbury, see Cambridge University Library, MS Ee. ii. 4 fols. 49-191, and Oxford, Bodleian Library, MS lat. Theol. 3.
57 Scholars tend to locate the date of publication loosely, circa 970, however, Julia Barrow has made the case for a more precise date of 966, Julia Barrow, 'The Chronology of the

has shown that it owed an origin to ideals of reform which had spread from Cluny and Flanders.[58] But the *Regularis Concordia* only acquired extensive influence in England, after it was published at a national synod of bishops, abbots, and abbesses supported by King Eadgar (c.959-75) and Queen Ælfthryth (r.963-975) at the Old Minster, Winchester.

We can safely assume that this customary was eventually adopted and observed by some forty-six Benedictine houses across Anglo-Saxon England.[59] However, it is because we cannot be sure of the precise nature of observance outside the centres where copies or versions of that national customary have survived that this book takes the approach of reading the Latin text of the *Regularis Concordia* as a lens on practices at Winchester, assuming that it connects us most immediately to Æthelwold's aspirations for the Old Minster, and to conditions which likely shaped the experiences of boys who entered that house from the mid-tenth century.[60] For a wider view of conditions across England, I will turn to evidence of later copies of that customary and examine the translations and local versions of the *Regularis Concordia* which both confirm the influence of that customary across England while also indicating how observance of that document evolved in and adapted to different conditions and generations.[61] A glossed copy of the Latin *Regularis Concordia* which was in use at Canterbury in the eleventh century has potential to disclose how its rules on children were enforced locally for example.[62] Two surviving fragmentary copies of

Benedictine Reform', in *Edgar, King of the English, 959-975: New Interpretations*, ed. Donald Scragg (Woodbridge, 2008), pp. 211-33.

58 Thomas Symons, 'Sources of the Regularis Concordia', *Downside Review* 59 (1941), pp. 14-36, 143-70 and 264-89.

59 Though there was an absence of monasteries in the far north until the Conquest. See, David Farmer, 'The Progress of the Monastic Revival', in David Parsons (ed.), *Tenth Century Studies* (London, 1975), pp. 10-19, esp. p. 10. See also, Catherine Cubitt, 'The Tenth Century Benedictine Reform in England', *Early Medieval Europe*, 6 (1997), pp. 77-94.

60 RC, pp. 2-3.

61 No 'original' copy of RC survives, all extant copies belong to later tenth or eleventh century moments of copying, see Gneuss, *Handlist*, nos. 59e (p. 33), 65 (p. 34), 332 (p. 63), 363 (p. 67), 925e (p. 141).

62 Gneuss, *Handlist*, no. 363, p. 67 (London BL Tiberius MS. A.iii). The Tiberius MS forms the basis of a printed edition by Lucia Kornexl, *Die Regularis Concordia und ihre Altenglische Interlinearversion mit Einleitung und Kommentar*. Münchener Universitätsschriften. Philosophische Fakultät. Texte und Untersuchungen zur

the *Regularis Concordia* composed in the vernacular at an unidentifiable house provide similar opportunities, revealing conditions which may have been important in another late tenth or early eleventh century context.[63] We also possess evidence of an alternative Anglo-Saxon customary. Abbot Ælfric of Eynsham (c.955-1010), a self-acclaimed student of Bishop Æthelwold and alumnus of the Old Minster at Winchester, composed the *Epistula ad monachos Egneshamnenses directa* (henceforth, EME or *Epistula ad monachos*) in the early eleventh century.[64] While he based this on the *Regularis Concordia*, since we know he had also adjusted it for the benefit of boys and men who lived at Eynsham in c.1005, we can treat it as a local customary, and can understand that its contents inform us about the particular disciplinary, liturgical, and educational conditions of the boys who lived at that house during his abbacy too.[65]

We might well ask whether and how far primary sources also give us access to communities of religious women. Æthelwold's preface to the Latin *Regularis Concordia* offers us the statement that 'not only monks *but also nuns*, under abbots *and abbesses*' were 'to be of one mind as regards monastic usage [...] lest [there should be] differing ways of

---

Englischen Philologie 17 (München, 1993).
63 For these two copies, see Gneuss, *Handlist*, no. 65, p. 34 (Cambridge, Corpus Christi College MS 201), no. 363, p. 67 (London, BL Tiberius MS. A.iii)
64 Ælfric of Eysnham, *Epistula ad monachos Egneshamnenses directa*, ed. H. Nocent, with C. Elvert and K. Hallinger, in *Consuetudinum Saeculi x/xi/xii Monumenta Non-Cluniacensia*, ed. Kassius Hallinger, 7.3 (Siegburg, 1984), pp. 155-85; ed. and trans. Christopher A. Jones, in EME. The oldest surviving copy of this work, from Worcester, is now contained in CCCC MS 265, see Richard Gameson, *The Manuscripts of Early Norman England (c. 1066-1130)*, British Academy Post-doctoral Fellowship Monograph (Oxford: University Press, 1999), no. 65, p. 62. Abbot Ælfric of Eynsham described himself as an alumnus of Winchester and Æthelwold in his *Excerptiones de arte grammatica anglice* (EGA, p. 1: 'Nos contenti sumus, sicut didicimus in scola Aethelwoldi (sic), venerabilis praesulis, qui multos ad bonum imbuit/We are content it is just as we learnt in the school of Æthelwold, that venerable bishop, who instructed many to good' (my translation). He also does so in his customary, the *Epistula ad monachos* (EME, pp. 110-1: 'Sed nec audeo omnia vobis intimare, quae in scola eius [Æthelwoldi] degens multis annis de moribus seu consuetudinibus didici/Nor do I dare to convet to you all those things that I learned about customs and usages while abiding for many years in his [i.e. Æthelwold's] school'.
65 For a good introduction to Ælfric, his life and writings, see Joyce Hill 'Ælfric: His Life and Works', in *A Companion to Ælfric*, ed. Hugh Magennis and Mary Swan (Leiden, 2009), pp. 35-65.

observing the customs of one rule and one country'.⁶⁶ This discloses that he had expected girls and women as well as boys and men to observe these regulatory documents. Again, it also demonstrates that he had actively encouraged contemporaries to work towards an ideal of uniformity. This still leaves us with a problem, however. Beyond the confines of the prologue we have little evidence to illustrate the extent of shared observance by men and women. The Latin *Regularis Concordia* itself was entirely directed at male categories – or boys and men. It does not readily express how girls and women applied its contents, and it does not readily seem to give us access to their conditions.⁶⁷ Fortunately for us, the surviving prescriptive record provides some direction. Joyce Hill has recently drawn attention, for example, to a series of additions which were incorporated into a surviving fragmentary copy of a vernacular version of the *Regularis Concordia*.⁶⁸ She has shown that many of these take the form of intrusive 'feminisations', and has postulated that these additions, which were probably first added in the form of either marginal or interlinear annotations before being integrated into the text, were made, if not by religious women themselves, then certainly for the benefit of communities of religious girls and women, giving us rare insight into their practices, and the ways in which girls' experiences might have varied from those of boys.

We can also ask prescriptive documents whether the Norman Conquest of England constituted a watershed in child oblation practices and experiences.⁶⁹ The autobiographical account of the life of Orderic

---

66 RC, pp. 2-3: 'Non solum monachos verum etiam sanctimoniales, patribus matribusque constitutes [...] ut concordes aequali consuetudinis usu [...] ne impar ac varius unius regulae ac unius patriae'. For Barbara Yorke's suggestion that, 'Æthelwold ... consciously adopted the Carolingian ideology of one God, one king, and one rule', see, *Bishop Æthelwold: His Career and Influence*, ed. Barbara Yorke (Woodbridge, 1997), pp. 39-40.
67 Gretsch, *Intellectual Foundations*, pp. 125-7; Nicola Robertson, 'The Benedictine Reform: Current and Future Scholarship', *Literature Compass* 3 (2006), pp. 287-8.
68 Joyce Hill, 'Rending the Garment and Reading by the Rood: *Regularis Concordia* Rituals for Men and Women', in *The Liturgy of the Late Anglo-Saxon Church*, ed. Helen Gittos and Marvin B. Bedingfield, HBS subsidia. 5 (London, 2005), pp. 53-64.
69 Knowles, *The Monastic Order*, pp. 111-3; Janet Burton, *Monastic and Religious Orders in Britain 1000-1300*, CMT (Cambridge, 1994), pp. 21-5; Rodney M. Thomson, 'The Norman Conquest and English Libraries', in *The Role of the Book in Medieval Culture*, ed. Peter Ganz (Turnhout, 1986), 27-40; Richard Eales and Richard Sharpe,

Vitalis reminds us that we have little reason to expect any dramatic collapse in the custom of oblation itself. We can expect that the Norman invaders and their clerical and monastic followers were familiar with the practice, and subscribed to the custom in their own recently reformed communities in Normandy.[70] We can expect too that there was no dramatic change in the underlying make-up of England's Benedictine communities in the immediate context of King William's conquest (1066-1087).[71]

The Norman invasion did not precipitate the immediate and sudden replacement of whole religious communities in England, but rather the gradual replacement of those who held the highest monastic offices. Even in a small number of cases where religious leaders died at or in the immediate aftermath of the Battle of Hastings, as was the case with Abbot Alfwyn of the New Minster, Winchester (1064-1066), and Abbot Leofric of Peterborough (d. 1066), they were often initially replaced by local English candidates, such as Wulfric of New Minster (1066-1072) and Brand of Peterborough (1066-1069). In most cases, continental alternatives only began to acquire leadership over Benedictine communities once those who had held or acquired office in the immediate aftermath of the invasion had died.[72] This was the case at Abingdon in 1071, for example, when Abbot Ealdred was replaced by Æthelhelm of Jumieges after encouraging a revolt against the king.[73] Despite the mixed fortune of English heads

---

Canterbury and the Norman Conquest: Churches, Saints and Scholars, 1066-1109 (London: Hambledon, 1995), pp. 145-58.

70 We can perhaps identify some Norman oblates by name, including the Archbishop's two nephews, Lanfranc II and Paul Abbot of St Albans (d.1093), and others such as Gilbert Crispin (c.1055-1117), later Abbot of Westminster.

71 Hugh Thomas, *The Norman Conquest: England after William the Conqueror* (Lanham Md, 2008), p. 120 and also Henry R. Loyn, *The English Church, 940-1154* (Harlow, 2000), pp. 76-7.

72 For more on the negative impact of the Conquest on some religious communities, the replacement of their abbots and heads of house, and the spoliation of lands and disruption to their rights, privileges, and their benefactors, see Emma Cownie, *Religious Patronage in Anglo-Norman England, 1066-1135* (Woodbridge, 1998), pp. 37-41 (Abingdon), 54-5 (St. Peter's, Gloucester), 66-8 (Bury St. Edmunds), 81 (St. Albans), 99-100 (St, Augustine's, Canterbury), 109-119 (The Fenlands: Ramsey, Peterborough, Crowland, and Ely).

73 Cownie, *Religious Patronage*, pp. 40-1. For other replacements of religious office holders with continental candidates, including at St. Peter's of Gloucester in 1072, St. Albans in 1077, Peterborough and St. Augustine's in 1070, and Thorney Abbey in 1066, see Cownie, *Religious Patronage*, pp. 54, 81, 100, 111-13, 121.

of house, a select number of abbots (or bishops of monastic sees), and, we can imagine, a larger number of other, and much less visible holders of monastic office, including teachers, managed to retain control of religious communities for some while longer. These include, for example, Worcester under Bishop Wulfstan (1062-1095), Bury St. Edmunds, under Abbot Baldwin (1065-1098), Burton under Abbot Beorhtric (d.1085), and also Crowland under Abbot Ulfcytel (1051-1085), his English successor Ingulf (1085-1110) and, after the rule of the Norman Geoffrey of St. Evruolt (1110-1124), under a series of English successors, including Waltheof of Crowland (1124-1138) and Eadward of Ramsey (1142-1175). Ramsey Abbey also stands out among its contemporaries, where a long succession of English abbots, interrupted only briefly by the rule of Herbert of Losinga (1087-1091), managed to retain control over that community until the death of Abbot Aldwin (1091-1113).[74]

Benedictine nunneries appear to have fared similarly. Most transitions of power appear to have occurred naturally, and over the course of time. Indeed, some English candidates appear to have held office at the Abbeys of Barking (Abbess Ælfgifu d.1114) and Wherwell (an 'Ælstrita' was abbess until c.1113) decades after the Conquest, allowing a greater degree of stability in the underlying makeup of their communities and perhaps a degree of continuity in their observance of pre-Conquest religious customs.[75]

A degree of continuity in office holding at certain communities should not be taken to mean that there was no significant change in the practices of England's Benedictine houses, however. The Conquest did herald changes, but many appear in the documentary record to have emerged in a limited and delayed way, and most visibly, in the case of boys and male houses, after the promotion of Abbot Lanfranc of Bec

---

74 For Anglo-Saxon leadership in more houses, including Tavistock (1082), Chertsey (1084), Crowland (1085), Pershore (1085), Bath (1087), Benet St. Holme (1089) among others, and in the light of holders of high monastic office elsewhere in England see Cownie, *Religious Patronage*, pp. 66-8, 109-10, 114-15, 119; Knowles, *Heads of Religious Houses*, pp. 23-4, 28, 31, 33, 36-8, 40, 42, 43, 45, 47, 51-2, 56-8, 60-2, 67, 70, 72, 76, 79-81, 83.

75 Barking's Abbess Ælfgyth died in c.1114, Abbess Ælstrita/Æthelthryth controlled Wherwell Abbey in c.1113, and Abbess Godgifu ruled Wilton for a brief period from 1067 and was succeeded by c.1093 by Matilda, see Knowles, *Heads of Religious Houses*, pp. 208, 219, 222-3.

to the archiepiscopacy of Canterbury (c.1070-1089) and with his composition in around 1077 of a new framework of customs known as the *Constitutiones*.[76] Since these nominally replaced the *Regularis Concordia* at Christ Church Priory, the emergence of the *Constitutiones* in c.1077 appears at first sight to have effectively ended an earlier set of ideals to maintain a uniformity of religious custom. Emma Mason has shown that Wulfstan of Worcester responded by organising a confraternity of houses in order to secure observance of the *Regularis Concordia* at Worcester, Evesham, and possibly Winchester, along with a few others.[77] But Lanfranc's customs signalled that contemporary bishops and abbots could impose new rules on their houses (including Bishop Herbert, who claims to have brought customs from the Abbey of Fécamp to Norwich), allowing greater fragmentation in the disciplinary, liturgical, and educational conditions of religious children across England.[78]

Manuscript evidence suggests that the *Constitutiones* had a wider significance, and was acquired by other abbots and houses, by Anglo-Normans who were particularly inclined to support his reforms, by communities with a recent history of foundation or monastic conversion, including St. Albans, Battle Abbey, and Durham Priory by c.1083, and the libraries

---

76 Lanfranc of Canterbury, *Constitutiones*, ed. and trans. David Knowles and Christopher N. L. Brooke, *The Monastic Constitutions of Lanfranc*, OMT (Oxford, 2002), p. vii. Knowles and Brooke use the two earliest and most closely related manuscripts, Durham Cathedral Library B.iv.24 (which was copied by Eadmer of Canterbury in c.1091), and Hereford Cathedral Library p.v.i (which was copied for Battle Abbey c.1100), see Gneuss, *Handlist*, nos. 248 (p. 52), 268.2 (p. 56) and Gameson, *The Manuscripts of Early Norman England*, no. 268, p. 85 and no. 319, p. 91.

77 E. Mason, *Wulfstan of Worcester, c.1008-1095* (Oxford, 1990), pp. 131-5, 139-45, 197-200; see the confraternity agreement here: B. Thorpe (ed.), *Diplomatarium Anglicum Aevi Saxonici* (London, 1865), p. 615. See also, Arnold Klukas, 'The Continuity of Anglo-Saxon Liturgical Traditions as Evident in the Architecture of Winchester, Ely, and Canterbury Cathedrals', in Jean Pouilloux (ed.), *Les Mutations Socio-Culturelles au Tournant des Xie-XIIe Siécles: Études Anselmiennes* (Paris, 1984), pp. 111-123.

78 'Usus et consuetudines Fiscannensis ecclesie sciatis teneri a fratribus nostris apud Norwicum/ You should know that the uses and customs of Fécamp are observed by our brothers at Norwich', Anstruther, *Epistolae Herberti de Losinga*, no. 34, pp. 68-9; trans. Symonds, *Letters of Bishop Herbert*, no. 34. p. 65. It should be noted that while Herbert accepted the idea of fragmentation, Richard Pfaff has found no evidence to confirm that this was true, however, see Pfaff, *Liturgy in Medieval England*, p. 205.

of Rochester and Bury St. Edmunds by c.1123.[79] It is possible that the *Constitutiones* even came to shape the lives of boys at houses which had initially resisted change and otherwise retained an Anglo-Saxon leadership. William of Malmesbury (c.1095-1143), reminds us of this possibility, for example, in his *Vita Sancti Wulfstani*, where he mentioned that Bishop Wulfstan of Worcester (1062-1095) had later sent his student, Nicholas (later prior, c.1116-1124), to study the new customs of Canterbury.[80] The *Constitutiones* could therefore have been transmitted to other houses in ways which might have echoed earlier ideals of uniformity. But since its reach has left little trace in the documentary record, and since part of this evidence suggests that its transmission took place, not by exchange of documents, but on an inter-personal level, and by virtue of the movements of religious students into and between different religious houses, it would not perhaps be sensible to assume it as a basis of study here.

The *Constitutiones* will therefore only be considered significant in this work in terms which recognise that this document is representative of Lanfranc's organisation of the community of boys and men at Christ Church, Canterbury. It will primarily serve as a parallel Anglo-Norman source to an earlier body of regulatory texts connected to Æthelwold of Winchester, including the *Old English Rule* and the *Regularis Concordia*, and it will serve the purpose of enabling a comparison between two of the most important centres of pre- and post-Conquest monastic life in England. This may seem a very obvious line of direction, but, curiously, no publication appears to have undertaken such a comparison in this way before. It is not entirely clear why. The *Constitutiones* offer us a view of customs which give an impression that Lanfranc had encouraged development and elaboration in the disciplinary, liturgical, and educational

---

79 Margaret T. Gibson, *Lanfranc of Bec* (Oxford, 1978), pp. 173-4; Alan J. Piper, 'The Durham Cantor's Book', in *Anglo-Norman Durham, 1093-1193*, ed. David Rollason, Margaret Harvey and Michael Prestwich (Woodbridge, 1994), 79-80. See Hereford Cathedral Library MS P.V. I. fols. 1-28 (from Battle Abbey c.1100) and Durham Cathedral Library MS B.IV.24 fols. 12-73 (composed by Eadmer of Canterbury in c.1096), in Gameson, *The Manuscripts of Early Norman England*, no. 268, p. 85 and no. 319, p. 91. *Constitutiones*, pp. xxiii-xxv.
80 William of Malmesbury, *Vita Sancti Wulfstani*, in *Lives of SS. Wulfstan, Dunstan, Patrick, Benignus and Indract*, ed. and trans. Michael Winterbottom and Rodney M. Thomson, OMT (Oxford, 2002), pp. 132-3.

architecture which surrounded boy oblates. This is perhaps best characterised by Lanfranc's decision to include a chapter on how to perform an oblation, a feature which finds no parallel in any original Anglo-Saxon composition, affording significant insight into the shape and significance of oblation rituals in the late eleventh century:

> Offerendus puer, facta sibi prius corona, minibus portans hostiam, et calicem cum vino, sicut mos est, post evangelium sacerdoti, qui missam celebrat, a parentibus offeratur. Qua oblatione a sacerdote suscepta, involvant predicti parentes manus pueri in palla, qua altare coopertum est, et cuius pars anterius pendet, et tunc suscipiat eum abbas. Quo facto prefati parentes coram Deo et sanctis euis statim promittant, quod per se, vel a se per suppositam personam susceptum ordinem puer nunquam reliquat; neque se ei aliquid scienter daturos unde puer, quod absit, perire possit [...] Dehinc ducatur ad radendum et vestiendum, sicut nostri ordinis consuetudo est.[81]

If this chapter offers evidence of conditions which cannot be recovered from Anglo-Saxon materials, this evidence does at least allow us to consider conditions which were significant to boys' lives in that precise context. With respect to Lanfranc's particularly unusual decision to describe 'the typical boy' who arrived wearing a cloak (*cappa*), a fur piece (*pellis*), and even a mantle (*clamis*) – items of clothing that might have belonged to boys from wealthy families – the *Constitutiones* would even seem to allow us to consider the socially exclusive nature of the oblations that took place under his eye.[82]

---

81 *Constitutiones*, pp. 162-5: 'If a child is to be offered to the monastery he shall first be tonsured, and then, bearing in his hands a host and chalice with wine in it, as is the custom, he shall be offered by his parents after the Gospel to the priest celebrating Mass. When the offering has been received by the priest, his parents shall wrap the child's hands in the cloth which covers the altar and which hangs down in front, and then the abbot shall accept him. When this is done the parents shall straightaway promise before God and his saints that the child shall never abandon the monastic life through their agency or that of anyone representing them, and that they will never knowingly give him anything that might lead – heaven forbid! – to his ruin [...] Then the child shall be taken to be shaven and clad in our monastic fashion'.
82 *Constitutiones*, p. 111.

INTRODUCTION: MONASTIC CHILDHOOD

In a study focussed on understanding the experiences of an illiterate or semi-literate demographic of boys and girls, and in light of the aims of chapter three on Latin instruction in particular, it will be important to account as fully as possible for evidence of child literacy and for materials which have the potential to give us our most direct access to a context of teaching and educational experience. We are fortunate in this regard that we possess several well-known school-texts thought to have been composed for the benefit of monastic children between c.950 and 1200. Indeed, there are so many that it will only be possible to consider here the nature of a few, and those few in particular which have perhaps attracted most controversy.

Twenty years ago, Scott Gwara and David Porter declared that a schooltext known as the *Colloquia* – a Latin text composed by a monastic teacher known as Ælfric Bata (fl.1005), and which took the form of a series of situational dialogues intended to help boys speak Latin with confidence – 'offer[ed] the richest information about the social nexus that produced much of Anglo-Saxon literature'.[83] Unfortunately, and as Michael Lapidge once recognised, Bata has 'never received the kinds of attention which he deserves'.[84] In fact, the *Colloquia* have more often succeeded in attracting criticism for their apparent lack of originality, and in terms which have disapproved of their repetitive nature and of the expletives of dialogue no. 25 in particular - which anticipated that students would engage with Latin lessons on how to call each other 'turds' (*stercus*).[85] This criticism has perhaps given ground to the idea that this school-text is a less worthy source of study, is less useful to the social historian, is less 'representative' of

---

83 Ælfric Bata, *Colloqiua*, ed. and trans. Scott Gwara and David Porter, *Anglo-Saxon Conversations: The Colloquies of Ælfric Bata* (Woodbridge, 1997), p. 1.
84 ÆlfBColl, p. 1, fn. 4; cf. Michael Lapidge, 'The Study of Latin Texts in Late Anglo-Saxon England I: The Evidence of Latin Glosses', in *Latin Learning and the Vernacular Languages in Early Medieval Britain*, ed. Nicholas Brooks (Leicester, 1982), p. 128.
85 ÆlfBColl, p. 136-159, at pp. 136-9: 'You are always doing soemthing worthless. You never came from good or noble people. You are not a good person. You are a turd! You are a devil [...] I would like you to be totally beshat and bepissed for all these words of yours!/Semper agis quod nil valet. Numquam venisti de bonis hominibus nec de nobilibus. Unus stercus es, et non bonus homo! Unus diabolus es [...] Ego vellem, ut totus esses caccatus et mintus pro his omnibus verbis tuis!'. For more on this historiography, see Christopher A. Jones, 'The Irregular Life in Ælfric Bata's Colloquies', *Leeds Studies in English* 37 (2006), pp. 241-60.

contemporary pedagogy, and so is also necessarily disruptive to any attempt to understand children's material and educational conditions in Anglo-Saxon England.[86]

Gwara's and Porter's own studies of Bata's *Colloquia* have dismissed some of these previous objections.[87] They have argued strongly for a need to re-evaluate these materials in terms which recognise their pedagogic context, not in terms which measure how far such content satisfies modern expectations of literary elegance or good religion.[88] They have also problematised concerns about originality. While Gwara and Porter have shown that Ælfric Bata had borrowed material from exemplars, leaning on works he had very probably encountered himself as a student – such as the *Colloquia de raris fabulis retractata* (which he used in twelve of his forty two dialogues), and the *Colloquium* of Ælfric of Eynsham – they have demonstrated that Bata had also effectively constructed an entirely new school-text.[89]

Gwara and Porter have also argued that Bata's unusual compositional choices – his fondness of repetition and expletives, and his descriptions of arguments between students and teachers and of corporal violence were part of Bata's pedagogic method. In the place of considering that Bata's texts were too repetitive to be useful or were intended to corrupt

---

86 ÆlfBColl, p. 15. Gwara and Porter give the example of Caroline White, who considered that Bata had 'ruined' Ælfric of Eynsham's *Colloquium* in the attempt of adapting it for his own school: Caroline L. White, *Ælfric: A New Study of his Life and Writings* (Boston, 1898), p. 98. They also point to William Stevenson who wrote 'no plea can save a man capable of pages like that', in his *Early Scholastic Colloquies, with Introduction by W. M. Lindsay*, ed. William Henry Stevenson (Oxford, 1929), pp. 52, 62-3.
87 ÆlfBColl, pp. 14, 17, 22.
88 ÆlfBColl, pp. 19-24, esp. 22.
89 Gwara and Porter have shown that Bata only borrowed extensively from exemplars for dialogue no. 16*. See dialogue nos. 1, 2, 8, 9, 10, 11, 16*, 18, 19, 20, 21, and 23 in, ÆlfBColl, pp. 80-1 (fn. 3, 5, 6, 8), 82-3 (fn. 9, 10), 96-7 (fn. 53), 98-9 (fn. 59, 60), 106-7 (80, 83, 84), 108-9 (fn. 85, 86, 87, 88, 89, 90), 116-9 (fn. 107)*, 118-9 (fn. 110), 120-1 (fn. 111, 112, 114, 115), 122-3 (fn. 116, 117, 118, 120), 128-9 (fn. 129, 130, 133, 134), 130-1 (fn. 136, 137, 139, 140, 141). For Gwara's and Poter's identification of possible – if uncertain – quotations, allusions to and/or notable intersections with the *Excerptiones de arte grammatica anglice* of Ælfric of Eynsham (EGA), see dialogue nos. 3, 5, 8, 9, 23, 24, 25, 27, 28 in, ÆlfBColl, pp. 82-3 (fn. 12, 13, 14), 84-5 (fn. 23), 88-9 (fn. 38, 39), 96-7 (f. 55), 98-9 (fn. 58), 100-1 (fn. 67), 128-9 (fn. 135), 132-3 (fn. 143), 134-5 (fn. 144, 145), 140-1 (fn. 165), 156-7 (fn. 300), 162-3 (fn. 320), 166-7 (fn. 335, 337).

future generations of teachers and student-readers, Gwara and Porter have shown that we are better served by considering that Bata's work was intentionally repetitive, and not only reflected boys' experiences of the liturgy, but represented the ways in which contemporary teachers instructed boys by rote. They have also argued that Bata's expletives and descriptions of school arguments may have provided relatable and memorable contexts of conversation, and were intended to serve readers with different levels of Latin comprehension.[90] The result of their studies means therefore that we can recognise how the *Colloquia* give us access to students' conditions and educational experiences, and represent the ways in which teachers like Bata expected boys to speak.[91]

Given the large number of saints' lives about religious women and men who grew up in monastic environments and which were composed between the tenth and twelfth centuries, it will also be useful to recover this body of material for the present study. Their usefulness as sources on childhood has often been calculated in terms which consider saints' lives to be 'unoriginal' or irredeemably dependent on literary *topoi*, and so they are often thought to be unrepresentative of the conditions and experiences of contemporary children. These informed assumptions can make them challenging sources to handle, but we can still use saints' lives if we treat them as contemporary texts as well. They are contemporary texts in the sense that saints' lives composed and read in our period likely played an important formative role in themselves, providing religious audiences

---

90 ÆlfBColl, pp. 14-15, 34-43.
91 ÆlfBColl, pp. 80-1: 'Composuit pueris hoc stilum rite diversum, qui vocatur Bata Ælfricus monachus brevissimus, qualiter scolastici valeant resumere fandi aliquod initium latiniatis sibi/In short, one called Ælfric Bata, a very short monk, wrote these appropriately varied pieces for boys, so as students they might take up some introduction to speaking Latin', and 170-1 'Hoc constitui et meatim disposui sermonem hunc vobis iuvenibus, sciens scilicet quosque pueros iugiter suatim loquentes adinvicem ludicra verba sepius quam honorabilia et sapientiae apta, quia aetas talium semper trahit ad inrationabilem sermonem [. . .] Et carius est illis, si eis licitum eriit ludere et iocare cum suis sociis et suis similibus insipienter et in hoc maxime letantur/I have written and arranged these speeches in my own way for you young men, knowing that boys speaking to one another in their way more often say words that are playful than honourable or wise, because their age always draws them to foolish speech [. . .] And if they are allowed they would rather play and joke foolishly with their pals and peers, and in this they take great pleasure'.

with models of religious behaviour. The optimal portraits of childhood presented in contemporary lives also offer important witnesses to contemporaries' inheritance and acceptance of ideals of childhood, and describe behaviours which contemporaries hoped children might adopt over the course of childhood.

Saints' lives can also be useful as organising documents, providing materials useful to comparing differences in contemporary expectations of boys and girls. Many of the saints' lives of Goscelin (fl. 1058-1107), a monk of the Flemish Abbey of Saint Bertin who settled in England shortly before the Norman Conquest, were devoted to religious girls and women.[92] These even appear at times to have been anchored in his own contemporary observations of women's religious practices. But even if we have no means to determine how far they describe the lives of actual girls, they still provide an important source of evidence for ideals of girlhood, and give us a valuable point of access onto expectations which might have shaped girls' and women's experiences and identities.

While the ideals they contain were intended to be difficult to achieve, we can also consider that they were meant to be anchored in a credible reality, and were perhaps even expected to have been realisable to a few. This may depend on the extent to which individual saints' lives give us access to credible models of behaviour, but it allows us to remain open to that possibility. Joyce Hill has argued recently, for example, and in the case of several hagiographies composed during our period, that some saints' lives, and especially those composed within living memory of the saint in question, might have a capacity to describe episodes from the lives of actual children.[93] It is on these occasions in particular then, and where saints' lives refer to the misbehaviours of saints or present us with idiosyncratic accounts of particular events, that we can approach saints' lives with

---

92 For an outline of Goscelin's career, see Moniker Otter, *Goscelin of St. Bertin: The Book of Encouragement and Consolation [Liber Confortatorius]*(Cambridge, 2004), p. 5.

93 See Joyce Hill, 'Childhood in the Lives of Anglo-Saxon Saints', in *Childhood and Adolescence in Anglo-Saxon Literary Culture*, ed. Susan Irvine and Winfried Rudolf (Toronto, 2018), pp. 139-61, esp. p. 161: 'The formulaic treatment . . . tell[s] us more about literary tradition than about historical reality, but even so, in the lives of some saints, especially those written at no great chronological remove from the saints themselves, we can perhaps allow that there are occasional touches of humanity, and one or two rare glimpses of the contemporary conditions of boyhood and adolescence'.

the view that they might even throw light onto the actual disciplinary, liturgical, and educational experiences of contemporary children.

Regardless of the genre to which any individual source belongs, the surviving documentary base which relates to religious childhood is not as adequate as we might hope. Before I proceed onto the main study itself, it will therefore also be useful to show how I signpost the uncertain significance of arguments which these and other sources allow us to entertain. While it is the case that no study on medieval children can hope to support the kinds of argument one could expect to find in a study centred on the lives of literate religious adults, it is particularly important to recognise that any attempt to recover evidence of the dynamics of childhood experience in England necessarily involves asking questions and orchestrating arguments that depend on a degree of interpretation, and on interpretation of sources which cannot be corroborated with independent material. I therefore employ terms of qualification such as 'possible', 'perhaps', 'probably', and 'might' in order to ensure that it is constantly made clear to readers the hypothetical nature of the positions I take in the chapters which follow. My use of these terms in this way, may, at times, seem excessive, but given the nature of our sources, and our difficulty in understanding how surviving sources give us access to the lives of contemporary children, I determine that it is essential, and not only so that this study accurately reflects the uncertain nature of any conclusions these sources can support, but so that it makes clear my own awareness of those fundamental uncertainties too.

CHAPTER ONE: DISCIPLINE AND BEHAVIOUR

In this first chapter, on monastic discipline, I ask how primary sources give us access to and allow us to understand how children integrated into the behavioural norms of monastic communities. In the past, scholars have approached questions like this through the evidence of monastic prescriptions, supporting a view of monastic houses as controlled environments where supervision and violence played a central role. Prosper Lorain held this view of the monastery in his study of prescriptions related to the continental Benedictine house of Cluny, for example, where he characterised life as one of 'continual surveillance, operating at all times', with no child ever 'able to act without the company of at least one adult and another boy'.[1] More recently, however, scholars have approached experiences of discipline through more anecdotal documents, and have emphasised the importance of learning in joining monastic routines and adopting norms of behaviour.[2]

This chapter adopts these directions. First, it explores monastic prescriptions, asking how contemporaries expected children to integrate

---

1 Prosper Lorain, *Histoire de l'Abbaye de Cluny : Depuis da Fondation jusqu'à sa Destruction à l'Époque de la Révolution Française* (Paris, 1845), p. 131: 'Une surveillance continuelle, exercée à toute heure ... l'enfant ne pouvait faire un pas sans être au moins accompagné d'un maître et d'un autre enfant'.
2 For examples see, Stephen Jaeger, *The Envy of Angels: Cathedral Schools and Social Ideals in Medieval Europe, 950-1200* (Philadelphia, 1994), pp. 4-16; see also Michael Kobialka, 'Staging Place/Space in the Eleventh-Century Monastic Practices', in *Medieval Practices of Space*, ed. Barbara A. Hanawalt and Michal Kobialka (Minneapolis, 2000), pp. 128-148, esp. pp. 130-32; and Valerie I. J. Flint, 'Space and Discipline in Early Medieval Europe', in ibid, pp. 149-165.

into daily rounds, adopt norms of behaviour, and experience conditions of punishment. I then assess a body of more descriptive sources, asking whether these confirm impressions of religious childhood based on prescriptions and also enable us to understand the role of teachers and of education in shaping boys' experiences of corporal violence.

Anglo-Saxon England: Infancy

The youngest children to enter monastic houses during the Anglo-Saxon period appear to have been born into minsters in the first few centuries after England's conversion to Christianity. Early insular collections of canon law, including the laws of the Greek Archbishop of Canterbury, Theodore (c.669-690), reveal this in penances assigned to religious women who fell pregnant inside a monastery.[3] Bodies of canon law which were written in the late Anglo-Saxon period do not confirm that this continued, but they still anticipated that very young infants would join. The *Collectio Wigorniensis*, for example, written by the circle of Archbishop Wulfstan of York (d.1023), recognised that very young infant boys were being offered to religious houses (*oportet tamen infantes...suscipi*), and ensured that their oblations had a legal basis.[4] Anecdotal evidence woud seem to confirm this. Eadmer of Canterbury, later prior of Christ Church Canterbury, appears to have joined his house on the threshold of infancy and boyhood, around the age of five or six.[5] What is more, the monks of Ely writing in the twelfth

---

3 For the Canons of Theodore, which were written in Latin before being translated into Old English in the tenth-century, see Alan J. Frantzen, *The Anglo-Saxon Penitentials: A Cultural Database* (http://www.anglo-saxon.net/penance/TCTH8558_151b.html): 'Munuc oðþe nunne gyf heo bearn gestreonen vii gear beten/ If a monk or religious woman produce a child let them make penance for seven years' (my translation).
4 J.E.Cross and A.Hamer (eds.), Wulfstan's Canon Law Collection *(Anglo-Saxon Texts,* 1999), p. 94: 'Oportet tamen infantes cum voluntate et consensu parentum, immo ab ipsis parentibus...sub testimonio plurimorum suscipi/It is fitting however that infants with the will and sonsent of parents, ideally from their own parents, should be received under the testimony of many'.
5 Born in c.1060, he tells us that he witnessed a fire that destroyed much of Christ Church Cathedral in c.1067 and was 'still a little boy' (*cum adhuc in scholis puerulus essem*) after he after he had witnessed the elevation of St. Dunstan's body during ther abbacy of Scotland of St. Augustine's (c.1070-1087), see W. Stubbs, *Memorials of*

century remembered Abbot Thurstan (r.1066-1072) as having begun his religious life in infancy at their house in the late Anglo-Saxon period too (*vitam ab infantia...servavit*).[6]

To understand what contemporaries might have expected of such infant boy oblates who entered religious communities after c.950, we might first turn for guidance to the *Regula Benedicti*, where *infantes* appears to have been a preferred form of reference to religious children. As we have noted previously, this rule encourages us to imagine that a first experience of monastic discipline might have depended on the oblation ritual described in chapter 59 of the *Regula*. That being so, however, the *Regula* does not tell us quite how infants might have adjusted into the patterns of daily life they likely encountered. The *Regula Benedicti* is useful in that it points us toward moments of first encounters in their lives. It reminds us of the significance of boys' adjustments from secular life to monastery. But neither chapter 59 of the *Regula* on the oblation ritual, nor the translated version of that chapter we have seen previously and which was composed by Bishop Æthelwold in the *Old English Rule*, discloses how contemporaries expected infant boys to integrate into their houses afterward.

A potentially revealing reference in chapter 45 of the Latin *Regula Benedicti* anticipated that *infantes* might have entered and learnt monastic routines proper to a choir and were beaten (*bapulere*) for making a mistake in recitation of a psalm, responsory, or antiphon in that context.[7] But if this were the case in the sixth century, however, and at communities which closely followed the language of the *Regula* in England or Europe, Æthelwold's version in his own *Old English Rule* did not follow suit. Instead, Æthelwold replaced the original Latin reference to an

---

Saint Dunstan, Archbishop of Canterbury (London, 1874), pp. 202, 212, 413.
6   See, Blake, *Liber Eliensis*, pp. 169, 231; trans. Fairweather, *Liber Eliensis*, pp. 202-212.
7   RSB, c. 45, pp. 154-5: 'Si quis dum pronuntiat psalmum, responsorium, antiphonam, vel lectionem fallitus fuerit, nisi satisfactione ibi coram omnibus humiliatus fuerit, maiori vindictae subiaceat, quippe qui noluit humilitatem corrigere quod negligentia deliquit. Infantes autem pro tali culpa bapulent/If anyone makes a mistake when he recites a psalm, responsory, antiphon, or reading, unless he is humbled by making satisfaction right there before all, he should be subject to more serious punishment, since he has refused to correct, in humility, an error made through carelessness. Children who make such mistakes should be whipped'.

CHAPTER ONE: DISCIPLINE AND BEHAVIOUR

infans with a reference in Old English to *geonge men* instead.[8] The phrase *geonge men* had a broad semantic range, and could have related to anyone of any sex deemed to be of an 'early stage of life'. It is possible, therefore, that Æthelwold had not entirely precluded 'infant boys' from these broad expectations. But this does not seem likely.[9] The phrase *geonge men* departed from Æthelwold's own preferred use of the term *cild* for references to *infantes* elsewhere in the *Regula Benedicti*, and it effectively removed entirely the visibility of 'infants' from a context of violence in a contemporary prescriptive context.[10]

In order to examine the significance of changes apparent in this very fluid context of age-related terms, we could consider the most influential contemporary framework on the terminology of the human lifecycle, Isidore's *Etymologiae* or 'Etymologies'. Although Isidore's scheme provided for six distinctive stages of human development, moving from *infantia* (infancy), *pueritia* (childhood), *adolescentia* (adolescence), *iuventus* (youth), *gravitas* (maturity), and *senectus* (old age), he recognised a significant degree of overlap between them.[11] He distinguished *infantia* from *pueritia* by understanding that infants should be unable to speak, for example, and also grouped those stages together, allowing for interchangeability, in recognition that both belonged to a pre-adolescent and non-procreative stage of life.[12] While we might

---

8   RSB, c. 45, pp. 154-5; OERB, c. 45, lines 9-10, p. 71: 'Geonge men for swa geradum gylte swingelle þolian/ young men, for failures such as these, should suffer a whipping' (my translation).
9   For a definition, see DOE: adj. *geong* + n. *mann:* 'in the early stage of life or growth, young, lit. young *man* or young *person* (of any sex), youth, boy, adolescent, and referring to an individual in training and not yet capable of full work'.
10 Abbot Ælfric of Eynsham also employed the term *geong mann* to translate the Latin 'adolescens' in his own school-text, see EGA, p. 301.
11 Isidore of Seville, *Etymologiae sive Originum*, ed. Migne, PL 82, xi, pp. 415-7 ; trans. Stephen Barney, J. A. Beach and Oliver Berghof., *The Etymologies of Isidore of Seville* (Cambridge, 2006), bk. xi, p. 241. Attesting to this influence, Æfric of Eynsham, a student of Winchester, appears to have borrowed these definitions for his own Grammar Glossary of Latin-Old English words, giving *unsprecende cild* for *infans*, and *cildhad* for *pueritia*, *cnihthad*, *iungling*, and *samgung* for *pubetenus* and *adolescens*, and *geoguþ* for *iuvens* - distinguishing boys from adults by their lack of beards, see EGA, pp. 61, 273, 301, 304.
12 Isidore of Seville, *Etymologiae sive Originum*, ed. Migne, PL 82, xi, p. 416: 'Infans dicitur homo primae aetatis; dictus autem infans quia adhuc fari nescit [...] Puer, a

therefore have been able to explain replacement of *infans* with another term attached to a pre-adolescent stage of life, the *Old English Rule* presents us with more problematic evidence for Æthelwold's adoption of a vernacular term with a semantic range that included post-adolescents. Isidore's scheme did not allow for this much overlap between 'infants' and post-pubescent *adolescentes* (adolescents) or *iuvenes* ('youths' or 'young men').[13] He classified this group either according to chronology, beginning from the age of fourteen, or in terms of acquiring the physical signs of and so belonging to an adult stage of reproductive maturity, distinguishing adolescents from children in reproductive terms and *iuvenes* from younger adolescents in terms of their greater age, including anyone up to around twenty eight to thirty, and their acquisition of mature responsibilities.[14]

These distinctions in Latin age-related terms do not fit neatly with Æthelwold's contemporary response. While it is possible that Æthelwold's text shows us how contemporary readers understood the term *infantes*, conflating childhood with early adulthood in a very broad life-stage, it is more reasonable to assume that it reveals his different, if unclear, understanding of the place of 'infants' within the prescriptive disciplinary context of the *Regula Benedicti*, and an intention to replace expectations of corporal violence for young children by redirecting them for older youths. We should be careful not to assume with too much certainty of course that

---

puritate vocatus, quia purus est, et necdum lanuginem floremque genarum habens'; trans. Stephen Barney, J. A. Beach and Oliver Berghof, bk xi, p. 241: 'It is called an infant, because it does not yet know how to speak [. . .] A boy is so called from purity, because he is pure and still retains, without the hint of a beard, the bloom of the cheeks'.

13   Isidore of Seville, *Etymologiae sive Originum*, ed. Migne, PL 82, xi, pp. 415-7.
14   Isidore of Seville, *Etymologiae sive Originum*, ed. Migne, PL 82, xi, pp. 416: 'Puberes a pube, id est, a pudendis corporis nuncupati, quod haec loca tunc primum lanuginem ducunt. Quidam autem ex annis pubertatem existimant, id est, eum puberem esse qui quatuordecim annos expleverit', 417 'Iuvenis vocatus, quod iuvare posse incipiat . . . Sicut autem triginta perfectae aetatos est annus in hominibus'; trans. Stephen Barney, J. A. Beach and Oliver Berghof, bk xi, p. 241: 'Those who have reached puberty are so called from pubes, that is, the private parts, for this is the first time that this area grows hair. There are those who calculate puberty from age, that is, they take someone who has completed his fourteenth year', 242 'A youth is so called because he begins to be able to help . . . in human beings the thirtieth year is the time of full maturity'.

CHAPTER ONE: DISCIPLINE AND BEHAVIOUR

he had intended to ignore children in chapter 45. In fact, where evidence for other interpretations of the Latin *Regula Benedicti* survives in the documentary record (for example, in glosses added to later copies of the Latin *Regula*), it is clear that other contemporaries continued to include children in this prescription. For this, we can consider the evidence of annotations made to chapter 45 in a copy of the Latin *Regula* which was in use at Christ Church Canterbury in the second half of the eleventh century, for example.[15] Close study of this copy by Henry Logeman has shown that it preserves a distinctive apparatus of interlinear Old English glosses, providing readers with *cildra* in place of the *infantes* in the Latin *Regula* and *geonge men* in chapter 45 of the *Old English Rule*.[16] *Cild* is clearly far closer to the original *infantes*. It is a direct cognate of the modern word 'child' and, similar to Isidore's Latin framework, would have allowed contemporaries to include children of all pre-adolescent ages, ensuring that the youngest oblates were also subject to disciplinary conditions in the choir.[17]

While we cannot know therefore quite what Æthelwold might have intended with his rather surprising choice of terminology, we can see that the Latin *Regula* gave rise to several different contemporary responses, and that there was a great degree of interchangeability in use of terms relating to age in the late Anglo-Saxon period. It is difficult to be certain whether this means that these differences had implications for the disciplinary experiences of the young children who entered contemporary choirs; it is only in the event that we can assume that they show how the Latin *Regula* was understood differently in different contexts, that contemporary prescriptions allowed for variation in children's conditions, and that religious

---

15 *The Rule of St. Benet: Latin and Anglo-Saxon Interlinear Version*, ed. Henry Logeman, EETS o.s. 90 (London, 1888), pp. xxxii, xli. Now contained in London, British Library, MS Cotton Tiberius A.iii (fols 118r-63v). For the provenance of this MS, Gneuss, *Handlist*, no. 363, pp. 67-68.
16 *Rule of St. Benet: Latin and Anglo-Saxon*, ed. Logeman, c. 45, p. 79: the gloss appears in the edition as follows, 'infantes autem pro tali culpa vapulent/cildra ... for swilcum gylta beimbeswungen'.
17 DOE: n. *cild*: '(1) child, an infant or young person, referring to unborn child, to male children, religious boys, school-boys, (2) offspring, (3), youth of noble birth, (4) a personal name'. *Rule of St. Benet: Latin and Anglo-Saxon*, ed. Logeman, p. xxxiv: Logeman recognised that its vocabulary was in many places 'very different' to Æthelwold's translation.

from different houses departed from one another in their handling of rules on discipline for young infants, that we might also consider that infants or young boys encountered slightly different disciplinary regimes depending on which house they joined in the late Anglo-Saxon period.

The *Regula Benedicti* and *Old English Rule* were not the only sources of regulation which were available to monasteries of this date, however. We have seen that they also interacted with and were checked by the *Regularis Concordia* of Winchester. But the *Regularis Concordia* only provides a slight extension to our view of monastic 'infants', focussing on just a single reference, where Æthelwold required the choir to perform a short liturgical service known as the *Trina Oratio*, before the monastic Office of Tierce:[18]

> *Infantibus* autem ecclesiam intrantibus, aedituus primum sonet signum; peractis tribus a *pueris* oraminibus, uti prius a senioribus gestum fuerat, dispositi singuli in locis suis campana pulsata incipiant horam Tertiam.[19]

This section suggests that very young boys, potentially of infant age, might have been expected to enter religious houses, integrate into a choir structure, and contribute to structured liturgical services at the Old Minster in Winchester. We cannot, of course, assume that the term *infans* related to infants in this particular case, and in distinction to the *pueri* who were introduced into the passage shortly afterwards. But even if we *were* to suppose that this shows that infant boys were expected to enter into liturgical routines shortly after oblation, Æthelwold's phrasing still obstructs our view of their activities (apart from simply 'entering' the church). The *Regularis Concordia* does not clearly prescribe what *infantes* should contribute, and the presence of the preposition 'a' appears rather to have confined a requirement of performance of the *Trina Oratio* to *pueri*

---

18 Christopher Jones sets out the constituent parts of the *Trina Oratio*, see EME, p. 153. For a discussion of the *Trina Oratio* and its development, see Thomas Symons, 'A Note on the Trina Oratio', *Downside Review* 42 (1924), pp. 67-83.
19 RC, p. 16: 'As the children enter the church the sacrist shall ring the first bell; and when they have said the *Trina Oratio* in the same way as the seniors have done, all shall take their places and the bell shall be rung for them to begin Tierce'.

alone, leaving us with the question of what, if anything, might have been expected.

Boyhood

This lack of positive prescriptive evidence for infants in either the *Old English Rule* or *Regularis Concordia* means that prescriptive documents before the Conquest only provide reliable evidence for Æthelwold's intentions to subject an older, and perhaps more numerous, category of *pueri* or 'boys' to monastic norms. Indeed, the *Regularis Concordia* assumes boys were subject to monastic regulations and normative expectations of behaviour. We can see that boys, or *pueri*, were expected to acquire the skills necessary for participating in monastic routines in the choir, for example. Choirs were normally divided, of course, but it is worth mentioning that the text required boys to split up into two manageable groups, on opposing right- and left-hand sides (*pueri dexteri chori ... et sinister*). Each side of choir appears to have constituted a mixture of adults and children, perhaps with a view to enabling senior brethren to supervise the activities of each grouping, and providing seniors with a means of identifying and arranging which children should do what and when (*omnes fratres dexterioris chori, scilicet seniores ac iuniores*).[20]

Æthelwold's references to the choir also allow us to consider how boys observed a daily round and encountered a hierarchical order in the choir arranged by seating. This presents itself at times directly, in requirements that boys should be 'assigned to their *own* spaces' (*dispositi singuli in locis suis*), and keep to their positions in the 'order' of their choir (*residentibus cunctis in sedilibus suis ordinatim*).[21] But we also find it indirectly, in references which imply particularisation of their conditions and subject boys to their own forms of supervision, with two seniors required to act as

---

20 For the eleven occasions in which *pueri* appear in choir see RC, pp. 13-4, 16, 23, 28, 35-6, 51, 61. RC, pp. 36-7: 'All the brothers of the right-hand-side choir, that is to say, both seniors and juniors'. I owe thanks to Dr Benjamin Thompson for the idea that the organisation of boys in choir provided a means of determining when they contribute to the liturgy.
21 RC, pp. 16 'All shall take their places', and 13 'All, ranged in order in the stalls'.

their 'guardians' on either side of their choir (*pueri dexterioris chori cum uno custode illud peragant; sequenti die dominica residui pueri sinisterioris chori cum custode*).[22]

The *Regularis Concordia* suggests that *pueri* were expected to enter several environments in the complex of the Old Minster at Winchester, requiring them to learn a pattern of routines for daily life and undertake a series of separate activities for washing, eating, and sleeping in mundane spaces of the cloister, refectory, and dormitory, in addition to the liturgy.[23] The *Regularis Concordia* did not detail these extra-liturgical rounds with completeness. The purpose of a customary was to outline the plan for a liturgical life rather than for daily activities. But it signposts enough of these daily rounds so as to allow us to recognise how conditions in these routines played a role in introducing boys into their communities.

Indeed, references to the activities of *pueri* in the *Regularis Concordia* allow us to recognise that boys learnt daily rounds that were different from their seniors. We can see, for example, that part of boys' own routines in the *Regularis Concordia* required boys to accustom themselves at an early age to using the toilet at set times of the day.[24] We could extend this evidence for boys' routines further still, including prescriptive measures which expected boys to accustom themselves to bathing and washing their faces and hands at fixed junctures: these prescriptions required that boys share only the company of their *magister* or 'teacher' – individuals who were required to supervise and instruct oblates in how to wash – and on a strictly separate basis from adult brethren, who were to wash at another time and individually (*Dehinc psalmodiis dediti facies suas, uti mos est, lavent schola universa cum magistro et abbate; seniores vero unusquisque semotim*).[25]

There are places in the documentary record, particularly in school-texts

---

22 RC, p. 61: 'The children of the right hand choir with their master shall carry it out, and on the following Sunday the other children, those of the left hand choir, with the other master'.
23 For a reconstruction of the daily *horarium* in winter, see RC, pp. xliii-xli, 13-24, 30-5.
24 RC, pp. 14, 16, 45-6: 'Egressa schola cum magistro ad necessitudinis usum, ceteri . . . in ecclesia resideant/ When the schola with their master leave the church for the necessity of nature, the rest . . . shall remain in the church'.
25 RC, pp. 14, 45-6, esp. 16: 'The entire *schola* with their master and the abbot shall wash their faces as is customary, intent on the psalms as they do so. As for the seniors, let each one [do so] separately'.

written for students' instruction in Latin, which add to this picture of the daily round in more surprising ways. The *Colloquia* of Ælfric Bata, which we have mentioned briefly in the introduction, for example, account in one dialogue for the hours between dinner and Vespers, when Bata permitted boys to play (*ludere*).[26] Bata's dialogue tells us that this was often conceded on saints' feast days, fostering positive associations with those festivals, and was subject to boys meeting certain conditions of behaviour, requiring evidence of their ability to request it, as well as completion of learning tasks. Bata suggests this play allowed boys to escape supervision, and use a material culture of toys made available for this purpose. These seem to have included a ball (*pila*) and a hoop (*trocho*), which connect to childhood in a very relatable way, as well as a stick or rod (*baculum*) and a flail (*flagellum*). While Bata described boys using these last items to control the ball or hoop, it is interesting to note here that he chose words which he connected to items used in a disciplinary context, as tools of correction. Bata tells us nothing else, sadly. But in referencing objects which mirror the use of rods and flails by teachers in behavioural management, his *Colloquia* offer a glimpse onto how teachers might even have exploited the conditions of play to nudge boys into accepting such tools as part of the normal fabric of behavioural management.

Pueri also occur in prescriptions which suggest that boys would need to share duties with a wider community of seniors, in a way that might have fostered a more corporate and choir-centred monastic identity. The

---

[26] see, ÆlfBColl, pp. 94-5: 'Domne magister, licet nobis ludere paulipser, quia modo scimus bene nostros acceptos et nostras lectiones et responsoria nostra et antiphonas nostras? Etiam licet, quod festivitas est: ideo vobis licentiam de modo hac vice iocandi usque ad signum verspertinum/ Bene est nobis modo, quod vivimus. Pergamus omnes simul iocare foris cum baculis nostris et pila nostra seu trocho nostro/ Tu puer, commoda mihi unum baculum, et ego accomodare volo tibi duos baculos statim, si vis/ Habeo satis, et si tu vis mecum ludere trocho, ego dabo tibi unum flagellum, ut in invicem ambo possimus iocare. Si vis cum pila ludere, commodabo tibi et pilam meam et baculum meum ad ludendum: Master, sir, let us play a little while - since we very well know our assignments, lections, responses, and antiphons already/ Very well, you may, because it is a feast day. I now give you permission this time to play until the Vespers signal/ Now it is good to be alive! Let's all go together to play outdoors with out sticks and our ball or hoop. You, boy, lend me a stick, and I'll give you back two sticks right away, please, I have plenty. And if you want to play with a hoop together, I'll give you a flail so we can both play taking turns. If you want to play with a ball, I'll lend you both my ball and my stick to play with'.

Regularis Concordia suggests that common routines centred on the choir, and were signposted in the Old Minster's complex through the manipulation of its 'soundscape' or heard environment. Æthelwold's customary expresses this through mention of 'signals' (*signa*). Thomas Symons, editor of the critical edition and translation of the *Regularis Concordia*, quietly assumed that many of these *signa* were 'bells', describing them as such. But since he did not explore the significance of these particular items, and given that there have been only a select number of publications which have surveyed and drawn attention to the significance of *signa* and the variety of forms they likely took (as gongs, cymbals, and bells), it will be useful to confirm the significance of Symons' terminology here, and consider how *signa* might have enabled boys to learn routines of liturgical performance after oblation.[27]

In order to identify 'bells' in the soundscape of Winchester in c.970, we are helped by the fact that the Latin *Regularis Concordia* occasionally provided nouns such as *campana* (bell) and *tintinnabulum* (little bell) which indicate their place and role in signalling certain offices.[28] We are also helped by the survival of fragmentary vernacular versions of the *Regularis Concordia* and continuous vernacular glosses to Latin copies of that customary which allow us to see how contemporaries writing in a slightly later generation understood and perhaps practised the terms and customs which the *Regularis Concordia* set down. As we shall see later, at least one glossator used the Old English term 'belle' to translate many of the *signa* in a Latin copy (i.e. London Tiberius MS A.iii which refers in one instance to '*þonne se belle cnelle, beon hi ealle gegaderode to primsancge*').[29] Joyce Hill, meanwhile, has shown that yet another copy, in the form of vernacular version of the *Regularis Concordia* (in the unprinted MS CCCC 201) provided slightly different, often more specific, and perhaps more realistic readings of *signa* and even of *belle,* employing terms such as a 'bench' or *tabula,* or a gong or

---

27 Joyce Hill, 'Lexical choices for Holy Week: Studies in Old English Ecclesiastical Vocabulary' in *Lexis and Texts in Early English: Studies Presented to Jane Roberts,* ed. Christian J. Kay and Louise M. Sylvester (Amsterdam, 2001), pp. 117-127.
28 RC, p. 16: 'Campana pulsata/The bell shall be rung' and 'Tintinnabulo a priore percusso/Then the prior shall strike the little bell'.
29 Schröer, 'De consuetudine monachorum', p. 296: 'When the bell knells, let them all be gathered to sing Prime' (my translation).

CHAPTER ONE: DISCIPLINE AND BEHAVIOUR

cymbal where the glossator of MS Tiberius had used *belle*, but also using *belle* in other places and contexts, confirming their presence and use in the community for which that vernacular version had been written.[30]

The *Regularis Concordia* also distinguished between the qualities and modalities of monastic *signa* employed at different times and in different spaces. The *Regularis Concordia* assigned, for example, where, when, and whether *signa* might have been percussive or silent, and did so by using what we might call sounding verbs, or verbs relating to hearing, with forms such as *pulsare* (to pound),[31] *percutere* (to strike),[32] *sonare* (to sound),[33] *advocare* (to call),[34] and *audire* (to hear)[35] notifying the community to gather. But it also appears to have done so by using less

---

30 Joyce Hill, 'Lexical choices for Holy Week: Studies in Old English Ecclesiastical Vocabulary', pp. 120-1: 'The Tiberius text, not surprisingly, is as unspecific as the Latin which it glosses and to which it is generally faithful, but the translation (of CCCC 201), which is characterised by a tendency to specify and explain, uses precise terms [...] For example... where the Latin has *facto signo* and the Tiberius gloss *gedonum tacne*, the CCCC 201 text has *mid beacne on þære formellan þæt getacnige*. Symons translates the Latin freely (indeed, inaccurately) as 'the bell shall be rung', but it is clear that in the community in which the Old English translation originated – and perhaps in other communities too – a bell was not used [...] what is in fact being referred to in the Old English explanatory translation is a wooden instrument, often used for signals in monasteries, and referred to elsewhere in the *Regularis Concordia*, as in other consuetudinaries of this date, as a tabula', and 'when *facto signo* occurs again and is glossed as *gedonum tacne* (in Tiberius), the translation in CCCC 201 is the specific *sconylle* (shoe-bell)' and for more on the presence of cymbals, see p. 121 '*Donec tintinnabulum pulsetur* [...] is accurately glossed in Tiberius A.iii as *oð þæt belle si gecnylled*, but is carefully adjusted in the CCCC 201 translation to *swa seo cymbalum sy geslægen* to reflect... the use of a small cymbal or portable gong which was struck, rather than a bell'.
31 RC, pp. 13: 'Continuatim pulsetur tintinnabulum/The little bell shall be rung continuously', 'Pulsatis reliquis signis/The remaining bells shall be rung', 15 'Pulsato signo congregentur ad Primam/At the sound of the bell, come together for Prime', 'Signo pulsato/Then the bell shall ring', 16 'Campana pulsate incipient horam Tertiam/The bell shall be rung for them to begin Tierce', 21 'Pulsatis signis celebrant Sextam/The bells being rung, Sext shall be said', 'Finita Missa pulsetur primum signum Nonae/After Mass the first bell for None shall be rung'.
32 RC, p. 22: 'Tintinnabulo a priore percusso/Then the prior shall strike the little bell'.
33 RC, pp. 13: 'Sonetur secundum signum/The second bell shall be rung', 'Primum sonet signum/Ring the first bell', 22 'Signa dum sonant/While the bells are ringing'.
34 RC, p. 19: 'Mox signorum motu fidelem advocantes plebem missam incohent/The bells shall ring to call the faithful together and the mass shall begin'.
35 RC, p. 16: 'Antequam illud audiatur signum/Before the bell is heard', 'Usque dum audiunt signum ad induendum/Until the sound of the bell for vesting'.

percussive verbal forms for what could have been other silent kinds of *signa*, such as *facere* (to make),[36] and *dare* (to give),[37] and verbs which might have depended on the use of a bodily gesture, occurring where and when the author of the *Regularis Concordia* might have expected that the community was already gathered.[38]

The *Regularis Concordia* also describes the use of *signa* in ways which suggest that Æthelwold had intended them to create a variety of effects useful to recognising specific offices. We might detect this, for example, in prescriptions requiring that some *signa* ring once and others 'continuously' (*continuatim pulsare*), and that, on some occasions, one could ring individually, but at other times a larger number could ring 'all together' (*omnia signa*).[39] Similar evidence survives in other monastic customaries, such as Abbot Ælfric of Eynsham's *Epistula ad monachos*. Written for the new foundation at Eynsham in c.1005, this customary depended on and shared much of Æthelwold's framework on *signa*, and, perhaps unsurprisingly, appears to have expected *signa* to play a similar function. Indeed, it affords a view onto a similar complex of variations in the soundscape of his own community at Eynsham, and appears to have anticipated that some would be singular (*signum*), while others worked in the plural (*omnia signa pulsentur*).[40]

Scholarship originating in anthropology has also long drawn attention to the significance of ritual gestures in the formation of 'communal

---

36 RC, pp. 17: 'Facto signo a priore/At a sign from the prior', 'Facto signo agant orationem/Then, when the bell is rung, there shall be a space for prayer', 23 'Facto signo a priore/At a sign from the prior'.
37 RC, pp. 21: 'Donec iterum dato signo Nonam agant/Until None which shall be recited when the second bell has rung', 23 'Rursumque dato tintinnabuli signo/When the little bell rings again'.
38 RC, pp. 31, 21. Æthelwold also distinguished occasions for when the *tabula*, a board listing the daily chores of the brethren, 'was to be sounded out' (*pulsetur*), see RC, p. 20.
39 RC, pp. 13: 'Continuatim pulsetur tintinnabulum/The little bell shall be rung continuously', 28-9 'Omnibusque signis motis agatur Missa/Then all the bells shall peal and the Mass shall be celebrated'.
40 For all references to bells, see EME, pp. 110-11, 117-8, 118-9, 134-5, 140-1, 142-3, e.g. p. 110-11: 'Usquequo signum Tertie insonverit/Until the bell for Tierce rings', and 118-19 'Ad nocturnam et ad Vesperam uti ad Missam omnia signa pulsentur/All the bells are rung at Nocturns and Vespers just as they are at Mass'.

identities'.[41] These studies have considered that ritual gestures can function as a type of private language, providing a behavioural node around which individuals could show their acceptance of norms of behaviour. The *Regularis Concordia* appears to set down on occasions throughout the monastic complex these kinds of behaviours – ritual gestures which Æthelwold appears to have either associated with boys in particular, or which he expected brethren to express, and which, by extension, he appears to have expected that boys might encounter and would have been important to their behavioural learning after oblation.[42]

Æthelwold's prescriptions indicate that expression of ritual gesture took on a relatively fixed form of routines, repeating on a daily and seasonal basis and beginning from the moment brethren arose from bed, when he expected them first of all to sign themselves with the Holy Cross.[43] The *Regularis Concordia* expected the liturgical community to partake in ritual silences proper to the cloister, where brethren were not permitted to speak between Vespers on one evening and Chapter on the following day.[44] The *Regularis Concordia* expected a similar course of ritual actions to be performed by those who entered the communal office of Chapter in the chapterhouse, requiring attendant brethren, upon entering, to turn east, salute the rood or crucifix, and lower their heads in the direction of the abbot or presiding senior.[45] Indeed, it expected a large

---

41 For example, Talal Asad, 'On Ritual and Discipline in Medieval Christian Monasticism', *Economy and Society* 12 (1983), pp. 287-327.
42 For example, see RC, pp. 13: 'Trinitatis reverentia ab omnibus legitime teneatur/The reverence to the Trinity shall be duly observed by all', 'Residentibus cunctis in sedilibus suis ordinatim/All, ranged in order in the stalls', 15 'His vero finitis subsequatur letania quam universi, more solito prostrati humiliter nullo except/Then the bell shall ring for the Litany at which all without exception shall humbly prostrate themselves as it the custom', 17 'Tunc residentibus cunctis legatur martyrologium, quo dicto surgentes omnes/When the brethren are seated, the Martyrology shall be read; all shall then rise'.
43 RC, p. 11: 'Primum sibi signum sanctae crucis imprimat per Sanctae Trinitatis incovationem/He shall first of all sign himself with the sign of the Holy Cross, invoking the Holy Trinity'.
44 RC, p. 54-5: 'Silentium diligenti cura in claustro custodiant; nam et omni tempore a primo pulsu Vespertinalis Synaxis silentium teneatur in claustro usquequo Capitulum finiatur alterius diei/Keeping strict silence in the cloister. For from the first bell of the Vesper Office silence must always be kept there until after the Chapter of the following day'.
45 RC, p. 17: 'Convenientes ad Capitulum ipso praecedente, versu facie ad orientem

number of these ritual observances to focus on the space of the choir, where the *Regularis Concordia* required members to genuflect in unison,[46] and prostrate themselves on the floor, every day after Prime throughout the year, and a further eight times a day and every day during Lent.[47] We find these expectations and a similar picture of behavioural learning in Abbot Ælfric of Eynsham's later customary for Eynsham too. Here, Ælfric appears to have expected his brethren to conform to similar acts of genuflection in their choir (*omnes pariter surgentes genua flectent*),[48] to learn to walk with bare feet during processions (*nudipedalia*),[49] and to share in requirements to lie prostrate on the ground in the choir space (*prostrati*).[50] Indeed, this regulatory picture of ritual gesture is supported by more anecdotal evidence contained in a document known to specialists as the *Monasteriales Indicia*. This manuscript, now London BL Cotton Tiberius MS A. III (fols. 97v-101v), contains an extensive list which witnesses the development and transmission by c.1050 of a system of sign language in Anglo-Saxon England, revealing unique details like boys' dietary access to meat before adulthood, and learning of 127 non verbal gestures - with two fingers pointing to the eyes representing their teachers, and the little finger representing themselves.[51]

---

salutent crucem et ceteris undique fratribus se vultu inclinato humilient/All shall come together for the Chapter, the prior leading. Turning to the east they shall salute the Cross and with bared heads abase themselves before one another'.

46 RC, pp. 12 'Tunc flexis genibus in loco congruo et consueto/Then, kneeling down in his proper and accustomed place', 13 'Flectentes genua post quinque psalmos, facto signo a priore/Genuflecting at a sign from the prior after each set of five psalms', 17 'Subiungentes Gloria et flectentes genua si tempus ita dictaverit/With the *Gloria* at the end, the brethren making a genuflection if the season of the year demands it'.

47 RC, pp. 15: 'His vero finitis subsequatur letania quam universi, more solito prostrati humiliter nullo excepto, signo pulsato compleant/Then the bell shall ring for the Litany at which all without exception shall humbly prostrate themselves as is the custom', 38 'Post quod letaniam agant prostrati/ After this they shall recite the Litany, prostrate'.

48 EME, pp. 116-17: 'All shall rise together and genuflect'.

49 EME, pp. 126-7: 'Parasceve etiam debent exercere nudipedalia usquequo crux adoretur/ On Good Friday they should also go barefoot until the cross is venerated'.

50 EME, pp. 122-3: 'Cotidie post expletionem uniuscuiusque hore duos psalmos prostrati solo oratorii peroremus devoti/Everyday from Ash Wednesday [until Maundy Thursday (feast days excepted)], at the conclusion of every hour we are to prostrate ourselves on the floor of the church and fervently recite two psalms'.

51 It contains signs which enabled monks to indicate food, clothing, books, tools, different groups of people (including children, who were signed with the little finger), see

CHAPTER ONE: DISCIPLINE AND BEHAVIOUR

The *Regularis Concordia* suggests that boys' experiences of monastic discipline at the Old Minster also depended in their round on participation in a 'school' (*schola*). Æthelwold provided some four individual references to a 'school' in the course of his *Regularis Concordia*, and appears to have associated that term with *pueri* or boys, with a dedicated 'guardian' (*custos*), and with at least one dedicated 'teacher' (*schola cum magistro*) who appears to have been required to supervise and instruct them.[52] The prologue of the *Regularis Concordia* indicates that the *schola* was expected to occupy itself in 'reciting psalms' (*Sed solito cum tota schola* [. . .] *psalmodiis inserviendo*), but, sadly, neither the prologue nor the customary as a whole tell us much more about its shape and disciplinary role.[53]

Studies originating in the late-nineteenth and twentieth centuries often assumed that monastic schools were physical spaces controlled by teachers.[54] Indeed, studies of Anglo-Saxon England have often adopted descriptors like 'classroom' and 'schoolroom', giving tacit approval to those impressions.[55] Despite our historiography, however, these forms

---

D. Banham, *Monasteriales Indicia: The Anglo-Saxon Monastic Sign Language* (1991), pp. 22-23, and for Banham's argument on eating meat see, 74-75; For direct evidence of meat-eating oblates, see also 'adhuc carnibus vescor, quia puer sum', in ÆlfColl, p. 46.

52 Symons postulated that some references to the *schola* refer to a school of trained adult singers rather than boys, but I find no overwhelming reason to follow the position, see RC, pp. 8: 'Nec ipse custos cum singulo aliquo puerulo sine tertio qui testis assistat migrandi licentiam habeat, sed solito cum tota schola [. . .] eat/Nor shall the master himself be allowed to be in company with a boy without a third person as witness; but let master and *schola* go together . . .', 14 'Egressa schola cum magistro ad necessitudinis usum/When the *schola*, with their master, leave the church for the necessity of nature', 16 'Dehinc psalmodiis dediti facies suas, uti mos est, lavent schola universa cum magistro et abbate/Next, the entire *schola* with their master and the abbot shall wash their faces as is customary, intent on the psalms as they do so', 21-2 'Surgentes a mensa vacent lectioni aut psalmis iuxta praeceptum regulae/Rising up from the meal, they shall give themselves to reading or to the psalms, according to the ordinance of the Rule', 42: 'Itemque schola idipsum latine, *Sanctus Deus*/And the *schola* repeating the same in Latin, *Sanctus Deus*', 48 'Postea descendat abbas cum schola canente letanias quinas ad fontes benedicendos/Afterwards the abbot shall go down with the *schola* to bless the font, singing the five-fold Litanies', 57 'Postea descendat abbas cum schola canente letanias quinas ad fontes benedicendos/The abbot and *schola* shall then go down to bless the font, singing the five-fold Litanies'.

53 RC, p. 8: 'But let master and *schola* go together in the accustomed manner [. . .] reciting the psalms'.

54 i.e. Arthur Leach, *The Schools of Medieval England* (London, 1915).

55 For illustrations of this problematic terminology, see Patrizia Lendinara, 'Instructional

of organisation are not obvious in the prescriptive record. The *Regularis Concordia* does not obviously associate the school with any single fixed location or even a series of locations, and, in fact, it more often assumed that the *schola* was a group rather than a part of the material complex. Indeed, Ælfric, in his own dependent customary, the *Epistula ad monachos*, described the *schola* in fluid terms, indicating that the *schola* moved around the monastic complex separately from seniors (*schola simul et seniores singillatim*), and was able to engage in a daily round not connected to experiences of Latin instruction.[56]

Neither the *Regularis Concordia* nor the *Epistula ad monachos* allow us to be certain of how teachers or guardians managed and corrected the behaviours of boys in a *schola*, however. In fact, Æthelwold's customary only reveals an effort on his part to manage the behaviours of seniors. It prohibited seniors from taking 'immature youths' (*iuvenculi*) along with them on journeys.[57] It restricted all senior monks from embracing or kissing oblates of any pre-adult age (*adolescentes vel pueruli*).[58] Indeed, it required that no guardian should be left alone with a single boy, adding that they should always have at least one other boy as a companion.[59] These prescriptions have attracted deep concern in the past. They have been

---

manuscripts in England, the tenth and eleventh-century codices and the early Norman ones', in *Form and Content of Instruction in Anglo-Saxon England in the Light of Contemporary Manuscript Evidence,* ed. Patricia Lendinara, Loredana Lazzari, and Maria A. D'Aronco (Turnhout, 2007), p. 71; Gernot Wieland, 'The Glossed Manuscript: Classbook or Library Book?', *ASE* 14 (1985), pp. 153-73; and also John Contreni, 'The Carolingian School: Letters from the Classroom', in *Carolingian Learning, Masters, and Manuscripts,* ed. John Contreni (Aldershot, 1992), pp. 84-111.

56 EME, pp. 110-11: 'The children together as a group, the senior monks individually'.
57 RC, p. 7: 'Iterantes vero non iuvenculos sed adultos quorum admonitione meliorentur secum in comitatu ducant/Again, let the brethren take with them as companions on a journey not youths but grown-up persons from whose conversation they may take profit'.
58 RC, p. 7: 'Domi vero degentes, non solum fratres sed etiam abbates, adolescentes vel puerulos non brachiis amplexando vel labris leviter deosculando, sed caritativo animi affectu sine verbis adulatoriis reverenter cum magna cautela diligant/In the monastery moreover let neither monks nor abbots embrace or kiss, as it were, youths or children; let their affection for them be spiritual, let them keep from words of flattery, and let them love the children reverently and with the greatest circumspection.
59 RC, pp. 7-8: 'Nec ipse custos cum singulo aliquot puerulo sine tertio qui testis/Nor shall the master himself be allowed to be in company with a boy without a third person as witness'.

CHAPTER ONE: DISCIPLINE AND BEHAVIOUR

considered as revealing of Æthelwold's anxiety at Winchester about a history of abuse of seniors' power, and as elements of a fresh initiative to prevent and punish it alongside associated problems of favouritism and victimisation in England's emerging network of reformist Benedictine houses.[60] Although we cannot know the precise details prompting Æthelwold to restrain religious in this way, at the outset of a document which declared the ambitions of a monastic reform, his prohibitions against adults make his (and also Ælfric's) lack of direction for teachers on how to manage the behaviours of oblates even more puzzling.

This vacuum of evidence relating to boys' experience in a *schola* context leaves us in a difficult position. It means that we are not only unable to understand how *magistri* might have attempted to discipline their schools or teach boys about matters relating to monastic discipline, but also of being unable to understand whether *magistri* were ever expected to adhere to a shared set of disciplinary principles. Without any guidance from the *Regularis Concordia*, we could even speculate that Æthelwold might have *deliberately* allowed this vacuum, and had either intended to impose his own disciplinary views on his contemporaries on a more interpersonal basis, or had intended to allow *magistri* and/or *custodes* across England to act semi-autonomously, imposing their own disciplinary systems onto boys instead.

Ælfric of Eynsham, student of Winchester, teacher of boys at Cerne Abbas, Abbot of Eynsham, and one of the most prominent authors of late Anglo-Saxon England, composed a number of influential school-texts which might help us answer these questions in part, by asking how he and contemporary teachers sought to manage their own 'school' groups in this surprisingly empty regulatory context:

> Inceditis morigerate cum auscultaveritis ecclesie campanas, et ingredimini in orationem, et inclinate suppliciter ad almas aras, et state disciplinabiliter, et concinite unanimiter, et intervenite pro vestris erratibus et egredimini sine scurrilitate in claustrum.[61]

---

60 Patricia Quinn recognised a sexual dynamic in her *Better than the Sons of Kings*, esp. pp. 155-194, at 155. Maria Lahaye-Geusen also devotes a sub-section of a chapter in her *Das Opfer der Kinder*, pp. 417-426, esp. 420-32 and at p. 431.
61 ÆlfColl, p. 48: 'When you hear the bells of the church, bow humbly before the holy

This short section of Ælfric's *Colloquium*, a Latin school-text which constituted a single Latin dialogue intended to help students to learn how (and what) to speak in the language, is demonstrative of the potential of school-texts as an alternative source on monastic discipline to prescriptive regulations in late Anglo-Saxon England.[62] In this section in particular, we can see that Ælfric's *Colloquium* contains a wealth of information with regard to contemporary disciplinary practices. It demonstrates that Ælfric had understood a connection between systems of discipline and experiences of Latin education, and exploited this in the context of the monastic school in order to shape boys' behaviours.

We should be clear that Ælfric's school-text does not create an entirely original disciplinary system, we can see that his work leans on structures which can be found in a prescriptive context. In the section given above, for example, we can immediately recognise routines and ideals of behaviour which conform with and seem to extend from the *Regularis Concordia*. For one, Ælfric's school-text explicitly associated boys' observance of a round with their hearing of bells, and he appears to recognise in them a function considered above, to co-ordinate boys on their daily routines. Ælfric's insistence that boys observe a fixed series of ritual gestures upon entering the church and choir, that is that they should first 'bow', then 'stand', and 'sing together', in specific places, times, and in order, appears to correlate closely with and support an understanding of ritual gestures which we have set out above too.

This short section also reveals what appear to be more general expectations of boys' behavioural learning that are not often conveyed by a prescriptive source-base. It indicates, for example, that boys' behavioural learning should include the need to acquire and exercise spatial awareness. We see this particularly clearly, for example, where Ælfric's fictional *magister* insists that boys should adapt their behaviour to the church spaces they

---

    altars, stand with discipline and sing together, intercede for your faults and leave without buffoonery into the cloister'.

62 Joyce Hill has argued the *Colloquium* was part of a 'triad' of grammatical school-texts including Ælfric's *Grammar*, *Glossary*, and *Colloquium*, 'Ælfric's Grammatical Triad', in *Form and Content of Instruction in Anglo-Saxon England in the Light of Contemporary Manuscript Evidence*, ed. Patrizia Lendinara, Lorendana Lazzari, and Maria Amalia D'Aronco (Turnhout, 2007), pp. 285-307. It should be noted, however, that they are only found united in one manuscript (Oxford St. John's MS 154).

CHAPTER ONE: DISCIPLINE AND BEHAVIOUR

entered and left. His expectation, that boys should change their behaviour in particular, suggests that monastic boys were not only encouraged to acquire a heightened level of spatial and behavioural awareness, but to know also when to maintain behaviours and for how long, to learn the moments and spaces in which they were needed, and to learn too when their seniors expected them to adjust their conduct as those and any other unspoken expectations changed.

Ælfric's decision to focus on boys' behaviours in the church could even express a contemporary anxiety about the locations of misbehaviour. This concern appears to centre on the conduct of boys in sacred spaces, or spaces which adults such as Ælfric might have thought of as sacred, but which untutored boys might not have valued as such or to the same degree themselves. We could recover evidence for this anxiety, for example, beneath the surface of Ælfric's *Colloquium*, and in directions that boys should observe a series of fixed ritual routines as they entered the church, and to focus on making a prayer or bowing to the altars as they entered together, and, indeed, that boys ought to avoid 'buffoonery' (*scurrilitas*) when inside and around the threshold of a church too.

The longer *Colloquia*, a school-text composed by his only known student, Ælfric Bata, were based on Ælfric of Eynsham's *Colloquium*, and demonstrate that teachers played an active role in creating norms of discipline. They also show that Ælfric's attitudes, anxieties, and his subscription to the importance of entering sacred spaces were, in a narrow sense, successfully reproduced by at least one successive generation of students in a monastic *schola*:

> Facite, et pulchre in oratorio et refectorio, nusquam sine licentia discurrentes, et in dormitorio similiter et in omni loco vos custodite.[63]

This passage, taken from dialogue no. 6 of Bata's *Colloquia*, echoes and provides visible testimony of his own formation under Abbot Ælfric of Eynsham, whom he called 'his teacher' (*Ælfricus Abbas meus fuit magister*).[64] Bata's text is not a perfect mirror image of his teacher's, how-

---

63 ÆlfBColl, pp. 92-3: 'Act nicely in the chapel and refectory, in the dormitory and everywhere else, never running about, without permission'.
64 Bata referred to Ælfric of Eynsham in the prologue to his own version of Ælfric's *Colloquium* which is now contained in Oxford St. John's College MS 154, fol. 204

ever. Its differences are as important, and they tell us about his own choices as an author. This section demonstrates his similar attitudes to, and perhaps shared anxieties about oblate behaviour in sacred space, but his dialogue also reveals conceptions of misbehaviour and correction which are not visible in the works of Ælfric of Eynsham. Where Ælfric had discouraged vague 'buffoonery', Bata's text described with greater precision that running (*discurrere*) was especially discouraged (and, perhaps, most commonly observed). By indicating that boys required permission (*non sine licentia*), Bata also reveals to us that running might at times have been acceptable. This view can be extended even further. Across the forty-one dialogues of the *Colloquia*, Bata also accounts for stealing, telling lies, spreading gossip, wasting time idly, failing to memorise or recite lessons, hiding or otherwise staying in bed, ignoring bells, not singing when expected, or distracting others with inappropriate gestures as being equally commonplace. Indeed, Bata describes occasions where boys refused to recognise a mistake, blamed others for their own actions, and questioned a teacher's authority.[65] He thus provides us with a view of a disciplinary system of greater and more credible complexity. Indeed, he sheds light onto thought systems where it is not just fictional boys' misbehaviours which appear to be subject to disciplinary outcomes, but where disciplinarians appear to be subject to norms of policing and behavioural management as well.

Some questions remain: quite where did their norms come from, on what basis did they construct them, and indeed how widely were expectations surrounding the management and formation of boys' behaviours shared by teachers throughout Anglo-Saxon England. On the first of these questions, Nathan Ristuccia has confirmed that contemporary teachers did in fact turn to the prescriptive record for their disciplinary principles. He has argued, for example, that dialogue no. 4 of the *Colloqiua* of Ælfric Bata was grounded on Bata's close reading of chapter 2 of the

---

recto: 'Hanc sententiam Latini sermonis olim Ælfricus Abbas composuit qui meus fuit magister sed tamen ego Ælfric Bata multas postea huic addidi appendices/Abbot Ælfric, who was my teacher, once composed this sentence of a Latin sermon, but I, Ælfric Bata, have added many sentences as appendices to it' (my transcription and translation); cf. ÆlfBColl, p. 2.

65 ÆlfBColl, pp. 83-5.

Regula Benedicti, which was itself based on II Timothy 4:2 – encouraging abbots to 'reprimand, implore, and reprove' poorly behaved brethren (i.e., *arguere, obsegrare* [sic], *increpare*).[66] Bata appears therefore to have mined the *Regula* for principles which related to the abbot and the management of a monastic community, adopting them as a model for teachers and for the management of monastic schools instead:

> O magistri, nolite provocare ad iracundiam filios vestros cum superflua austeritatis duritia, sed mensurate et cum bonitate aliquando increpentes, aliquando arguentes, aliquando obsecrentes, et aliquando flagellantes.[67]

Insofar as dialogue no. 4 reveals Bata's adoption of this procedure, it also reveals that Bata had chosen to rearrange and add to them. For one, Bata's revised order encouraged teachers to use 'reproof' before 'reprimand' and 'imploring' (i.e. (3) (1) (2)), and Bata also appears to have added a fourth element, introducing the verb *flagellare* or 'to flog/beat' to his list. In doing so, Bata significantly transformed the verbal corrective centre of gravity of the original framework of the *Regula* and in a way which has gone unrecognised by Ristuccia. What this shows, however, is that Bata had brought his *Colloquia* into line, not with the Latin *Regula*, but with the version of chapter 2 as it appears in Æthelwold's *Old English Rule*, and with Æthelwold's own addition of *witnian*, or 'to torment or plague with violence' in particular.[68] Similar to how the *Colloquium* of Ælfric of Eynsham appears to have intersected with the *Regularis Concordia* then, the contents of the *Colloquia* of Ælfric Bata suggest that teachers had also explored Æthelwold's *Old English Rule* in order to construct disciplinary principles in the absence of any clearer prescriptive authority, and, what is more, they indicate that teachers used the vehicles of their school-texts

---

66 RSB, c. 2, pp. 24-5. For the original identification, see Ristuccia, 'Ideology and Corporal Punishment', 375, 377-8; OERB, c. 2, p. 13: 'Þrea and witna and halsa and cid'.
67 ÆlfBColl, pp. 86-7: 'Masters, do not provoke your sons to anger with needlessly harsh sternness, but discipline with moderation and kindness, sometimes rebuking, sometimes reproving, sometimes entreating, and sometimes whipping'.
68 OERB, c. 2, p. 13: 'Þrea and witna and halsa and cid'. BT: v. *witnian*: 'to punish, torment, plague'.

in order to ensure that their principles continued to have influence, and wherever and for as long as they played a role in experiences of Latin education.

In the absence of evidence for other contexts in which violence could be imposed on boys in the prescriptive record, it could also be useful to ask whether school-texts give us access to teachers' views on and boys' experiences of violence. Bata's syntactical choices, and his positioning of 'flogging' at the end of a long clause of less obviously violent and seemingly milder verbally-signifying corrective methods in dialogue no. 4 of his *Colloquia* could suggest that he had also viewed it differently to Æthelwold, locating it in a position of *final* rather than second resort. Supporting this view, Irina Dumitrescu has argued that Bata's own *magister* provides evidence for a preference of threats and forms of deterrence rather than violent correction. What is perhaps more significant about Ælfric of Eynsham's own writings, however, is that this evidence occurs in more elementary school-texts on grammar like the *Excerptiones de arte grammatica anglice* (EGA), and so they may even represent the experiences and intended learning outcomes of a significantly younger demographic of 'uneducated boys' (*inscientes pueruli*).[69]

Irina Dumitrescu has shown that the *Excerptiones de arte grammatica anglice* integrated a series of striking mnemonics into examples of Latin inflection and conjugation which threatened and reminded students of the possibilities of violent correction in the event of poor behaviour. She has drawn attention to this in a section 'on verbs' for example, where Ælfric introduced students to the concept of active and passive verbal forms, and where he used images of pain and violence in order to facilitate student understanding of the active voice through *weorc*, signifying 'labour', and the passive voice through *þrowung*, meaning 'suffering'.[70]

---

69 EGA, p. 1: 'Ego deputo hanc lectionem inscientibus puerulis, non senibus, aptandam/ I determine that this work has been suitably prepared for untutored boys, not old men' (my translation).
70 Irina A. Dumitrescu, 'The Grammar of Pain in Ælfric Bata's Colloquies', *Forum for Modern Language Studies* 45 (2009), p. 241. BT: n. *weorc*: 'work, operative action', n. *þro[e]wung*: 'feeling, suffering, suffering which is painful', see EGA, pp. 119-22: '*Verbum* ys word, an dæl ledenspræce mid tide and hade butan case getacniende oððe sum ðing to donne oððe sum ðing to þrowigenne ... *significatio* ys ... hwæt þæt word getacnige, dæde oððe þrowunge [...] *activa verba*, þæt synd dædlice word, þa

CHAPTER ONE: DISCIPLINE AND BEHAVIOUR

Ælfric had also sought to demonstrate to boys how those forms differed by scaffolding his instruction with powerfully relatable examples, describing the active form in terms of how he 'will cane' students (i.e. *verbero, ic swinge*) and the passive in terms of boys' experience of being caned (i.e. *verberor, ic eom beswungen*).[71]

These occasions in Ælfric's *Excerptiones de arte grammatica anglice* strongly imply that violence had a tangible place in contemporary boyhood, and there are occasions in Ælfric Bata's *Colloquia* that would support this view too. We can turn, for example, to the evidence of dialogue no. 28, where Bata's school-text appears to authorise the immediate beating of a boy who was accused of theft:

[*Puer*]
Ecce, habemus virgas nunc, domne
[*Magister*]
Vultis vos flagellare eum?
[P]
Etiam statim, si debemus.
[M]
Sumite virgas duas et stet unus in dextera parte culi illius et alter in sinistra, et sic invicem percutite super culum eius et dorsum, et flagellate eum bene prius, et ego volo postea[...]
[M]
Percute, tu stulte, melius. Deridet verbera vestra, et ea non sentit omnino.[72]

---

geswuteliað hwæt men doð [and] geswutelað min weorc [...] *passiva verba*, þæt synd þrowiendlice word [...] þa word eac sume... habbað þrowiendlice getacnunge, swaswa ys: *vapulo*, ic eom beswungen/ *Verbum* means 'word', it is a part of Latin speech with tenses and conditions without cases and which signifies either something 'to do' or something 'to suffer/feel'... *significatio* means what the word signifies, whether a 'deed' or a 'sufferance' [...] *activa verba*, is a term for doing words, which convey what we do and which convey our labours, for example, [...] *passiva verba*, is a phrase which is for feeling words [...] words [which] can also have some signification of suffering, just like the verb: *vapulo*, meaning 'I am beaten' (my translation).
71 EGA, pp. 119-22: 'I beat [others]', and 'I am beaten' (my translations).
72 ÆlfBColl, pp. 164-7 esp. 166-7: 'Here, we have got some rods now, sir/ Are you willing to whip him?/ Yes, sir. Right away, if we must/ Take two rods. One boy stand on the right side of his ass (sic) and one on the left. Take turns like this beating his ass (sic) and back. First you two beat him well and I will afterwards [...] Hit harder, you fool! He is

This peer-sourced beating is shocking. Indeed, it is easy to see why it might previously have been dismissed as a 'burlesque' of reality, and as an unreliable witness to the role of violence in boys' lives.[73] There are, however, good reasons for taking this dialogue seriously. Irina Dumitrescu, for example, has shown we can situate the dialogue against the backdrop of the far harsher treatment of thieves in contemporary royal law codes – which prescribed that so-called 'men' of twelve years of age should be punished with death.[74] Just as compelling, however, is the account of victimisation which Bata wrote for the passage which followed. Here, the boy discontinued his appeal, and turned instead to what appears to have been intended as an oblate monologue - revealing Bata's considerable insight into the damaging effect of violence on boys' psychological well-being:

> [*Puer*] Amodo, pater, cessare ab hac fraude volo, pro qua hec patior. Satis sum modo flagellates et punitus hac vice [...] Iam moriturus sum [...] Hoc est mihi malum nunc. Karius esset mihi mortuum [...] Nullus mihi protectionem prebet nec defensionem prestat, nullus adminiculum tribuit, nullus malis meis succurrit. Desertus sum, ab omnibus amicis meis et proximis et notis et propinquis [...] Ego deposita facie sileo et taceo. illi non quiescunt, sed amplius seviunt [...] Modo sanguis meus in terra manat, cum lacrimis cruor stillat.[75]

making fun of your blows. He does not feel them at all'.
73 For one, Katherine O'Brien O'Keeffe has argued that the Colloquia are a 'burlesque'. This view has been strongly contested by Michael Lapidge, David Porter, Scott Gwara, and Christopher Jones, see: C.A.Jones, 'The Irregular Life in Ælfric Bata's Colloquies', *Leeds Studies in English*, 37 (2006), pp. 241-60.
74 Dumitrescu, 'Grammar of Pain', pp. 239-253. This age threshold for identifying a child as being criminally responsible can be seen under kings Æthelstan (925-939) and Cnut (c.1016-1035), see Dorothy Whitelock, *English Historical Documents I, c. 500-1042* (rev. ed., London, 1996), (VI Æthelstan), c. 2, no. 37, p. 428: 'No thief who steals over twelve pence and is over twelve years of age is to be spared ... we are to kill him and take all that he owns'; (Cnut II, 'Secular Laws') c. 49, nos. 20-1, p. 464: 'Every man over the age of twelve is to give an oath that he will not steal or be an accessory to theft'.
75 ÆlfBColl pp. 167--9: 'Father, from this moment I will stop the lying I am suffering for. I have been beaten and punished enough this time [...] I am about to die [...] This is hurting me! I would rather be dead now than to bear such lashes. Woe is me! Why was I ever born? [...] No one offers me protection or gives me any defence, no one gives me help, or eases my troubles. I have been deserted, by all my friends, my family, aquaintances and kin [...] I cast my face down and say nothing. Instead of ceasing to attack me,

Here, Bata constructs a situational dialogue through which boys could learn how to express their distress in Latin. He recognises that violence, if tipped into extremes - signified here by the drawing of blood and isolation and ignoring of boys - had the potential to result in long term harm which he described later as 'anxiety of mind', bound in great trouble, and overwhelmed by ills and miseries (*angustia mei animi turbat me*).[76] Bata's recognition of the potential impact of violence is surprising in a documentary landscape that usually accounts for violence passingly, as an uncontested norm. It suggests that he at least questioned its advantages, and it offers a view of attitudes of more credible complexity than has sometimes been allowed. It also forces us to ask whether the extremity of violence described in dialogue no. 28 connects us to conditions and experiences which were typical. Urging us to caution in particular is the fact that dialogue no. 28 is an exception. Indeed, Bata describes the imposition of corporal violence on a boy in just this one case, and in the case of one dialogue out of a total of some forty-one. We might consider therefore that dialogue no. 28 represents an exceptional experience, important perhaps to teachers' intentions to demonstratively punish in particularly grave circumstances, but not necessarily a frequent occurrence. Bata's involvement of several boys to punish an individual would even seem to express an acceptance of forms of violence which spread the effects of punishment to several boys as witnesses and administrators of violence. Bata's dialogue could therefore also connect us to conditions of punishment for theft that were deliberately inclusive, and intended to ensure that the *memory* of violence itself would play a part in preventing any other boys from theft and from a need for harsher punishment.[77]

At the same time, and since we lack corroborating sources, Bata's *Colloquia* could simply give witness to methods that were confined to

---

they only grow more vicious [...] Now my blood lies on the earth and my blood drips with tears'.

76 ÆlfBColl pp. 166-7: 'circumseptus erumna magna/ oppressus infelicitate et angustiis'.
77 For an anthropological view of the role of pain and memory in medieval pedagogy, see Mary Carruthers, 'Reading with Attitude: Remembering the Book', in *The Book and the Body*, ed. Dolores W. Frese and Katherine O'Brien O'Keeffe (London, 1997), pp. 1-33, at pp. 14-15; Mary J. Carruthers, *The Book of Memory: A Study of Memory in Medieval Culture* (rev. ed., Cambridge, 2008), p. 129.

his school. This need not surprise us. The *Colloquium* and *Colloquia* demonstrate that boys' experiences of discipline and their conditions of violence depended to some extent on their own teachers, and they may have been especially dependent given that we lack evidence of a prescriptive document authorising teacher's responsibilities. We should be careful too, perhaps, not to preclude entirely the possibility that these school-texts give us access to disciplinary conditions which shaped boys' experiences more widely still. The *Colloquium* of Ælfric of Eynsham and the *Colloquia* of Ælfric Bata testify to the ways in which religious teachers and their students shared and transmitted ideals of discipline among themselves. They show how school-texts authorised situations where violence could (and perhaps should not) be legitimately administered. Indeed, they also show how school-texts played a role in filling a regulatory vacuum left by documents like the *Regula Benedicti*, the *Old English Rule*, and the *Regularis Concordia,* informing views about behavioural learning and violence wherever they came into use. While we cannot say with confidence therefore that the works of Ælfric and Bata connect us to a shared culture of discipline in late Anglo-Saxon England, their texts suggest that boys' disciplinary conditions and experiences would have depended on similar sources, on their teachers, on their teachers' school-texts, and, ultimately, on a shared framework of prescriptive sources which those teachers turned to for guidance on matters of disciplinary enforcement.

Anglo-Norman England:

In this section, the *Constitutiones* form a similar bedrock to the *Regularis Concordia* for a study of disciplinary systems at Christ Church Canterbury after the Norman Conquest. Greater dependence on the *Constitutiones* for insight into a single post-Conquest environment in this section does not present a serious limitation, however. In fact, unlike the *Regularis Concordia*, and as we have seen in the previous chapter, Lanfranc's *Constitutiones* offer an outline for a contemporary oblation ritual, and, in doing so, provide us with a more immediate view onto boys' anticipated first encounters with a monastic context.

Lanfranc's rite of oblation shows that boys who entered Christ Church were, from the moment and duration of that ritual, subject to the regulatory framework of the *Constitutiones*.[78] The rite itself does not disclose that the youngest oblates were expected to be capable of observing any forms of monastic discipline. As we have seen in the introduction to this study, Lanfranc described boy entrants in his prescription for a ritual of oblation, but did not require very much from them. Whether tutored or not, experienced in religious behaviours or not, Lanfranc's ritual of oblation did not expect boys to express an understanding of monastic norms, save for submitting to being tonsured and wearing a monastic habit. It is a ritual which seems to allow for the oblations of very young children, potentially of infant age. Indeed, anecdotal evidence would support that possibility. We see this in the case of a complaint against the oblation of two infant boys 'barely weaned and beyond the cradle' which we know had been made to Pope Alexander III (c.1159-1181) by the monks of the nearby abbey of St. Augustine's in Canterbury in 1178, for example.[79] But Lanfranc's *Constitutiones* frustrate direct attempts to assertain how infant boys might have first become subject to his own prescriptive rules. While the *Constitutiones* are fuller and more detailed in their attempt to frame boys' oblations than its predecessor, suggesting that children's conditions became more dependent on a prescriptive authority after the Conquest, and that Lanfranc allowed far less room for monks to act autonomously in shaping the experiences of boys in their care, Lanfranc adds little to our understanding of the conditions of care which we might have expected such boys to encounter.

Infancy

In the same way we have seen that the *Regula Sancti Benedicti* employed the term *infantes* as a preferred form for children, so too Lanfranc's

---

78 *Constitutiones*, c. 105, pp. 162-5.
79 see 'bulla ne pueri infra aetatem xv annorum recipiantur in habitum monachalem/Bull si that boys under the age of fifteen should not be received into the monastic habit', issued by Pope Alexander as a result of the complaint, recorded further in C. Hardwick and Thomas of Elmham (eds.), *Historia Monasterii Sancti Augustini Cantuariensis* (London, 1858), no. 58, p. 427.

Constitutiones appear to have used *infantes* and *infans* as preferred terms of reference for monastic boys. This terminology might first seem to suggest that Lanfranc had followed the Latin *Regula Benedicti*, and that he had authorised the use of beatings on 'infants' whenever they made a fault in the choir at Christ Church, Canterbury:

> In choro presente abbate nisi precepto eius nullus eos [infantes] percutiat.[80]

This does not appear to be the case, however. On closer inspection of the *Constitutiones,* Lanfranc's uses of terms like *infantes* appears imprecise. Lanfranc's imprecision only becomes clear if we appreciate in particular the unlikelihood that 'infants' would have been able to carry out all other prescribed duties attached to *infantes*. Instead, Lanfranc's *Constitutiones* appear to have used the term *infans* and *infantes* on a generalised basis, as a shorthand for 'boys', mirroring almost all of the contemporary anecdotal records and alternative monastic customaries I have found for oblates, such as Nicholaus of Abingdon (fl.1130-58), Hugh Candidus of Peterborough (c.1095-1160), Richard of Ely (c.1177x94), John of Ely (d.1170), and, indeed, all the boy oblates who were subject to the later customs of Abingdon Abbey in c.1219, who were categorised as *pueri*.[81]

Naturally, we could assume that Lanfranc's use of *infans* therefore precludes a direct view of conditions and expectations which may have been important to any infants, in distinction to older and more capable oblates. There is, however, one occasion which takes the form of a single prescription on the engagement of one *infans* after Sext, where Lanfranc's *Constitutiones* might provide a window:

---

80 *Constitutiones*, c. 109, pp. 172-3: 'When the abbot is present in choir no one shall strike a child'.
81 This customary rather unusually also allowed boys to make noise during the main meal before Vespers '*sonum pueri ad prandium fecerint*/let the boys make noise at dinner', for this and all other references to pueri in this customary see, 'de obedieniariis abbatiae abbendonsis', in Stephenson, *Chronicon de Abingdon*, vol. ii, pp. 346-7, 349, 356, 361-2, 371, and 404. Manuscript now London BL Claudius MS B. Vi.

Post Sextam nullus in claustro loquatur donec infantes de monasterio exeant, et minimus eorum alta voce *Benedicite* dicat.[82]

The significance of this passage for us lies in Lanfranc's use of the superlative form of comparison *minimus* to assign a liturgical duty to a child. Needless to say, this appears to have demanded an individual who was to be at a particularly early point of his monastic life. Its importance in this chapter also lies in the fact that it appears to reveal a dynamic not obvious from the earlier *Regularis Concordia* – that 'infants' might have participated in a daily round. This portrait also seems credible. Lanfranc appears to expect little of this individual. The performance of this 'youngest' of the boys was to occur in an outlying space rather than in the choir or church, and this 'youngest' boy was only explicitly required to signpost the end of a monastic office. The occasion allows us to consider that young boys were prepared so that they could join in aspects of liturgical routines on a piecemeal basis. We could suppose that, in order to do so, they were expected to learn a few enabling, short, and accessible elements of liturgical Latin during their round, and prepare for a performance debut on this less intimidating and lower risk threshold of a daily Office.

Boyhood

The prescribed actions of this youngest boy are also useful because they allow us to consider the nature of a developmental gap represented here – a gap between the duties of this infant and the duties of all other and older *infantes* represented in this consuetudinary.[83] This gap provides a helpful view onto Lanfranc's changing expectations, shedding light onto how boys were expected to learn liturgical routines on a piecemeal basis

---

82 *Constitutiones*, c. 2, pp. 8-9: 'After Sext no one shall talk in the cloister till the children come out of church and the youngest of them says aloud "Bless ye the Lord"'.
83 For all references to boys (*infantes* and *pueri*) in relation to the choir-space including those which imply their presence, or directly required it*, see *Constitutiones*, c. 2, 4-9, esp. 6-7*; c. 3, pp. 12-13; c. 9, pp. 20-1; c. 19, pp. 28-9; c. 20-2, pp. 32-3*; c. 25, pp. 40-1*; 28-31, pp. 42-3*; c. 33-9, pp. 52-3*; c. 46-9, pp. 66-7*; c. 55, pp. 74-5*; c. 57, pp. 80-1*; c. 62-5, pp. 86-7*; c. 81, pp. 106-7*; c. 82, pp. 110-1*.

once they outgrew the duty of saying *Benedicite*. Lanfranc suggests, for example, that 'boys' (*infantes*) were eventually expected to integrate fully into the choir. His descriptions of its structure suggest that this also organised boys into two groups, occupying the right-hand and left-hand sides (*in dextro choro omnibus per ordinem et sic in sinistro*) similar to that of the Old Minster at Winchester encountered above.[84] Each of these sides of Christ Church's choir appears to have constituted a mixture of seniors and boys, and these appear to have organised the seniors in a hierarchical system of seating beginning from the 'lowest' of all choir places (*in loco ... ultimus omnium*).[85]

Lanfranc never made clear whether a hierarchy might have informed boys too. It is likely that Lanfranc had arranged boys as a group. Lanfranc's text expresses boys' distinctive status in the choir through his use of phrases such as *ordo seniorum*, or 'the community of seniors', and through terms implying a separable view of the seniors (who stand with youths) and boys (who stand with their teachers).[86] Lanfranc also appears to have assigned to boys and adults different times of arrival into the choir (*infantes expectent/ ingressis infantibus in chorum*),[87] and, on other occasions too, he appears to have expected seniors and boys to hold different areas of seating. Indeed, Lanfranc suggested on one occasion that seniors occupied places nearest to the altar (*priores a parte altaris sint, reliqui post eos sicut est ordo eorum*),[88] and so, we might assume by extension, that he intended children to occupy the space beside them, furthest away from the holy

---

84 See for example in arrangements for the celebration of feasts of twelve lessons, *Constitutiones*, c. 77, pp. 102-3: 'All in order on the right of the choir, and then those on the left'.
85 *Constitutiones*, c. 99, pp. 146-7.
86 *Constitutiones*, c. 28-31, pp. 42-3: 'In matutinis laudibus, cum incipiunt psalmum Laudate Dominum de celis, vadant magistri inter infantes, qui et versi sint ad priores, sicut et ipsi infantes; iuvenes vero, qui in custodia sunt, mixtim sint in ordine seniorum/ At lauds, when the psalm Laudate Dominum is begun, the masters shall join the children and face the seniors with them; the young monks under ward shall be mingled with the seniors',
87 *Constitutiones*, c. 2, pp. 6-7: 'Incumbentes terre infantes expectent/Wait on their knees for the children'; c. 25, pp. 40-1: 'Cum infantes loti fuerint ... ingressis chorum infantibus/When the children have washed ... when the children have entered the choir'.
88 *Constitutiones*, c. 55, pp. 78-9: 'Priores a parte altaris sint, reliqui post eos, sicut est ordo eorum/The seniors shall be nearest to the altar, and the rest behind them in order'.

CHAPTER ONE: DISCIPLINE AND BEHAVIOUR

sanctuary.

The *Constitutiones* give us grounds for considering that boys' experiences in the choir were particularised further still through systems of discipline and supervision. Unlike the *Regularis Concordia*, Lanfranc's *Constitutiones* do not detail how many seniors were required to watch over each group of boys in the choir. His *Constitutiones* only clearly required that a number of *magistri* or 'teachers' enter the choir alongside boys (*pueri cum magistris suis primi ingrediantur ecclesiam*) and that only these figures should have supervisory responsibilities over them (*remanentibus infantibus cum magistris suis in choro, qui ante missam debent esse induti*).[89] Just one occasion, relating to arrangements specific to Lauds on Maundy Thursday, requiring teachers to join the boys and face the senior community, seems to suggest that *magistri* did not ordinarily stand in amongst or mixed in with boys, but were otherwise expected to take seats belonging to the senior *ordo*.[90] Whether or not this tells us where teachers were usually expected to stand and why, however, and how this might have enabled supervision of boys, we cannot know.

Like the *Regularis Concordia*, Lanfranc's customary appears to subject boys to a separate daily round, requiring them to observe particular arrangements for washing, combing, eating, and to attend a *schola* and Chapter in the mundane spaces of the religious complex.[91] The *Constitutiones* also appear to have enabled boys' familiarisation with the

---

89 *Constitutiones*, c. 81, pp. 106-7 : 'The children and their masters shall be the first to enter the church' ; c. 62-5, pp. 86-7 'While the children, who should be vested before Mass, remain with their masters in choir'.
90 *Constitutiones*, c. 28-31, pp. 42-3: 'Vadant magistri inter infantes, qui et versi sint ad priores, sicut et ipsi infantes/The masters shall join the children and face the seniors with them'.
91 For all references to washing and combing, see *Constitutiones*, c. 9, pp. 20-1; c. 10, 22-3; c. 19, pp. 28-9; c. 20-2, pp. 32-3; c. 23, pp. 32-3; c. 25, pp. 40-1; c. 40-5, pp. 60-1 and 64-5; c. 55, pp. 74-5; c. 56, pp. 78-9; c. 57, pp. 80-1; c. 82, pp. 110-1; for direct references to boys engaging in a Divine Offices and other corporate celebrations, see c. 2, pp. 4-7 (Prime); for references to boys engaging in the celebration of mass services see also, c. 2, pp. 8-9 (High Mass); c. 28-31, pp. 46-7 (On Maundy Thursday); c. 46-9, pp. 66-7 and 70-1 (On Holy Saturday); c. 62-5, pp. 86-7 (On Feasts); for references to boys' taking of a *mixtum* in addition to attendance in the corporate meal in the refectory, see c. 32, pp. 48-9; c. 33-9, pp. 52-3; c. 46-9, pp. 70-1; c. 55, 74-5; c. 56, pp. 80-1; references to the school, see c. 32, pp. 48-9; c. 82, pp. 110-1; c. 109, pp. 172-3.

liturgical aspects of the daily round through a similar manipulation of the soundscape.[92] The *signa* of Canterbury would also seem likely to have constituted bells. I say likely, rather than certainly, because we can only infer it from the ways in which they occur in this document, and because *signa* appear to be articulated in a similar way to the *Regularis Concordia*; *signa* attracted an association with percussive verbal forms signposting an auditory effect (*pulsare*, *sonare*, and *tangere*), they appear in different kinds and numbers, and Lanfranc gives the impression that they helped members to identify Regular Offices.[93] We see this at several places in chapter 2 of the *Constitutiones*, for example, beginning with the requirement that a small signal be rung at daybreak by the church warden (*illuscente autem die pulsetur a custode ecclesie parvulum signum modice*).[94] They include too a *signum* that was to be sounded later in order to indicate when the community should prepare for Tierce (*sonet signum ad apparatum Tercie*).[95] Even before this Office, Lanfranc had required another 'sign', described as the 'smallest' (*pulsetur a secretario modice signum minimum quod skillam vocant*),[96] to call seniors to church, and before an even greater *signum* (*pulsetur maius signum ad horam*) reminded boys to join the choir in particular.[97]

In addition to sound, the *Constitutiones* suggest that light may also have played a role in a multi-dimensional disciplinary system. Lanfranc reserved the terms *laterna* and *luminares* for arrangements on the supervision of boys. He required that every two boys should carry at least one lamp between them whenever and wherever they went outside the

---

92 For references to those *signa* which may have constituted bells, see *Constitutiones*, c. 2, 4-9; c. 3, pp. 12-3; c. 8, pp. 18-9; c. 9, pp. 18-9 and 20-1; c. 10, pp. 20-1; c. 11-3, pp. 21-3; c. 17, pp. 24-7; c. 19, pp. 28-9; c. 20-2, pp. 32-3; c. 23, pp. 32-3; c. 25, pp. 34-7; c. 28-31, pp. 44-7; c. 33-9, pp. 54-5; c. 40-5, pp. 58-61; c. 46-9, pp. 64-9; c. 50, pp. 70-1; c. 51, pp. 70-1.

93 *Pulsare*, was by far the most common form used, but for examples of each of these types, see *Constitutiones*, c. 2, pp. 6-7; c. 81, pp. 104-5.

94 *Constitutiones*, c. 2, pp. 4-5: 'When day is breaking the small bell shall be sounded lightly by the warden of the church'.

95 *Constitutiones*, c. 2, pp. 6-7: 'The bell rings for preparation for Tierce'.

96 *Constitutiones*, c. 2, pp. 6-7: 'The sacrist shall sound lightly the smallest bell which is called the *skilla*'.

97 *Constitutiones*, c. 2, pp. 6-7: 'The large bell shall ring for the hour'.

CHAPTER ONE: DISCIPLINE AND BEHAVIOUR

hours of daylight (*duobus una laterna sufficiat*),⁹⁸ so that boys could see, and could also be more 'carefully guarded by their teachers' (*infantes in capitulo cum luminaribus diligenter a magistris custodiantur*).⁹⁹ The *Constitutiones* also allow us to suppose that boys still entered into their own dietary regime at Canterbury. Brooks and Knowles, in their critical edition of the *Constitutiones*, have previously drawn attention to an additional opportunity for boys to take food, appearing to occur in two periods, after Tierce and morning mass.¹⁰⁰ In addition to this, however, the *Constitutiones* also suggest boys could take suppers in the refectory up to an hour earlier than the rest of their seniors, after high mass rather than after Vespers, and enjoyed other smaller breaks for a *mixtum*, or 'the measure of bread and drink' (*quantitas panis et potus*), which Lanfranc

---

98 *Constitutiones*, c. 109, pp. 170-1: 'One lantern shall suffice for two'.
99 *Constitutiones*, c. 3, pp. 10-1: 'The children shall be carefully looked after by their masters in the chapter-house with lights burning'; for other references to these illuminations, see c. 2, pp. 4-7 'Infantes et iuvenes cum luminaribus, veniant in ecclesiam/ The children and young monks with lanterns shall enter the church'; c. 28-31, pp. 44-5 'Lucescente die, ita ut pueri et iuvenes sine laternis possint exire/When day breaks, so that the children and young monks can go about without lanterns', and 'Stet unusquisque in loco suo usquequo magister infantum laternas accensas in chorum deferat, et ipsis infantibus tribuat/Everyone shall stand in his place until the master of the children brings lighted lanterns into choir and gives them to the children'; c. 46-9, pp. 66-7 'Laternam portare debet unus de magistris pueroum/This lantern shall be carried by one of the masters of the children'; c. 109, pp. 172-3 'Collacatis in lectis suis assistant magistri dum sint cooperti; in nocte cum accensis candelis/When they go to bed their masters shall be present, with candles lit if it be night, until they have the bed-clothes over them'.
100 *Constitutiones*, pp. xxiii-xxv, at xxiv. For all references to boys taking a *mixtum*, see c. 2, pp. 8-9: 'Post orationem vadant in refectorium accipere mixtum ebdomadarii coquine et mense lector [. . .] in potestate abbatis vel prioris sit utrum et ipsi mixtum accipere, et statutam ebdomadariis debeant quantitatem panis et potus habere/ After prayer the weekly kitchen servers and the reader at table go to the refectory for their mixtum [. . .] the abbot or prior shall have the power to decide whether they too shall receive the mixtum and the measure of bread and drink allotted to the weekly servers'; c. 29-31, pp. 48-9: 'Quo completo, vadant in refectorium accipere mixtum/ After this they shall go to the refectory for the mixtum'; c. 55, pp. 74-5: 'Post Terciam sumant mixtum pueri, et infirmi qui ieiunare non possunt/After Tierce the children and the sickly, who cannot fast, shall receive the mixtum'; and also c. 57, pp. 80-1: 'Post Tertiam pergant infantes et minuti sanguine, et infirmi, quibus licentia data est, accipere mixtum/After Tierce the children and those who have been bled, and the sick who have permission, shall go to partake of the mixtum'.

only otherwise allowed to those ministering at altars.[101]

The *Constitutiones* provide a map of ritual gestures similar to the *Regularis Concordia*, suggesting that Lanfranc also expected boys' behaviours to be informed by learning and shared expression of monastic behaviours. Lanfranc's customary contains more direct references to gestures expected of boys, however, and described more behaviours belonging to mundane areas of a daily round. These included the washing of hair, hands, and feet, for example, but they extended to gestures similar to those anticipated by the *Regularis Concordia*, seen above, and belonging to spaces adults thought sacred – including common acts of genuflection and the taking up of holy water upon entering church.[102] A majority of references appear to have been required of all rather than of boys in particular, but again, in requiring all to participate, and by requiring boys to be present when such gestures were to be expressed, the *Constitutiones* show how these ritual gestures might have shaped boys' behavioural learning. Within this category, for example, we can include requirements that brethren, the choir, or all perform ritual

---

101 *Constitutiones*, c. 46-9, pp. 70-1: 'Qua facta vadant infantes in refectorium, si aliqui adeo parvi sunt, ut usque post Vesperas expectare non possint/ When this is done the children go to the refectory, if there be any so young as to not be able to wait until after Vespers'; c. 2, pp. 8-9 'Post orationem vadant in refectorium accipere mixtum ebdomadarii coquine et mense lector [...] in potestate abbatis vel prioris sit utrum et ipsi mixtum accipere, et statutam ebdomadariis debeant quantitatem panis et potus habere/ After prayer the weekly kitchen servers and the reader at table go to the refectory for their mixtum [...] the abbot or prior shall have the power to decide whether they too shall receive the mixtum and the measure of bread and drink allotted to the weekly servers'.

102 For all direct references to behavioural requirements placed upon boys, see *Constitutiones*, c. 2, pp. 6-7: 'Cum vero infantes loti fuerint, et se pectinare inceperint pulsetur maius signum ad horam. Accedentes et ipsi ad aquam benedictam in chorum veniant, et dimisso signo omnes simul tres orationes faciant/When these have washed and begun to comb their hair the large bell shall ring for the Hour. Then the children shall take holy water and enter the choir and when the bell ceases all shall say the Three Prayers together'; see also c. 9, pp. 20-1; c. 10, 22-3; c. 19, pp. 28-9; c. 20-2, pp. 32-3; c. 23, pp. 32-3; c. 25, pp. 40-1; c. 40-5, pp. 60-1, 64-5; c. 55, pp. 74-5; c. 56, pp. 78-9; for genuflection, see c. 25, pp. 38-9 'Deinde a pueris cantetur antiphona *Cum angelis*, in fine tantum antiphone genua flectentibus/Then the children shall sing the antiphon *Cum angelis*, genuflecting only at the end of it'; for obeisance, see c. 33-9, pp. 52-3 'curvati supra formas decant in silentio *Kyrieleison* (sic)/Bowing of their desks they shall say in silence *Kyrie eleison*' and 'petitur venia ab omnibus supra formas/All shall bow over their desks'; for additional requirements of 'silence' too, see c. 82, pp. 110-1 'In scolam suam redeant, et cum silentio sedeant/Return to their school, sitting in silence'.

bows and inclinations (*inclinare ante et retro*),[103] and that they undertake at times a more profound type of bow, requiring them to lean with their backs forward over choir stands (*curvantes supra formas*).[104] We can include too requirements that brethren undertake demonstrative prayers (i.e. *faciat orationem*);[105] that they prostrate themselves on the ground (i.e. *prosternant se cuncti in terram*),[106] initiate and carry out processions while unshod (i.e. *vadant nudis pedibus/ discalcient se omnes*),[107] make ritual halts for prayer (i.e. *faciant stationem*),[108] and frequently make the sign of the cross (i.e. *signo sancte crucis in nomine domini*).[109]

The *Constitutiones* also suggest that boys' experiences of monastic discipline were shaped by groups of supervisors similar to those which we have seen were prescribed by the *Regularis Concordia*. Lanfranc appears to have envisaged that the abbot (or [arch]bishop), as well as the prior, subprior, claustral prior, 'roundsmen' (or *circatores*), and cantor(s), would

---

103 *Constitutiones*, c. 32, pp. 52-3 'Inclinantes se ante et retro/Doing double obeisance'; c. 33-9, pp. 56-7 'Ante et retro faciant, et postea sessum vadant; quibus abbas similiter potum ferat osculans eorum manus/Make a double obeisance and then go to their seats, whereupon the abbot shall bear drink likewise to them, kissing their hands'.
104 *Constitutiones*, c. 8, pp. 16-7: 'Factaque oratione, supra formas/When the prayer has been said by the monks kneeling over their benches'; c. 28-31, pp. 42-3 'Prosternant se super formas/They shall prostrate themselves over their desks'; c. 28-31, pp. 48-9 'Supra formas/They kneel over their desks; c. 29-31, pp. 44-5 'Curvantes se supra formas/Bow over their desks'.
105 *Constitutiones*, c. 55, pp. 76-7 'Quo dicto inclinantes se faciant orationem/After this they shall bow down and pray'; c.77, pp. 102-3 (priest) 'Faciat orationem suppliciter inclinatus/[The priest] shall make the prayers bowing down'.
106 *Constitutiones*, c. 8, pp. 18-9 'Prosternant se cuncti in terram/All may prostrate themselves on the ground'; c. 8, pp. 18-9 'Lector etiam ante analogium [prosternat]/The reader prostrates before the lectern'; c. 10, pp. 22-3 'Ab omnibus flexis ad terram genibus/All shall kneel down in worship'; c. 32, pp. 48-9 'Inclinantes se flexis ad terram genibus adorent Christum in pauperibus/Bowing down they shall adore Christ in the poor'; c. 40-5, pp. 62-3 'Tunc omnes petant veniam, flexis ad terram genibus/Then all shall kneel on the ground and bow'.
107 *Constitutiones*, c. 20-2, pp. 32-3 'Discalcient se omnes/All shall take off their shoes'; c. 40-5, pp. 58-9 'Ad Primam pulsata tabula surgentes nudis pedibus vadant ad monasterium/When the board has been sounded for Prime all shall go barefoot to the church'.
108 *Constititiones*, c. 25, pp. 40-1 'Et ingressi ecclesiam faciant iterum stationem/And entering the church they make another halt'.
109 *Constitutiones*, c. 28-31, pp. 46-7 'Signo tantum Sancte Crucis in nomine Domini/Over which only the sign of the cross has been made in the name of the Lord'.

have a role to play in policing the behaviour of boys in the different spaces of the monastic complex boys entered and wherever those seniors held influence.[110] Lanfranc's *Constitutiones* also give clear examples of the kinds of behaviours disciplinary authorities were to correct in seniors and which we could suppose he might, at some point before adulthood, have considered problematic in boys too. Relating to the duties of the claustral prior, for example, Lanfranc indicated that misbehaviours could be identified according to the appropriateness of a bodily gesture and the illicitness of a conversation. Lanfranc's customs on the infringements which may have been common before c.1077 but which he had hoped his brethren would in future avoid included a series of asserted errors such as not walking reverently (*non reverenter incedere*),[111] not leaving with their hoods on as was custom (*non valeant capitiis capita ... ut mos est*),[112] and remaining where they should not (*non debeat, ibi remanserit*).[113]

The *Constitutiones* also referred to a *schola* on multiple occasions,[114] but

---

110 The prior could supervise teachers and boys in school, see *Constitutiones*, c. 3, pp. 10-3: 'Deinde debet per claustrum et in capitulum ire, ac videre qualiter se habeant magistri et infantes, et per loca alia ubi necessarium esse perspexerit/The [the prior] should go through the cloister and chapter-house to see how the children and their masters do, and whithersoever else he may judge necessary'. For the duties of the claustral prior, see c. 83-4, pp. 114-5 'Quecunque maior prior, dum in monasterio est, concedere potest vel prohibere, ulcisci culpas vel indulgere, hec quoque prior claustra absente eo facere potest, exceptis maioribus causis, quas vel ipsius maioris prioris vel abbatis iudicio reservare debet/All permissions, prohibitions, punishments and remissions that may be given by the great prior when he is at home may be given by the claustral prior in his absence, save for matters which he should reserve for judgement by the great prior or abbot'. For the duties of the roundsmen or circas/circatores, see *Constitutiones*, c. 85, pp. 116-9.
111 *Constitutiones*, c. 83-84, p. 114-15: 'Unde bene possit observare qui sint, qui non reverenter incedunt/So as to note who they are who do not walk reverently'.
112 *Constitutiones*, c. 83-84, p. 114-15: 'Et qui, in exitu ecclesie, ut mos est, non velant capitiis capita sua/And who do not put up their hoods, as the custom is, on leaving the church'.
113 *Constitutiones*, c. 83-4, pp. 114-15: 'Egresso toto conventu, accepta absconsa si nox est, vadit per criptam et cetera membra monasterii, ubi suspicio potest esse, per claustrum, capitulum, ceterasque officinas subtiliter observando, ne aliquis frater, qui non debeat, ibi remanserit/When all the community has left, he should take a dark lantern if it be night and go through the crypt and other such parts of the church as may harbour irregularity, through the cloister, also, chapter-house and other offices, looking carefully to see that no brother remain there who should not'.
114 *Constitutiones*, pp. 6, 48-50, 56, 126, 128.

CHAPTER ONE: DISCIPLINE AND BEHAVIOUR

Lanfranc provided more information than had the *Regularis Concordia* on how he thought behaviours in the *schola* ought to be managed. Like Æthelwold, Lanfranc insisted on creating safeguards against adults who might encounter boys in the complex and who were charged with the care of the school, allowing only the abbot, prior, and dedicated teachers or *magistri* and a head teacher to speak directly with boys (*Unus, super alios magister, sit magister eorum maturus et discretus*).[115] Lanfranc mirrored the *Regularis* in that the number of teachers should always approximate the number of boys - ideally this meant they should provide at least one *magister* for every two boys.[116] But Lanfranc was clearer in outlining that teachers were not to confine themselves to Latin instruction, requiring them to undertake disciplinary responsibilities and supervise boys wherever they went or needed to go.[117] Lanfranc's frequent use of a reflexive possessive, *sui magistri*, to describe boys' *own* teachers, would suggest further still that he had not only expected many senior brethren to participate in the instruction of oblates, but had given seniors the care of their own

---

115 *Constitutiones*, c. 109, pp. 172-3: 'A monk of mature age and known discretion shall be their head master' and 'In nullius manum aliquid dent; de nullius manu aliquid accipiant nisi abbatis, prioris maioris, magistri eorum/They shall not give anything to anyone, nor receive anything save from the abbot, great prior, and their masters'.

116 *Constitutiones*, c. 109, pp. 170-1: 'Quocunque pergunt infantes unus magister inter duos infantes sit/Whithersoever the children go a master shall be between every two'.

117 For references to supervision in dorms, the chapter, and choir, and in procession in that order, see *Constitutiones*, c. 82, pp. 110-11: 'Magister tamen infantum si viderit transire horam, qua sonitus a priore fieri solet, surgat, et quam quietius possit infantes excitet, virga tantummodo tangens pannos/If the master of the children see that the hour is passing at which the signal is wont to be given by the prior, he should rise and rouse the children as quietly as may be, simply touching with his rod their bedclothes'; c. 3, pp. 10-11: 'Infantes in capitulo cum luminaribus diligenter a magistris custodiantur/The children shall be carefully looked after by their masters in the chapter-house with lights burning', and c. 28-31, pp. 42-3 'Vadant magistri laudibus, qui et versi sint ad priores, sicut et ipsi infantes; iuvenes vero, qui in custodia sunt, mixtim sint in ordine seniorum/The masters shall join the children and face the seniors with them; the young monks under ward shall be mingled with the seniors; for the procession which would welcome a visiting dignitary see also, c. 81, pp. 106-7 'Pueri cum magistris suis extremi veniant/The children with their masters shall come last'; see also Palm Sunday and Holy Saturday, at c. 28-31, pp. 44-5 'Usquequo magister infantum laternas accensas in chorum deferat et ipsis infantibus tribuat/Until the master of the children brings lighted lanterns into choir and gives them to the children' and c. 45, pp. 66-7 'Hanc laternam portare debet unus de magistris puerorum/ This lantern shall be carried by one of the masters of the children'.

specific groups of boys too.[118]

Lanfranc's choice of vocabulary for his school also indicates quite differently from the *Regularis Concordia* that the *schola* at Christ Church Canterbury might have possessed a more physical dimension. We can detect this dimensionality, for example, through Lanfranc's use of the accusative case in a formula indicating that he had required boys to *go into* a school (*infantes divertant cum magistris suis in scolam suam*)[119] and return *into* a school as a fixed environment (*in scolam suam redeant*).[120] If this were the case, sadly, the *Constitutiones* do not easily allow us to confirm it, for they offer no satisfactory picture of where the school might have been located. It is possible that Lanfranc had not expected that location to be fixed, and had expected that it should move throughout the monastic complex, perhaps according to the needs of the senior community. Exhaustive survey of all references to the *schola* and to points in the daily round when Lanfranc required boys to study could offer us at least two different potential locations. It might have been in the cloister at Christ Church, for example, given that a series of references allude to the cloister as a place where boys were sometimes expected to read.[121] But Lanfranc's customs indicate that boys might have also studied in the

---

118 *Constitutiones*, c. 25, pp. 38-9: 'Pueri vero accedentes stabunt versis vultibus ad ipsas reliquas cum magistris suis/The children shall draw near and stand facing towards the relics with their masters', and at c. 62-5, pp. 86-7 'Remanentibus infantibus cum magistris suis in choro, qui ante missam debent esse induti/The children, who should be vested before Mass, remain with their masters in choir'.
119 *Constitutiones*, c. 32, pp. 48-9: 'Egressi refectorium infantes divertant cum magistris suis in scolam suam/ As they leave the refectory the children shall turn aside to their school with their masters'.
120 *Constitutiones*, c. 82, pp. 110-11: '[Infantes] factis solitis orationibus in scolam redeant et, cum silentio sedeant donec abbas de lecto surgat/After the usual prayer [the children] return to their school, sitting in silence till the abbot rises'; c. 23, pp: 32-3 'Infantes quoque post capitulum suum descendentes de dormitorio, hoc intervallo in scola sua sedeant et legant/The children likewise, coming down from the dormitory after their chapter, shall sit during this interval in their school and read'.
121 *Constitutiones*, c. 2, pp. 6-7: 'Pueri vero primitus alte legant, et postea si opus fuerit cantent. Omni tempore antequam legant infantes nullus in claustro legat aut cantet, nisi in silentio/The children shall begin by reading aloud, and afterwards, if need be, practise the chant. No one shall ever read or rehearse the chant in the cloister, save in silence, until the children begin to read'; c. 40-1, pp. 60-1 'Sedeant in claustro, non loquentes, sed cantantes aut legentes/They shall sit in the cloister, not speaking but chanting or reading'.

CHAPTER ONE: DISCIPLINE AND BEHAVIOUR

chapterhouse, providing them with an enclosed space more suitable during bad weather, and allowing them to practise their liturgical assignments at a distance from their seniors.[122]

Regardless of location, Lanfranc's *Constitutiones* suggest that teachers were chosen with care. We find this, for example, in a prescription which echoes chapter 31 of the *Regula Benedicti* on the office and qualities of the ideal cellarer, requiring that *magistri* of Christ Church Canterbury should be mature (*maturus*), should possess discretion (*discretus*), and should be capable of understanding when and how to indulge boys and when to punish them for faults of delinquency (*qui auditis clamoribus culpas delinquentium moderata discretione sciat vel punire vel indulgere culpas delinquentium*).[123] Chapter 109 of the *Constitutiones* expanded significantly on the apparatus of the *Regularis Concordia* and provided a framework of expectations of boys' behaviours in the *schola* too. These prescriptions reveal more about the aspired context of learning for boys which was intended to be quiet and isolating. Lanfranc not only required that boys should be seated, but that they should be seated apart from one another ([*infantes*] *separati ab invicem ita sedeant*), and in a way which may have been intended to discourage peer-based interaction.[124] Lanfranc's prescriptions also placed great emphasis on controlling boys' movements and conversation. He not only required that boys should not get up from their seats without command or permission (*non de loco in quo sedet surgat de loco in quo sedet sine precepto vel licentia surgat*), but suggested that they also should not make clamours or signs to their peers.[125]

---

122 *Constitutiones*, c. 3, pp. 10-11: 'Infantes in capitulo cum luminaribus diligenter a magistris custodiantur, canantes quod necessarium erit/The children shall be carefully looked after by their masters in the chapter-house with lights burning, practising such chant as may be necessary'.
123 RSB, c. 31, c. 116-7; *Constitutiones*, c. 109, pp. 172-3: 'He shall be skilled to punish or remit their faults when they are accussed as a discreet moderation may suggest'.
124 *Constitutiones*, c. 109, pp. 170-1: 'They shall sit apart from one another'.
125 *Constitutiones*, c. 109, pp. 170-1: 'Seperati ab invicem ita sedeant, ut alter alterum nec manibus, nec vestibus contingere possit. Infans infanti non signo innuere, non verbo aliquid dicere, nisi vidente atque audiente magistro, presumat; non de loco in quo sedet sine precepto vel licentia surgat/They shall sit apart from one another, in such a way that no one can touch his neighbour either with his hands or his clothes. No child shall make a sign to another, nor say a word to him, unless the master can see and hear him, nor shall a child rise from his place save under order, or with permission'.

Lanfranc did not forbid noise altogether, and insisted that boys should read aloud their lessons (*qui cum legere inchoant, alte aliquandiu legant*), but he appears only to have allowed this on the occasion that teachers wanted boys to memorise a passage or rehearse sequences of sacred scripture.[126]

As I have mentioned briefly above, there are occasions in Lanfranc's prescriptions which suggest that *magistri* were to supervise and manage boys' behaviours elsewhere in the monastery. These occasions give us further opportunities to build a view of the behaviours which Lanfranc disapproved of in oblates and of the procedures which he expected to operate in order to manage boys when misbehaviours arose outside the school. We find this, for example, in the case of Lanfranc's prescriptions in chapter 109, where Lanfranc outlined punishments for the late arrival of individual boys into the choir. This tells us that Lanfranc considered a boy to be late if he did not enter choir before the *Gloria* of the first psalm had been recited. It also tells us that, should boys be late, Lanfranc preferred that the boy's teacher or *magister* should in fact normally be punished in the boy's stead:

> Si post versum, qui ante cibum dicitur, ingrediuntur refectorium, vel post Gloriam primi psalmi ad horas intrant chorum, ipsi quidem ad loca sua vadant, solito more inclinent; magister vero eorum ad loca, que tardantibus instituta sint, eat.[127]

This prescription suggests that Lanfranc employed an unusual form of disciplinary correction, requiring the scope of punishment to expand onto individuals other than any single individual who might have committed an error. We cannot say with certainty what Lanfranc might have intended here. Lanfranc's efforts to manage disruption in a sacred space may disclose anxieties similar to those which we have considered in relation to Ælfric of Eysnham in the section above. What is clear, however, is that Lanfranc's

---

126 *Constitutiones*, c. 109, pp. 170-1: 'When they begin to read they shall for a space read in a loud tone of voice'.
127 *Constitutiones*, c. 109, pp. 172-3: 'If they enter the refectory after the verse that is said before meals, or enter choir after the *Gloria* of the first psalm, they shall go to the places appointed for those who come late'.

CHAPTER ONE: DISCIPLINE AND BEHAVIOUR

system functioned to offset the need for violence in choir and in the middle of an Office, and might have been intended to remind teachers in particular to ensure that boys arrived on time at liturgical services.

What is less obvious in the *Constitutiones* is how Lanfranc expected teachers to correct boys or impose corporal violence. Like the *Regularis Concordia* of Winchester, the *Constitutiones* nowhere offered explicit guidance on how and to what extent each of these visible infractions should have been handled. Apart from his suggestion that *magistri* should know when to indulge or punish a boy for a fault, a suggestion which would seem to imply that they could punish boys on a relatively reactive basis, and according to their own personal judgement, Lanfranc's *Constitutiones* otherwise only seem to allow us the view that boys' punishments were decided upon at an office known as the Chapter.

The senior Chapter likely played an important formative role in boys' experiences of violent correction. But, sadly, we know little else about the role of this Chapter in boys' lives for certain. At times, Lanfranc's prescriptions even seem to confuse our view of conditions, and point us towards the co-existence of at least three different types of Chapter at Christ Church, dividing Canterbury into three discrete disciplinary groups. These seem to expect one Chapter for seniors (*maiores in maiori capitulo*)[128], another for boys,[129] and yet another Chapter for 'servants' (*capitulum servientum*),[130] or for those who held senior offices in the monastery, allowing for a degree of oversight of the activities of teachers of the boys and youths, as well as the cantor, the sacristan, and the prior.

If these references allow us to consider that there may have been distinct Chapters for men and boys, Lanfranc's *Constitutiones* also appear to suggest that boys were expected to enter the senior Chapter. This evidence can only be inferred from Lanfranc's singular insistence that

---

[128] *Constitutiones*, c. 109, pp. 172-3: 'Their elders are in theirs [their chapter]'.
[129] For all references to the children's chapter see, *Constitutiones*, c. 2 pp. 8-9, c. 23 pp. 32-3, c. 94 pp. 136-7, c. 109 pp. 172-3, c. 112 pp. 180-1, c. 113 pp. 188-9.
[130] *Constitutiones*, c. 83-4, pp. 112-3: 'Quotiens res expostulate, tenet aut teneri iubet capitulum de omnibus servientibus, qui intra officinas monasterii conversantur, et secundum merita delinquentium, eo iubente, vindicate inferuntur/When need arises he holds, or causes to be held, a chapter of all servants who work in the offices of the monastery, and punishment is inflicted at his order according to the deserts of those culpable'.

corporal violence should 'not be delegated to boys, youths, or novices'.[131] But this prohibition is sufficient to indicate that Lanfranc had expected those groups (i.e. children, youths, and novices) to be present. Indeed, this might even disclose that Lanfranc had expected boys to enter the senior Chapter for that very reason; that he intended for boys to learn from the senior round as a proxy for their own, and that he had perhaps required them to observe senior disciplinary routines at a stage before they were subject to the arrangements of senior Chapters themselves.

The *Constitutiones* do seem to confirm on this occasion that Lanfranc had expected the boys' own Chapter to be closely aligned with that of their seniors. Lanfranc's insistence that boys ought to be whipped in their own Chapter *in the same way* that seniors were in theirs (*in capitulo suo vapulent sicut maiores in maiori capitulo*), demonstrates that assumption clearly.[132] But this, sadly, is also as much as Lanfranc's *Constitutiones* tell us about the shared nature of the two disciplinary meetings. Since we know that the two Chapters were connected, however, and since we are given some reason to consider that Lanfranc had expected boys to enter the senior Chapter, we can perhaps extend our view of boys' disciplinary experiences further, by exploring in more detail the better described senior Chapter, and by taking a view, on a very contingent understanding, that the conditions which shaped senior men might have been shared by boys to some corresponding extent.[133]

Lanfranc's prescriptions on the senior Chapter required all misbehaviours to be measured according to two categories, depending on whether a fault could be thought light (*si culpa levis sit*) and could be remitted, or whether a fault was grave (*si gravis culpa sit*), and needed to be punished

---

131 *Constitutiones*, c. 106, pp. 166-7: 'Disciplinam corporalem inferat quicumque ille sit cui ab abbate vel priore iniungitur, hoc observato, ne infantibus vel iuvenibus aut novitiis id facere iniungatur/The abbot or prior shall appoint him who is to administer punishment, taking care that neither child, nor junior, nor novice is bidden'.

132 *Constitutiones*, c. 109, pp. 172-3: 'They are flogged in their chapter, as their elders are in theirs'.

133 For these chapters of the *Constitutiones*, see c. 99-100, pp. 146-53; c. 106, pp. 164-7; c. 107, pp. 168-9; c. 109, pp. 170-3. For the reading of the RSB at Chapter, see c. 89, pp. 128-9: 'Lecta vero in capitulo, et exposita predicta sententia/After the aforementioned passage has been read in Chapter and expounded'.

CHAPTER ONE: DISCIPLINE AND BEHAVIOUR

demonstratively.[134] According to this framework, 'light' misbehaviours could be corrected privately and outside the office of Chapter, but if reported at Chapter, they could either be indulged, or corrected with a non-physical punishment, such as a temporary prohibition against solo liturgical performances in choir.[135] Lanfranc's *Constitutiones* suggest that grave misbehaviours, transgressions considered serious, and which were also so commonly known that they could not be resolved privately, would need to be resolved publicly, and with violence.[136]

Sadly, Lanfranc's *Constitutiones* do not tell us quite what (mis)behaviours might have been considered grave and how known they needed to be to attract such treatment. Nor, indeed, does he tell us whether grave faults might have been weighed and punished similarly in boys as in senior men. All his customary provides is a form of procedure for conducting the correction of grave faults in senior brethren. This offers us a view of a series of ritual *formulae* and behavioural gestures Lanfranc might have expected boys to learn and which he required adults to perform in the event that they were accused of a grave fault. Lanfranc also detailed what forms corporal punishment could take in the senior Chapter – that seniors could be scourged either with a single stout rod while lying in an undergarment, that they could be beaten with a bundle of finer rods sitting with a bare back, and/or that they could undergo a form of penance, continuing until

---

134 For these, see *Constitutiones*, c. 95, pp. 140-1; c. 99-100, pp. 148-53.
135 For Lanfranc's arrangements on light faults, see *Constitutiones*, c. 95, pp. 140-1; and also c. 99-100, pp. 146-9, esp. pp. 146-7: 'A communi mensa separetur [. . .] In monasterio et in capitulo, in loco ubi solet esse sit, aut ultimus omnium, aut inter utrunque, secundum quod culpa fuerit, et abbas preceperit. In ecclesia missam non celebret, epistolam vel evangelium vel lectionem non legat, responsorium non canat, antiphonam super psalmos non imponat, nec aliquid huiusmodi, nisi cum ceteris agat/He eats apart from the rest [. . .] In church and Chapter he shall be either in his usual place, or last of all, or somewhere between the two, according to the measure of his fault and the command of the abbot. In church he shall not celebrate Mass, nor read Epistle, Gospel, or lesson; he shall not sing a responsory nor begin an antiphon to the psalms, nor do anything of the kind save along with all the others'.
136 For Lanfranc's arrangements on grave faults, see *Constitutiones*, c. 99-100, pp. 148-53, esp. 148-9: 'In capitulo ante abbatem in conventu examinetur. Et communi iudicio frater ille corporalem disciplinam acriter patiatur/The offence shall be examined before the abbot in Chapter in a meeting of the brethren, and the brother who is condemned by the judgement of all shall suffer severe corporal punishment'.

rescinded at another meeting of Chapter.[137]

Lanfranc appears to have recognised that his system did not always function as intended, and there are occasions in the *Constitutiones* which set out a series of increasingly serious alternative punishments that could be adopted at the senior Chapter in the event that an individual either refused to accept culpability and/or expressed aggression.[138] In these events, Lanfranc advised that the individual in question should be removed from Chapter by force, placed into isolation and, indeed, further corrected with violence in a cell arranged for this purpose (*in carcerem*).[139] If brethren continued to reject these disciplinary structures, Lanfranc reserved the option to expel an individual from the monastery altogether (*vel de monasterio expelli*).[140] It is the case, of course, that we have no means of determining how far these procedures found an analogue in the junior Chapter at Christ Church, Canterbury. While it would be difficult to imagine that this context of punishment bore no resemblance to the conditions which shaped the lives of the boys who were expected to eventually enter into such arrangements, and while I would argue that such forms should therefore contribute to our understanding of how boys integrated into a disciplinary system at Christ Church, we should recognise that Lanfranc's prescriptions only strictly point to the importance of the Chapter as a context for the experiences of correction of adults.

If the prescriptive record of this period cannot throw more light on the role of the Chapter or improve our understanding of how and why contemporaries used violence on boys, contemporary works of history and even saints' lives could prove more helpful. These not only serve to confirm that teachers used a similar framework of consequences for misbehaviour in boys, but shed light on how violence could intersect with experiences

---

137 *Constitutiones*, c. 106, pp. 166-7: 'Suscepturus iudicium aut sola grossiori virga super staminiam verberetur, et prostratus iacet, aut pluribus gracilioribus virgis, et nudus sedeat, utrumque ad arbitrium eius qui preest ordini, considerata qualitate et quantitate culpe/He who is to undergo punishment shall be scourged either with a single stout rod while he lies in his shift on the ground, or with a bundle of finer rods while he sits with his back bare. In each case he is punished at the discretion of the superior, who should consider the degree and the magnitude of the fault'.
138 *Constitutiones*, c. 99-100, pp. 152-3.
139 *Constitutiones*, c. 99-100, pp. 152-3: 'Into the prison'.
140 *Constitutiones*, c. 99-100, pp. 152-3: 'Or to expel him from the monastery'.

CHAPTER ONE: DISCIPLINE AND BEHAVIOUR

of doctrinal learning. One account of Richard of Ely in his *Liber Eliensis* gives shape to the kinds of behaviour which may have entailed serious faults, for example. We see this where Richard explains an event at his house, sometime during the rule of Abbot Simeon (1081-1093), when an adolescent monk (*adolescens*) called Eadwine, who was in the care of an English *magister* known as Siward, had dysregulated into a fit of rage during recital of a monastic Office in the choir. Richard tells us that Eadwine launched an attack on the abbot, hit his responsive teacher with a *tabula* (a tablet containing the list of choral duties), and proceeded to bite one of the elderly monks who had then attempted to restrain him. In doing so, Richard confirms forms of supervision by teachers, a preference for reducing and containing problems in the choir space, and the use of restraint against oblates who defied ordinary disciplinary expectations or displayed aggression. The episode, Richard informs us, was not repeated or escalated further - but resolved by means of diagnosis of wider misbehaviour. Eadwine had been the victim of another, more clearly blameworthy, and supposedly demonic boy who, monks agreed, had been pulling him by his cowl - allowing Eadwine to reintegrate without further consequences.[141]

It is worth noting too, that saints' lives throw light onto areas of discipline not otherwise disclosed by Lanfranc's customs, such as teacher perceptions on the utility and impact of corporal punishment. The two post-Conquest versions of the *Miracula Sancti Dunstani* by Osbern (c.1050-1090)[142] and Eadmer (c.1060-1126)[143] of Christ Church Canterbury, the *Lectiones in Natale Sancte Eormenhilde* of Goscelin of Saint Bertin[144], and the *Mircula Sancti Erkenwaldi*,[145] all contain parallel accounts of the use of corporal discipline, for example, and indicate that monastic houses instituted what Osbern of Canterbury in particular

---

141 Blake, *Liber Eliensis*, pp. 208-209, at 209; trans. Fairweather, *Liber Eliensis*, pp. 246-7.
142 Osbern of Canterbury, *Miracula Sancti Dunstani*, in *Memorials of Saint Dunstan Archbishop of Canterbury*, ed. William Stubbs (London, 1874), pp. 140-2.
143 Eadmer of Canterbury, *Miracula Sancti Dunstani*, in *Memorials of Saint Dunstan*, ed. Stubbs, pp. 229-30.
144 Goscelin, *Lectiones in Natale Sancte Eormenhilde*, in *Goscelin of Saint Bertin: The Hagiography of the Female Saints of Ely*, ed. and trans. Rosalind Love, OMT (Oxford, 2004), pp. 20-1.
145 *Miracula Sancti Erkenwaldi*, in *The Saint of London: The Life and Miracles of St. Erkenwald*, ed. George E. Whatley (Binghamton, 1989), pp. 103-9.

called a 'custom' of ritual beating of oblate boys (*mos in ecclesia tunc temporis erat*) occurring on a fixed time of day and point of the year (*prima diei hora ... durius punerit*).¹⁴⁶ Like the compositions of his near-contemporaries, Osbern's work indicates that boys themselves did not consider beatings on these occasions justified, and disliked the idea that they could neither reduce their beating nor obtain the intervention of more sympathetic seniors (*nec spes intercessionis*).¹⁴⁷ Osbern's use of the first person in his own account distinguishes his own writings from those of his contemporaries too, implying that Osbern experienced these rituals of beating in his *own* boyhood even (i.e. *mane ad magistros intravimus vapitulari pro culpis quas commiseramus*);¹⁴⁸ indeed, the adoption of a parallel narrative by Eadmer suggests that those customs might have continued to have an influence for some time, continuing at Canterbury long after the Norman Conquest.¹⁴⁹

What is also interesting about these parallel narratives centred on the lives of boys at Ely and Canterbury, however, is that each of their authors described the intervention of empathetic saints who either halted all punishment or retrospectively punished teachers for their callousness. Osbern recorded, for example, that boys had cried out for a remedy from Dunstan and were then saved by him from all punishment (*remedium crediderunt ut ad memoriam dulcissimi patris Dunstani confugiam facerent ... ad illum multis lacrimis eius clementiam postulantes*).¹⁵⁰ Goscelin recorded too that the boys of Ely had attempted to avoid punishment on the feast day of Saint Eormenhild of Ely (d.700) and 'took refuge together at that kindly mother's tomb, crying out and begging for their deliverance' (*ad*

---

146 Osbern of Canterbury, *Miracula Sancti Dunstani*, in *Memorials of Saint Dunstan*, ed. Stubbs, pp. 140-2: 'There was a custom in the church at that time', and 'On the first hour of the day ... he punished [us] harshly' (my translation).
147 Osbern, *Miracula Sancti Dunstani*, in *Memorials of Saint Dunstan*, ed. Stubbs, pp. 140-2: 'There was no hope of intervention' (my translation).
148 Osbern, *Miracula Sancti Dunstani*, in *Memorials of Saint Dunstan*, ed. Stubbs, pp. 140-2. 'In the morning we went in to our teachers to be beaten for the faults which we had committed (my translation).
149 Eadmer, *Miracula Sancti Dunstani*, ed. Stubbs, pp. 229-30.
150 Osbern, *Miracula Sancti Dunstani*, in *Memorials of Saint Dunstan*, ed. Stubbs, pp. 140-1: 'Believing it a remedy, they made refuge at the tomb of their most sweet father, Dunstan ... crying out at that place for his mercy and shedding many tears' (my translation).

ipsius benignissime matris sepulchrum pariter confugere, clamantes et orantes pro sui liberatione).¹⁵¹ While they did not avoid a violent beating in this instance, Goscelin's *Vita* asserted that Eormenhild intervened later, and bound up the limbs of the teacher who had punished them, removing his bonds after he had apologised to the boys and once they had prayed to Eormenhild on his behalf.¹⁵²

By describing boys' seeking out and receiving of saintly help, these materials disclose that rituals of violence might even have served that very purpose. They indicate how experiences of violence, and either the threat of violence or the imposition of violence, might have been intended to shape boys' awareness of the power of prayer and intercession beyond the narrow confines of enabling boys to maintain behavioural norms or identify sources of authority. They disclose that violence may have intersected with a previously undetected, but perhaps established framework of educational methods which might have allowed teachers to *manufacture* disciplinary contexts useful to encouraging boys to learn how to pray and to view local saints as effective sources of protection from harm.¹⁵³

---

151 Goscelin, *In Lectiones de Natale Sancte Eormenhilde*, ed. and trans. Love, pp. 20-1.
152 Goscelin, *In Lectiones de Natale Sancte Eormenhilde*, ed. and trans. Love, pp. 20-1: 'His actis, sub sequenti nocte ubi se lectulo composuit, ecce prepotens Eormenhilda, memor factorum, pedes illi veloces ad persequendum et manus ad torquendum, forties quam compedibus et manicis ferries constrinxit [...] Mane autem pueros ad se convocat, veniam suppliciter efflagitat, et ut se ad tumbam piissime domine Eormenhild deferant, ibique pro se intercedant, lacrimabiliter implorat. At illi ut invalidis viribus alii brachiis eius et humeris, alii tibiis se subicientes, ferebant sullimem miserabili spectaculo ad sancta Eormenhilde presentiam ibique aliquandiu psalmodiantes et orantes impetraverunt ei salutem pristinam, ut rediret gressibus propriis qui venerate minibus alienis/After this was all over, the following night when he was lying on his bed, lo! mighty Eormenhild mindful of his deeds, bound up the feet that were so quick to pursue and hands so hasty to punish more tightly than any iron shackles or fetters could [...] In the morning he summoned the boys to him, and humbly begged their forgiveness, and tearfully implored them to carry him to the tomb of the most holy lady Eormenhild, and there to plead for him. And they, although of feeble strength, some of them lifting his arms and his shoulders, and some his legs, carried him aloft, a wretched spectacle, into the presence of St. Eormenhild, and there for some time begged for the restoration of his health, chanting psalms and praying, so that he who had come there in the hands of others went away again on his own feet'.
153 The account of Goscelin goes further than the others and describes how the teachers, once halted and punished by the saint, begged the boys themselves to pray to Saint Eormenhild and ask for her intercession on his behalf, see Goscelin, *In Lectiones*

If Eadmer experienced this form of punishment at Canterbury after the Conquest, his record suggests he may also have witnessed its tranformation under Lanfranc's successor, Archbishop Anselm (c.1093-1109). In his *Vita Sancti Anselmi*, for example, Eadmer described an occasion when the archbishop had been approached by another abbot for advice on dealing with misbehaviour:

> Quidam abbas secum...loqueretur...de pueris in claustro nutritis verba consereret adiecit, "Quid obsecro fiet de istis? Perversi sunt, et incorrigibiles. Die et nocte non cessamus eos verbarentes, et semper fiunt sibi ipsis deteriores". Ad quae miratus Anselmus, "Non cessatis" inquit "eos verberare? Et cum adulti sunt quales sunt?", "Hebetes" inquit "et bestiales". At ille, "Quam bono omine nutrimentum vestrum expendistis; de hominibus bestias nutrivistis". "Et nos" ait "quid possumus inde? Modis omnibus constringimus eos ut proficiant et nihil proficimus", "Constrigitis". "Dic quaeso nichi domine abba, si plantam arboris in horto tuo plantares, ex mox illam omni ex parte ita concluderes ut ramos suos nullatenus extendere posset? Cum eam post annos excluderes, qualis arbor inde prodiret?", "Profecto inutilis, incurvis ramis et perplexis". "Et hoc ex cuius culpa procederet nisi tua, qui eam immoderate conclusisti? Certe hoc facitis de pueris vestris. Plantati sunt per oblationem in horto ecclesiae, ut crescant et fructificent Deo. Vos autem in tantum terroribus, minis, et verberibus undique illos coarctatis, ut nulla penitus sibi liceat libertate potiri. Itaque indiscrete oppressi, pravas et spinarum more perplexas infra se cogitationes congerunt, fovent, nutriunt [...] Sic et vos si pueros vestros cupitis ornatis moribus esse, necesse est ut cum depressionibus verberum, impendatis eis paternae pietatis et mansuetudinis levamen atque subsidium".[154]

---

de Natale Sancte Eormenhilde, ed. and trans. Love, pp. 20-1: 'Mane autem pueros ad se convocat, veniam suppliciter efflagitat et ut se ad tumbam piisime domine Eormenhilde deferant, ibiqur pro se intercedant'.

154 see R.W.Southern (ed. and trans), *The Life of Anselm, Archbishop of Canterbury* (Oxford, 1972), pp. 37-38: 'A certain abbot...said something about the boys brought up in the cloister, adding, "What, I ask you, is to be done with them? They are incorrigable ruffians. We never give over beating them day and night, and they only get worse and worse". Anselm replied with astonishment, "You never give up beating them? And what are they like when they have grown up?", "Stupid brutes" he said, "but what can

CHAPTER ONE: DISCIPLINE AND BEHAVIOUR

Eadmer's account reveals that a contrast of attitudes to corporal discipline had emerged at Christ Church by the early twelfth century. On the one hand, he recognised that many of his contemporaries resorted to violence as a tool of correction in light of irregular behaviour among oblates. On the other, he suggested that Anselm rejected corporal punishment almost entirely. Anselm, he tells us, favoured a less interventionist approach, allowing a natural course of intellectual and physical growth to achieve much of an intended outcome of behavioural formation - without causing long term psychological and perhaps even physical harm. Anselm would not appear to have been alone in this, of course. We can recognise some of this anxiety in the *Colloquia* of Bata a generation earlier. But Eadmer sets Anselm apart by means of his acceptance of variation of boys' behaviours and his replacement of violence with kindness, concluding that responsiveness to boys' needs was more likely to lead to boys' acceptance of behavioural norms and foster healthy development. And while Eadmer's account does not confirm whether Anselm's philosophy resulted in any change at Canterbury, we can see that Eadmer certainly advocated for it. Indeed, as author, Eadmer ensured that these attitudes to discipline and behaviour not only gained significant potency, placed in the mouth of a saint, but permanency in the written record, acquiring potential to shape teachers' views and boys' experiences wherever and for as long as his *Vita Anselmi* enjoyed readership.

we do about it?...We use every means to force them to get better, but without success", "You force them? Now tell me, my lord abbot, if you plant a tree-shoot in your garden and straight away shut it on every side, so that it has no space to put out its branches, what kind of tree will you have in later years when you let it out of its confinement?", "A useless one, certainly, with its branches all knotted and twisted", "And whose fault would this be, except yours, for shutting it in so immoderately? For this, without doubt, is what you do with your boys. At their oblation, they are planted in the garden of the Church to grow and bring forth fruit for God. But you so terrify them and hem them in on all sides with threats and beatings that they are utterly deprived of their liberty, and being thus injudiciously oppressed, they harbour and welcome and nurse within themselves evil and crooked thoughts, like thorns [...] So, if you want your boys to be adorned with good habits, you too, besides the pressure of blows, must apply the encouragement and help of fatherly sympathy and gentleness".

Communities of Religious Women: Infancy

Girls, especially those of royal or aristocratic background, appear to have been offered to Benedictine houses at much younger ages than we can see for boys, and the timing of their oblation rituals would seem to provide us with an immediate point of difference in the conditions of girls' religious lives. Several hagiographies of female saints from the late Anglo-Saxon period, including those of Saint Eadgyth (d.984) and Saint Wulfhild (d.1000), indicate that royal girls sometimes entered religious houses as soon as they had been weaned.[155] We can see this in Goscelin's *Vita Sancte Edithe Virginis*, for example, in relation to an account of a pregnant mother who reportedly promised her unborn child to the Abbey of Wilton. At the infant's baptism, Bishop Ælfheah of Winchester (and later Archbishop of Canterbury c.1006-1012) noticed the girl's fascination with tapers that were burning during the ceremony. He named her Brihtgifu (meaning 'Bright-gift'). The bishop, interpreting her fascination as an expression of her desire to join the religious life, insisted that she be oblated to Wilton after she was weaned (*post ablactacionem*) to be nurtured from infancy to become Christ's bridegroom (*infantulam soli deo desponsandam nutrite*).[156] Indeed, we find more evidence of oblation during infancy in the case of the tenth-century religious girlhood of Saint Eadgyth, whose extremely young infant age at oblation, at just two years, has been widely accepted, and which is described in detail in the same *Vita Sancte Edithe Virginis* (or 'Life of the Holy Virgin, Eadgyth):

> Sistitur ergo bima infantula ut in florido prato hostia lactea, ut in divina libra dragma aurea. Que, ut arca Dei, a dextris et a sinistris in reflexa, recto impetus de medio splendencium colorum solum

---

155 Goscelin, *Vita Sancte Wulfhilde*, in 'La Vie de Sainte Vulfhilde par Goscelin de Cantorbery', ed. Mario Esposito, *Analecta Bollandiana* 32 (Paris, 1913), pp. 14-5: 'Nata et ablactata traditur virginibus Vultonie educanda/After having been born and weaned, she was given to the virgins of Wilton to be educated'.

156 This account describes the life of Abbess Brihtgifu of Wilton (c.984-1065), whom Goscelin is extremely likely to have met and known for many years as a teacher at Wilton, see, 'De Brihtgiva nuperrime abbatissa in tricessimo eius nata', in 'La légende de ste Édith en Prose et Vers par le Moine Goscelin', ed. Arnold Wilmart, *Analecta Bollandiana* 56 (1938), p. 99.

velum excipit et pro corona capiti imponit [. . .] Tum rex sorore, de conjuge facta in conventu angelorum et hominum parvulo Christo parvulam suam desponsant [. . .] reliquitur Deo sua pupilla, que et inter ipsa materna ubera a seculi illecebra exempta, voce psallaret prophetica "Pater meus et mater mea dereliquerunt me, Dominus autem assumpsit me".[157]

Again, Goscelin presented the two year old as a central, willing, and surprisingly (and perhaps unrealistically) active agent in her own monastic oblation, 'turning' (*reflexa*), picking up (*excipit*), and placing (*imponit*) a religious veil purposefully on her own head. This account of oblation was written long after the events it describes in c.1079.[158] But even if the date of composition means that it cannot be treated as a reliable source for a tenth-century oblation, or of Eadgyth's agency in choosing it, and even if Eadgyth never experienced this precise oblation ceremony, Goscelin's account seems likely to have been based on features which were accepted by religious women at Wilton. Her age may not have been typical of the many other non-royal girls who likely entered Benedictine abbeys in the tenth or later centuries, and we must be careful not to assume so, but Goscelin's acceptance of her age in his account of Eadgyth's age oblation to Wilton is significant, and should be taken seriously.

This evidence for girls' young ages at points of entry into Benedictine houses before and after the Conquest would also conform well with cartulary evidence of transactions which secured seemingly dependent girls

---

157 Goscelin, *Vita Sancte Edithe Virginis*, in 'La légende de ste Édith en Prose et Vers par le Moine Goscelin', ed. Arnold Wilmart, *Analecta Bollandiana* 56 (1938), pp. 44-7; ed. and trans. Stephanie Hollis, W. R. Barnes, Rebecca Hayward, Kathleen Loncar, and Michael Wright, *Writing the Wilton Women: Goscelin's Legend of Edith and Liber Confortatorius* (Turnhout, 2004), pp. 26-31: 'The little two-year old girl was put down therefore like a milk-white sacrificial victim. She, like the Ark of God turning aside neither to the right nor to the left, with unwavering purpose, picked out only the veil from the midst of the splendid colours and put it on her head as a crown. [. . .] Then the king, with the woman who had been his wife but was now his sister, betrothed their little child to the infant Christ [. . .] The little girl was left to God, and she, cut off from the enticements of the world in the bosom of her mother, could have sung with the prophetic voice of the psalmist "My father and my mother have left me, but the Lord has taken me up"'.
158 For an outline of Goscelin's career, see Moniker Otter, *Goscelin of St. Bertin: The Book of Encouragement and Consolation [Liber Confortatorius]* (Cambridge, 2004), p. 5.

to Shaftesbury Abbey after 1086.¹⁵⁹ Indeed, it also fits comfortably with evidence found in contemporary letter collections which describe oblation rituals in women's houses as requiring little more than that a girl should be presented at the altar by her parents (*ad altare tamen oblatae fuerunt*).¹⁶⁰ It also correlates with the use of the term *infantes* in later monastic customs from women's houses, such as from Barking Abbey in c.1413 - where oblation-like practices seem to have continued relatively undisturbed into the late medieval period.¹⁶¹

This nexus of evidence supporting infant oblation clearly has implications for our understanding of potential differences in girls' experiences of monastic discipline in women's houses in our period. It raises some expectation, for example, that their young ages at oblation might have had a corresponding influence on the provisions of child-care women provided. Goscelin's saints' lives support this view in fact, and offer accounts of girls' religious infancies indicating that women's religious communities provided levels of care not visible in the documentary record for male houses. In his *Translatio Sancte Edithe Virginis*, for one, Goscelin accounted for an infant (*in infantia apud monasterium*) raised at Wilton under the supervision of one of the younger religious women whom he described as a nurse

---

159 For analysis of London BL Harley MS 61, and a dating of these oblations to c.1089x1121, see Kathleen Cooke, 'Donors and Daughters: Shaftesbury Abbey's Benefactors, Endowments and Nuns, c.1086-1130', Anglo-Norman Studies, 12 (1990), pp. 29-31. This cartulary records the donartions of land with daughters (cum filia) - with 11 examples showing these being conducted by fathers, apparently alone. It also records names, which can be cross references with the Domesday Book and PASE project (Prosopography of Anglo-Saxon England) to recover an idea of the social backgrounds of these oblated girls - many of whom appear to be of post-Conquest Norman parentage as daughters of tenants-in-chief, including Serlo de Burci, Goscelin de Rivera, and Roger de Berkeley, though some, such as Harding fitz Alnoth, Leofwine de Bristowe, and Ailuf (possibly, Alfwulf) appear to have been relatively wealthy and of Anglo-Danish background. Harding Fitz Alnoth can be seen in Domesday holding several estates in the Wiltshire area in both 1066 and c.1086 (http://opendomesday.org. Accessed July 2016).

160 See, H.V.Clover and M.T.Gibson, (eds. and trans), *The Letters of Lanfranc* (Oxford, 1979), no. 53, p. 167.

161 For references to '*infantes*' and '*iuvenculae*' or 'adolescents' see, J.B.L.Tolhurst (ed.), *The Ordinale and Customary of the Benedictine Nuns of Barking Abbey: Oxford University College, MS 169* (Woodbridge, 2010), vol. i, pp. 14, 27, 34.

CHAPTER ONE: DISCIPLINE AND BEHAVIOUR

(*nutrix*).[162] He suggested that she had a cell of her own (*cella*), a room which he described as having had a previous purpose, serving as a 'shrine' devoted to Saint Eadgyth's mother, Abbess Wulfthryth of Wilton (d.1000) (*Wulftrudis sacrarium*). Goscelin also described an occasion when the infant girl had fallen seriously ill there, and where, he had imagined further, and after she had recovered, that the infant girl had wandered (*vagari*) out of her confinement and into Wilton's complex, encountering other religious women, and making interruptive demands for food (*edulium poscere*). This account provides for surprising details of a system of care for infants and conditions of religious infancy at Wilton in the eleventh century. Goscelin's references to the infant's 'demands for food', and his subsequent description of how senior religious women had sought to find her a dish of 'curds' or 'coagulated milk' (*lacteo coagulo*) present us with a portrait of a particularly young individual who might have only recently been weaned. Goscelin does not appear to have expected that such a girl

---

162 Goscelin, *Translatio Sancte Edithe Virginis*, in 'La légende de ste Édith', ed. Wilmart, c. 17, pp. 292-3: 'Supradicti rebellionis supradicta et adhuc superstes propinqua in infantia sua apud hoc monasterium in gremio nutricis mori videbatur febricata. Hanc videns una priorum in exitum hanelantem: "Aufer, ait, ab hac cella morientem, quia hoc non funeratorum speleum, sed domne Wlftrudis decet haberi sacrarium, unde illa celo reddidit spiritum". Idne errori ascribatur an fidei, patet note virtutus mater, qualis hic habeatur meriti. At mulier procurrens seminecem coram opifera proicit Editha. Ibi cum triduo quasi funus immotum servaretur, et nil preter exitum vel beate virginis respectum prestolaretur, subito expectata, vel desperata, salus regreditur. Cepit parvula quasi a morte respirare, diem luminibus scintillare, vagitu edulium poscere; sumtoque lacteo coagulo, convaluit destinata sancta Edithe oblatio'; trans. Hollis, et al., *Writing the Wilton Women*, p. 86: 'The above-mentioned and still surviving relative of the above-mentioned rebellious man, when in her infancy she was being cared for in this monastery by her nurse, seemed to be dying of fever. One of the leading sisters, seeing her gasping for breath on the point of expiring, said: "Take the dying child away from this cell; this is not a burial-cave, but it ought to be preserved as a shrine of the lady Wulfthryth, since here she returned her spirit to heaven'. Whether this should be ascribed to error or to faith, the lady is known to be of remarkable virtue, whatever the merits of this action. But the woman ran and cast the half-dead child before Edith the aid bringer. When it had remained motionless there for three days as if dead, and the only alternative to death that was expected was the intervention of the holy virgin, suddenly her health – despaired of, or hoped for – returned. The little girl began to breathe as if returned from death, to look upon the daylight with sparkling eyes; she began to wander about demanding food, and having eaten some curds she regained her strength for her future as an oblate of Saint Edith'; Knowles, *Heads of Religious Houses*, p. 222.

would have been subject to a routine. In fact, Goscelin does not appear to have subjected her to a(ny) disciplinary system at all. Indeed, Goscelin's account of the girl's wandering and calling out for food – behaviours which we could reasonably expect would have broken acceptable monastic norms if undertaken by adults – attracted no suggestion on his part that she would have needed to undergo a form of punishment. Goscelin's descriptions of her being soothed by religious women point us rather in an opposing direction. They disclose that religious houses might not in fact have sought to impose a similar framework of discipline on all members, did not expect very young girls of infant age to be subject to normative conditions, and did not expect them to recognise, let alone value, monastic routines.

Girlhood

To understand the conditions of older girls, we can return to prescriptive materials seen above, and approach terminology relating to *pueri* in Latin customaries and *cild* in the *Old English Rule*, in terms which suppose that girls participated in an apparatus designed for the 'child'. Rohini Jayatilaka has previously shown, in fact, that several surviving copies of the Latin *Regula Benedicti* show traces of adaptation for use by women and give visible testimony to the participation of girls in a prescriptive context.[163] These adapted copies are especially significant because feminine adjustments not only reveal that religious girls were governed by the *Regula Benedicti* but because they also reveal *how* they were.

In the case of contemporary copies of the Latin *Regula Benedicti*, scholars have identified several adaptations which suggest that women participated in contemporary regulations by simply replacing masculine

---

163 Rohini Jayatilaka argues that 'the Old English Rule was rapidly adapted to female use and extensively copied and was soon more freely available than the original male version', see Rohini Jayatilaka 'The Old English Benedictine Rule: Writing for Women and Men', *Anglo-Saxon England* 32 (2003), pp. 147-87 esp. pp. 185-6. At least one copy was probably also adapted for a community of religious vowesses, however, see 'Old English Benedictine Rule', pp. 186-7. For more on the terminology of female religious, see Sarah Foot, 'Language and Method: the Dictionary of Old English and the Historian', in *Dictionary of Old English: Retrospects and Prospects*, ed. M. J. Toswell and Antonette di Paolo Healey (Kalamazoo, MI, 1998), pp. 73-87.

elements with feminine equivalents. We can see this particularly clearly, for example, in two unprinted copies of bilingual versions of the *Regula* which are now contained in Cambridge, Corpus Christi College MS 178, and in Oxford, Corpus Christi College MS 197. These not only reveal a 'feminisation' of pronouns in Latin headings to chapter 45, *De his qu[a]e fallunt[u]r in oratorio,* 'On those [girls] who make a fault in the church', but indicate that contemporaries believed that girls should be subject to conditions of corporal punishment, and, in the case of chapter 45 of the *Regula,* that girls should be beaten if they made mistakes in their liturgical performances in choir.[164]

We can ask similar questions of surviving copies of the *Regularis Concordia*, and consider whether they also tell us how girls and women might have participated in its conditions. We might ask, for example, whether surviving copies of the *Regularis Concordia* challenge the idea that girls were required to split up into more manageable groups on the right- and left-hand sides of the choir. We might ask too whether or not choirs were to constitute a mixture of adults and girls, and whether their groups were organised to create a hierarchical environment. We might ask, indeed, whether they tell us girls followed their own daily routines, and were subject to the care of 'teachers', 'guardians', or the multiplicity of other disciplinary authorities mentioned in the *Regularis Concordia*.

Sadly, these copies provide few answers. Two fragmentary vernacular translations of the *Regularis Concordia,* now preserved in London, British Library Cotton Tiberius MS A. iii (corresponding to pp. 14-19 of RC or pp. 112-13 of EME) and in Cambridge, Corpus Christi College MS 201 (corresponding to pp. 36-43 of RC or pp. 124-133 of EME) contain examples of feminine vocabulary similar to those present in contemporary copies of the *Regula Benedicti*. They reveal that girls and women adapted their copies and participated in prescriptions in ways similar to the *Regula,* often simply by adding to Latin terms for male agents – for male monks,

---

164 Several examples are printed in Jayatilaka, 'Old English Benedictine Rule', pp. 152 (Oxford MS CCC, 197, fol. 69r: 'De his que falluntur in oratorio'), and 154 (Cambridge MS CCC, 178, p. 393: 'De his que fallunter (sic) in oratorio'); Cambridge MS CCC, 178, pp. 393-4, at 394: 'Geonge men for swa geradu[m] gylte swingelle þolian', and also Oxford MS CCC, 197, fol. 69v: 'Geonge m[en] for swa geradum gylte swingelle þolian'.

male abbots, male brothers – with a parallel apparatus of female equivalents.[165] We can see the results of this process of adaptation quite clearly for example where the Old English fragments of the *Regularis Concordia* anticipated that their audiences would include an 'abbess' (*abbodysse*), a community of 'sisters' (*geswyster*) or 'female monks' (*mynecena*) and a group of senior women or office holders which included a 'reader' (*rædestre*).[166] They therefore raise the possibility that girls participated in similar ways:

(Tiberius MS A. iii)
Þonne þa ... geendode fram þam cildum, þonne hringe me þa oþer

---

165 For the fragment present in Tiberius MS A. iii, (fols. 173-6), see Arnold Schröer, 'De consuetudine monachorum', *Englische Studien: Organ für englische philologie* 9 (1886), pp. 290-6, at 294-6. For the fragment now in CCCC 201 (pp. 1-7), see Julius Zupitza, 'Ein weiteres Bruchstück der *Regularis Concordia* in altenglischer Sprache', *Archiv für das Studium der neueren Sprachen und Literaturen* 84 (1890), pp. 1-24, at pp. 2-16. Lucia Kornexl has also recognised feminine adaptations in her 'The *Regularis Concordia* and its Old English Gloss', *ASE* 24 (1995), pp. 95-130. See also Joyce Hill (On CCCC MS 201), 'Rending the Garment and Reading by the Rood: *Regularis Concordia* Rituals for Men and Women', in *The Liturgy of Late Anglo-Saxon England*, ed. Helen Gittos and M. Bradford Bedingfield (London, 2009), pp. 53-64. For each instance of feminisation visible in Tiberius MS A. iii, see Schröer (Tiberius MS A. iii), 'De consuetudine monachorum', p. 296: 'Anim[a]e fratrum et sororum nostrarum requiescant in pace'. For those in CCCC MS 201, see Zupitza, 'Ein weiteres Bruchstück', pp. 10 'Abbode oððe abbodyssan; þa gebroðra oððe þa geswysterna', 11 'Þæs abbodes oððe þære abbodyssan dome', 12 'Sy husl geseald ægðer ge þam gebroðrum ge geswysternum; nime se abbod oððe seo abbodisse þa gebroðra oððe þa geswysterna þe hi wyllan; æfter æfensange gan þa gebroðra oððe ælce geswyster', 13 'Þam geendedum se abbod oððe seo abbodisse on heora setlum sitten ... and hi æfter þan arisan and eallum gebroðrum oððe geswysternum wæter to heora handum gesellen; mynecena þonne, þeah him swage rad scrud ne gebyrige, gan hi þeah for arwyrðnesse þæs mæran dæges mid taporum and mid storcillan and swylc þincg be þaere halgan rode ræde swylce him þearflic sy to gehyrenne ...', 14 'Scence se abbod oððe seo abbodysse æne eallum gebroðrum oððe geswysternum heora hand cyssende. Þære þenunge geendedre sitte se abbod oððe seo abbodesse ... arise þonne se þe þam gefere yldest bið and scence þam abbode oððe þære abbodessan/ Gange seo abbodysse to cyricean mid hyre geswysternum', 16 'Þonne mon ræde: "Partit[a]e sunt vestimenta mea", þa twegen diaconas þe standað on twa healfe þaes altares toteon þaet getreagode hræ[g]l'.

166 Zupitza, 'Ein weiteres Bruchstüch', pp. 2-16; DOE: n. *abbodesse*: 'abbess'; BT: n. *gesweostor*: 'sister', n. *mynecenu*: lit. 'female monk' – i.e. a woman religious; the male pl. *munecas* and feminine pl. *munecena* are equivalent', n. *rædestre*: 'female reader'.

stunde, heom eallum sittendum on heore settlum endebyrdlice.¹⁶⁷

(CCCC MS 201)
Acwuncenum eallum leohtum, gan twa cild [...] to þan suþportice singan, hludre stefne: *Kyrieleison* (sic) [...] Þisum geendedum, andswarige eal chor: *Christus dominus factus est.*¹⁶⁸

While the term *cild* in these contexts does not reveal an obvious element of 'feminisation', we can appreciate that neutral gender terminology relating to children might have shaped the conditions of girls. These terms would allow us to suppose that girls entered the choirs in parallel to boys, and joined hierarchical orders expressed in their arrangements of their seating (*healdan heora endebyrdnesse*).¹⁶⁹ These would also allow us to imagine that girls observed their own daily routines, including using the toilet at fixed times of day, as well as bathing and washing their faces and hands at particular junctures. They would also let us suppose that girls contributed to liturgical activities and encountered a similar index of ritual gestures, from 'first setting on themselves the sign of the holy rood' (*ærest he onsette him sylfum þæt tacn þære halgan rode*),¹⁷⁰ 'bending their knees' in church (*mid gebigendum cneowum*),¹⁷¹ 'making a procession with tapers and censers and such things' (*gan hi ... mid taporum and mid storcillan and*

---

167 Schröer, 'De consuetudine monachorum', p. 295: 'Then, once this has been completed by the children, a *signum* shall be rung for the hour, and all shall be seated in their seats, in order' (my translation).
168 Zupitza, 'Ein weiteres Brüchstuch', p. 6: 'When all the lights have been extinguished, two children shall go to the south-porticus to sing with loud voices: *Kyrieleison* (sic) [...] Once these things have been finished, the whole choir shall answer: *Christus dominus factus est*'.
169 Zupitza, 'Ein weiteres Bruchstück', p. 3: 'They should keep their orderliness' (my translation); and see also Schröer, 'De consuetudine monachorum', p. 295: 'eallum sittendum on heore settlum endebyrdlice/with all sitting on their seats in orderliness' (my translation). DOE: n. *ende-byrdnes*: 'order/ arrangement, rank, priority/precedence, procedure/proper conduct, management, a natural course'.
170 Schröer, 'De consuetudine monachorum', p. 294 (my translation).
171 Schröer, 'De consuetudine monachorum', p. 295 (my translation); and Zupitza, 'Ein weiteres Bruchstück', pp. 9, 15.

swylc þincg),[172] and 'going to Prime with unshod feet' on Good Friday (*gan to heora primsange unscodum fotum*).[173] They would also imply that girls' learning of those routines and behaviours might also have been helped by the monastic soundscape as we explored it above through the manipulation of 'bells' struck at different times to create a variety of effects (i.e. *þonne se belle cnelle, beon hi ealle gegaderode to primsancge*).[174]

These adapted fragmentary copies also expected children to enter 'school' structures, subjecting them to conditions of supervision under dedicated 'teachers':

(BL Tiberius MS A. iii)
Ga seo scola mid heora *magistrum* to þare gewunelican neode and belifan þa oþer innon cyrcean on heora gebedum.[175]

(CCCC MS 201)
... and siððan heora rædinge georne rædan oð sconylle.[176]

For all these potential conditions, however, it is the case that the prescriptive source base provides no means to determine whether, let alone how far, girls' experiences followed these expectations. While the survival of references to schools and teachers encourages the idea that girls encountered that structure, there is little anecdotal evidence to support it. We have already seen in the *Translatio Sancte Edithe Virginis*, for example, that Goscelin had accounted for a girl's infancy at Wilton as having been confined to structures we do not find in contemporary prescriptions, that is to say, to a cell or *cella*, and to the care of a young religious woman or

---

172 Zupitza, 'Ein weiteres Bruchstüch', p. 13 (my translation).
173 Zupitza, 'Ein weiteres Bruchstüch', p. 14 (my translation).
174 Schröer, 'De consuetudine monachorum', p. 296: 'When the bell knells, let them all be gathered to sing Prime' (my translation).
175 Schröer, 'De consuetudine monachorum', p. 296: 'Let the school go with a *magister* to the toilet for its needs, while the others [seniors] remain inside the church in prayer' (my translation).
176 Zupitza, 'Ein weiteres Bruchstüch', p. 10: 'After afterwards, let them go to study in prayer' (my translation).
Zupitza, 'Ein weiteres Bruchstüch', p. 10: 'After afterwards, let them go to their readings until the shoe-bell rings' (my translation).

nutrix. His accounts of older girls at Wilton provide a similar picture. His *Vita Sancte Edithe Virginis* described Eadgyth's educational experiences in ways which allow us to consider that she might have also experienced her education at Wilton in the solitary occupation of a cell (*cella*) or a little chamber too (*cubiculum*).[177] Goscelin was quite consistent in this vocabulary. He nowhere allowed us to imagine that Eadgyth could have experienced a formal education in any collective unit alongside peers, and never broke from a pattern of references which would have allowed his description of her life at Wilton to conform better to the *Regularis Concordia*. Goscelin tells us that Eadgyth might have had an interior teacher, in the form of Wilton's own abbess, incidentally her own mother, Wulfthryth (d.1000), and he tells us that she had access to an exterior set of teachers – or chaplains and bishops. In the case of both sets of teachers, Goscelin only ever accounted for a private type of instruction of Eadgyth, and in the case of her male chaplains in particular, he discloses that teachers might only have instructed girls like her through a window in their

---

177 Goscelin, *Vita Sancte Edithe Virginis*, in 'La légende de ste Édith', ed. Wilmart, p. 47: 'In ecclesie gremium, in virginale collegium, in divinum gymansium, in scolas virtutum'; trans. Hollis et al., *Writing the Wilton Women*, p. 30: 'She was gathered into the bosom of the church, the college of virgins, the divine training school, the schools of virtue'. For images of the little chamber, see Goscelin, *Vita Sancte Edithe Virginis*, in 'La légende de ste Édith', ed. Wilmart, pp. 45: 'Dilexit me rex et introduxit me in cubiculum suum'; trans. Hollis et al., *Writing the Wilton Women*, p. 29: 'The king has loved me and brought me into his bedchamber'; Goscelin, *Vita Sancte Edithe Virginis*, in 'La légende de ste Édith', ed. Wilmart, pp. 60-1: 'Post vigiliarum sollemnia ... post psalmodie, orationum ac lacrimarum holocausta medullata – non primum regnum Dei querebat – quasi de cubiculo Domini ad exteriora exit officia'; trans. Hollis et al., *Writing the Wilton Women*, pp. 36-7: 'After the celebration of vigils ... after the fat-burnt offerings of psalmody and prayers – for she sought first the kingdom of God – she went forth to her exterior duties as if from the chamber of the Lord'. See also reference to a closed little chamber where her clothes were thought to have been kept at Goscelin, *Vita Sancte Edithe Virginis*, in 'La légende de ste Édith', ed. Wilmart, p. 71: 'Rediviva flamma faciem suam illuminat et clauso cubiculo intus stepere intus grassari, ardour inimicus ceperat'; trans. Hollis et al., *Writing the Wilton Women*, p. 43: 'The revived flame flared up and became self-sustaining, and in the closed room the destructive head began to roar and rage inside the chest'; and see another reference to chamber made in relation to the place of her death at p. 95: 'Totumque cubiculum suavitate replere'; trans. Hollis et al., *Writing the Wilton Women*, p. 59: '[The place where she offered her blessed soul like incense to her Father in the highest does not cease to give forth fragrance and] fill the whole chamber with sweet odours'.

chambers or cells (*per fenestram*).[178]

It is possible that some girls entered a more communally orientated system of education centred on an abbey 'school' and dedicated teacher, in closer agreement with the language of the *Regularis Concordia* and the later *Constitutiones*. But the earliest and clearest source of evidence supporting this emerges at Barking Abbey after the Norman Conquest, in Goscelin's *De Translatione Sanctarum*, commissioned by its abbess, Ælfgifu (c.1050-1114):

Erat huic dudum puellulae et coetaneae scolae monasterialis

---

[178] Goscelin, *Vita Sancte Edithe Virginis*, in 'La légende de ste Édith', ed. Wilmart, p. 49: 'Mater illi non auro rutilos crines impedire non aurea lammina vel gemmis in fronte dependentibus arcem crucis obnubilare ... pro stibio pudorem docebat, pro variis ornatibus litterarum ac virtutum decore hanc preparabat'; trans. Hollis et al., *Writing the Wilton Women*, p. 32: 'Her mother did not desire to load her reddish hair with gold, nor to obscure the stronghold of the cross with a gold plate or jewels hanging over her forehead, nor to crown her with the finery of the married state ... in place of purple, in place of cosmetics for the face and eyes, she taught her modesty; in place of a range of adornments she preferred to adorn her with the splendour of learning'; Goscelin, *Vita Sancte Edithe Virginis*, in 'La légende de ste Édith', ed. Wilmart, pp. 50-1: 'Auctoritate quoque sancta flagrancie Edgari, inter sacerdotes Wiltonie qui precedebant arcam federis Domini, ministri dominici tabernaculi, pollebant duo, tam morum quam scientie philosophia venerandi, quorum alter Radbodo Remensis de Sancto Remegio alter memoratur Benna Treverensis canonicus de Sancti Paulini Patrocinio [...] Hi condigna reverentia vicissim erudiebant alumnam spiritus sancti; hi portabant pedibus eius lucernam verbi Domini, ut, accensis lampadibus scripturarum, lectis gradibus virtutum, niteretur ad etherei regis solium [...] eruditor pudicus a foris per fenestram docebat et audiri magis quam videri assueverat, ut sancti pudoris vernulam decebat. Ornabant aures eius margaritis celestibus mater interius, magister exterius'; trans. Hollis et al., *Writing the Wilton Women*, p. 32: 'Among the priests of Wilton who went in procession before the Ark of the Covenant of the Lord, ministers of the Lord's tabernacle, there were twin instructors who were of special weight by Edgar's authority, venerable for their wisdom both in life and in scholarship, of whom one is remembered as Radbodo of Rheims, from St. Remegius, the other as Benno, canon of Trier under the patronage of St. Paulinus [...] These men took turns to teach, with worthy reverence, this pupil of the Holy Spirit; these men brought to her feet the light of the word of God, so that by the light of the lamps of the scriptures and by choosing the steps of the virtues, she might advance towards the throne of the eternal king [...] The chaste teacher instructed her from outside through a window and accustomed himself to being heard rather than being seen, as was appropriate for the young pupil with her holy modesty. Her mother within and her teacher from outside adorned her ears with heavenly pearls'.

magistra, bonae memoriae.[179]

In the same way that we find this account of a school at Barking comprised of a teacher (*magistra*), later referred to as Wulfruna, and a number of young girls (*puellulae*), we find evidence for similar structures later in the twelfth century and at women's houses which belonged to new monastic orders. Abbot Aelred of Rievaulx (c.1110-1167) accounted for a nun who grew up at the Gilbertine Priory of Watton in c.1150 and who was apparently educated there in a similar collectivising system. Though Aelred did not use the descriptor *schola* or 'school' as such, he described what seem to be equivalent conditions; a space set apart for the instruction of a group of girls of similar age (*aliae [puellae]*), and governed by several dedicated teachers (*magistrae*).[180] The salient features of both Goscelin's early twelfth century and Aelred's late twelfth century accounts of religious education in a female house strongly imply that structures similar to those anticipated by the *Regularis Concordia* and *Constitutiones* might have shaped the disciplinary conditions and contingent experiences of religious girls at some point. Girls' experiences of supervision and correction might thus have come to conform with the *Regularis Concordia* and *Constitutiones* and to parallel those of contemporary religious boys in a period coterminous with the lifetimes of Goscelin and Aelred.

These same authors are also witnesses to ideals in girls' behaviours, and describe gestures which contemporaries expected girls to learn in their religious environments from their teachers or supervisors. Goscelin describes a series of behavioural ideals in his *Liber Confortatorius* to the young religious woman, Eafe of Wilton (fl. 1058-1125), for example:

---

179 Goscelin, *De Translatione vel Elevatione Sanctarum Virginum Ethelburgae, Hildelithae et Wlfhildae*, in 'Texts of Jocelyn of Canterbury which Relate to the History of Barking Abbey', ed. Marvin Colker, *Studia Monastica* 7 (1965), p. 453: 'There was at that time a teacher [Wulfruna] of good memory of the monastic school of young girls and associate students' (my translation).

180 Aelred of Rievaulx, *De Sanctimoniali de Wattun*, ed. Migne, PL 195, cols. 791-2: 'Furabatur magistrarum oculis horas, ut vel indulgeret, vel signis inordinatis difflaeret, aut vacaret fabulis, aut inutile aliquid aliis suaderet'; trans. Boswell, *Kindness of Strangers*, p. 453: 'She wasted hours in plain view of her teachers, either doing nothing, or making naughty signs, or telling stories, or persuading others to waste time'.

> Ubi vero inter quattuordecim virgines, coruscantibus cereis tanguam syderibus et lampadibus supernis, ad dominicas nuptias trepida et penultima accessisti ac, populosa caterva sollemniter expectante, pignus fidei divine cum sacrata veste induisti, ille humilis habitus, ille tremebundus accessus, ille suffusus vultus, tamquam ab igneo throno Dei sedentis super cherubim, sapienter metuentis, altius viscera me percussere cum hoc epithalamico carmine admirabilis gratie: "Ipsi sum desponsata, cui angeli serviunt, et annulo suo subarravit me". Tacitus sum rore celesti et fervore irriguo flevi. Continuata quoque silentia tua, sollicita continentia, frequens psalmodia, pia magistre testimonia, magis accenderunt vota mea.[181]

In this passage, we find evidence of the acquisition of a complex of ritual gestures Eafe had apparently mastered by the time of her confirmation at Wilton in c.1065. Here, Goscelin identified himself as one of Eafe's behavioural influences, alongside a more dedicated 'teacher' or *magistra*, and emphasised her learning and successful reception from them of a series of expressive monastic gestures centring on her control over the body and voice. In terms of managing Eafe's misbehaviours, Goscelin's *Liber Confortatorius* recalled that he had been able to discipline her by means of vexing (*irritare*) and correcting (*corrigere*).[182] Goscelin's recollections

---

[181] Goscelin, 'The *Liber Confortatorius* of Goscelin of Saint Bertin', ed. Charles H. Talbot, *Analecta Monastica* 37 (1955), p. 28: trans. Otter, *Liber Confortatorius*, p. 23: 'But when you walked up to the Lord's wedding, with trepidation, the penultimate of fourteen virgins, with glittering candles like the stars and constellations above; when, before a large crowd waiting in solemn silence, you put on the sacred vestment, it was as if from the fiery throne of God sitting above his cherubim, I was struck to the quick with this wonderously beautiful epithalamium: "I am given in marriage to him whom the angels serve, and he has wedded me with his ring". I was touched by the heavenly dew and wept in tearful fervor (sic). And as I continued to witness your silence, your careful continence, your singing of the psalms and the praises of your teacher, my desire was inflamed even more'. N.b. Otter's translation does not meet Goscelin's word for word but this is largely because Goscelin practised a very idiosyncratic Latin style, hard to replicate in modern English, which indulged a contemporary interest in lofty poeticism, often at the expense of verbal precision.

[182] Goscelin, *Liber Confortatorius*, ed. Talbot, p. 27: 'Memor, dignaberis hec nostra monumenta respicere, estimato me tecum Wiltonie coram sancta domina nostra Eadgyda aut etiam in hac pudica serie residere, te alloqui, te exhortari, te consolari', and p. 28: 'Meministi, anima mi dulcissima, ut primo tuam irritaverim infantiam, securus me facile correcturum tam piam animam'; trans. Otter, *Liber Confortatorius*, pp. 21-2:

therefore not only provide a useful window onto an individual girl's behavioural formation, but they provide a view of discipline centred on the use of verbal forms of correction. This emphasis is shared more widely in the hagiographic record too. Indeed, an anonymous *Vita Beate Sexburge*, composed by a monk of Ely in c.1107, suggests in two accounts of an ideal religious girlhood, that verbal conditions of discipline and correction were preferred as a means to shape girls' behaviours in the early twelfth century:

> In annis itaque puellaribus [...] Caribdim ipsa sine vitio persequebatur. Non lasciva, non garrula, sed sobria et modesta [...] Non iuvenibus cincinnatis arridebat nec applaudabat procis forma delicatis.[183]

The author of the *Vita* appears to have considered the face, aspects of personal appearance, and degrees of chattiness to be highly indicative of a state of continence. Indeed, the work articulates the author's own anxiety about chastity, and about girls' and women's relationship with sexual continence in particular:

> Variis modis [...] iracundas patientes blanditiis correptione aggreditur. Iurgia et lites blando sermone conciliabat [...] Lascivum verbum et inhonestum nulla earum producebat garrulas ac procaces converti sepius hortabatur. Que in perverso opere persistebat, a sororum sequestrabat consortio, vincebaturque pudore in publico quas obiurgatio non corrigebat occulta.[184]

'[Whenever] you will deign to look at these my letters, you will believe me with you at Wilton, before our holy Lady Edith, sitting chastely by your side, speaking with you, admonishing you, consoling you', and 'You remember, my sweetest soul, how I first vexed you when you were a child, quite certain I could easily correct such a pious soul'.

183 Anon., *Vita Beate Sexburge Regine*, in *Hagiography of the Female Saints of Ely*, ed. and trans. Love, pp. 139-40: 'In the years of her girlhood [...] she passed through the Charibdis of the vices herself without vice. Not lustful, or prattling, but sober and modest [...] She did not smile at youths with curly locks, nor show her approval of suitors comely in form'.

184 Anon., *Vita Beate Sexburge Regine*, ed. and trans. Love, pp. 180-1: 'By various means [...] she approached the hot-tempered with kind words, the stubborn with punishment. She settled arguments and disputes with a gentle word [...] She frequently exhorted the over-talkative. She separated from the company of sisters any

What is perhaps just as noteworthy about this work, however, is that the author of the *Vita Beate Sexburge Regine* also provides a verbal centre of corrective gravity. Here, we find a contemporary portrait of Seaxburh as a model disciplinarian and as someone who could have used an index of verbal methods of correction on the poorly behaved girls subject to her care. In addition to this, Goscelin's *Vita Sancte Edithe Virginis* provides yet another opportunity to explore potential systems of punishment in an account of a girl-thief who, Goscelin claimed, had once attempted to steal a linen cloth which had been kept at Wilton Abbey as a relic of Saint Eadgyth:

> Muliercula, sola ibi relicta et ex solicitudine furto contigua, excerpit, tibieque involutum spoilium abducit. Mox divina compes fugientem constrinxit et furtigerulum pedem radicitus fixit [...] pallore, temore, gemitu crimen prodit [...] resolvit.[185]

This account of a girl-thief is useful to us too because it provides a basis of comparison with Ælfric Bata's school *Colloquia* and with dialogue no. 28 in particular, where he accounted for the beating of a boy for theft. As with Bata's account, Goscelin seems to recognise that a girl of Wilton would ordinarily have been punished for theft, but his account, quite unlike Bata's, assigned no corrective act of violence to the hands of a dedicated female religious disciplinarian. Instead, Goscelin constructed a miraculous intervention, allowing the long-dead figure of Saint Eadgyth to behave as disciplinarian, and denying us an opportunity to ascertain who might have impressed correction, and what disciplinary processes, if any, might have ordinarily played a role.

At first sight, this account does seem to give ground to the idea that corporal punishment might have been less significant to the experiences

---

who persisted in wrong behaviour, and anyone who could not be corrected by private rebuke was dealt with by public shaming'.
185 Goscelin, *Vita Sancte Edithe Virginis*, in 'La légende de ste Édith', ed. Wilmart, pp. 100-1; trans. Hollis et al., *Writing the Wilton Women*, p. 62: 'A girl left there alone and in her solitude became inclined to theft and took it and tied the spoils around her shin. Suddenly divine fetters bound her as she tried to flee and rooted the thieving foot to the spot [...] she confessed her crime with a trembling paleness of complexion [...] and [her foot] released'.

of religious girls. If that was the case, however, it would be difficult to imagine that violence was not used at all. Post-Conquest sources do describe occasions of the use of violence, and, indeed, Abbot Aelred of Rievaulx's (c.1147-1167) later twelfth century account of the pregnancy of an oblate nun who had grown up at Watton Priory from the age of four, confirms the presence of violence in the experiences of girls of low social status. Although he confirms the place of violence only in the course of his attempt to explain why the young woman had become pregnant, his account is particularly useful because it focussed blame on and so described in unusual detail her formative disciplinary experiences. It blamed a failure to remain sexually continent on the girl's lack of acquisition of an interest in the *Regula Benedicti*,[186] it laid blame on her teachers (*magistrae*) who, Aelred claimed, had initially employed a mixture of both verbal chastisements (*corripere verbis*) and beatings (*urgere verberibus*), but who had eventually erred by giving up on correcting their young charge. It also laid blame on the grounds that, by 'closing up their ears and eyes', the girl's teachers had effectively suspended normative expectations of religious behaviour, and had given tacit licence to her behavioural autonomy as she passed adolescence.[187]

---

186 Aelred of Rievaulx, *De Sanctimoniali de Wattun*, ed. Migne, PL 195, cols. 791-2: 'Nullus ei circa religionem amor, nulla circa ordinem sollicitudo circa Dei timorem nullus affectus'; trans. Boswell, *Kindness of Strangers*, p. 453: 'No love for religious life, no concern for the rule, no inclination to honor (sic) God'.

187 Aelred of Rievaulx, *De Sanctimoniali de Wattun*, ed. Migne, PL 195, cols. 791-2: 'Corripitur verbis sed non corrigitur; urgetur verberibus, sed non emendator ... disciplina ordinis premebatur, et ad exterioris hominis honestatem utcunque servandam cogebatur invita. Omnie ei ex timore constabant, ex amore nihil. Et iam nubilis facta, interioribus exterior, otiose quietis, seriis ludicra praeponebat'; trans. Boswell, *Kindness of Strangers*, p. 453: 'She was reproached by words but not corrected; injured by beatings but not chastened ... She was restrained by the discipline of the order, and forced against her will to maintain some external semblance of decency, but all such constraints worked on her through fear, none through love. By the time she was a teenager (i.e. of marriageable age) she preferred the superficial to the spiritual, play to reflection, and the silly to the serious'. See also Aelred of Rievaulx, *De Sanctimoniali de Wattun*, ed. Migne, PL 195, col. 791: 'Ubi tunc tuus custodia disciplinae vigilantissimus sensus? Ubi tot tam exquisite ad excludendam vitiorum materiam machinamenta? Ubi tunc illa tam prudens, tam cauta, tam perspicax cura, et circa singula ostia, fenestras angulos tam fida custodia ut sinistris etiam spiritibus nigari videretur accessus? Elisit totam industriam, una puella, quia *nisi Dominus custodierit civitatem, frustra vigilat qui custodit eam* [...] Ubi timor? Ubi amor? Ubi illius sanctae

In addition to presenting us with this account of violence, however, Aelred's account raises questions about the nature of Anglo-Saxon and earlier Anglo-Norman practices.[188] Up until now, we have seen that the lives of pre-Conquest saints tend not to describe shared structures of correction, and give rise to an impression of more individualised systems of behavioural instruction, of private correction, of violence towards girls like the nun of Watton, who were of low social status, and a preference for verbal disciplinary actions with respect to royal saints. These differences seem so stark that we should ask whether they represent real differences in disciplinary conditions between the eleventh and twelfth centuries, or whether instead the differences that they indicate are more an accident of genre and the chance survival of records.

We may partly resolve questions about the representativeness of our sources if we recall evidence seen earlier in this section for the use of corporal violence on girls in the context of feminine word forms added to copies of the *Regula Benedicti*, and if we also recognise that several post-Conquest authors believed that violent punishments were important to girls before the Conquest. Indeed, post-Conquest records may allow us to consider more than this, that girls of royal status were treated differently to those of lower status.[189] It is well known, for example, that certain lives of royal saints describe royal girls as being relatively independent of the normative structures of their religious communities. We find evidence for this kind of

---

congregationis reverentia? Ubi beati pontificis qui te huic monasterio tradidit sauvis memoria? [...] Quid plura? Heu! Claudite aures, virgines Christi, oculos operite'; trans. Boswell, *Kindness of Strangers*, pp. 453-4: 'Where, father, was your most diligent concern for the maintenance then? Where then were your many ingenious devices for eliminating occasions of sin? Where then was that care so prudent, so cautious, so perspicacious, and that supervision so strict in regard to every door, every window, every corner, that it seemed to deny access even to evil spirits? One girl made a mockery of all your efforts, father, because "except the Lord keep the city, the watchman waketh but in vain" [...] Where was the respect, where was love, where was reverence for that holy congregation? Where was the sweet memory of the blessed bishop who had given you to the convent? [...] What next? Alas! She goes out. Block your ears, virgins of Christ, and close your eyes'.

188 For further discussion of the episode, see Giles Constable, 'Ailred of Rievaulx and the Nun of Wattun', in *Medieval Women*, ed. Derek Baker (Oxford, 1978), pp. 205-26.

189 Katherine, O'Brien O'Keeffe, 'Leaving Wilton: Gunhild and the Phantoms of Agency', *Journal of English and Germanic Philology* 106 (2007), pp. 203-223.

exemption in Goscelin's late eleventh century account of the *Vita Sancte Edithe Virginis*, where he described Bishop Æthelwold of Winchester's attempt to verbally chastise Eadgyth of Wilton for wearing a purple gown in the station of a royal princess instead of the habit of a religious.[190] But we also find evidence for difference in the treatment of royalty in Osbert of Westminster's (d.1158) mid-twelfth century *Vita Sancte Ædburge Virginis* (the 'Life of the Blessed Virgin, Eadburh', d.960). Osbert provided an account of a royal girl's misbehaviour and detailed her subsequent subjection to corporal punishment at Nunnaminster. He described that the prioress, rather than any other dedicated guardian, had discovered the young girl at one time trying to read without supervision between offices. The prioress assumed the role of disciplinarian, 'beating [Eadburh] severely with her hand' (*grandis alapis percussione cohercet*).[191] In doing so, Osbert's account suggests that under normal circumstances girls who were offered to houses of religious women could encounter reactive forms of corporal punishment.

After this, however, Osbert's *Vita* added a scene which appears to have entirely transformed the system of correction which the prioress had previously been able to uphold:

> Commoverat enim illam zelus disciplin[a]e et domus Dei, ut nulla

---

190 Goscelin, *Vita Sancte Edithe Virginis*, in 'La légende de ste Édith', ed. Wilmart, c. 12, p. 70 : 'Aliquando premoneret, "O filia, non his itur ad talamum Christi induviis, nec exteriori cultu delectatur sponsus celestis". Illa, interni conscia habitatoris ... tali memoratur elogio respondisse, crede, O pater reverende, nequaquam deterior mens Deo aspirante sub hoc habitabat tegmine quam sub caprina melote. Habeo Dominum meum, qui non vestem sed mentem attendit ... Vir sensit Deo afflatus presentientis in virgine gratie auctoritatem nec ausus contristrare supernam in illa'; trans. Hollis et al., *Writing the Wilton Women*, pp. 42-3: [Æthelwold] 'Once warned, O daughter, not in these garments does one approach the marriage chamber of Christ, nor is the heavenly bridegroom pleased with exterior elegance"; she, conscious of her indwelling guest [...] is reported to have replied in these words: "Believe, reverend father, a mind by no means poorer in aspiring to God will live beneath this covering than beneath a goatskin. I possess my Lord, who pays attention to my mind, not to the clothing [...] The man inspired by God recognized (sic) the authority of grace excelling in the virgin, and not daring to distress the heavenly guardian within her'.
191 Osbert of Clare, *Vita Sancte Ædburge Virginis*, in *Royal Saints of Anglo-Saxon England: A Study of West Saxon and East Anglian Cults*, ed. Susan Ridyard (Cambridge, 1988), p. 267 (my translation).

earum privatis in oratio vacaret officiis ... cum principis filiam esse cognosceret, toto in terram copore prostrato postulans indulgentiam, accusat delictum et confitetur culpam.[192]

Upon discovering the royal identity of Eadburh, Osbert imagined that the prioress of Nunnaminster would have needed to prostrate herself on the ground in order to beg Eadburh for forgiveness.[193] Osbert's *Vita* indicates therefore that, while religious girls of non-royal status might ordinarily have been subject to such experiences, a royal status, and Eadburh's position as daughter and sister to Anglo-Saxon kings, meant that some girls were not. Osbert assumed that a privileged royal status, similar to conditions of infancy seen above, would have disrupted the operation of disciplinary systems at houses of women religious, and that girls of royal birth could not or perhaps should not have been treated similarly to non-royal girls. His *Vita* also implies that particularly privileged girls might not have participated in other conditions outlined by a contemporary body of monastic prescriptions - like chapter 45 of the *Old English Rule* on the beating of *geonge men* in choir - and that violent correction might not have played as tangible a part in the formation of their behaviours as they might have done in the lives of a larger number of contemporary girls and boys of lower status.

---

192 Osbert of Clare, *Vita Sancte Ædburge Virginis*, ed. Susan Ridyard, p. 267: 'For a zeal for discipline and the house of God had provoked her [the prioress] so that none of them might spend time in prayer in private ... when she had recognised that she [Eadburh] was the daughter of the King, she prostrated herself to the ground with her entire body, petitioning for her [Eadburh's] forgiveness, admitting her offence and confessing her guilt' (my translation).
193 Osbert of Clare, *Vita Sancte Ædburge Virginis*, ed. Susan Ridyard, pp. 98, 267.

CHAPTER TWO: LITURGICAL FORMATION

In this chapter, I focus on the liturgical experiences of religious children, and ask whether and how oblates might have become masters in the liturgical programmes of their houses. I explore what knowledge children were expected to acquire, and what role liturgical experiences might have played in facilitating children's emergence into senior communities. The organisational principle adopted here mirrors and intersects with that of the previous chapter. This, in part, is intended to recognise that many of the documentary texts and environmental structures which have been of interest to that chapter, such as the *Regula Benedicti*, the monastic choir, the daily round, and 'school', provide important bases for consideration here. But this also allows us to consider childhood development in a more realistic way, showing how experience in the liturgy supported and extended from conditions in monastic discipline.

Although the *Regula Benedicti* has previously offered a point of entry for understanding structures of monastic discipline, it provides almost no ground for launching a study into children's liturgical development. Much of its liturgical framework ignored children, and focussed on *fratres* or 'brethren' and the 'whole' community instead. The *Regula* is therefore only helpful in providing a view of the general structures of a liturgical life in a monastery, indicating that liturgical activity would centre on membership of the choir (*sociari choro*) and focus on a need to sing psalms (*psallere*) in a continual service of prayerful intercession with God.[1] The *Regula* suggests that the Psalter was to be recited each week in the course

---

1 RSB, c. 19, 43, pp. 90-1, 146-9

of eight daily meetings known as Divine Offices.² These offices were to be held at regular intervals or 'hours' (*horae*) and their timing adjusted over the course of the year, depending on measures of daytime. It also tells us that routines were expected to begin in the middle of the night (Nocturns), continuing with a series of intervals in between for reading, prayer, eating, and manual labour, at day-break (Lauds, or Matins), at the first hour of the day (Prime), at third, sixth, and ninth hours (Tierce, Sext, Nones), at dusk (Vespers), and concluding in the late evening (Compline).³

Anglo-Saxon England: Infancy

As we have seen in chapter one, just a single reference in chapter 45, relating to the beating of *infantes* who had made a mistake in recitation of a psalm, responsory, or antiphon in choir, provides a context where the *Regula* assumed that infant boys would participate in liturgical routines after oblation.⁴ But we have also seen that the Anglo-Saxon corpus makes it difficult to understand whether infant oblates observed these expectations in a contemporary context. Æthelwold removed this reference to *infantes* from his own translation, and allowed it to point to a wider or older demographic of *geonge men* instead. Another copy of the Latin *Regula* which attracted a vernacular response for the 'child' indicates that this reference to *infantes* had been understood differently elsewhere, and might have included infants in the liturgy by virtue of expecting (all)

---

2 RSB, c. 16, pp. 78-9: 'As the prophet says, "I praised you seven times a day". This sacred number will be completed by us if we fulfil our duties of service . . . and concerning the night-time vigils, the prophet also says "I rose in the middle of the night to confess your name"'.
3 RSB, c. 16, pp. 78-9.
4 RSB, c. 45, pp. 154-5: 'Si quis dum pronuntiat psalmum, responsorium, antiphonam, vel lectionem fallitus fuerit, nisi satisfactione ibi coram omnibus humiliatus fuerit, maiori vindictae subiaceat, quippe qui noluit humilitatem corrigere quod negligentia deliquit. Infantes autem pro tali culpa bapulent/If anyone makes a mistake when he recites a psalm, responsory, antiphon, or reading, unless he is humbled by making satisfaction right there before all, he should be subject to more serious punishment, since he has refused to correct, in humility, an error made through carelessness. Children who make such mistakes should be whipped'.

CHAPTER TWO: LITURGICAL FORMATION

'children' to enter the choir, but these do not provide particularly strong grounds for accepting the participation of infants either.[5]

As we have also seen in the context of discipline, the *Regularis Concordia* contains just one occasion where we might consider infants were introduced into choral structures and expected to memorise liturgical texts necessary for reciting a service called the *Trina Oratio*:[6]

> *Infantibus* autem ecclesiam intrantibus, aedituus primum sonet signum; peractis tribus a *pueris* oraminibus, uti prius a senioribus gestum fuerat, dispositi singuli in locis suis campana pulsata incipiant horam Tertiam.[7]

In the same way that we have asked about its disciplinary significance, this passage would also seem to encourage us to think about children's earliest liturgical experiences. The passage appears to offer grounds from which we could speculate that young boys, potentially of infant age, entered liturgical communities and choral spaces, and observed and/or began to contribute to choral activities at Winchester's Old Minster once they had learnt by heart a certain enabling body of liturgical text.[8] But its imprecision, particularly in relation to *infans* and *puer*, and what each of them were supposed to do during this service, also means that we can understand very little for certain.[9]

Boyhood

With no precise reference to *infantes* in the *Regularis Concordia*, we can hardly begin to suppose infants entered choirs, let alone consider that

---

5 OERB, c. 45, lines 9-10, p. 71; *Rule of St. Benet: Latin and Anglo-Saxon*, ed. Logeman, c. 45, p. 79.
6 For a brief outline of the history of the *Trina Oratio*, see Christopher Jones EME, p. 153.
7 Symons assumes these refer to the same group of children, see RC, p. 16: 'As the children enter the church the sacrist shall ring the first bell; and when they have said the *Trina Oratio* in the same way as the seniors have done, all shall take their places and the bell shall be rung for them to begin Tierce'.
8 RC, p. 16.
9 RC, p. 16.

they might also have been expected to learn the threefold *Trina Oratio*. It is safer, therefore, to assume that the *Regularis Concordia* only discloses what Æthelwold expected an older or broader category of *pueri* or 'boys' to contribute to its performance.[10] The *Regularis Concordia* described this duty in some detail, expecting boys to learn by heart the Seven Penitential Psalms, for one. These prescriptions also expected boys to learn groups of other texts alongside them, requiring them to recite a first group of psalms (i.e. Pss. 6, 31, and 37) along with the *Pater Noster* and a collect, a Latin text which they were to learn to sing on behalf of the souls of monks. It also required them to master a second unit of the *oratio* (Pss. 50 and 101), which was to be recited with the *Pater Noster* again. This, the *Regularis Concordia* explains, was to be sung with a Latin collect sung on behalf of both the king and queen.

This performance deserves attention. Historians of later centuries might find mention of the king and queen rather unsurprising, but it is highly unusual here. England's early kingdoms did not confer equivalent status to queens. King Eadgar (r.959-975) and Queen Ælfthryth (d.1001) were the first monarchs of a still consolidating England to be crowned together in 973, undergoing a coronation of deliberately imperial ambitions in the Roman city of Bath. In this moment, Ælfthryth gained a status that was unprecedented, becoming England's first annointed Queen. Boys' performance of this collect on her (and the king's) behalf in a document from c.966 therefore reveals the importance of monastic houses in forming a new relationship between Church and emerging State. Indeed, it shows that religious leaders used their powerful monastic network to recognise and exalt the status of kings and queens, to sacralise further the increasingly religious nature of the monarchy, and prepared oblates for performance of the central mechanism of that bond, using their prayers to bind the monarchy to monastic interests, and intercede with God on their behalf for the kingdom's future.[11]

---

10 For the role of the Psalter in the monastic liturgy, see George Hardin-Brown, 'The Psalms as the Foundation of Anglo-Saxon Learning', in *The Place of the Psalms in the Intellectual Culture of the Middle Ages*, ed. Nancy Van Deusen (New York, 1999), pp. 1-24.

11 For more on the role of the monastic reform in sacralising England's monarchy, particularly relating to Eadgar's education in a reformist monastery, and of the borrowing

To this innovative collect, the *Regularis Concordia* added a third *oratio* (Pss. 129 and 142), requiring boys to perform the *Pater Noster,* another Latin collect sung on behalf of those who have died, the *Kyrie eleison* and also the *Preces* (Pss. 1:11-14), and it expected boys to have prepared for two other performances of the *Trina Oratio* according to similar arrangements, in the afternoon at Tierce and in the evening after Compline.[12] These references reveal that the *Trina Oratio* was important to fostering in boys not only a school, but a monastic and national identity too.

Sadly, the *Regularis Concordia* denies us a clear understanding of how and when, and whether Æthelwold might have expected boys of different ages to learn the skills and texts necessary for its complete recitation on these three occasions each day. Intersecting with the previous chapter on monastic discipline, however, contemporary school-texts may help further, and describe aspects of boys' participation in the liturgy that seem to confirm that boys trained and then sung parts in a piecemeal fashion:

> Petite libros vestros cito, et in scamnis vestris sedentes legite, et firmate acceptos vestros, ut properanter reddere valeatis cras in primo mane [...] modo scimus bene nostros acceptos et nostras lectiones et responsoria nostra et antiphonas nostras.[13]

These sections of Bata's *Colloquia* afford a more precise view onto a method of memorisation for the liturgy that boys likely pursued in order

---

of a Carolingian idea of the *via regia*, see Molyneux, *Formation of England*, pp. 191-192; see also, T. F. X. Noble, 'The Monastic Ideal as a Model for Empire: The Case of Louis the Pious', *Revue bénédictine*, 86 (1976), pp. 235-50. For an origin to studies on the sacralisation of kingship through coronation and consecration ordines, see E. H. Kantorowicz, *The King's Two Bodies: A Study in Medieval Political Theology* (Princeton, NJ, 1957), pp. 77, 89-90. In England, the works of Smaragdus of St. Mihiel appear to have been key transmittors of Carolingian politcal theology into monastic circles, see J. Bovendeert, 'Royal or Monastic Identity? Smaragdus' *Via regia* and *Diadema Monachorum* Reconsidered', in R. Corradini, R. Meens, C. Poessel and P Shaw (eds.), *Texts and Identities in the Early Middle Ages* (Vienna, 2006), pp. 239-51. It should be noted that the *Regularis Concordia* mentions *Via regia* in relation to Eadgar's education at Abingdon Abbey when he was ten years old.

12 RC, pp. 13, 16, 23.
13 ÆlfBColl, pp. 85-6: 'Quick, get your books and sit in your seats. Read and memorise your assignments so that first thing tomorrow morning you can recite quickly [...] we very well know our assignments, lections, responses, and antiphons already'

to perform at the Divine Offices. It accounts for individual boys working through discrete sequences which they call *accepti*, memorising (*firmare*) passages needed for a particular element of the liturgy the next day, and practising out loud by reading (*legere*) - though not necessarily understanding the texts - within their school.[14] This dynamic also presents itself in dialogues nos. 1 and 5 in a way that potentially also connects liturgical preparation to boys' daily round. Here, Bata describes boys memorising and practising prayers around a monastic complex 'as a custom' (*orationes nostras facere secundum nostram consuetudinem*).[15] They also point to boys' preoccupation at some stage with practising the Seven Penitential Psalms, which Bata hoped they would sing whenever they washed their hands (*manus nostras vii psalmos cantantes lavimus*).[16]

This evidence for training in the *Trina Oratio*, connecting us to the *Regularis Concordia*, is not likely to be a coincidence.[17] But these inferences push the limits of what we can understand securely. What we can see, is that boys' everyday lives likely reinforced and enabled their liturgical progression. These documents suggest too that the non-liturgical round was more important to boys, and to their liturgical development, than is often appreciated. Indeed, they seem to have allowed them to rehearse in a perhaps more forgiving space, and before mistakes entailed potentially violent consequences in choir.

Aside from small duties like the *Trina Oratio*, the *Regularis Concordia* does not allow us to explore fully how boys contributed to the eight regular Offices which took place each day. References to the Offices in this customary often followed and preceded prescriptions which mentioned boys - requiring them to perform duties like the *Trina Oratio*, which occurred

---

14 ÆlfBColl, pp. 87, 95
15 ÆlfBColl, pp. 80-1: 'Make our prayers following our custom'
16 ÆlfBColl, pp. 90-1: 'We washed our hands while we sang the seven [penitential psalms]'.
17 RC, p. 13: 'Donec quidem pueri introeunt ecclesiam unum continuatim pulsetur tintinnabulum, ipsi quoque pueri ingress, ut Trinitatis reverentia ab omnibus legitime teneatur, trina utantur oratio. Finitis vero orationibus a pueris . . . cunctis in sedilibus suis . . . canentibus quindecim psalmos graduum . . . trina partitione uti superiores septem [psalmos]/The bell shall be rung . . . until the children enter the church, and when they have all come in they too shall sing the *Trina Oratio* so that reverence to the Trinity shall be observed by all. When they have finished the *Trina Oratio* . . . all now seated shall recite the fifteen Gradual Psalms . . . in three-fold division, just as the Penitential Psalms were said'.

CHAPTER TWO: LITURGICAL FORMATION

either before or after three Offices. But Æthelwold's text does not disclose how boys observed the Offices themselves.[18] This silence of performance and performers in the *Regularis Concordia* might represent an inherited silence rather than any intent; it echoes the nature of the arrangements for Offices which were set out in the *Regula Benedicti* which had only vaguely required brethren to recite at Offices. More intentionally, it could also have ensured that the *Regularis Concordia* avoided problems in houses with variable numbers of oblates (with Winchester's Old Minster schooling at least six simultaneously, and Bury St. Edmunds caring for just two boys, Oswald and Ordric, when it was founded under King Cnut in c.1020) which may have resulted from setting down a more rigid framework.[19] In any case, it still leaves us in a position of being unable to tell whether, let alone how far, boys might have been expected to contribute.[20]

Just as we have proceeded in the chapter on discipline and in the section above, again, in order to have some direction on boys' performances at monastic Offices, we can explore the evidence of contemporary schooltexts. These documents are potentially useful to us not only because they were intended to help boys speak Latin – and in some cases, to paraphrase liturgical and biblical texts – but because they also appear to have been intended to enable boys to talk about their liturgical rounds. We find one such occasion in the *Colloquium* of Abbot Ælfric of Eynsham, for example:

[*Puer*]
Psallam omni die septem sinaxes cum fratribus et occupatus sum lectionibus et cantu.[21]

---

18 RC, p. 16.
19 These two boys, named as Oswold and Ordric appear to have been removed from Benet St. Holme at the request of the local bishop Æthelwine to help found (with the patronage of one of Cnut's newly appointed earls, Thorkell) a new community of 13 monks at Bury St. Edmunds (with the number symbolic of the apostles and Christ) - this appears, on the evidence of surviving charters attached to Bury's Custom's, in the manuscript London BL Halrey 1005, at 198r-v
20 For this and other offices, see RSB, c. 8, pp. 58-9 (Nocturns), chs. 17-8, pp. 80-5 (Prime), c. 18, pp. 84-5 (Tierce, Sext, Nones), c. 18, p. 87 (Vespers), c. 18, p. 87 (Compline).
21 ÆlfColl, p. 19: 'I sing every day, at each of the seven offices, with the brothers, and I keep myself busy with reading and song' (my translation).

This sentence appears to have imposed upon a boy a voice in which he was able to assert that he could sing parts of the Psalter (*psallam*) and make at least one contribution to all monastic Offices.[22] Ælfric does not make clear how old this fictional boy might have been at the point that he might have uttered such words. Ælfric's language only indicates that he might have been able to do so by the end of boyhood. His sentence may also only represent an aspired picture of development, and may only have been intended to serve to encourage boys to aim for that objective; to seek to acquire liturgical proficiency, and indeed to begin to measure their progress in the liturgy in this way, through a calculation of how often and in how many Offices they contributed to liturgical life. This seems more likely when we turn for comparative evidence to the school-texts of a later generation, for example, to the educational intentions revealed by the *Colloquia* of his student Ælfric Bata:

[Puer]
Nos legimus, et cantavimus tota die, et scripsimus aliquid ante Primam et post Primam usque ad Tertiam et quando edituus pulsavit signum primum, tunc ilico sine mora surreximus et ivimus ad latrinam, et postea manus nostras vii psalmos cantantes lavimus [. . .] et postea induimus nos cum vestimentis ecclesiasticis ad missam, et cantavimus missam et sinaxes cum aliis fratribus.[23]

As we have noted previously, Bata's *Colloquia* were dependent upon Ælfric's *Colloquium* for part of their content, and Bata's dialogue here is strongly indicative of his similar aspirations for boys' learning of the Psalter, evident in his reference to their singing of psalms, and their contributions to Divine Offices. This dialogue allows us to identify Prime, the morning mass, and at least two of the later minor offices. The first ten dialogues of Bata's *Colloquia* reinforce this picture further still – supporting

---

22 While Ælfric only mentions seven offices, it is possible that he rolled Lauds and Prime into a near continuous morning office. ÆlfColl, pp. 44-8. RC, pp. 15-7.
23 ÆlfBColl, pp. 88-91: 'We read and sang all day, and we wrote something before Prime and after Prime till Tierce. When the sacristan beat the first signal, we got up right away and went to the toilet. Afterwards we washed our hands while we sang the seven [Penitential] Psalms [. . .] and afterwards we put on our church vestments for mass. We sang mass and the holy office with the other brothers'.

the idea that contemporaries across Anglo-Saxon England expected boys to participate in every monastic Office over the course of an entire day by the time they reached adulthood.[24]

The *Regularis Concordia* gives us more space to ask whether and how far boys might have been expected to recite 'together', and as a distinct liturgical community, as opposed to performing in harmony with seniors. We might be able to explore this dynamic, for example, on the one occasion where the *Regularis Concordia* outlines preferences for the manner of boys' performances on the daily round, with respect to their performance of the *Trina Oratio* at Compline, which, we are told, was to be said 'first by the boys, and [only] then by the seniors'.[25] Indeed, this modality also appears to have been important to prescriptions relating to the annual round, and with respect to the celebration of the most solemn occasions, on feast days which were undertaken just once a year, where, as we shall see below, boys were expected to narrate and impersonate biblical agents in contemporary liturgical dramas.

In the past, scholars have forwarded the argument that boy oblates were an important enabling constituent in the development of religious theatre and catalysts in the emergence of a new class of ritual play which conferred mnemonic advantages.[26] We can see this expecation underlying sequences now contained in a document called the *Winchester Troper*, composed in part by the oblated monk Wulfstan, Cantor of Winchester, for example. This musical compendium, which contains some of the earliest surviving forms of musical notation (*neums*), witnessing the

---

24 For dialogues 1-10, see ÆlfBColl, pp. 80-109.
25 RC, p. 23: 'Agant primum pueri tres orationes, post pueros agant fratres'.
26 This has been the case in particular in relation to the origin of a feast known as 'Boy Bishop' on Holy Innocents which scholars have inferred from a musical compendium commonly known as *The Winchester Troper*, see Edward Rimbault, 'The Festival of the Boy Bishop in England', *Camden Miscellany* 7 (1875), pp. 1-34. Arthur Leach, 'The Schoolboys Feast', *Fortnightly Review* 59 (1896), p. 128. Charles M. Gayley, *Plays of Our Forefathers: And Some of the Traditions Upon Which They Were Founded* (New York, 1968), p. 55. Edmund Chambers argues that this monastic context was vital in the development of theatrical traditions, see Edmund K. Chambers, *The Medieval Stage* (rev. ed., New York, 1996), I, p. 339. *The Winchester Troper* is now contained in, CCCC, MS 473. Weston Library Macherras r. Pal 8 135 OS; Susan Rankin, *The Winchester Troper: Facsimile Edition and Introduction* (London, 2007).

significance of Benedictine houses in that historical development during the tenth century, indicates that Æthelwold had tasked boys with memorising a series of liturgical sequences prior to the feast day of Holy Innocents (December 28th) in order to lead the entire community in performance of introits for the offertory of the mass. As part of this liturgical drama, the rubrics tell us that boys sung sequences which required them to animate the words of the child martyrs in particular, encouraging them to inhabit and to align themselves with biblical *oblati* in recreation of scriptural events that recount their deaths on the orders of King Herod (Matthew 2:16-18).[27]

The *Regularis Concordia* also reveals this expectation in prescriptions which required boys to animate the voices of biblical figures and identify on an associative basis with the Hebraic Boys of Jerusalem who welcomed Christ on Palm Sunday (Matthew 21:1-11 and 15-16). We can see this association particularly clearly, for example, in Æthelwold's prescriptions for the greater procession around the cloister of the Old Minster, where he required boys to begin the antiphon *Pueri hebraeorum portantes ramos olivarum obviaverunt domino* ('The Hebraic boys, bearing olive branches, went out to meet the Lord').[28] Boys' roles in these biblical associations appear to have extended further still, and – whether or not boys understood the significance of church sacraments – animated the antiphon as agents of biblical drama by requiring boys to join a service of mass and 'meet' the Lord in the form of the Eucharistic offering.

References in the *Regularis Concordia* to the organisation of the choir during another office known as *Tenebrae* provide another basis in which boys appear to have been allowed a prominent role in a liturgical drama.[29] According to the *Regularis Concordia*, at Nocturns (i.e. the night

---

27 For example, CCCC, MS 473, fols 17v-18r: 'Filii carissimi dominum melos pangite una voce dicentes, ex ore fecisti laudare nomen tuum et lacta triumphantes de hoste vipereo flore aeterne virginitatis eos in caelesti gloria suscepisti'.
28 RC, p. 35: 'Post benedictionem aspergantur benedicta aqua et tus crematur, dehinc pueris inchoantibus antiphonas, *Pueri Hebraeorum*, distribuantur ipsae palmae et sic, maioribus antiphonis initiatis, egrediantur/After the blessing the palms shall be sprinkled with holy water and incensed. While the children begin the antiphons *Pueri Hebraeorum* the palms shall be distributed. Then the greater antiphons shall be intoned and the procession shall go forth'.
29 RC, pp. 36-7.

CHAPTER TWO: LITURGICAL FORMATION

Office) on Maundy Thursday all the lights in the monastery were to be extinguished in order to ensure memorability and encourage the boys into a state of mind which Æthelwold described emotively as, 'terror at the darkness' (*tenebrarum terror*):

> Nihilque iam cereorum luminis remanente, sint duo ad hoc idem destinati pueri in dextera parte chori qui sonora psallant voce: *Kyrie eleison*, duoque similiter in sinistra parte qui respondeant: *Christe eleison*, nec non et in occidental parte duo qui dicant: *Domine miserere nobis*, quibus peractis respondeat simul omnis chorus: *Christus Dominus factus est oboediens usque ad mortem* [...] Quibus tertio finitis, agant tacitas genuflexo more solito preces.[30]

Æthelwold explained that this rite was intended to educate and dramatically recreate the moment of Christ's death and entombment in the choir of the Old Minster.[31] What is significant about this passage for us, however, is that the *Regularis Concordia* appears to have required a process of preparation and selection. The text's requirement, that six boys should be 'designated' (*destinati*) to different roles and places, allows us to consider that boys were organised to undertake different components, and to either sing or say the *Kyrie eleison*, or other subsequent parts, in co-ordination with one another and with the rest of a mixed community of brethren who remained in the choir.[32] This evidence for boys' separation in singing parts of the liturgy, their physical separation from one another, and from their wider community, provides a view onto an often

---

30 RC, pp. 36-7: 'When all the lights have been put out, two children should be appointed who shall stand on the right hand side of the choir and shall sing *Kyrie eleison* with a clear voice; two more on the left hand side who shall answer *Christe eleison*; and, to the west of the choir, another two who shall say *Domine miserere nobis*; after which the whole choir shall respond together *Christus Dominus factus est oboediens usque ad mortem* [...] When this has been sung for the third time the brethren shall say the *preces* on their knees and in silence as usual'.
31 RC, pp. 36-7.
32 The Latin text only provides references to saying (*dicere*) but a requirement for a sonorous voice would suggest that *dicere* might be understood better as a reference to a precise form of liturgical signing or chanting. Joyce Hill has shown that the Old English translator of the Latin text in CCCC 201 was inclined to specify *singan* where the Latin offered *dicere*, see Hill 'Lexical choices for Holy Week: Studies in Old English Ecclesiastical Vocabulary', p. 120.

unrecognised dynamic in the monastic liturgy, revealing that boys experienced the liturgy *differently* from one another, and in ways which may have also fostered idiosyncratic liturgical identities.

We find evidence for this type of selectivity of liturgical experience again in a passage shortly afterward, as part of an observance known as *Quem Queritis* ('Whom do you seek') which was to begin during Nocturns on Easter.[33] This rite required four professed brothers (*fratres*) to dramatise the discovery of Christ's empty tomb (Matthew 28:1-10). One of these was to play an angel, and three remaining brothers were to animate the biblical figures of the three women who searched for and found Christ's empty tomb. According to the *Regularis Concordia*, once the angel had found that Christ had gone and had arisen from death, the three brothers were to proclaim Christ's resurrection to the world by singing in the direction of boys and senior brethren who represented the microcosm of the world in choir. Shortly after this, and integrated into observances for the dawn Office of Matins, the *Regularis Concordia* required a single 'boy' to complete the dramatic liturgy at the break of day by saying – alone – the verse *Surrexit Dominus de Sepulcro* ('The Lord has risen from the tomb').[34]

It is in this moment that the *Regularis Concordia* offers us another opportunity to consider Æthelwold's assumed dynamics of performance

---

33 RC, pp. 49-51: 'Dum tertia recitatur lectio, quattuor fratres induant se, quorum unus, alba indutus ac si ad aliud agendum, ingrediatur atque latenter sepulcri locum adeat ibique, manu tenens palmam, quietus sedeat [. . .] Aguntur enim haec ad imitationem angeli sedentis in monumento, atque mulierum cum aromatibus venientium ut ungerent corpus Jhesu [. . .] incipiat mediocri voce dulcisone cantare: *Quem quaeritis?/* While the third lesson is being read, four of the brethren shall vest, one of whom, wearing an alb as though for some different purpose, shall enter and go stealthily to the place of the 'sepulchre' and sit there quietly, holding a palm in his hand [. . .] Now these things are done in imitation of the angel seated on the tomb and of the women coming with perfumes to anoint the body of Jesus [. . .] he shall begin to sing softly and sweetly: "Whom do you seek?".

34 RC, p. 51: 'Quinque psalmis iure peractis cum antiphonis sibi rite pertinentibus, capitulo etiam a presbytero, versuque: *Surrexit Dominus de sepulcro,* ut mos est a puero dicto, initietur antiphona in evangelio, qua peracta dicatur collecta/ When five psalms have been duly sung with their appropriate antiphons and when the chapter has been said by the priest and the verse: *Surrexit Dominus de sepulcro* by one of the children, as is the custom, the antiphon to the *Benedictus* shall be intoned and, after it, the collect shall be said'.

and some of its implications for our understanding of the role of the liturgy in boys' liturgical development. That just one boy appears to have been required to take on this role, while a minimum of five other boys who were required for the service of *Tenebrae* remained silent in the choir, makes it possible to recognise that Æthelwold had expected a need to select a boy from his peers, allowing the liturgy to shape that single boy differently from any other.

These frameworks for Maundy Thursday and *Quem Queritis* also seem to allow us to recognise a developmental role for hierarchies of performance in the boys' choir. Individual boys at Winchester who learnt their *accepti*, who could impress, and obtain extraordinary experiences as soloists, distinguished their own particular childhoods, acquiring particular developmental experiences. Solo recitations may not only have provided boys with unique experiences therefore, but could have enabled the development of specific liturgical identities too. If it is possible to question whether the *Regularis Concordia* allows us to make these considerations, we are fortunate to possess in dialogues no. 13 and 25 of Bata's *Colloquia* sources which would suggest that the judgement of boys' qualities of performance was a normal expectation:

> [Puer]
> Lectus et positus in tabula fui ad secundam lectionem et ad quintum responsorium et sic feci.
>
> [Puer]
> Quintam lectionem legit iste meus socius et secundum responsorium cantavit [...] pueri, sicut heri in tabula positi et inscripti et lecti fuerunt.[35]

Alongside this dialogue, which recognises the selection of boys to particular performances in Divine Offices, it is also useful to consider dialogue no. 25, which indicates that Bata had expected boys to evaluate themselves

---

35 ÆlfBColl, pp. 110-1: 'I was chosen and put on the slate for the second lection and the fifth response and so I performed them/This classmate of mine read the fifth lection and sang the second response [...] the boys both read and sang in the order they were chosen and written down on the slate yesterday'.

and their peers on a comparative basis of liturgical ability:

> [Magister]
> Non est tam vetus sicut tu es in annis, sed tamen melius et rectius et pulchrius legit et cantat et loquitur quam tu agis. Duodecim annos habet aetatis et non plus, et tamen non est tam fatuus sicut tu, qui quindecim annos aut se[x]decim modo portas in dorso tuo.[36]

Here, we can see Bata in the attempt of encouraging boys to compete, and become aware of a performance-based hierarchy which governed boys' liturgical contributions according to the 'correctness' (*rectius*) and 'beauty' (*pulchrius*) of their singing. These were qualities which were sought after more widely too, and indeed, we can see that Byrhtferth of Ramsey Abbey lauded such qualities in his narrative on the boyhood of Saint Oswald.[37] It is the case here, however, that Bata's dialogues point us in a direction indicating that Anglo-Saxon teachers might even have encouraged the emergence of competitive dynamics. It might be expected at this point to note that this consideration leans upon a unique source, constituting an otherwise unsupportable line of argument. It might be expected to note too that Bata's school-text indicates rather than demonstrates any actualities. But we can also recognise that these features occur in a school-text intended for student consumption. It is this context of use which connects this school-text with boys as students of Latin and as performers of a monastic liturgy. It is with this context that the liturgical content of Bata's *Colloquia* acquires its significance, and, indeed, it is a context where the *Colloquia* can be seen to give ground to the idea that selectivity, judgement of performance capabilities, and dynamics of

---

36 ÆlfBColl, pp. 138-41: 'He is not as old in year as you, but still he reads, sings, and speaks better, more correctly and more beautifully than you do. He is twelve years old, no more, and still he is not a loudmouth like you who now carry fifteen or sixteen years on your back'.

37 Byrhtferth, *Vita Sancti Oswaldi*, in *Vita Sancti Oswaldi*, in *Byrhtferth of Ramsey: Lives of St Oswald and St Ecgwine*, ed. and trans. Michael Lapidge, OMT (Oxford, 2009), pp. 50-1: 'Tria in uno dono Dei habebat dona, ut autumno: vocis pulchritudinem et pulchritudinis suavitatem et altitinem cum vocis modulatione/He had these three gifts in one bequest, as I suppose, namely beauty of voice and sweetness of beauty, and depth (or height) of voice, with an appropriate sense of modulation'.

competition played a powerful formative role in shaping boys' liturgical development before adulthood.

If a dynamic of selectivity of the type considered above can be sustained by the documentary base, and if it can be located through the *Regularis Concordia* as having been important to boys at the Old Minster at Winchester, it is important to recognise that other contemporary consuetudinaries, such as Abbot Ælfric's *Epistula ad monachos*, do not allow us the exact same perspective. Instead, his customary indicates that smaller choirs could not replicate exactly the routines of monastic sees like the Old Minster:

> In Cena Domini, duos pueros psallere sonora voce: *Kyrrieleison* (sic) in australi porticu duosque respondere: *Christeleison* (sic), in boreali porticu, et in occidentali parte duos fratres reboare: *Dominus miserere nobis*, et omnem chorum simul repespondere *Christus Dominus factus est obediens usque ad mortem*.[38]

Ælfric's customary seems to reveal that boys' experiences of the liturgy were deeply informed by the sizes of their choirs and by differences in the capacities of their cantors to select boys from other boys and privilege particular individuals with extraordinary duties. While Ælfric appears to have felt able to incorporate many observances we have seen above at the Old Minster, his customary exhibits a divergence from Æthelwold's prescribed model. For one, he reduced the number of boys required for the service of *Tenebrae* on Maundy Thursday, from six to just four, requiring two seniors (*duo fratres*) to take the place of two *pueri* who recited *Domine miserere nobis*.[39]

---

38 EME, pp. 126-7: '[On Maundy Thursday] two boys are to sing from the southern porch (sic) of the church: *Kyrie eleison*, in full voice, and two respond from the northern porch (sic): *Christe eleison*, and from the western side two brothers sing back: *Domine miserere nobis*, and the whole choir responds as one: *Christus Dominus factus est obediens usque ad mortem* '. N.b. for more on Jones' use of the term porch instead of the more correct *porticus* see fn. 33 below.

39 It is worth mentioning that Joyce Hill has also undertaken a careful analysis of references to the positions of the boys in this passage, pointing to Ælfric's greater specificity in describing their location in the south and north porticus, not a porch, as Jones (mis)translates in this passage, or simply to the right or left of the choir, as the Latin *Regularis* holds. She demonstrates that EME shares this greater specificity only with the

Ælfric's changes suggest that, for the most elaborate services, boys participated in his choir on a different level. In doing so, Ælfric forces us to consider that boys might not often have constituted a *schola* large enough to have been able to divide into three couplets for this service and, indeed, the *Epistula ad monachos* discloses a context where the availability of singers and an ability to select performers for their 'better' voices was quite limited. This nexus of evidence, which anticipates reduced numbers and reveals reduced choices, and which either indicates that boys made up a smaller proportion of the choir, or that the choir as a whole was smaller, reminds us of the significance of differences in institutional conditions in shaping boys' liturgical experiences across Benedictine England. This consuetudinary from c.1005, and indeed cartulary evidence we have seen above of just two boys at Bury St. Edmunds in c.1020, afford a view which suggests that, while boys' experiences in reformed houses might have depended upon a single prescriptive framework, they were not 'uniform' in terms of actual practice throughout England, but varied, evolved, and adjusted according to local circumstances and patterns of oblate recruitment.

Anglo-Norman England: Infancy

The *Constitutiones* allow us to explore questions relating to boys' liturgical conditions, experience, and development at the archiepiscopal seat of Christ Church in similar ways. In some respects, Lanfranc's regulations are more useful to us than the *Regularis Concordia*, and reveal more about

---

vernacular translation of the Latin *Regularis Concordia* in CCCC 201, albeit lacking its reference to a *westheowag* instead of a 'western part' or *occidentali parte*, which, Hill suggests, could reveal how boys were rather expected to sing from a high western walkway contained in a tower with an upper floor in the nave of the monastery where that translation was made. For an analysis of this difference and a comparison of responses to this passage in the contemporary written record see Hill, 'Lexical choices for Holy Week: Studies in Old English Ecclesiastical Vocabulary', pp. 122-3: 'The translation in the Corpus manuscript is rather more vivid and seems to reflect actual practice within a real architectural space. The boys are sent not simply to the right and left of the choir, but into the north and south porticus, for which Latin loan words are used [. . .] The Old English translator was not alone in envisaging the use of a porticus for two of the pairs of boy singers, since Ælfric similarly sites them in *australi porticu*'.

the particular characteristics of the liturgical lives of infants. This would seem to be the case, for example, where the *Constitutiones* offer a foundation for considering the earliest experiences of oblates, in a prescription which we have seen in chapter one, on the performance of *Benedicite* after the office of Sext:

> Post Sextam nullus in claustro loquatur donec infantes de monasterio exeant, et minimus eorum alta voce *Benedicite* dicat.[40]

The significance of this passage for this particular chapter lies in its potential to reveal what infant boys might have been expected to know and do (and how) at a superlative stage of liturgical training. Lanfranc's advice on the performance of *Benedicite* serves as a useful entry point into questions relating to infant-boys' encounters with formal liturgical duties, offering a window onto a relatively unexplored context of boys' liturgical contributions outside the choir-space at that stage. It also encourages us to recognise a dynamic of selection. Lanfranc's direction for just one *infans* appears to authorise the preparation of just a single individual, and so supports a view that routines of selection were important to boys at Lanfranc's community, from a visibly much earlier stage of boyhood and monastic training than has been noted previously from the *Regularis Concordia*.

Boyhood

Since Lanfranc's *Constitutiones* do not offer the kind of vocabulary necessary for distinguishing between the liturgical duties of infants and boys elsewhere, however, we can only continue to examine references to *infantes* and *pueri* collectively, and in cautious terms which understand that they at least represent a broadly defined 'boy' demographic. This provides a basis from which we can recognise that the *Constitutiones* provide a larger picture of boys' liturgical learning than the *Regularis Concordia*, suggesting,

---

40 *Constitutiones*, c. 2, pp. 8-9: 'After Sext no one shall talk in the cloister till the children come out of church and the youngest of them says aloud "Bless ye the Lord"'.

again, that Lanfranc had sought to regulate boys' experiences more precisely than his predecessors.[41] This document indicates, for example, that boys were expected to memorise and recite a wide variety of liturgically significant texts of different lengths. Chapters 1 to 6 of the *Constitutiones*, which concentrated on boys' activities in the ordinary Offices, appear to have required knowledge of now familiar elements, such as the *Trina Oratio*, and the Seven Penitential Psalms which were integral to it, but Lanfranc also required additional contributions from boys, including that they should have learnt about and performed a Litany of Saints every day after Prime and after Sext.[42]

To begin, however, it may be useful to cross-examine rules in the *Constitutiones* which upheld requirements present in the *Regularis Concordia*, that boys perform the *Trina Oratio*. This duty, as we have described in more detail in the section immediately above, required a preceding degree of learning by heart of a number of Latin texts including the *Pater Noster*, *Kyrie eleison*, the *Preces*, and a number of Latin collects. The Penitential Psalms were still divided into these groups, but Lanfranc's prescriptions on its performance were different:

> [Infantes] accedentes et ipsi ad aquam benedictam in chorum veniant, et dismisso signo, omnes simul tres orationes faciant.[43]

The dynamics of this performance of the *Orationes* before Tierce are perhaps emblematic of all references to the *Orationes* visible in the *Constitutiones*.[44] Lanfranc only ever required boys to recite in harmony with

---

41 *Constitutiones*, c. 2, pp. 4-9; c. 3, pp. 12-13; c. 19, pp. 28-9; c. 20-2, pp. 32-3; c. 25, pp. 38-41; c. 28-31, pp. 44-5; c. 33, pp. 52-3; c. 46-9, pp. 66-7; c. 55, pp. 74-5; c. 57, pp. 80-1.

42 *Constitutiones*, c. 2, pp. 6-7: 'Infantes et iuvenes cum luminaribus suis veniant in ecclesiam, et facta oratione cantent Primam, et psalmos familiares cum collectis suis et septem psalmos, et letaniam/The children and young monks with lanterns shall enter the church, and when a prayer has been said they shall sing Prime, and the psalms for relatives with their collects, and the seven penitential psalms, and the litany', pp. 8-9: 'Dicatur ab infante letania/One of the children shall say the litany'.

43 *Constitutiones*, c. 2, pp. 6-7: 'Then [the children] shall take holy water and enter the choir, and when the bell ceases all shall say the Three Prayers together'.

44 For the *Trina Oratio* before Nocturns, Tierce, and after Compline, see *Constitutiones*, c. 92, pp. 132-3: 'Factis tribus orationibus, que fiunt ante nocturna/When the three prayers before Nocturns have been said' (Nocturns); c. 2, pp. 6-7 (Tierce); and c. 33-9,

their seniors. He nowhere repeated an expectation visible in the *Regularis Concordia* that boys perform the *Trina Oratio* as a liturgical group, and he appears nowhere to have allowed boys to intone this service on a closely associative basis or in a way which would have effectively allowed boys to mark the opening of Nocturns and Compline, at the *termini* of the liturgical day. The *Constitutiones* appear instead to confine our view of their participation, suggesting, at face value at least, that boys engaged in a more united dynamic of performance with seniors. These details suggest that the *Trina Oratio* played a different role in boys' lives at Canterbury compared to Anglo-Saxon Winchester, and that it served to reinforce in boys' minds their place as part of a larger community, contributing to a much more corporate liturgical identity rather than one based on a school.

In a similar way, chapters 1 to 6, on the arrangement of ordinary days, allow us to ask what the *Constitutiones* expected of boys' participation in a monastic liturgy centred on the Divine Offices. Of all Offices, however, the *Constitutiones* are only clear in expecting boys' presence and engagement in choir at Prime. Again, this section implies that boys were expected to adhere to a united mode of engagement in this Office, and we find this, for example, where the *Constitutiones* required 'brethren' and 'boys' and 'youths' to all enter church and 'sing' Prime *together*.[45]

Boys are less visible when it comes to asking about their participation in other Divine Offices. To be clear, the *Constitutiones* are not entirely silent, and do at times seem to imply their presence. These occasions might even allow us to locate boys in choir during the periods in which each of the remaining Offices were observed. But the evidence is limited.[46] The *Constitutiones* do not provide concrete evidence of Lanfranc's expectations

---

pp. 58-9: 'Post Completiorum tres orationes solito more faciant; prior tabulam percutiat tribus ictibus post orationes infantum/After Compline the three prayers shall be said as usual, and the prior shall strike the board thrice after the children's prayers' (Compline).

45 *Constitutiones*, c. 2, pp. 4-7: 'Surgentes fratres in nocturnalibus suis, et infantes et iuvenes cum luminaribus suis, veniant in ecclesiam, et facta oratione cantent Primam/ Then the brethren, rising in their night shoes, and the children and young monks with lanterns shall enter the church, and when a prayer has been said they all sing Prime'.

46 For an occasion where boys' presence at Nocturns is implied, see *Constitutiones*, c. 3, pp. 12-13.

for boys' performances in these Offices, for example, but they do reveal that boys were expected to learn and master various modalities of recitation which would have been useful to engaging in those remaining hours. Lanfranc's choice of verbs to describe *how* the youngest of the infants was 'to say' (*dicere*)[47] the *Benedicite*, rather than 'sing', for example, and, indeed, how boys were 'to sing' (*cantare*)[48] on some occasions on the daily round, and 'to make' (*facere*)[49] prayers on others, and on others still, 'to intone' (i.e. *inchoere*)[50] or simply 'to begin' (*incipere*) the singing or the utterance of verses are highly suggestive of a pattern of regular practice intended to enable public performance in the choir - mirroring practices which we can see more clearly in a pre-Conquest context, through Bata's Latin school-text.[51] It would, of course, be unwise to argue that such glimpses of liturgical engagement make a fact of this. But they do confirm that boys were expected to learn several modes of chant, in addition to memorising liturgical sequences, all of which was needed for engagement in the Divine Offices more completely.[52]

---

47 *Constitutiones*, c. 2, pp. 4-9: 'Facta oratione/When a prayer has been said', 'Minimus eorum alta voce *Benedicite* dicat/The youngest sais aloud "Bless ye the Lord"'; 'Dicatur ab infante letania/One of the children shall say the litany'.

48 *Constitutiones*, c. 2, pp. 4-9: 'Infantes ... cantent Primam/The children ... shall sing Prime'; c. 25, pp. 38-9 'Incipiant pueri, et qui cum eis sunt, antiphonam *Osanna filio David* [...] Deinde a pueris cantetur antiphona *Cum angelis*/ The children and those with them shall begin the antiphon *Hosanna filio David* [...] Then the children shall sing the antiphon *Cum angelis*'; c. 25, pp. 38-9 'Canant pueri de loco apto, et qui precepto cantoris cum eis erunt, *Gloria, laus* [...] pueri, *Israel es tu rex* [...] Item pueri, *Plebs ebrea tibi* [...] Item pueri, *Cetus in excelsis*/The children and others with them in a suitable place at the direction of the cantor shall sing *Gloria, laus* [...] the children singing *Israel tu es rex* [...] the children *Plebs Hebrea tibi* [...] The children *Cetus in excelsis*';

49 *Constitutiones*, c. 2, pp. 4-9 'Facta oratione/When a prayer has been said'.

50 *Constitutiones*, c. 19, pp. 28-9: 'Inchoante infante *Exurge Domine*/A child shall intone *Exurge Domine*'; c. 57, pp. 80-1: 'Inchoet infans *Exurge, Domine*/One of the children shall intone *Exurge, Domine*'.

51 *Constitutiones*, c. 33-9, pp. 52-3: 'Statim puer incipiat antiphonam *Calicem salutaris*/ One of the children shall at once begin the antiphon *Calicem salutaris*'; c. 55, pp. 74-5 'Qua facta incipiat infans antiphonam *Exurge, Domine*/ When this is done one of the children shall begin the antiphon *Exurge, Domine*'.

52 It may be worth pointing out that pre-Conquest Latin and vernacular versions of the *Regularis Concordia* sometimes disagreed on their use of verb for performance, so it is not unlikely that the Latin terms present in the *Constitutitones* were understood by contemporaries in ways which are no longer obvious to readers today. See for example,

CHAPTER TWO: LITURGICAL FORMATION

The *Constitutiones* offer some ground to challenge an impression that the liturgy played a smaller role in signalling difference between boys and seniors. But this difference manifests itself in Lanfranc's customary in a more confined way than appears to have been the case in the *Regularis Concordia*. It hardly occurs in the context of prescriptions relating to the daily liturgical round, for example. Lanfranc appears to have allowed his consuetudinary to express separateness between boys and seniors on the daily round only through a non-liturgical mechanism – through differences in their time of arrival into choir.[53] Instead, we find occasions of difference are more characteristic of Lanfranc's prescriptions on festivals of heightened solemnity. The result of a distinction between his treatment of boys on a daily and annual round means that, on the surface at least, Lanfranc would seem to have expected that boys would experience a much sharper contrast between those two kinds of round. Indeed, it suggests that boys' opportunities for experience as soloists, and as a distinctive liturgical group, might even have centred on once-a-year feasts and on elaborate processional rituals:

> Finita antiphona: *Occurrunt turbe*,
> Incipiant pueri, et qui cum eis sunt, antiphonam: *Osanna filio David*
> [...]
> Quam antiphonam chorus repetat, et similiter genua flectat.
> Deinde a pueris cantetur antiphona *Cum angelis*
> [...]

Hill, 'Lexical choices for Holy Week: Studies in Old English Ecclesiastical Vocabulary', p. 120: 'The translator of the text in CCCC 201 is more inclined than the Latin text of the Tiberius gloss to specify the singing of the liturgy: compare *singen* with *cweþan* for Latin *dicant*; *bið gesungen* with *bean geendude* for Latin *fuerint finite*; *sy . . . gesungen* with *si gedon* for Latin *agatur*'.

53 *Constitutiones*, c. 25, pp. 40-1: 'Cum infantes loti fuerint, et ad tersoria ire ceperint, pulsante maius signum secretario, surgant omnes de sedilibus suis, et ingressis chorum infantibus faciant prius orationem, postea cantent Nonam/When the children have washed and begin to go towards the towels, the sacrist shall ring the big bell and all shall rise from their seats, and when the children have entered the choir they shall pray first and then sing None'; c. 28-31, pp. 44-5 'Veniant in chorum curvantes se supra formas in ordine suo quousque infantes veniant/Coming to the choir bow over their desks in order till the children come'; c. 86, pp. 122-3 'Incepto unoquoque versu, cantor ante et retro faciat, et omnes infantes inclinent/When the verse is begun the cantor makes a double bow, and all the children bow'.

> Canant pueri de loco apto, et qui precepto cantoris cum eis erunt:
> *Gloria laus;* et similiter chorus respondeat
> Pueri: *Israel tu es rex,*
> et chorus: *Cui puerile,*
> Item pueri: *Plebs ebrea tibi,*
> et chorus: *Cui puerile.*
> Item pueri: *Cetus in excelsis,*
> et chorus: *Gloria laus.*[54]

Appearances can be deceiving, and this contrast could easily be a product of silences in Æthelwold's and Lanfranc's editorial decisions, but this section, taken from Lanfranc's directions on the greater procession on Palm Sunday, is, in many ways, emblematic of a visible divide in the nature of the written record for boys' liturgical activities after the Conquest. Although boys were no longer responsible for singing the part of the Hebraic boys, as they had in the *Regularis Concordia*, the *Constitutiones* appear to have allowed boys to take a leading role in liturgical events and express themselves as a distinctive liturgical group, separate from the adult choir. This particular string of liturgical duties also appears to constitute the most cognitively and behaviourally demanding service required of boys in the liturgical calendar of any insular prescriptive source surviving from our period. It appears not only to have required the whole community of choir boys to be trained to carry out an extensive group of Psalter-based prayers, but required them to coordinate their prayers in public view in

---

54 *Constitutiones*, c. 25, pp. 38-9:
 'When the antiphon: *Occurrunt turbe* is done,
 the children and those with them shall begin the antiphon: *Hosanna filio David*
 [...]
 The choir shall repeat the antiphon and genuflect in like manner.
 Then the children shall sing the antiphon: *Cum angelis*
 [...]
 The children and others with them in a suitable place at the direction of the cantor shall sing: *Gloria, laus*; and the choir shall answer in turn.
 The children singing: *Israel tu es rex,*
 and the choir: *Cui puerile.*
 The children: *Plebs Hebrea tibi,*
 and the choir: *Cui puerile.*
 The children: *Cetus in excelsis,*
 and the choir: *Gloria, laus.*

the city of Canterbury, on an alternating basis with their seniors.

Lanfranc's *ordo* for Palm Sunday also serves to represent a pivot in the *Constitutiones* towards the procession as a new centre of gravity in boys' lives.[55] Lanfranc's *Constitutiones* elaborated on a longer procession on Palm Sunday than had the *Regularis Concordia*, which was confined to the cloister. Instead, Lanfranc subjected boys to a walk up to the walls and gates of the city of Canterbury and back to the cathedral church, involving a series of ritual halts, and requiring boys to learn and memorise a large number of ritual gestures.[56] Lanfranc's arrangements for this procession offer an especially useful window too onto the ways in which processions might have informed boys about their status:

> Precedant famuli cum vexillis,
> sequatur conversus ferens situlam cum aqua benedicta;
> alii duo portantes duas cruces;
> item duo cum duobus candelabris, accensis desuper cereis;
> alii duo ferentes duo thuribula igne et thure referta.
> [...]
> Duo subdiaconi portantes duos textus evangeliorum;
> post quos laici monachi,
> deinde infantes cum magistris;
> post quos ceteri fratres precedentes abbatem, qui ultimus procedit,
> duo et duo, sicut sunt priores.[57]

---

[55] For all major references to processions associated with 'infantes' and 'pueri', see *Constitutiones*, c. 19, pp. 28-9; c. 20-2, pp. 32-3; c. 25, pp. 34-5; c. 46-9, pp. 66-7; c. 55, pp. 74-7; c. 62-5, pp. 86-7; c. 68, pp. 94-5; c. 72, pp. 96-7; c. 81, pp. 104-9.

[56] *Constitutiones*, c. 25, pp. 34-41, esp. pp. 36-7: 'Cum autem perventum fuerit ad ipsum locum fiat statio a toto conventu/When they reach the starting-point of the procession all the community halts in position', pp. 36-7 'Interim cantore incipiente canatur antiphona *Pueri ebreorum*/Meanwhile the cantor shall begin and the two antiphons *Pueri Hebraeorum* shall be sung' and also 'Cantore autem incipiente antiphonam *Occurrunt turbe*/When the cantor begins the antiphon *Occurrunt turbe*', pp. 38-9: 'His dictis, inchoet cantor responsorium *Ingrediente Domino*/ When this is done the cantor shall intone the responsory *Ingrediente Domino*'.

[57] *Constitutiones*, c. 25, pp. 36-7:
'The servants go first with banners;
a converse follows with a bucket of holy water;
two others bear two crosses;
yet another two bear two candlesticks with lighted candles;
and two more carry thuribles filled with fire and incense.

Lanfranc's arrangements here for Palm Sunday communicate boys' place in a monastic and liturgical hierarchy. They show that he had located boys as part of the most elite group of the monastery and that boys held a status above lay brethren – who were not professed members of the choir – but below senior professed brethren. His *ordo* shows that boys were a core part of the liturgical community, separate from non choral servants who led bearing flags at the front. His customary also shows that boys were expected to lead the choir in effect, walking three units ahead of the abbot, who was to humbly follow behind everyone else, emphasising his solitary authority at the end. Lanfranc's arrangements also indicate that processions signalled boys' *lack* of office or adult status, separating them from monastic converts at the head of proceedings who could carry objects of sacred significance, and emphasising the privileges of those who monopolised duties in bearing holy texts and vessels.

Lanfranc also appears to have observed an elaborate ritual *Tenebrae* which, as we have seen in the *Regularis Concordia* above, had been required on Maundy Thursday at the beginning of the *Triduum* at the end of Holy Week:

> Tot candele accendantur ante altare, quot antiphonas, et quot responsoria cantari oportet [. . .] Per singulas antiphonas, et singular responsorial, extinguantur singule candele.[58]

The broad arrangements for this service will be familiar. Like Æthelwold, Lanfranc had required the lights of the monastery to be put out in order to create a dramatic period of darkness in Canterbury's cathedral church, educating boys or reminding informed members of the community of the death and entombment of Christ. Lanfranc's *Constitutiones* reveal

---

[. . .]
Two sub-deacons carrying two gospel books;
after them come the lay monks,
then the children with their masters;
after them the rest of the brethren two and two in conventual order before the abbot, who walks last'.

58 *Constitutiones*, c. 28-31, pp. 42-5: 'Candles shall be lighted before the altar according to the number of antiphons and responsories to be sung [. . .] At every antiphon and every responsory a candle shall be put out'.

differences, however. The *Constitutiones* no longer conferred on boys a particular role in this liturgical performance, for example. Lanfranc required no separation of boys in the choir, or any parallel observance of singing from different parts of the choir or church space. Where the *Regularis Concordia* had required oblate-singers, Lanfranc insisted that trained cantors should begin *Traditor autem* and then the choir as a whole should say *Kyrie eleison* without modulation. Indeed, he appears to have included boys only as part of the whole choir, allowing them to respond to the cantor as a single unit, without revealing distinctions in attainment, status, or age.[59]

Lanfranc's arrangements for *Tenebrae* do, however, particularise the presence of boy-oblates in an indirect way, by referring to the lanterns which Lanfranc had expected boys to carry after *Tenebrae* had been observed:

> Candele extinguantur in toto monasterio, preter unam, que in choro ardeat; que et ipsa, cantore incipiente antiphonam *Traditor autem,* extinguatur. Finita antiphona curventur super formas sub silentio dicentes *Kyrieleison* (sic); *Pater noster;* preces: *Ego dixi, Domine*; psalmum *Miserere mei, Deus,* solum sine *Gloria Patri*; collectam: *Respice, quesumus, Domine* [...] Stet unusquisque in loco suo usquequo magister infantum laternas accensas in chorum deferat, et ipsis infantibus tribuat.[60]

This section allows us to recognise that Lanfranc had allowed boys'

---

59 *Constitutiones,* c. 28-31, pp. 42-5: 'Cantore incipiente antiphonam *Traditor autem,* extinguatur. Finita antiphona curventur super formas sub silentio dicentes *Kyrieleison* (sic)/When the cantor begins the antiphon *Traditor autem,* [the last remaining candle] shall be put out. When the antiphon is done they shall bow themselves over the desks, saying in silence *Kyrie eleison*'.
60 *Constitutiones,* c. 28-32, pp. 42-5: 'The candles shall be put out in the whole monastery save one, which burns in the choir; it too, when the cantor begins the antiphon *Traditor autem,* shall be put out. When the antiphon is done they shall bow themselves over the desks, saying in silence *Kyrie eleison* and *Pater noster,* together with the *preces Ego dixi, Domine,* the psalm *Miserere mei* without doxology and the collect *Respice, quesumus, Domine* [...] Everyone shall stand in his place until the master of the children brings lighted lanterns into choir and gives them to the children'. For each of the three days of the *Triduum,* see *Constitutiones,* c. 28-31, pp. 42-5 (Thursday); c. 40-5, pp. 58-9 (Friday); c. 46-9, pp. 66-7 (Saturday).

carrying of lanterns to alter the effect of the *Tenebrae* and to disrupt the darkness of the liturgical environment which had been created by putting out the candles of the monastery. The boys' lamps intersected with a disciplinary system of supervision encountered previously, in chapter one, but they appear here to have had a symbolic value in the context of a liturgical drama.[61] Lanfranc appears to have allowed boys' lanterns to end a dramatic ritual, providing the few sources of light which remained in the monastic complex on each of the night offices at the end of Holy Week. Whether or not we can assume that boys recognised this result, Lanfranc would seem to have allowed boys to become, even if only temporarily, among the most prominent figures of their monastery, and singular light-bearers around the precincts of Christ Church until the dawn.

Lanfranc's prescriptions for once-a-year festivals also seem to indicate that a dynamic of selection and individual performance in choir, similar to that considered in relation to the *Benedicite* previously, and in relation to the *Regularis Concordia* in late Anglo-Saxon England, may have continued to play a role as boys integrated further into liturgical routines. We can recognise this potential, for example, in requirements of selection for Ash Wednesday, when he required just two boys to begin the litany (*incipiant duo infantes letaniam*),[62] and also for the first Sunday of Lent, when he required a single boy to intone the antiphon *Exurge Domine* (*inchoet infans antiphonam*).[63] We also see it for Maundy Thursday, when a single boy was required to begin the hymn *Dei fide qua vivimus* (*inchoet statim infans ymnum*),[64] we see it in prescriptions for Rogation days, where Lanfranc required a boy to begin the antiphon *Exurge Domine* (*incipiat infans antiphonam*),[65] on Whit Monday, when he expected another boy to

---

61 For all references to lanterns or illuminations and association of the boys with lights, see *Constitutiones*, c. 2, pp. 8-9; c. 3, pp. 10-11; c. 28-31, 43-5; c. 46-9, pp. 66-7; c. 109, pp. 170-1.
62 *Constitutiones*, (Ash Wednesday) c. 19, pp. 28-9: 'Two of the children shall begin the Litany'.
63 *Constitutiones*, (First Sunday of Lent) c. 20-2, pp. 32-3: 'A child shall begin the antiphon'.
64 *Constitutiones*, (Maundy Thursday) c. 28-31, pp. 44-5: 'One of the children straight-away intone the hymn'.
65 *Constitutiones*, (Rogation days) c. 55, pp. 74-5: 'One of the children shall begin the antiphon'.

perform *Exurge Domine* (*inchoet infans Exurge Domine*).⁶⁶ Indeed, we see it too in prescriptions for feasts of a third rank, when Lanfranc stipulated that two boys should sing a short responsory together and apart from their choir (*duo pueri decant breve responsorium [. . .] ad Laudes, duo pueri breve responsorium, sive sit propria hystoria sive non. Et ad Vesperas similiter*).⁶⁷ This picture of selectivity in the boy-choir across these festival days conforms with a picture set out in chapter no. 109 of the *Constitutiones*, where Lanfranc expected the cantor of Christ Church to prepare the school for the liturgy.⁶⁸ If we can permit ourselves to assume a degree of internal coherence in Lanfranc's *Constitutiones*, we can link this expectation with sections of the *Constitutiones* describing how the cantor assigned choir services, showing how the cantor decided who and how many were to sing the solo chants:⁶⁹

> Ipsius est omnes fratres in tabula ad omnia officia annotare, non considerato conversationis ordine, aut voluntate eorum, sed secundum quod ei visum fuerit, honestatem et edificationem in hoc vigilanter consideranti.⁷⁰

Lanfranc's references here allow us to reconstruct the operation of the

---

66 *Constitutiones*, (After Sext on Whit Monday) c. 57, pp. 80-1: 'One of the children shall intone *Exurge Domine*'.
67 *Constitutiones*, c. 73, pp. 98-9: 'Two children shall say the short responsory [. . .] At Lauds two children shall sing the short responsory, whether it be a proper one or no, and similarly at Vespers'.
68 *Constitutiones*, c. 109, pp. 172-3: 'Cantor quoque, cum in scolis eorum est, potest librum in quo cantari aut legi debet dare eis et accipere ab eis/The cantor likewise, when he is in their school, may give or receive from them the book from which they are to read or sing'.
69 *Constitutiones*, c. 62-5, pp. 88-9: 'Cantor provideat quot et qui, que singulariter cantanda sunt, cantent/The cantor shall arrange who, and how many, are to sing the solo chants'; c. 66-7, pp. 92-3: 'Cantor quot et quos volverit ad se vocet/The cantor shall choose as many as he wishes, and whom he wishes, to stand with him'.
70 For all references to the cantor, see *Constitutiones*, c. 11-3, pp. 22-3; c. 62-5, pp. 88-9; c. 66-7, pp. 90-3; c. 86, pp. 118-9, 120-1; c. 109, pp. 172-3. See in particular *Constitutiones*, c. 86, pp. 118-23, esp. pp. 120-1: 'It is his task to put down the brethren for all duties on the tabula, paying no attention to their seniority or their personal wishes, but according to his best judgement having careful regard only to good performance and edification'.

liturgical environment of Christ Church and confirm the place of boys within it. These sections suggest that Lanfranc expected boys to have been subject to the cantor in training, and, to some extent or another, subject to formative assessments of ability. The *Constitutiones* do not tell us how a good performance might have been measured, and so we can only suppose that Lanfranc's requirements encouraged cantors to select boys for reasons of edification, but they show that Lanfranc had expected particularisation of boys' liturgical experiences at Canterbury, and suggest that he, like Æthelwold, had encouraged boys to emerge into individualised liturgical identities in addition to a more corporate one shared with seniors and expressed in the choir, albeit on the feasts of the annual rather than the daily round.[71]

Communities of Religious Women: Infancy

We can reasonably assume that girls were expected to engage in the *Opus Dei*, learn how to participate in eight liturgical Offices and eventually learn and sing the entire Psalter by heart over the course of each week as part of a constant round of intercessory prayer. But there are areas of the monastic liturgy where we can immediately assume that girls and women would have had a different role. At the heart of differences in the liturgical formations of girls and women lies the fact that a contemporary state of canon law prevented them from celebrating mass and performing auxiliary functions proper to deacons.[72] This means that we approach surviving prescriptions here with an understanding that girls and women could not have replicated rules directed at ordained clergy, and that only areas of monastic regulation centred on the choir might have been less problematic to female readers and allow us a build an idea of their parallel

---

71 For the assignation of duties, see *Constitutiones*, c. 11-3, pp. 22-3; c. 62-5, pp. 88-9; c.66-7, pp. 90-3; c. 86, pp. 118-9, 120-1.
72 For canonical prohibitions against women entering the sanctuary, see *Capitula Neustrica*, in MGH Capit. Episc. I, pp. 64, 107, 212-3, 215, 240, and III, p. 60. Mary Frances Smith, Robin Fleming, and Patricia Halpin, 'Court and Piety in Late Anglo-Saxon England', *Catholic Historical Review* 87 (2001), p. 601. This point is also made in Hill, 'Rending the Garment', p. 60.

experiences.

As we have already seen, the Anglo-Saxon corpus makes it difficult to understand the process by which infant oblates first encountered liturgical structures underpinned by the *Regula Benedicti* and *Regularis Concordia*. In his *Old English Rule*, Bishop Æthelwold appears to have adjusted the single reference to *infantes*, which might have required the presence of infant oblates in a monastic choir to the vernacular form *geonge men* instead. At the same time, we have also encountered a copy of the Latin *Regula* which may have seen use at a male community at Christ Church, Canterbury, and which appears to indicate that its Latin references to *infantes* had been understood differently, and related to 'children' instead.[73]

We have also seen that the Latin *Regularis Concordia* provides an equally inconclusive basis for exploring 'infant' participation in monastic liturgy – and while this occasion raises the possibility of the participation of very young infant girls too, and in the same way that it has allowed us to ask whether infant boys might have been expected to engage in choral structures and in a formal liturgical round, the Latin *Regularis Concordia* cannot be relied upon to establish that parallel.[74] In fact, in so far as we possess fragmentary copies of a vernacular version of the *Regularis Concordia* we know had been adapted for a female audience, and in so far as one of these also happens to cover this section of the *Regularis Concordia*, it would seem clearer that the late tenth or eleventh century scribes responsible for producing this vernacular version followed the line taken by the vernacular glossator of the Latin *Regularis Concordia*, and considered that this prescription should be interpreted broadly, to include all children:

> Witodlice, hringe ane bellan andfealdlice, oðþæt þa cildru in to cyrcean cuman. Eac swylce notigean þa sylfan cild þrymfealdum *oratio*.[75]

---

73 OERB, c. 45, lines 9-10, p. 71; *Rule of St. Benet: Latin and Anglo-Saxon*, ed. Logeman, c. 45, p. 79.
74 RC, p. 16.
75 Schröer, 'De consuetudine monachorum', p. 295: 'Let a bell ring continuously until the children have arrived into church. Then let the children begin the *Trina Oratio*' (my translation).

The vernacular fragment ignored and smoothed over differences between *infantes* and *pueri* in this section of the Latin *Regularis Concordia*.[76] It did not recognise the presence of especially young children, and it does not allow us to consider that the *Trina Oratio* informed the liturgical experiences of the youngest oblates. At most, mention of *cild* instead of *pueri* in relation to the performance of the *Trina Oratio* before Tierce offers us an opportunity for thinking about how older 'girls' participated in this duty. We have no reasons to assume that girls could not perform the *Trina Oratio* in close parallel to contemporary boys. This liturgical service would seem to represent an important context of liturgical learning and its importance could allow us to suppose that it played a role in girls' learning of Latin liturgical texts.

Girlhood

As we have seen above, the *Regularis Concordia* gives few indications about how far boys were expected to be present at and also contribute to the eight Divine Offices themselves and so we can only suppose how girls would have learnt that round too. In the same way that I have proceeded above, we are perhaps only placed to answer narrower questions of these prescriptive materials. We can turn, for example, to examine the likelihood of girls' parallel associations with biblical figures, and explore evidence which might point to girls' own place in dramatic monastic liturgies celebrated on the annual round in festival periods and encountered in the section above. That girls may have been allowed to participate in similar associations with the Hebraic Boys, and that their learning and performance of liturgical sequences might have also allowed them to identify with biblical figures, can perhaps be situated on a similar basis in the *Regularis Concordia*. We might do so, for example, through the evidence of prescriptions for Palm Sunday, and through those copies of a vernacular

---

76 Compare, RC, p. 16: 'Infantibus autem ecclesiam intrantibus, aedituus primum sonet signum; peractis tribus a pueris oraminibus/As the children enter the church the sacrist shall ring the first bell; and when they have said the *Trina Oratio*'.

version of Æthelwold's consuetudinary which had attracted adaptations for a female audience:

> Æfter þysum, þam cildon þisne antifen beginnendum: *Pueri Hebreorum*, syn þa palmtwiga todælede and swa þa lengran antifenas singende gan to þære heafodcyrican and ætforan þære dura geanbidigen oþ þæt þa cild, þe þider forð eoden singan: *Gloria, laus*.[77]

In this section, references to 'children' allow us to read its prescriptions in a way which understand that they could have been intended to include 'girls'. These vernacular prescriptions could therefore have expected girls to participate in a similar index of biblical associations, and could have allowed them to animate biblical figures, like the Hebraic boys who welcomed Jesus into Jerusalem. The section of the vernacular *Regularis Concordia* which covers Palm Sunday, and which expected 'children' to sing *Gloria laus* alone, apart from the rest of the seniors in the 'choir' and from within the church, could also allow us to imagine that girls might have been informed by school-based dynamics of performance, and could act as and identify with their own liturgical community.[78] One of our two surviving fragmentary copies which contains prescriptions for more dramatic liturgical events such as *Tenebrae*, on Maundy Thursday, may even be capable of telling us about a parallel of selectivity in the liturgy of women's houses. In the same way that the Latin text had 'designated' (*destinati*) six *pueri* to sing different parts in their couplets – the *Kyrieleison* (sic), *Christeleison* (sic), *Domine miserere nobis* and from different locations, to the south, north, and west of a 'choir', so also the vernacular fragment appears to have required the same number of six 'children' to perform the same liturgical parts we encountered in the section above, once the lights had been put out:

> Acwuncenum eallum leohtum, gan twa cild welgestemned and

---

77 Zupitza, 'Ein weiteres Bruchstück', pp. 3-4: 'After these things, and once the children have begun the antiphon: *Pueri Hebreorum*, the palm-twigs may be dealt out, and then, while singing the longer antiphons, [all should] go up to the main church and wait there in front of the doors until the children, who are to have gone in ahead of them, sing: *Gloria, laus*' (my translation).
78 Zupitza, 'Ein weiteres Bruchstück', pp. 3-4.

to þam foresceawode to þan suðportice mid gedremum swege singan hludre stefne: *Kyrieleison*, and gelice þa oðre twa on þam norðportice singan þus andswariende: *Christeleison*, and on þæm westheowage syn twegen on maran ylde, þe þis singen: *Domine, miserere nobis*. þisum geendedum, andswarige eal chor: *Christus Dominus factus est*.[79]

The fragment attests to the survival of observances which had first been articulated by Æthelwold in the *Regularis Concordia* of c.966x70, but this section reveals two changes which may have been important to the religious children who encountered it in a late tenth or eleventh century context. The first of these occurs in relation to the positions in which the 'children' were expected to stand. Unlike the Latin *Regularis Concordia*, which focussed on dividing boys between the left and right-hand 'parts' of the choir or church, the vernacular *Regularis Concordia* does not confirm the usual arrangement of boys taken from these two groupings. The author(s) of the vernacular copy appears instead to have allowed an arrangement similar to Abbot Ælfric in his *Epistula ad monachos*, which – as we have seen previously – had referred to the use of church porches (*porticus*) instead.

The second difference visible here is perhaps more significant, however, and takes the form of an addition which expected that the last two individuals who were to stand to the west of the liturgical community and sing *Domine miserere nobis*, should also 'be older' (*syn on maran ylde*). This detail is unique. It does not appear in any other copy of either the Latin or vernacular *Regularis Concordia*, or, indeed, we might add, in Ælfric of Eynsham's *Epistula ad monachos*. This makes it difficult to understand quite what the author might have intended, but two possibilities would seem likely. One, for example, could understand that the observances of the *Regularis Concordia* had moved closer to Ælfric's Latin customary, the *Epistula ad monachos*, requiring adult brethren or *fratres* to take

---

79 Zupitza, 'Ein weiteres Bruchstüch', p. 6: 'Once all the lights have been put out, two children with clear voices should go to the places previously shown them, that is, to the south-porticus, and with a melodious tune and a loud voice sing: *Kyrie eleison*, and likewise another two should sing at the north-porticus, thus responding: *Christe eleison*, and to the west of them there should be two of older age, who sing this: *Domine, miserere nobis*. Once all this has been completed, the whole choir will respond: *Christus dominus factus est*' (my translation).

up the final *Domine miserere nobis*. But, the passage also differs from Ælfric's consuetudinary. Instead of requiring two *fratres* to contribute, this copy would seem as likely to have required six 'children' like the original Latin *Regularis Concordia*, expecting that two of those children would need to be recognisably older or 'of greater age' than the others, and suggesting that Maundy Thursday might have even given visibility to individuals of different ages in the child-choir.

For all these signs of adjustment, however, and as much as we might consider that girls' practices are represented here, it is also the case that we simply cannot know if and how far this evidence intersects with their liturgical practices in distinction to boys. This means that we can only attempt to test some of these ideas by turning to alternative sources which describe liturgical activity in communities of Benedictine women. The *Liber Confortatorius* and hagiographic lives of Goscelin of Saint Bertin, for example, portray choirs as important frameworks for the development of a communal identity in women's houses. Indeed, Goscelin's writings on the community of Barking Abbey describe the layout of its choir space, and point to its confined but divided structure, indicating the presence of 'seats' (*sedes*), and noting that the tombs of former abbesses were kept 'in the middle of the choir' (*in medio choro*) so that they could be 'embraced' by the liturgical community (*Beata Wulfhilda ... cum beata Æthelburga amplectantur choream*).[80] These works confirm that women's liturgical communities at Barking were physically arranged in ways which approximated structures described in the *Regularis Concordia* – that is, that they were arranged into two manageable groups on the right- and left-hand sides, and these sources suggest that the choir space was likely an important

---

80 Goscelin, *Translatio Sancte Wulfhilde*, in 'Texts of Jocelyn of Canterbury', ed. Colker, p. 433: 'Beata Wulfhilda ad dextrum latus altaris ... cum beata Æthelburga in medio choro suam amplectantur choream et tota aeclesia'; trans. Vera Morton and Jocelyn Wogan-Browne, *Guidance for Women in Twelfth-Century Convents* (Woodbridge, 2003), p. 150: 'The blessed Wulfhild was placed at the right ride of the altar, with the blessed Æthelburh in the middle of the chancel embraced by her choir and the church'; see also Goscelin, *Visio Abbatisse Ælfgive*, in 'Texts of Jocelyn of Canterbury', ed. Colker, p. 454: 'Chorus circa eam [tumbam] psallentium gravabatur artiori loco. Nam vix poterat transiri inter sedes canentium te virginis mausoleum'; trans. Morton and Wogan-Browne, *Guidance for Women*, p. 154: 'The choir singing around the tomb was oppressed by the narrowness of the space. For it was scarcely possible to pass between the seats of the singers and the tomb of the virgin'.

environment to girls' and women's idea of sisterhood, connecting them physically with present and also past religious.

Goscelin's *Vita Sancte Edithe Virginis,* or 'Life of the Holy Virgin Eadgyth' might even allow us to account for areas of girls' extra-liturgical activities in ways that are not obvious in the prescriptive record, such as cloth-working. We find evidence of girls' and women's engagement in liturgical craft, for example, in a section where he recorded the survival of an alb, a ritual vestment which could be worn by those in clerical orders, and which he claimed had been crafted by Saint Eadgyth of Wilton herself:

> Sunt et aliae benignae caritatis eius reliquiae. Inter quae fecerat ibi ex bisso candidissmo albam, exemplar innocentie suae, praestantissimam auro, gemmis, margaritis ac perulis Angligenis a summo contextam, secundum fidem suam auream et sinceritatem gemmeam, circa pedes aureas apostolorum ymagines Dominum circumstantes, Dominum medium assidentem se vice suplicis Mariae affusam, dominica vestigia exosculantem.[81]

Whether or not it was actually a product of Eadgyth is something of a moot question. For us, it is sufficient that Goscelin – who was at least in a more convenient place to judge – accepted her skill-set in the crafting of an alb. Insofar as Goscelin saw Eadgyth's alb as a product of her life-long religious formation at Wilton from the age of two, and an 'example of her innocence' (*exemplar innocentie suae*) by the time of her death at around age thirty, we can also see that he had assumed that the alb represented her "Agency" and her acquisition and expression of skills which other young women like Eadgyth might have acquired over the course of their religious upbringing at Wilton.

Aside from the clear religious content of the embroidery which he

---

81 Goscelin, *Vita Sancte Edithe Virginis*, in 'La légende de ste Èdith', ed. Wilmart, p. 79; trans. Hollis et al., *Writing the Wilton Women*, p. 48: 'There are also other relics of her kindly love. Among these there is an alb which she made out of the whitest cotton, a symbol of her innocence, very striking with its gold, gems, pearls, and little English pearls, woven around the yoke in keeping with her golden faith and gem-like sincerity; around the feet, the golden images of the Apostles surrounding the Lord, the Lord sitting in the midst, and Edith herself prostrated in the place of Mary the supplicant, kissing the Lord's footprints'.

found, Goscelin's record of this alb suggests that religious women like Eadgyth had the capacity to engage in their liturgical environments in a very individualised way.[82] In fact, Goscelin's reference to an alb allows us to consider that girls used their craft skills to shape the liturgy. Indeed, it allows us to recognise that religious girls *altered* spaces of the sacred environment otherwise prohibited to them, confirming that religious girls and women participated in sacramental areas of liturgical activity more directly than is sometimes appreciated.

If Goscelin's *Vita Sancte Edithe* is not sufficient in itself to confirm the significance of this dimension of engagement, we can return to the vernacular fragment of the *Regularis Concordia* as another supporting base of evidence for the place of fabric-working in liturgical dramas. One study, by Joyce Hill, has in fact already drawn attention to the place of craft in the context of this source in Anglo-Saxon liturgical practice, through a close examination of a fragmentary copy which prescribed for a dramatic routine intended to animate a biblical episode – the Rending of Christ's Garment – on Good Friday, after Nones.[83]

This section contains a little explained feminine modification which may be important to understanding how religious women related to this liturgical drama. This modification occurs in the form of an incipit of John 19:24 – but the biblical incipit is not 'correct' in the context of this copy. Instead of requiring a deacon to read out the lesson as it appears in the Latin Vulgate: *Partiti sunt vestimenta mea*, or 'They [the men] have parted my garbs', the vernacular copy provided readers with a feminine form *Partit[a]e*. It appears, therefore, to have encouraged a lesson which replaced the male agency of the Latin Vulgate with an interpolated feminine agency, giving the reading *Partitę sunt vestimenta mea*, or 'they [the women] have parted my garbs' instead.[84]

---

82 This emphasis, and the idea of women's control and influence over religious life, over this aspect of the liturgy, over religious objects, and over spaces, and the clothing of ordained servants, has only recently been explored and developed in detail by Maureen Miller in her *Clothing the Clergy*, p. 172. There is clear evidence of the place of craft in a community of religious vowesses and young girls in the *Liber Eliensis*, ed. Blake, bk. ii, pp. 157-8.

83 Hill, 'Rending the Garment', pp. 53-64.

84 Julius Zupitza recognised this feminine form, though he did not explain it, Zupitza, 'Ein weiteres Bruchstück', p. 16: 'Æt þære þrowunge anginne ne secge se diacon *Dominus*

It is not entirely clear what this instance of a feminine adjustment expresses about the use and users of this text, and whether its significance should be confined to an unintentional scribal error, or whether it might represent something more deliberate. Since this adjustment appears never to have been corrected, we could explore the idea that the reading was acceptable or useful to its audience. On the surface, and without clearer access to its context, this reading allows us to ask whether religious girls and women were allowed to locate themselves in this drama. Indeed, it permits us to explore the possibility that it conveys how religious girls and women might have interacted in their liturgical services in similar ways to boys and men, and participated in dramatic services by imagining themselves as agents of biblical narratives too.[85]

Joyce Hill's study has also drawn attention to another addition present in this copy, requiring that a cloth should be constituted of at least two pieces 'sewn-up together' (*þæt getreagod hrægl*) so that they could be torn apart more dramatically once a deacon had recited *Partite sunt* (etc.).[86] It should be noted that this addition does not reveal any evidence of feminine word forms, and Joyce Hill's study does not recognise any feminine form or make any specific judgements about the connection this ritual may have had to a female audience.[87] Indeed, it may not relate to them, and

---

vobiscum, ac forðrihte, *Passio Domini nostri Iesu Christi*, secundum Iohannem and nan ne andswarige, *Gloria tibi, Domine*. Þonne mon ræde, *Partite sunt vestimenta mea*, þa twegen diaconas, þe standað on twa healfe þæs altares, toteon þæt getreagode hrægl, þe up on þam altare ligð under þære Cristes bec, on þæt gemet, þe þæs hælendes reaf todæled wæs, se abbod æfter þysum cweðe þa gewunelican *orationes*, þe æfter fyligeað . . . /At the beginning of the Passion, the deacon does not say *Dominus vobiscum*, but [says] forthrightly *Passio Domini nostri Iesu Christi*, according to John, and no one is to answer, *Gloria tibi, Domine*. When he reads, *Partite sunt vestimenta mea*, two deacons, who are to stand on the two halves of the altar, will divide up the sewn-together cloth which lay upon the altar under the Gospel book in the manner in which the Saviour's garb was divided, after these things, the abbot says the customary prayers, which follow after . . .' (my translation).

85 Zupitza, 'Ein weiteres Bruchstüch', p. 16; John 19:24.
86 Hill, 'Rending the Garment', 57-60; for this section, see Zupitza, 'Ein weiteres Bruchstüch', 16.
87 Hill, 'Rending the Garment', 59-60: 'The meaning of gestures was usually polyvalent, associative, variable from one observer to another, it is possible that other allusions instead or in addition were perceived by those watching [. . .] the actors who rend the garment are deacons who are within the sanctuary [. . .] no women could emulate this,

could owe its origins as part of a seamless vernacular translation which she has suggested had been carefully produced by a grammatically competent scribe.[88] Be that as it may, the addition here allows us, even if only on a notional level, to think about its place in a framework of modifications which include *Partite* and which we might connect to a female audience. There are good reasons why we might gain from an attempt to establish a connection between the evidence for a sewn-up cloth and a female audience of course. We have already seen above that Goscelin associated the working of textiles with communities of religious girls and/or women. This section would also allow us to connect a feminine reading of Gospel scripture (i.e. *Partitae*) with a context of sewing, and so could provide an opportunity to consider how religious might have contributed to their liturgical activities in corresponding ways. To be clear, we cannot be certain of these connections, not by any means. But these sources, both this fragmentary copy of the *Regularis Concordia* and Goscelin's *Vita Sancte Edithe Virginis*, provide grounds for thinking about the role of sewing and craft in girls' liturgical development, and they allow us to consider that young girls might have been expected to contribute crafts to liturgical dramas along a similar scale of proficiency, extending from tacking pieces of cloth to designing and completing richly embroidered albs.

and indeed their opportunities for dramatising the liturgy were more limited than those of men because there was so much of the liturgy which they could not perform'.

88 Hill, 'Rending the Garment', 55-6: 'In its origins then, this translation gives us an insight into life in a reformed monastery probably in the 980s or 990s [...] a copy of the translation was acquired by a reformed house of female religious who adapted it – not entirely systematically – for their own use by occasional interlineations and by marginalia which were then incorporated into the body of the text, whether by the scribe of CCCC 201 or by a predecessor [...] The incorporations are often awkward in terms of grammar and syntax – which is why I am sure they are additions later than the translation itself... the translator was far too careful to have allowed such disturbances of the Old English text'.

CHAPTER THREE: EDUCATION AND LITERACY

Scholarship on monastic education is vast. But in many ways, it remains concerned with fundamental questions about the nature of experiences in religious instruction. It continues to question whether it is appropriate to think of monastic education in terms which are perhaps most familiar to us today, as 'curricular' and 'programmatic'. It explores the importance of educational environments, like 'classrooms', and asks how far experiences of monastic instruction were aural-, or reading-based, dependent on books, or on memory, dependent on teachers and formal instruction, and it asks whether it was target-based, or was more variable in outcomes.[1] Michael Lapidge is perhaps one of the most significant contributors to this subject, and his extensive assessments of the nature of monastic education necessarily provide directions to consider here. Lapidge's studies have judged that boys' educations in Anglo-Saxon England constituted of two *foci* with mutually reinforcing objectives.[2] The first of these centred on

---

1 For some authorities on pre-Conquest monastic curricula, see Michael Lapidge, *Anglo-Latin Literature, 600-899: I* (London,1996), pp. 2-4; David Porter, 'The Latin Syllabus in Anglo-Saxon Monastic Schools', *Neophilologus,* 78 (1991), pp. 463-82; Patrizia Lendinara, 'Instructional Manuscripts in England: The Tenth- and Eleventh-Century Codices and the Early Norman Ones', in *Form and Content of Instruction in Anglo-Saxon England in the Light of Contemporary Manuscript Evidence: Papers Presented at the International Conference, Udine, 6-8 April 2006,* ed. Patrizia Lendinara, Loredana Lazzari, and Maria A. D'Aronco (Turnhout, 2007), pp. 59-113.
2 See the entry on 'Schools', in *The Wiley Blackwell Encyclopaedia of Anglo-Saxon England*, ed. Lapidge, Michael, John Blair, Simon Keynes, and Donald Scragg (rev. ed., Chichester, 2014), pp. 421-3, esp. pp. 421-2: 'The curriculum can be determined from various sources [and] from these various sources it can be deduced that the young oblate was set first to memorising the psalter, followed by the wisdom books (Sapientia,

an illiterate stage of elementary instruction, focussing on preparing boys for the choir. His studies consider that boys could experience a secondary type, centring on learning to read Latin and on acquiring knowledge useful to engaging on a deeper level with the Latin liturgy and to understanding Latin texts in general. Lapidge has argued that when a monastic boy completed a certain enabling measure of grammatical instruction, he reached a cross-roads, and at this stage, and depending on ability and on the availability of books and teachers, could either have been expected to advance into the study of metrical and poetic texts, or would have been allowed to settle into a less ambitious pattern of study of the psalms, or of singing and mastering the liturgy instead.

Past studies have left significant gaps in our understanding, however. For one, scholarship has shown remarkably little interest to connect a picture of formal Latin learning with boys' education in systems of religious thought. For another, greater attention by scholars on education in pre-Conquest houses has often meant that there is a lack of historiographical coverage on the same areas of monastic education in Benedictine houses after the Norman Conquest. Indeed, it is also often because studies have focussed on setting down a picture of Anglo-Saxon literacy, and because academics have been concerned with studying the most intellectually impressive individuals, that researchers have not given as much attention to the formative role of elementary areas of education or drawn attention to the significance and implications of evidence for illiteracy.

Sadly, the *Regula Sancti Benedicti* offers little support for initial expectations about monastic instruction. It provided next to no guidance for any dedicated environment of education, no formal programme of instruction, and no need for dedicated instructors. In fact, it contained

---

Proverbs, Ecclesiastes, Sirah, and the Book of Job). As progress in Latin continued, the somewhat more difficult poetic texts of the late antique curriculum (which were also studied in continental schools) would be studied, perhaps in a graded sequence of difficulty, beginning with the anonymous *Disticha Catonis*, and/or the *Epigrammata* of Prosper of Aquitaine, then the *Evangelia* of Juvencus, the *Carmen Paschale* of Caelius Sedulius, and the *Historia Apostolica* of Arator. This sequence could be amplified so as to include other Christian Latin poets: Avitus, Dracontius, Venantius Fortunatus, and Prudentius, and to these, at a later period, were added various works of Aldhelm and Bede. The only classical poets for whom there is any evidence of intensive study are Virgil and Persius'.

only references to reading which appear to concern senior brethren; when they could be allowed to study in private, and how books should be distributed to the senior monastic community at the beginning of Lent.[3] Only chapter 45 of the *Regula*, which we have encountered in relation to both discipline and the liturgy, and which assigned corporal punishment to *infantes* who made a mistake in the recitation of 'a psalm, responsory, or antiphon' in a choir, intersects with education and provides for an expectation that religious children were to acquire a functional degree of Latin literacy by memorising texts which were proper to the performance of those duties in the choir.[4]

Anglo-Saxon England: Boyhood

As we have seen in chapters one and two, Anglo-Saxon copies of the *Old English Rule* and glosses added to one copy of the Latin *Regula* obscure the presence of 'infants' and appear even to reveal some discordance. These differences reveal themselves in contemporary responses made to chapter 45 of the *Regula*, and in changes made to rules which suggest that learning of Latin chants was important either to 'young persons' or to 'children' (or both).[5] As we have seen too, Æthelwold's *Regularis Concordia* provided just one solitary reference to *infantes* who were expected to enter the

---

3 RSB, c. 48, pp. 160-3: The *Regula* appears to allow three periods in the day for reading from Easter to October (after Tierce and until Sext: 'Usque hora quasi sexta agent lectioni vacent', after the main meal: 'Qui voluerit legere sibi sic legat', and before Vespers: 'Agatur nona iterum quod faciendum est operentur usque ad vesperam'), two periods from October to Lent (between Prime and Tierce: 'Usque in hora secunda plena lectioni vacent', and after the main meal: 'Post refectionem autem vacent lectionibus suis aut psalmis'), and one period between Prime and Tierce which was allowed during Lent in addition to a general requirement that brethren read an entire book during any spare time (Accipiant omnes singulos codices de bibliotheca, quo ex integro legant/ let each brother receive his own book from the library and read it through entirely).
4 RSB, c. 45, pp. 154-5. For more on 'scales of literacy' and a discussion of what 'literacy' should and could be undertood to mean in medieval contexts, see David. N. Bell, *What Nuns Read: Books and Libraries in Medieval English Nunneries* (Kalamazoo Mich, 1995), esp. p. 60.
5 OERB, c. 45, lines 9-10, p. 71; *Rule of St. Benet: Latin and Anglo-Saxon*, ed. Logeman, c. 45, p. 79.

CHAPTER THREE: EDUCATION AND LITERACY

church before Tierce and perform the Latin texts which were integral to the *Trina Oratio*. Nonetheless, we have considered that the imprecision of its vocabulary here prevents us from making facts of infant participation and educational experience at this stage.[6]

There is more evidence in prescriptive and pedagogic sources to suggest that 'school' communities played a role in shaping the lives of boys in Benedictine houses. Intersecting with evidence already seen in chapter one, we have noted previously that the *Regularis Concordia* and Ælfric's *Epistula ad monachos* referred to boys (*pueri*) as the youngest group of individuals who were expected to participate in a *schola* structure, and they seem to refer too to groups of *magistri* and, in the case of Eynsham, to a single dedicated *magister*, who may have acted as cantor as well as a disciplinarian (*magistri/ magister scholae vel cantor*).[7] We have also seen, however, that neither consuetudinary provides the kinds of information which would have been useful to understanding the *schola*, and to understanding what, how, and when 'boys' might have been expected to study. The *Regularis Concordia* seems to allow up to three periods for private reading each day in its summer and winter cycles, after Nocturns, after Prime, and after the main meal of the day, but these occasions were directed at 'brethren' (*fratres*) rather than boys, and so it is only to the extent that these occasions reveal an educational routine of sorts that they allow us to imagine that boys' conditions corresponded to them in some way.[8]

If the *Regularis Concordia* did not provide overt guidance on the instruction of boys, we can perhaps work from an assumption, informed by the *Regularis Concordia* and evidence seen in chapter two, that boys' earliest experiences of Latin instruction were connected with memorising the liturgical Latin texts which that document directly

---

6 RC, p. 16.
7 For all references to the *schola*, see RC, pp. 8, 14, 16, 18. EME, pp. 110-1, 126-7, 134-5.
8 RC, pp. 15: 'Quibus finitis vacent fratres lectioni usque ad horam secundam/When these are finished the brethren shall give themselves to reading until the second hour', 21-2 'Surgentes a mensa vacent lectioni aut psalmis/Rising up from the meal, they shall give themselves to reading or to the psalms', 26 'Nocturnali peracto officio . . . fratribus psalmodiae deditis vel lectioni', 27 'Post haec egrediantur ecclesiam atque in lectione sacra animae profectum meditentur/They shall then leave the church and meditate on holy reading for the profit of their souls'.

associated with boys' performances in choir. This connection is immediately visible in an original Anglo-Saxon school-text on grammar called 'Beatus Quid Est' or 'What Is Beatus?', which used the opening lines of the Psalter (*Beatus Vir Qui*) to teach boys what the phrase meant, for example.[9] Contemporary saints' lives provide evidence of a similar emphasis of this study, and imply that religious boys were routinely expected to engage in a process of learning to understand either the Roman or Gallican versions of the Psalter.[10] The author 'B', writing his tenth-century *Vita Sancti Dunstani* pointed to this liturgical focus in his near contemporary portrait of Dunstan's boyhood at Glastonbury Abbey (c.910x25).[11] Indeed, some hagiographic writings, and particularly those which describe contemporary educational conditions with a more idiosyncratic and reflective detail, such as Wulfstan Cantor of Winchester's (c.960-1000) *Narratio de Sancto Swithuno*, suggest that boys' experiences of sacred text involved encounters with a wider variety of Latin liturgical text useful to church services, and so much so that Wulfstan characterised his own boyhood at Winchester in terms of preparing for local saints' festivals and translations and spending entire days focussed on sacred hymns.[12]

---

9   It opens "Beatus Quid Est? Oratio est. Et quae pars orationis? Nomen [...] Beatus masculinus quia in 'us' beatus vir qui non habit (sic) in consilio impiorum, non dicit quae, non dicit quod, sed dicit qui non abiit genere masculino'/ What is Beatus? It is speech. But which part of speech? Noun [...] Beatus is masculine because in 'beatus vir qui non abiit in consilio impiorum, it does not say a feminine 'who', nor does it have a neutral 'who', but it says 'who' does not abide in a masculine form' (transcription and translation are my own), see the unprinted manuscript London BL Harley MS 3271, fols. 93r-113v, esp. 93r and 97r. See also, Martha Bayless, 'Beatus Quid Est and the Study of Grammar in Late Anglo-Saxon England', in Vivien Law (ed.), *History of Linguistic Thought in the Early Middle Ages* (Amsterdam, 1993), pp. 67-110.

10 The Roman Psalter predominated in England before its slow replacement (except at Canterbury) with the Gallican Psalter after the Reform, see Hardin-Brown, 'The Psalms as the Foundation', pp. 1-24. For an edition of ink-based Old English glosses to the first fifty psalms, see Phillip Pulsiano, *Old English Glossed Psalters: Psalms 1-50* (Toronto, 2001).

11 'B', *Vita Sancti Dunstani, in Early Lives of St Dunstan*, ed. and trans. Winterbottom and Lapidge, pp. 14-5: 'Pueri dunstani parentes sacris eum litterarum otiis curiose contulerunt /His devout parents took care to give the boy Dunstan the leisure to devote to Sacred Letters'.

12 Wulfstan Cantor, *Narratio Metrica de Sancto Swithuno*, in *Frithegodi Monachi Breviloquium Vitae Beati Wilfredi et Wulfstani Cantoris Narratio Metrica de Sancto Swithuno*, ed. Alistair Campbell (Zurich, 1950) II, pp. 256-65: Wulfstan describes what

CHAPTER THREE: EDUCATION AND LITERACY

As we have also seen in chapter one, in relation to a corpus of school-texts in late Anglo-Saxon England, the contemporary record strongly implies that boys were also eventually expected to become *independent* users of Latin. Byrhtferth, a well-known schoolteacher of Ramsey Abbey (fl.986-1016), tells us this much in his early eleventh century school-text on lunar calculation, the *Enchiridion*. His description of a monastic education at Ramsey in c.1010 illustrates that the source base for boys' experience of grammatical learning was determined at some houses by a variety of resources. We see this in the *Enchiridion*, for example, where Byrhtferth remarked that at least some of his students had acquired their understanding of Latin grammar on the bases of two grammatical primers, one, which he disclosed as having been composed by 'Sergius', and which we might speculate was his commentary on Ælius Donatus's *Ars minor de octo partibus orationis* (A minor work on the eight parts of speech) (fl.450), and another, which he described simply as 'by Priscian' (fl.500), and which perhaps referred to his *Institutio de nomine et verbo* – a digest of rules on Latin nouns and verbs.[13]

Most useful to us in this chapter, however, is Ælfric of Eynsham's new school-text on Latin grammar, the *Excerptiones de arte grammatica anglice*.[14] This text was informed by educational practices at the Old Minster of Winchester, and is most significant to us as a source of evidence of boys' courses of learning of elementary grammar in a pre-Conquest context because it appears, on the basis of some fourteen complete or fragmentary manuscript copies which survive from before c.1150, to have attracted a wider transmission than *any* other known contemporary

---

he and his peers recited on the day of the translation of St. Swithun, 15th July 971 and recalled that 'Diem totum sacris expendimus ymnis laudentes dominum/we spent the entire day praising God with sacred hymns'.

13 Byrhtferth, *Enchiridion*, ed. Peter Baker and Michael Lapidge, EETS s.s. 15 (Oxford, 1995), pp. 120-1. Helmut Gneuss argues that Worcester Cathedral Library MS Q.5 which contains a copy of the *Institutio de nomine* was an educational compendium, Gneuss, *Handlist*, nos. 765, p. 114. There are only two other known copies of this work which survive from Anglo-Saxon libraries, see Gneuss, *Handlist*, nos. 326 (p. 63), 809.9 (p. 122).

14 For a date of composition in the last decade of the tenth century, see Clemoes, Peter, 'The Chronology of Ælfric's Works', in *The Anglo-Saxons: Studies in Some Aspects of Their History and Culture Presented to Bruce Dickens*, ed. Peter Clemoes (London, 1959), pp. 212-47.

school-text.[15] Its contents would also appear to be highly representative of contemporary pedagogic intentions at a relatively elementary level. As we have noted briefly in chapter one, on discipline, Ælfric had addressed and designed the text for an audience of 'uneducated boys, tender young boys and young children' (*insciens/tenellus puerulus/geong cild*). It therefore seems to offer an opportunity to explore courses of Latin learning that shaped boys from an early age, and not just in a single *schola* generation, but in successive generations, and wherever children encountered this school-text across England.[16]

The elementary nature of this school-text can be seen at its opening, where Ælfric crafted a seemingly original passage to help Old English speaking students learn the nature of letters (*stæfas*). He detailed what they looked like, how they were associated with sounds (*clypunge*) that could be voiced (*stemn*) and how, together, they formed words (*word*) that were the constituent part of complex sentences (*cwydas*). What is more, his chapter prompted teachers to give students a model example not just of the Latin alphabet, but of letters belonging to Old English (i.e. Þ, þ, æ, and ð). This learning intention echoes what scholars have long noted of the growing importance of a body of works from the mid tenth century which had been written in the vernacular, ensuring that students could still compose or engage in higher learning even if they struggled with Latin. Moreover, it demonstrates that Ælfric supported an ideal of fostering cultural unity through the teaching of oblates in England's monastic schools, mirroring the efforts of earlier reformers like Æthelwold to achieve a degree of standardisation of written English which, partly as a result of the linguistic disruptions of two conquests in 1016 and 1066, would not be achieved again until the modern period.[17]

---

15 For the critical edition which I use here, see Julius Zupitza, *Ælfrics Grammatik und Glossar: I Text und Varianten* (Berlin, 1880), or EGA. Ælfric notes his use of the *Excerptiones de Prisciano* in his preface EGA, pp. 1-3. For extant copies, see Gneuss, *Handlist*, nos. 13, 115, 182, 244, 331, 336, 414, 435, 441, 480, 494, 541, 868, 876.
16 EGA, pp. 1-2.
17 EGA, pp. 4-6; for more on the achievement of the monastic reform in standardising English, both through systematic translations of Latin texts, and in original compositions, see Molyneux, *The Formation of the English Kingdom in the Tenth Century*, p. 192: '[Æthelwold] appears to have cultivated standardized (sic) Old English spelling and vocabulary, with set translations of particular Latin words'. see also, H. Gneuss,

CHAPTER THREE: EDUCATION AND LITERACY

Like most pedagogic texts of this period, the *Excerptiones de arte grammatica anglice* was not what we could call an entirely 'original' work, however. Scholars such as Vivien Law have shown that Ælfric had depended for his structure and much of his Latin content on a small body of pre-existing Latin grammars, including Donatus' *Ars Minor*, and, most notably, a grammar known to us as the *Exerptiones de Prisciano*, a text which was probably of continental and Carolingian origin, and which represented an earlier attempt to digest a handful of advanced Late Antique school-texts on Latin grammar by Priscian, chiefly his *Institutio de nomine, pronomine et verbo* and his *Institutiones Grammaticae*.[18] Vivien Law has previously illustrated that Ælfric's *Excerptiones de arte grammatica anglice* departed from the *Excerptiones de Prisciano* and that Ælfric adjusted his exemplar thoroughly, introducing a large number of original elements.[19] But no one has previously undertaken a complete examination of these divergences, and for anyone who undertakes a line by line comparison of the *Excerptiones de Prisciano* and Ælfric's *Excerptiones de arte grammatica anglice*, it will quickly become clear why. Ælfric's changes are so great in number that they deserve a study of their own.[20]

Many of the adjustments are perhaps not entirely worthwhile exploring in our present context even; most are subtle, and involve everything from Ælfric's quiet decisions to reorder sentences and paragraphs, to his introduction of new material.[21] Many of Ælfric's choices in crafting his

---

'The Origins of Standard Old English and Æthelwold's School at Winchester', ASE, 1 (1972), pp. 63-83.

18 For more on the place of Priscian's *Institutiones Grammaticae* in this grammar, see Vivien Law, 'Anglo-Saxon England: Ælfric's *Excerptiones de Arte Grammatica Anglice*', *Histoire Épistémologie Langage* 9 (1987), pp. 51-5. For a critical edition of the *Excerptiones de Prisciano*, see David. W. Porter, *Excerptiones de Prisciano: The Source for Ælfrics Latin-Old English Grammar* (Cambridge, 2002), pp. 31-3.
19 Law, 'Ælfric's "Excerptiones de arte grammatica anglice"', pp. 56-8.
20 Law, 'Ælfric's "Excerptiones de arte grammatica anglice"', pp. 47-71. Vivien Law noted that such a comparison would be necessary: 'any attempt to assess the extent of Aelfric's (sic) Christianising activities must begin by comparing his text with that of the Excerptiones', see her 'Ælfric's "Excerptiones de arte grammatica anglice"', p. 58.
21 For an example of a doctoral study which has perhaps come closest to achieving a comparison between Ælfric's school-text and the *Excerptiones de Prisciano*, see Jeannine M. Bender-Davis, 'Ælfric's Techniques of Translation and Adaptation as Seen in the Composition of his Old English Latin Grammar', *Ph.D. Dissertation, Pennsylvania State University* (1985), pp. 233-41: '[Ælfric] transformed the original [source-text]

Excerptiones de arte grammatica anglice reveal an intention to ensure that his school-text was more consistent than his exemplar(s). They show that he felt it necessary to abbreviate overly lengthy areas of the *Excerptiones de Prisciano*, removing much (though certainly not all) of its Greek-derived Latin nouns and verbs. They also reveal a concern to balance his material. Ælfric added significantly to areas which had either attracted little or no coverage in the *Excerptiones de Prisciano*, such as the morphology of all verb conjugations and each of their active, passive, and deponent forms, and he expanded on areas which might have presented particular difficulty to young students, including the concept of gramamtical genders (masculine, feminine, and neuter), and Latin grammatical meta-language.[22]

Ælfric's choices can also be explained in terms of an intention to ensure that the school-text was relatable, and would function in an Anglo-Saxon religious context. We can see this in very specific areas which have previously attracted scholars' attention, and where Ælfric introduced into his Latin school-text references to historical Anglo-Saxon figures such as King Penda and the monk Bede, and more contemporary figures, such

from a text intended primarily for use by readers completely familiar with the Latin language, to a text equally accessible to those not familiar with that language ... he rearranges material ... providing illustrations ... and completely reorganizes the material [on conjugation], conveying the same general concepts but presenting them in a way less confusing for those not familiar with the language. [...] He deletes material of a more technical nature than he thinks will benefit students ... he consistently adds examples ... [and] Ælfric seems to have taken the greatest liberties ... to supply an explanation of a concept or grammatical term or form which the student simply could not do without'.

22 Ælfric gives considerable space to supporting instruction on words not only having gender (or *cynn*) but often different genders to that which they could observe in the world, and indeed, that they included a 'neutral gender' or 'naðor'. His lesson appears to have centred on reassuring students alarmed by the genders of Latin nouns, that their own language had gender too, and that words in Old English, such as '*wif*' or 'woman', which they might expect would be female were actually neuter in their own tongue, but more logically feminine in Latin (*femina*). He appears to have ignored Priscian's paradigms for key verbs too, preferring Donatus' novice friendly verbal paradigms, *amo doceo, lego* for the active and passive instead of those provided by the *Excerptiones,* On the Verb, Ælfric disagreed with Priscian and agreed with Donatus at several locations, including in his chapter *de Figura* (i.e. 'Donatus telð gyt ma to ðisum, *ni, nisi, sed/* Donatus says yet more on these matters in relation to *ni, nisi* and *sed*'), see EGA, pp. 87, pp. 119, 147-52, 190, 262; compare *Excerptiones,* c. 7, p. 180, c. 84, p. 224, c. 20, p. 286.

CHAPTER THREE: EDUCATION AND LITERACY

as King Eadgar, Archbishop Dunstan, and Bishop Æthelwold.[23] But we can see these intentions underlying the text as a whole, and, indeed, we can connect references to Eadgar, Dunstan, and Æthelwold with a body of references to the offices which those figures held. References to *rex* and to *episcopus* and *praesul* (which Ælfric equated with *bisceop*/bishop) reveal an intention to ensure that the school-text enabled discussion about those offices, for example, and may even have served to reinforce an awareness in boys of the significance of the monastic reform with which those three figures were associated.[24]

While I draw on the very significant researches of Vivien Law, Jeanine Bender-Davis and David Porter, each of which have drawn attention to and discussed the nature of some of Ælfric's additions, my own direct comparison of the *Excerptiones de arte grammatica* with the *Excerptiones de Prisciano* has allowed me to extend from those studies, exploring further how Ælfric updated the terms and names present in the *Excerptiones* in view of teaching boys.[25] Historians have already shown, for example,

---

23 Vivien Law has also argued that the grammatical school-text offers the scholar a 'rich quarry of material' and can and should be approached 'as an unconscious' source of historical information, see Law, 'Ælfric's "Excerptiones de arte grammatica anglice"', pp. 56-9. Vivien Law, *Grammar and Grammarians in the Early Middle Ages* (London, 1997), pp. 15-6; see also Vivien Law, 'The Study of Grammar', in *Carolingian Culture: Emulation and Innovation*, ed. Rosamond McKitterick (Cambridge, 1998), pp. 88-110.

24 EGA, p. 15 'Penda, Pending, Pendingas'; EGA, p. 15 'Hic Beda'; EGA, pp. 8-9 'Eadgarus, Adelwoldus ... rex cyning, episcopus bisceop ... hwa lærde þe? ... þonne cweðe ic Dunstan ... Hwa hadode de? ... he me hadode/Eadgar, Æthelwold, King, bishop. ...who taught you? ... then I say Dunstan ... who ordained you? ... he ordained me' (my translation). For examples of Ælfric's introduction of words related to *rex* and *episcopus*, see and compare these passages of the *Grammar* with the relevant section of the *Excerptiones de Prisciano*: EGA, p. 21 'Huius episcopi'; *Excerptiones*, p. 102; EGA, p. 39 'Praesul, bisceop, praesulis, bisceopes'; *Excerptiones*, c. 206, p. 114; EGA, p. 48 'Rex, regina'; *Excerptiones*, c. 219, p. 118; EGA, p. 116 'rex'; *Excerptiones*, c. 48, p. 180; EGA, p. 117 'Qualis est rex? Nescio quails est rex'; *Excerptiones*, c. 48, p. 180; EGA, p. 127 'Rex equitat, episcopus docet'; *Excerptiones*, c. 52, p. 206; EGA, p. 173 'Rex cyning þe rihtlice wissað his folce'; *Excerptiones*, c. 104, p. 236; EGA, p. 231 'Adest episcopa ... ecce venit rex'; *Excerptiones*, c. 56, p. 264; EGA: p. 258 'David rex'; *Excerptiones*, c. 1, p. 280; EGA: p. 272 'De rege loquitur episcopus; *Excerptiones*, c. 44, p. 302.

25 Jeannine M. Bender-Davis, 'Ælfric's Techniques of Translation and Adaptation as Seen in the Composition of his Old English Latin Grammar', *Ph.D. Dissertation, Pennsylvania State University* (1985); David. W. Porter, *Excerptiones de Prisciano: The Source for Ælfrics Latin-Old English Grammar* (Cambridge, 2002).

that Ælfric updated terms in areas including occasions where he replaced references to *Titheius, Orpheus, Odysseus,* and *Oleus* in two sections on proper nouns ending in –us and on vocative nouns ending in –ius, giving boys the religious examples of *Martinus, Benedictus, Augustinus* and *Laurentius, Dionisius,* and *Mauricius* instead.

But my own comparison reveals that Ælfric crafted his school-text in order to introduce vocabulary which he appears to have thought would have been particularly useful to boys in a Benedictine environment, playing a role in shaping boys' understanding of community and of religious behaviour and status as well as improving their knowledge of important religious objects and concepts.[26] These include the addition of community-identifying terms such as *socius, frater, faternitas,*[27] and they include too interrogative sentences cast in a style similar to Latin school-texts that took the form of dialogues, such as *quotus* (sic) *es in ordine monachorum?* which seem likely to have nudged students into developing an awareness of their own status.[28] They also include references, such as we find in a list on *temporalia,* which introduced church-specific jargon of Greek origin, such as *ebdomada* (i.e. εβδομάδα),[29] *ydropicus* (water-bearer) and *ydria* (water-vessel) (from ὕδωρ, 'water'),[30] and terms which seem likely to have been included in order to enable boys to describe holy-water and which, along with Ælfric's introduction of *haec turibula, pas storcyllan,* (i.e. 'thurible' or 'censer'), equipped students with an apparatus of words important to paraphernalia used in liturgical processions and ritual services.[31]

Historians have also shown that Ælfric deliberately introduced exemplifying sentences relating to corporal punishment. We have seen some of these before, of course, in relation to chapter one. But these references

---

26 Compare EGA, pp. 29 and 32; *Excerptiones,* c. 185, p. 106 and p. 108; EGA, p. 111; *Excerptiones,* c. 37, p. 174. For new references to *magister* see EGA, pp. 23-4 (several), 241, 280
27 EGA, p. 17; *Excerptiones,* p. 84.
28 EGA, p. 117: 'How high are you within the order of monks?'; compare *Excerptiones,* c. 48, p. 180.
29 EGA, p. 14; *Excerptiones,* pp. 66-7.
30 EGA, p. 68; *Excerptiones,* c. 259, p. 128.
31 EGA, p. 90; *Excerptiones,* c. 356, p. 156; and also EGA, p. 90; *Excerptiones,* c. 356, p. 156.

belong to a much larger body, and include references which recognise, exploit, remind, and also serve to threaten students of the experience of corporal punishment with a 'flail' or 'rod', crafting far more memorable Latin lessons on accusative cases, such as *hos pueros flagello* and *percutere te volo virga*.³² We see references of a much wider variety of forms too, and these included terms which intersect with and reinforce the significance of monastic prescriptions on discipline. We find this in a section on prepositions, for example, where Ælfric had introduced the phrase *secundum regulam vivo, æfter regole ic lybbe* ('I live according to the rule'), in order to nudge boys into accepting a similar view of documents like the *Regula Benedicti* and *Regularis Concordia*.³³ On a section on adverbs, we can see that Ælfric introduced material reinforcing the significance of boys' conditions and experiences of the liturgy. These include a paradigmatic sentence, *humiliter precatur, eadmodlice he bit* (lit. 'he prayed humbly') which built carefully upon boys' established familiarity with intercession and an index of ritual gestures.³⁴ They also include Ælfric's introduction of paradigmatic sentences, such as *O pueri, cantata bene* (Oh boys, sing well!), and his introduction of *sallio vel psallo, ic singe mine sealmas* (lit. 'I sing my psalms') in a section on verbs ending on -io.³⁵ Indeed, they include his introduction of paradigmatic sentences exemplifying uses of the preposition in-, such as *introibo in domum tuam, domine, ic gange in to ðinum huse, drihten*.³⁶ In each of these occasions, and on many others, Ælfric's additions reveal an intention to transform the contents of his Carolingian exemplar, and ensure that his own school-text intersected with boys' own disciplinary, liturgical, and educational experiences.³⁷

Research into this school-text undertaken by Jeanine Bender-Davis and Leslie Lockett has also recognised that the *Excerptiones de arte grammatica anglice* provides evidence of areas of doctrinal instruction which

---

32 See EGA, pp. 23-4: 'I [shall] beat these boys'; EGA, p. 169: 'I want to beat you with the rod'; compare *Excerptiones*, c. 101, p. 234.
33 EGA, p. 270; *Excerptiones*, c. 40, p. 300.
34 EGA, p. 223; *Excerptiones*, c. 2, p 248.
35 EGA, p. 192: 'I [shall] sing my psalms'; compare *Excerptiones*, c. 122, p. 242.
36 See EGA, p. 273; *Excerptiones* c. 54, p. 306; DRV: ps. 5:8 'I will come into thy house, [O Lord]'.
37 EGA, p. 273; compare *Excerptiones*, c. 53, p. 306.

Ælfric anticipated that boys would need to interiorise.[38] Leslie Lockett's ground-breaking study on *Anglo-Saxon Psychologies* has drawn particular attention to the fact that Ælfric's works contained theologically significant material and introduced readers to ideas on the (in)corporeality of souls, heavenly bodies and beings, and on the substantiality of the Eucharistic sacrifice.[39] Lockett has located part of this intention, for example, through a study of Ælfric's handling of grammatical material on 'substance' present in the *Excerptiones de Prisciano*, and has shown that Ælfric had not only deliberately simplified what he found, scaffolding what would be quite challenging for an audience of children, but presented information on the nature of substance in a way that conformed with his own theological position.[40]

My own examination of the *Excerptiones de arte grammatica* reveals that Ælfric had intended his school-text to enable a far wider number of encounters with forms of conceptual learning, however. It reveals that that school-text had a capacity to shape student responses to areas of conceptual knowledge which were also more foundational, and related to boys' understanding of Christian faith. It is possible to recognise that Ælfric's work was intended to inform students about concepts of 'heaven' and 'hell' and even of virginal status for example. We can recognise this potential in the *Excerptiones de arte grammatica anglice* where Ælfric introduced into his own school-text terms not present in the *Excerptiones de Prisciano*, such *caelum, caelistis,* and terms which would seem to have had nudged boys into acquiring an understanding of Christian concepts such as 'heaven'.[41] Indeed, we can find this same context of conceptual learning in another location, where Ælfric introduced complementary

---

38 For recognition of similar content which instructs readers on the concept of penitence, sin, church doctrine and desirable religious behaviours and her consideration of these in terms of Ælfric's teaching intentions, see Jeannine W. Bender-Davis, '*Ælfric's Techniques of Translation and Adaptation*', pp. 233-248, esp. pp. 241-46.
39 See Leslie Lockett, *Anglo-Saxon Psychologies in the Vernacular and Latin Traditions* (Toronto: University Press, 2011), p. 374: 'Ælfric of Eynsham pioneer[ed] the concept of the strictly incorporeal, unitary soul to a broad audience' and devoted himself (p. 402) 'to persuading his listeners that spiritual and imperceptible entities can also be real, and that the presence of Christ in the Eucharist is one such incorporeal reality'.
40 Lockett, *Anglo-Saxon Psychologies*, pp. 434-8, esp. pp. 437-8.
41 EGA, p. 17; compare *Excerptiones*, c.118 p. 92; see also EGA, p. 31; *Excerptiones*, p. 108.

terms such as *herebus, hell*. These seem likely to have been intended to play a supporting role, encouraging boys to interiorise ideas about the implications of two spheres of salvation and damnation.⁴²

In a similar way, a comparison of the *Excerptiones de Prisciano* with Ælfric's own school-text allows us to see that Ælfric had introduced terms into his *Excerptiones de arte grammatica anglice* which exemplified the 'chaste', the 'clean man' (*castus/clæne*) and 'chastity' (*castitas/clænnys*). These are terms for concepts which were likely valued by senior religious figures like Ælfric, and they are concepts which Ælfric might have considered important for an audience of pre-adolescent monastic boys too.⁴³ Indeed, Ælfric's introduction into his *Excerptiones de arte grammatica anglice* of Latin nouns which were closely attached to ideals of bodily and ritual purity, and to a chaste and/or virginal status, appears only to have been reinforced further by Ælfric's use of an innovative bilingual apparatus. His use of the vernacular allowed him to expand further on a complex of Latin terms on chastity and, indeed, to explain in more detail, the significance of nouns relating to it. We find this in his introduction of *hic, haec, et hoc cælebs, clæne oððe heofonlice*, for example, where Ælfric not only encouraged teachers and boys to assign to 'chastity' a positive value, but to associate chaste individuals on an etymological level with that which was 'heavenly' as well.⁴⁴

As a road map of boys' learning, the *Excerptiones de arte grammatica anglice* also suggests that Latin instruction under Ælfric was intended to shape boys' literary identities and their understanding of and relationship with biblical scripture. I have already noted above that Ælfric appears to have introduced into his school-text a number of references to singing, but it would seem equally important to recognise that Ælfric introduced material from the Psalter and Bible. Ælfric appears to have gone to considerable lengths to remove examples of classical Latin poetry which occurred in the

---

42 DOE: n. *hell*: 'hell'. EGA, p. 30; compare *Excerptiones*, c. 184, p. 106, where the *Excerptiones de Pisciano* only listed *abbisus* and *sinodus*. DOE: n. *hell*: 'hell'.
43 EGA, p. 17; compare *Excerptiones*, n. 164, p. 100. DOE: adj. *clæne*: 'clean, free from defilement' with secondary meanings including 'pure, ceremonially or ritually cleansed, free from sin, chaste, celibate, virgin', n. *clænnes*: 'moral purity, freedom from sin' or more specifically 'chastity'.
44 EGA, pp. 17, 37, 66; compare *Excerptiones*, c. 252, p. 128.

Excerptiones de Prisciano, and he replaced them with quotations and vernacular translations of quotations taken from the Psalter and from books of the Old and New Testament, including, most notably, the Gospels of Matthew and John. We can see this, for example, where Ælfric had introduced into his own school-text elements of the Psalter in a section on second conjugation verbs and the use of the preposition 'in' and 'ad' with the gerund in particular, citing psalm 125:1 (*in convertendo dominus captivitatem Sion, ad legendum*).[45] He also used psalm 40:11 (*tu autem, domine, miserere mei et resuscita me*) to demonstrate verbs which took the genitive as an object and, indeed, he further translated these psalms into Old English (i.e. '*þu soðlice, drihten, miltsa me and arær me*').[46] We can see this where he also cited psalm 126:1 among his examples on the uses of *nisi* (*nisi dominus custodierit civitatem/Buton drihten gehealde þa burh*).[47] We can see this too where Ælfric appears to have added a reference to psalm 12:4 ([*ne quando*] *obdormiam in morte/Þæt ic neafre on deaðe ne slape*).[48] We also find this in a section 'On defective Verbs', and specifically concerning the preterit of the verb *odire* (to hate), where Ælfric even seems to have departed from the position on the grammatical uses of *odium* (hate) forwarded by the *Excerptiones de Prisciano*, encouraging boys to view the Psalter (or ps. 118:113 in particular), not just classical Latin literature, as an authority on the correct use of Latin (*Ac we cweðað hwilon ic hæbbe on hatnunge, swa stent on ðam sealme, iniquos odio habui, þa unrihtwisan ic hæfde on hatunge*).[49]

If these additions confirm how Latin learning intersected with the liturgy and demonstrate that the Psalter was important to Ælfric's teaching method and to boys' experiences of grammatical instruction in the late tenth century, Ælfric's introduction into his *Excerptiones de arte grammatica anglice* of references which connected boys to other biblical texts also demonstrates that the experience of learning grammar was intended

---

45 EGA, p. 152; compare *Excerptiones*, c. 84-6, pp. 224-226.
46 EGA, p. 261; compare *Excerptiones*, c. 19, p. 284.
47 EGA, p. 262; compare *Excerptiones*, c. 20, p. 286.
48 EGA, p. 166; *Excerptiones*, c. 19-21, p. 286.
49 EGA, p. 205: 'But as we say sometimes "ic hæbbe on hatnunge", so also it stands in the psalm *Iniquos odio habui*, I have hated the unjust' (my translation); compare *Excerptiones*, c. 246, p. 130

CHAPTER THREE: EDUCATION AND LITERACY

to enable each generation of religious boys to handle Christian scripture more broadly, supporting both teachers and students by translating Latin paradigms from the Old and New Testaments into Old English. These additions include a reference to Genesis 45:6 for example, which Ælfric used to illustrate grammatical points on the use of numbers (*and Ioseph cwæð: adhuc resant anni quinque*).⁵⁰ We also find that he cited Job 10:1 on the use of *taedet* with the accusative case (*taedet animam meam vitae meae, cwæð Iob*).⁵¹ We can see that he used the Gospel of Matthew 16:24 in order to exemplify *tunc* or 'then' in the phrase '*tunc dixit Iesus/þa sæde se hælend*'.⁵² In addition to these, Ælfric added and translated into Old English a large number of biblical references (which I include here by order of appearance) from 2 Corinthians 12:16 (*etsi volvero gloriari non ero insipiens/gif þe ic wylle wuldrian, ne beo ic na unsnoter*),⁵³ as well as to John 11:15 (*etiam si mortuus fuerit, vivet*),⁵⁴ Genesis 2:15 (*tulit ergo dominus hominem/eornostlice, drihten genam þone mann*),⁵⁵ Genesis 2:1 (*igitur perfecti sunt caeli et terra et omnis ornatus eorum*),⁵⁶ Job 1:21 (*sicut domino placuit ita factum est/swaswa hit drihtne gelicode, swa hit is gedon*),⁵⁷ Mark 6:23 ([*licet*] *petieris dimidium regni meri/ðeah ðe ðu bidde healfne dæl mines rices*),⁵⁸ Genesis 22:16 (*quia fecisti rem hanc/fordan ðe þu dydest þys þing*),⁵⁹ Matthew 16:18 (*quia tu es Petrus/þæt þu eart Petrus*),⁶⁰ Matthew 23:37 (*gallina congregat pullos suos sub alas*),⁶¹ Isaiah 40:9 (*super montem excelsum ascende tu/ofer healice dune astih ðu*),⁶² and Ezechiel 2:9 (*vae mihi, quia tacui/wa is me þæt ic suwode*).⁶³ Ælfric also appears to have introduced an allusion to what appears to be Ephesians 4:10 (*qui descendit*

---

50   EGA, p. 206; compare *Excerptiones*, c. 1, pp. 310-12.
51   EGA, p. 207; *Excerptiones*, c. 13, p. 246.
52   EGA, p. 237; *Excerptiones*, c. 14, p. 246.
53   EGA, p. 262; *Excerptiones*, c. 15, p. 282.
54   EGA, p. 262; *Excerptiones*, c. 13, p. 282.
55   EGA, p. 263; *Excerptiones*, c. 17, p. 284.
56   EGA, p. 263; *Excerptiones*, c. 17, p. 284.
57   EGA, p. 263; *Excerptiones*, c. 17, p. 284.
58   EGA, p. 264; *Excerptiones*, c. 15, p. 285.
59   EGA, p. 262; *Excerptiones*, c. 20, p. 286.
60   EGA, p. 262; *Excerptiones*, c. 20, p. 286.
61   EGA, p. 273; Excerptiones, c. 55, p. 305.
62   EGA, p. 274; *Excerptiones*, c. 56, p. 306.
63   EGA, pp. 278-9.

super caelos/se astah ofer heafonas),⁶⁴ and, indeed, he appears to have introduced a number of references which referred to what 'Christ said', (e.g. *Crist cwæð be Judan, vae illi, wa him. He cwæð be þam ungeleaffullum Judeiscum, vae bovis, wa eow on wyrigunge*), and which could have been taken from a number of places such as, but not necessarily limited to, the Gospels of Matthew (18:7, 23:14, 23:15, 23:23, *inter alia*), Luke (17:1) and/or Mark (14:21).⁶⁵

In addition to this content, it is useful to recognise that Ælfric inserted into the *Excerptiones de arte grammatica anglice* his own paradigmatic sentences. These occasions are perhaps even more useful in demonstrating his expectation that boys would need to accept a system of religious belief. This can be seen, for example, in Ælfric's addition of nouns relating to 'faith', such as his introduction into a list of feminine nouns ending in –as of *credulitas, geleaffulnys* (lit. 'belief-fullness/faithfulness').⁶⁶ We also find evidence for this in Ælfric's additions on pronouns, where he introduced references to Christ, and the idea of 'Christ's sacrifice', e.g. *Christus se dedit pro nobis, a se expulit malos* ('Christ gave himself for us, he repelled evil doers from himself').⁶⁷ We also see this learning objective in Ælfric's introduction of *Deus/God* into exemplifying sentences for the verbs *timere* and *metui* such as, *timeo Deum, metuor a pueris nostris* (I fear God [and, correspondingly] I am feared by our boys).⁶⁸ We see it too in additions exemplifying the uses of *utinam*, such as *utinam amarem Deum, eala gif ic lufode God* ('Oh, if I loved God!'),⁶⁹ and we also see it in his addition on juratives, through his addition of *Iuro per Deum, ic swerige ðurh God* (lit 'I swear by God').⁷⁰ We see similar examples in his additions to a section on semi-deponents, passive verbs, and participles including *amare* such as *amans Deum* (lit. 'I love God', and 'loving God'),⁷¹ and those derived from *precari,* such as *precans, precatus Deum* (lit. 'praying,

---

64 EGA, p. 274; *Excerptiones*, c. 56, p. 306.
65 EGA, p. 278; *Excerptiones*, c. 56, p. 306.
66 EGA, p. 50; compare *Excerptiones*, c. 224, p. 120. BT: n. *geleaffulnes*: 'faithfulness, belief, trust'.
67 EGA, p. 95; *Excerptiones*, c. 13, p. 164
68 EGA, p. 123; *Excerptiones*, c. 5, p. 182.
69 EGA, 125; *Excerptiones*, c. 25, p. 192
70 EGA, 227; *Excerptiones*, c. 40, p. 262.
71 EGA, pp. 249; *Excerptiones*, c. 12, p. 270.

I have/he has prayed to God'),[72] and we see it slightly later still in the example of *amans Deum, amator Dei* (lit. 'loving God, a lover of God),[73] and in Ælfric's addition of a paradigm on feast days, *itaque epulemur in Domino* (lit. 'Let us feast in the Lord's name']).[74]

We find yet more examples in fact in Ælfric's chapter on prepositions, and on 'ad' for example, where he introduced the examples *ad patrem* and *ad Deum* (to the father, to God).[75] We find them in his addition of the paradigmatic sentence *extra legem Dei facit, ofer Godes æ he deð* (lit. 'he acted outside the law of God'). We see them in his addition of *de domo Dei* to describe a church as a 'house of God',[76] and in his addition of a sentence explaining Christ's Passion as a demonstration of faith, *propter fidem passus est, for geleafan he ðrowode* ('He suffered for [his/the] faith').[77] Indeed, we find it in another sentence, which drew on, if it did not also introduce to boys, the idea that prayer was a means of interceding with God on behalf of society, *pro hominibus oro, for mannum ic gebidde* (I pray on behalf of humankind). In a connected way, we find it in Ælfric's addition of the phrase *prope est dies Domini, gehende is Godes dæg* (lit. 'the day of the Lord is near/God's day is at hand').[78] This phrase, which describes a concept of a 'Final Day' of Judgement, otherwise known as the 'Eschaton' (i.e. from ἔσχατον, meaning 'the last [thing]'), is an idea that we know had troubled senior religious figures like Ælfric in a brief generational period c.990-1000, in the years running up to and just after he composed the *Excerptiones de arte grammatica anglice*. It would seem likely, therefore, that Ælfric's decision to introduce it into an elementary grammar reflects those contemporary fears, and reveals how Ælfric passed onto a succeeding generation a similar awareness and concern.[79]

---

72   EGA, p. 250; *Excerptiones*, c. 15-16, pp. 274-5.
73   EGA, p. 256; *Excerptiones*, c. 14, p. 272 and c. 27, p. 278.
74   EGA, p. 273; *Excerptiones*, c. 17, p. 284.
75   EGA, p. 269; *Excerptiones*, c. 19, pp. 292-4.
76   EGA, p. 272; *Excerptiones*, c. 33, p. 298.
77   EGA, p. 270; *Excerptiones*, c. 40, p. 300.
78   EGA, p. 270; *Excerptiones*, c. 30, p. 300.
79   For more on the Anglo-Saxon view of the millennium as the time of Judgement, see Edwin Duncan, 'Fears of the Apocalypse: the Anglo-Saxons and the Coming of the Millennium', *Religion & Literature* 31.1 (1999), pp. 15-23. For more specific studies on Ælfric of Eynsham, and his introduction of apocalyptic themes into his vernacular homilies, see Malcom Godden, 'Apocalypse and Invasion in Late Anglo-Saxon

These additions to the grammatical apparatus of the *Excerptiones* are indicative of Ælfric's intention to shape boys' religious *beliefs* as well as their knowledge of Latin grammar and vocabulary. The additions are indicative of a broader intention to ensure that boys viewed the Bible as an axiomatic Latin text, and as an ultimate authority on the correct use of Latin as well as a source of doctrinal validation. Not all scholars would concede that learning outcomes can be understood from these teaching intentions of course. But Ælfric's school-text does seem to be capable of sustaining these arguments, and it would seem to give us useful insight into dynamics that might have tied boys' experiences of instruction in grammar with their acquisition of religious learning at an elementary level.

We can also connect the contents of Ælfric's school-text with evidence from contemporary copies of the Psalter which attracted layers of educational glosses, and which suggest that boys were eventually expected to use their grammatical learning to engage in deeper interpretative study of sacred texts known as *exegesis*. Scholars have in fact already begun to approach surviving copies of Anglo-Saxon Psalters in this way, and increasingly take the view that Psalters reinforced lessons about the monastic context as their comprehension of Latin increased.[80] In some ways, this potential is not difficult to recognise – the Psalter was central to the daily liturgy, boys were tasked with memorising it from early childhood and they were expected to recite it daily. As we have already seen, Ælfric of Eynsham's school-texts, both his *Excerptiones de arte grammatica* and his *Colloquium* and also Ælfric Bata's *Colloquia* demonstrate that the Psalter was important to boys' Latin learning and intersected with their liturgical instruction. It is easy to recognise therefore that the Psalter, rich in models of obedience, with many verses beginning with very emotive requests for forgiveness and guidance, would have provided student-readers with influential models on how to construct, express, and vocalise personal and

---

England', in *From Anglo-Saxon to Early Middle English: Studies presented to E. G. Stanley*, ed. Malcom Godden, Douglas Gray, and Terry Hoad (Oxford, 1994), pp. 130-62.

80 Alice Jorgensen, 'Learning about Emotion from Old English Prose Psalms of the Paris Psalter', in *Anglo-Saxon Emotions: Reading the Heart in Old English Language, Literature and Culture*, ed. Alice Jorgensen, Frances McCormack, and Jonathan Wilcox (Farnham, 2015), p. 136.

CHAPTER THREE: EDUCATION AND LITERACY

religious feelings.[81]

Antonia Harbus and Tahlia Burnbaum's studies of Old English glosses added to the *Lambeth Psalter*, a copy of the Gallican Psalter identified by Patrick O'Neill as having served as a school-text, have argued that contemporaries encouraged readers to project a monastic filter onto many of the emotionally and behaviourally indicative Latin verbs and nouns which that Psalter contained.[82] Their interest in this copy has drawn particular attention, for example, to interlinear glosses which were added to psalms provided below, and which glossed verbs, such as *erubescere* (to redden) and *confundere* (to confound), in such a way that encouraged students to associate expressions of 'redness' and 'confusion' with ideals of behaviour:[83]

[Ps. 6:11]
ablysian hi vel gesceamige heom (i.e. 'let them blush or be ashamed')
Erubescant et conturbentur vehementer omnes inimici mei

aswarnian hi vel gesceamige heom
Et *erubescant* valde velociter.[84]

---

81 See Antonina Harbus, 'Affective Poetics: The Cognitive Basis of Emotion in Old English Poetry', in *Anglo-Saxon Emotions*, ed. Jorgensen, McCormack and Wilcox, p. 24.
82 Patrick O'Neill, 'Latin Learning at Winchester in the Early-Eleventh Century: The Evidence of the Lambeth Psalter', *Anglo-Saxon England* 20 (1991), pp. 143-66; Phillip Pulsiano, *Old English Glossed Psalters: Psalms 1-50* (Toronto, 2001).
83 Gneuss, *Handlist*, no. 517, p. 87; Tahlia Burnbaum, 'Naming Shame: Translating Emotion in the Old English Psalter Glosses', in *Anglo-Saxon Emotions*, ed. Jorgensen, McCormack, and Wilcox, pp. 109-126; Stephen J. Harris, 'Happiness and the Psalms', in *Old English Literature and the Old Testament*, ed. Michael Fox and Manish Sharma (Toronto, 2012), pp. 292-314.
84 Ps. 6:11: 'Let all my enemies be ashamed, and be very much troubled: let them be turned back and be ashamed very speedily'. For the Old English Gloss, see Pulsiano, *Old English Glossed Psalters*, (*siglum* I) p. 50. DOE: v. *ablysian*: 'to blush, be ashamed', *a-swarnian*: 'to be confounded, be ashamed'. BT: v. *ge-sceamian*: 'to blush, be ashamed'.

[Ps. 24:2]

sy aswæmed vel þæt me ne sceamige
Deus meus, in te confido non *erubescam*.[85]

[Ps. 30:18]

ic ne beo gescynd   *gescynd sceamian vel syn gescend*
Domine non *confundar* quoniam invocavi te. *Erubescant* impii et deducantur in infernum.[86]

[Ps. 34:26]

syn gescynde vel ablysian vel scamian (i.e. 'let them be put to shame, or blush, or be ashamed')
Erubescant et revereantur simul qui gratulantur malis, induantur

mid sceame vel mid gescændnysse
confusione et reverentia qui magna loquuntur super me.[87]

[Ps. 39:16]

sceame vel gescendnesse
Ferant confestim *confusionem* suam qui dicunt mihi, euge, euge.[88]

---

85 Ps. 24:2: 'In thee, Oh my God, I put my trust, let me not be ashamed'. Pulsiano, *Old English Glossed Psalters*, (*siglum* I) p. 300. DOE: v. *a-swæmnan*: '(1) to be troubled, to suffer grief, to languish, (2) to be confounded, put to shame, (3) to blush with shame, feel shame'.

86 Ps. 30:18: 'Let me not be confounded, O Lord for I have called upon thee'. Pulsiano, *Old English Glossed Psalters*, (*siglum* I) p. 395. BT: v. *ge-scendan*: 'to shame, put to shame, confound'.

87 Ps. 34:26: 'Let them blush and be ashamed together who rejoice at my evils. Let them be clothed with confusion and shame who speak things against me'. Pulsiano, *Old English Glossed Psalters*, (*siglum* I) p. 478. See *ge-scendan*, and also BT: n. *ge-sceandnysse*, 'shame, confusion'.

88 Ps. 39:16: 'Let them immediately bear their confusion that say to me, 'tis well, 'tis well'. Pulsiano, *Old English Glossed Psalters*, (*siglum* I) p. 582.

CHAPTER THREE: EDUCATION AND LITERACY

Studies of Old English glosses added to the *Lambeth Psalter* suggest that this emotional terminology prompted teachers to explain that the Latin noun *rubor* could mean both 'redness' and 'shame', encouraging boys to consider blushing as an exteriorisation of interior guilt or sin.[89] This type of evidence does not seem to have been confined to Latin verbs and nouns for shame, however. My own study of glosses added to this copy reveals that our view can be extended further to include evidence suggesting that teachers encouraged boys to engage in a basic level of biblical exegesis. We can find evidence for this sort of engagement in a number of Old English glosses for Latin terms which I provide again below for example, and which relate to 'land' and 'nobles/ princes' in psalms 32:10, 36:9 and 36:11:

[Ps. 32:10]
Dominus dissipat consilia gentium, reprobat autem cogitationes
ealdra (i.e. 'of the elders/seniors')
populorum, et reprobat consilia *principium*.[90]

[Ps. 36.9]
Quoniam qui malignantur exterminabuntur, sustinentes autem
ece lif (i.e. 'eternal life')
Dominum, ipsi haereditabunt *terram*.[91]

---

89 EGA, p. 47; compare *Excerptiones*, n. 219, p. 118; Jonathan Wilcox, 'An Embarrassment of Clues: Interpreting Anglo-Saxon Blushes', in *Anglo-Saxon Emotions*, ed. Jorgensen, McCormack, and Wilcox, p. 95.
90 Ps. 32:10 'The Lord bringeth to naught the counsels of nations and he rejecteth the devices of people and casteth away the counsels of princes'. Pulsiano, *Old English Glossed Psalters*, (*siglum* I) p. 424. DOE: n. *ealdor* 'someone in authority, superior, over others, a ruler, king, lord, prince, paterfamilias, apostles, parent, Christ, authority in a monastery, an abbot, abbess, dean'; note the use of *ealdor* for monastic seniors in OERB, c. 64, p. 123.
91 Ps. 36:9 'For the evildoers shall be cut off, but they that wait upon the lord shall inherit the land'. Pulsiano, *Old English Glossed Psalters*, (*siglum* I) p. 499. See DOEWC for extensive use in Ælfric's *Catholic Homilies*, see also OERB, c. 7 and 73, pp. 24, 133.

[Ps. 36:11]

heofonrice (i.e. 'heavenly kingdom')

Mansueti autem haereditabunt *terram*, et delectabuntur in multitudine pacis.[92]

These glosses framed the Latin of the Psalter in ways which departed from their literal meaning and projected monastic values onto them. Indeed, they suggest that contemporaries encouraged readers to turn away from a literal frame of reading in areas which described 'inheriting land', and towards a way of thinking which encouraged boys to take a more symbolic view, and understand 'inheriting eternal salvation' or 'the heavenly kingdom' instead. These glosses may also demonstrate that contemporaries sought to frame student encounters with references to 'nobles or princes' in the Psalter by orientating them towards an understanding of monastic seniors and religious elders, and as part of this wider practice of reading the Psalter reflectively. Such arguments are highly contingent, but these glosses show how the Psalter allowed for this instruction in a similar way to Ælfric's *Excerptiones de arte grammatica anglice*. They suggest that the experience of instruction in Latin likely played a fundamental role in shaping boys' developing religious identities, providing boys with an increasingly influential lens for understanding and policing monastic values and behaviours in the world around them as their comprehension of Latin improved.[93]

In focussing upon evidence suggesting that boys encountered a relatively fixed progress of learning, from memorising Latin sequences to reading Latin through the medium of sacred texts like the Psalter, we risk reinforcing an impression that all monastic students moved smoothly through their education, never encountering difficulty or exhibiting any resistance to their studies. This picture, of a kind of uncomplicated inertia in educational experience, is not particularly credible, however, and should not only be questioned, but revised, and in a way which draws attention to how the documentary base of this period also expresses a more nuanced

---

92   Ps. 36:11 'But the meek shall inherit the land, and shall delight in abundance of peace'. Pulsiano, *Old English Glossed Psalters,* (*siglum* I) p. 501. DOE: n. *heofonrice*: 'kingdom of heaven'.
93   Birnbaum, 'Naming Shame', p. 109.

CHAPTER THREE: EDUCATION AND LITERACY

reality. As much as Ælfric of Eynsham or teacher-users of his school-text might have hoped that boys would work through the *Excerptiones de arte grammatica anglice*, internalising all its grammatical content and acquiring a body of conceptual and religious thought, the *Colloquia* of Ælfric Bata present us with an account of one boy's literary development which draws our attention to a messier reality of student outcomes:

> [Magister]
> Scis tu loqui in Latina lingua?
> [Puer]
> Non utique nisi paulipser perpauca verba et non tantum sapio quantum legi et didici, quia multa oblitus sum propter ebitudinem ignorantie mee
> [...]
> Quamquam sim parvus ingenio, longa tamen meditatione pauca verba recognosco, sed hec regulariter secundum grammaticam respondere vel loqui non possum.[94]

Bata's words were not intended for an audience of illiterate students, and so this dialogue from his *Colloquia* should be read in a way that understands it was intended for an audience of learned Latin students. This means that Bata's school-text only accounts precisely for the experiences of those boys who did advance in their Latin instruction, who encountered his *Colloquia,* and who may have been expected to encounter in their studies the many other Latin texts which Bata's *Colloquia* cited, including the Psalter, Proverbs, Ecclesiastes, and Wisdom, as well as Ephesians, Timothy, II Thessalonians, II Corinthians, Deuteronomy, Genesis, Romans, and the Gospels of Luke and Matthew, among others.[95] But dialogue no. 16

---

94 ÆlfBColl, pp. 116-9: 'Can you speak Latin?/ Actually no, just a little, very few words. I do not understand as much as I read and learned, since I forgot a lot because of the dullness of my ignorance [...] Though I have little intelligence, I do recognize (sic) a few of those words when I concentrate on them, but I cannot answer or speak properly according to grammatical rules'.
95 Gwara and Porter identify a reference to ps. 110(10) in dialogue no. 4 for example, see ÆlfBColl, pp. 86-7 (fn. 29). Dialogue no. 25 constitutes an amalgamation of more than 126 references to individual verses taken from the book of Proverbs, see ÆlfBColl, pp. 116-7, 140-55. For references to Ecclesiastes, Sapientia, as well as Ephesians, I Timothy, II Thessalonians, II Corinthians, Deuteronomy, Genesis, Romans,

also illustrates a dynamic of failure and illiteracy. For one, it would seem to have been intended to give literate students licence to pass comment on boys who may not have advanced far in their Latin education. In doing so, the *Colloquia* therefore also point us in a direction which suggests that the experience of learning Latin grammar sharpened divisions in monastic schools. Bata's use of terms such as *pauca verba, propter ebitudinem ignorantie* and *secundum grammaticam* offer us a view onto how teachers responded to student failures in Latin learning, and exploited dynamics of competition between students to foster identities of attainment. They indicate that the process of learning grammar even allowed teachers like Bata to identify openly boys who had not made progress.[96] Indeed, this dialogue discloses that teachers may even have deliberately encouraged boys who did not progress in their learning to internalise that literary and monastic identity, one based on inability and illiteracy. Bata seems to approve here of what we might see as 'bullying' to convince students to resign themselves to Old English literacy, to the liturgy, to life with only internal prospects of promotion, without higher career advancement, and to identify themselves as 'slower' (*hebetudo*), less able or 'unable' to understand, and either slower to memorise or quicker to forget, and to think of themselves as being among the ignorant in their particular generation or community (*ignorantia, ignorare*).[97]

---

the gospels of Luke and Matthew, and Aldhelm of Sherborne's *Prosa et Versus de Virginitate*, see ÆlfBColl, nos. 4, pp. 86-7 (Ecclesiastes 1:1; Ephesians 6:1; I Timothy 5:1; II Timothy 4:2; Sapientia 1:1); 196-7 (Romans 8:15); 14, 112-3 (II Thessalonians 3:10); 15, 116-7 (Deuteronomy 32:7); 24, 132-3 (II Corinthians 6:7); 25, 136-7 (Luke 10:6); 28, 164-5 (Genesis 49:27); 29, 176-7 (Matthew 5:6 and 25:34); and for Aldhelm's *De Virginitate* see *Difficiliora Colloquia* in ÆlfBColl, nos. 4 (pp. 180-3), 5 (pp. 184-5), 7 (pp. 186-7), 9 (pp. 188-91).

96 Gwara and Porter isolate adjustments made by Bata to his *Colloquia* at ÆlfBColl, pp. 116-9 (fn. 107), they include additions of 'Docte' 'in Latina lingua', 'Puerosque instruentes', and the end of the dialogue 'Sermo divinus litteris litteratorum (id est grammaticorum) minime servit, et tamen nullus liber scriptus vel positus recte erit, nisi prius grammaticam artem didicerit, qui illum disponit/Divine speech hardly serves the letters of the teachers or grammarians. Still, no book is properly written or arranged unless the one who composes it first studies the grammatical art'.

97 ÆlfBColl, pp. 116-9: 'Ignoro autem litteras grammaticorum et exempla poetarum/ I do not know the letters of the grammarians or the exempla of the poets'; although Bata took this line verbatim from the earlier *Colloquia de raris fabulis Rectractata*, see ÆlfBColl, pp. 116-9 (fn. 107).

CHAPTER THREE: EDUCATION AND LITERACY

Anglo-Norman England: Boyhood

As we have seen in chapter one, Lanfranc's *Constitutiones* illustrate far more clearly an intention to regulate boys' educational conditions than the *Regularis Concordia*. For one, they suggest that boys were expected to join a complex of educational structures at Christ Church, Canterbury. These included a *schola*, which could be understood as physical spaces of learning and as a time in the daily round set aside for boys' study, overseen by a community of teachers or *magistri*. Lanfranc's consuetudinary is particularly useful, however, in that it gives us a clearer view of when and how often Lanfranc expected boys to attend this educational structure. The *Constitutiones* appear, for example, to have required boys to enter their school at two fixed periods in their daily round. The first of these periods occurred after Prime and continued until a *signum* was rung for Tierce, and a second period of study appears to have occurred after Nones and may have continued until a *signum* alerted boys and their *magistri* to attend Vespers at dusk.[98]

It also confirms that boys' experiences of Latin education centred to a significant extent on the liturgy, and that experiences of Latin learning continued to be intended to enable boys' engagement with the choir. Post-Conquest hagiographies continue to support this view too, and describe an ideal in monastic education of an early occupation with the 'study' of 'sacred letters'. The *Vita Sancti Aldhelmi*, composed by the Italian émigré Faricius of Arezzo, who was cellarer at Malmesbury in c.1100 and later Abbot of Abingdon (c.1100-1117), supplies one such account for example, locating the place of 'letters' in an elementary stage of boys' learning, preceding a potentially much longer course of instruction:

> Post hec annis succedentibus puer ablactatur et sacris litterarum studiis a genitore Christianissimo traditur . . . tantum aperuit ingenium ut doctoris animus in se ipso saepe miraretur nimium, quod tam facile caperet, tam memoriter retineret que sibi ostendebat per singulos dies [. . .] Trium quippe proprietate linguarum, non solum vulgaritate, ceterum etiam litterarum dogmate, sanctissimus

---

98 *Constitutiones*, pp. xxxv-xxxvi.

iste peritus extitit. Miro denique modo Graie facundie omnia idiomata sciebat, et quasi Grecus natione scriptis et verbis pronuntiabat [...] Latine quoque scientie valde potatus, etiam aliquis eo melius nequaquam usus est post Virgilium [...] Prophetarum exemplaria, Davidis psalmos, Salomonis tria volumina, Hebraicis litteris bene novit et legem Moysaicam. Musice autem artis omnia instrumenta ... aliis varietatibus melodie fieri possunt et memoria tenuit et in cotidiano usus habuit.[99]

We should perhaps question the representativeness of this content. Faricius' arrangement of a well-resourced monastery, able to provide an extensive education stretching from elementary rudiments in letters to advanced areas of the *quadrivium*, including learning in musical instruments, law, as well as Greek and Hebraic letters, may not entirely reflect either his own experience of teaching and/or learning in England or records of Aldhelm's seventh century upbringing. But its salient educational features, and its recognition in particular of the place of biblical text in boys' earliest encounters with Latin letters, are familiar to us from pre-Conquest progressions. Faricius supplies us with an ideal which still anticipated that boys who entered monasteries without much learning could expect a total formation in letters. He seems to expect too that that instruction would not only provide boys with a functional literacy useful to memorising liturgical texts, but allowed some boys to study grammar and read at a more advanced level.

For the period 1050 to around 1120, our best evidence for the shape and content of grammatical education continues to lie in the group of

---

99 Faricius of Arezzo, 'Vita S. Aldhelmi', ed. Michael Winterbottom, *Journal of Medieval Latin* 15 (2005), p. 100: 'In the years after the boy was weaned he was given ... to the study of sacred letters ... and he understood as easily as he retained in his memory whatever was revealed to him in instruction each day [...] this most holy man was masterful in the rules of three tongues, not only in his own English but indeed [...] In a miraculous way of fertile grace he knew all the idioms of Greece, as if a Greek by nation in his writing and pronunciation ... He absorbed knowledge of Latin too, and in this, indeed, after Virgil, there was no one who could be thought better [...] He knew well the exemplars of the prophets, the psalms of David, the three volumes of Solomon, Hebraic letters and Mosaic law. He held too in his memory and practised daily many varieties of melody through all the instruments of the art of religious music' (my translation).

school-texts on grammar composed in England between 992 and 1010.[100] The most widely attested of the grammatical primers of the period remains Ælfric of Eynsham's *Excerptiones de arte grammatica anglice*. Aside from the fact that this text had been widely available in pre-Conquest libraries and that it was still present within them after the Conquest, the school-text continued to attract new copies, and appears to have been transmitted to new foundations after the Conquest, including the community of regular canons at Exeter c.1070 and the Norman Benedictine foundation of William St. Calais at Durham sometime after c.1083.[101] Studies have also shown that almost half of all extant copies of the *Excerptiones de arte grammatica anglice* contain signs suggesting that they continued to see a purpose in instruction up until the mid-twelfth-century.[102] Tony Hunt has done important work to this effect, and while he has recognised that glosses added to copies of an educational text do not necessarily reflect the activities of a school, he has shown that many of the additions support a view of continued use in monastic contexts.[103]

At the same time, copies of the *Excerptiones de arte grammatica anglice* which attracted annotations, and which were produced after the Conquest, also indicate that there were changes in the educational and social environments of the houses where they remained useful. Tony Hunt, for one, has argued that change in boys' experience of Latin instruction through these copies is visibly marked by the appearance of a thoroughly revised version of the school-text which was composed by a single scribe at the turn of the twelfth century (c.1100x10) surviving in a single unprinted manuscript,

---

100 Rodney Thomson observed that Anglo-Saxon libraries were 'eccentric', see Rodney Thomson, 'The Norman Conquest and English Libraries', in *The Role of the Book in Medieval Culture*, ed. Peter Ganz (Turnhout, 1986), p. 29.
101 i.e. MSS Exeter H.h.1.10, and Durham Cathedral Library B.III.32, see Gneuss, *Handlist*, nos. 13 (p. 28), 244 (p. 52).
102 Tony Hunt analyses two copies (MSS London BL, Cotton Faustina A.x, and Cambridge University Library Hh.1.10) which reveal evidence of scribal activity after the Conquest, see Tony Hunt, *Teaching and Learning in Thirteenth Century England I: Texts* (Cambridge, 1991), pp. 8-9 and esp. pp. 101-11, and 111-8.
103 Melinder Menzer, 'Ælfric's English Grammar', *Journal of English and Germanic Philology* 103 (2004), 106. Patrizia Lendinara, 'The World of Anglo-Saxon Learning', in *The Cambridge Companion to Old English Literature*, ed. Malcom Godden, and Michael Lapidge (Cambridge, 1991), 264-81; for French annotations see, EGA, pp. 29/17, 30/1, 33/12, 34/3&6, 35/7, 80/10, 81/1.

Cambridge, Trinity College MS R.9.17.[104] Although we cannot identify the house to which it belonged, since a majority of copies which do have a known place of origin or provenance can be identified with a monastic community, it would seem likely to be the product of a monastic scribe.[105] This copy is of particular interest, however, not just because it represents a significant editorial adjustment, but because it reveals something about the changing needs of the community where it was made and used.[106] The scribe would appear to have still valued the vernacular as a medium of instruction. This much seems clear from the fact that they chose to retain many of Ælfric's Old English synonyms for Latin nouns and verbs. But the copy also provides a window onto a new scribal context, and onto a series of editorial decisions indicating that contemporaries had come to centre their interests in the *Excerptiones de arte grammatica anglice* on its Latin content. The composer had recognised its concise and comprehensive scope and had sought to ensure that the school-text provided an even more concise basis for supporting Latin instruction. But the removal of much of Ælfric's vernacular or 'bi-lingual' apparatus, and evidence for the excision of all of its Old English meta-language, its commentary on Latin grammatical concepts, and its vernacular translations of exemplary Latin sentences, show that Ælfric's authorised method for teaching Latin had also become less useful to its post-Conquest audience.

In fact, the disappearance of much of the Old English content in this copy coincides with evidence for the contemporary appearance in this,

---

[104] Tony Hunt has printed all Anglo-Norman glosses, see Hunt, *Teaching and Learning Latin I*, p. 26; see Gneuss, *Handlist*, no. 182, p. 45: (s. xi/xii).

[105] For all the copies which can be identified with a monastic community, see Cambridge, University Library, Hh.1.10 (orig. Canterbury, see Hunt, *Teaching and Learning Latin*, p. 100); Durham Cathedral Library MS B.III.32 (see Gneuss, *Handlist*, no. 244, p. 52: orig. Canterbury), BL Harley 107 (Gneuss, *Handlist*, no. 414, no. 74: orig. South-East England), Oxford, St. John's College 154 (Gneuss, *Handlist*, no. 686, no. 107: prov. Durham). By contrast, only one can be identified as having belonged to a non-monastic house at some point in its life, but even this has been associated with a monastic house (i.e. Cambridge, University Library, Hh.1.10, see Gneuss, *Handlist*, no. 13, p. 28).

[106] Tony Hunt thought that it was 'probably written at the very beginning of the twelfth century', but argued, seemingly unaware of the slight contradiction, that 'Ælfric's Old English Grammar obviously did not outlive the Conquest', see Hunt, *Teaching and Learning Latin I*, pp. 26, 100.

and in three other copies of the *Excerptiones de arte grammatica anglice* of a complementary apparatus of glosses in Norman French.[107] Although one of these MSS has been associated with a house of regular canons at Exeter, the addition of a French apparatus appears to have been widespread, and would seem likely to offer a view onto a dynamic of change in the context of monastic education in the late eleventh century, when French speakers – as boys and/or teachers – might have begun to enter monastic schools in sufficient numbers and on a consistent enough basis that they began to have a visible impact on the established material culture of Latin instruction.[108] As we have noted, we find evidence for this emerging dynamic in several copies, but we can consider them emblematic of those added to a copy of the *Excerptiones de arte grammatica anglice* now contained in Cambridge, University Library MS Hh.1.10, thought to have been copied at Christ Church, Canterbury before travelling to Exeter.[109] At some stage, this copy acquired a complete system of Norman French forms alongside Ælfric's framework of Old English paradigms for Latin forms, and, ultimately, it provided readers with a similar comparison of active and passive Latin verbs for *amare*, beginning with the first conjugation and the French verb *aimer* for example (i.e. *iu aim, tu aimes, zil aimet*), and complementing an inherited apparatus on the English verb *lufian* (i.e. *ic lufie, þu lufast, he lufiað*/I love, you love, he loves).[110]

While these changes to the Anglo-Saxon apparatus of the *Excerptiones de arte grammatica anglice* suggest that boys' experiences of Latin

---

107 These are Cambridge, University Library, Hh.1.10 (Gneuss, *Handlist*, no. 13, p. 28), Cambridge, Trinity College R.9.17 (Gneuss, *Handlist*, no. 182, p. 45), BL, Cotton Faustina A.x fols. 3-101 (Gneuss, *Handlist*, no. 331, p. 63), BL Julius A.ii fols.10-135 (Gneuss, *Handlist*, no. 336, p. 64).

108 For more on Anglo-Norman glosses, see Hunt, *Teaching and Learning Latin I*, pp. 11-2, 16, at 16: 'This is the first study devoted to the role of Anglo-Norman and Middle English glossing in the teaching and learning of Latin. It provides a conspectus of materials ... host texts and reproduces as accurately as possible the glosses themselves'. See also Hunt, *Teaching and Learning Latin I*, p. 26.

109 Gneuss, *Handlist*, no. 13, p. 28. Hunt, *Teaching and Learning Latin I*, p. 100: 'This interesting adaptation of the grammar to the new cultural language of French has not been sufficiently appreciated ... MS CUL Hh.1.10 ... has additions in three languages in the twelfth century and ... may have come from Christ Church, Canterbury'.

110 Hunt, *Teaching and Learning Latin I*, pp. 111-8, esp. 111-3.

instruction continued to be defined by a pre-Conquest material base for some time after the Norman Conquest, the emergence of new languages into monastic schools and the slow transformation of the basis of instruction indicates that a series of social changes were playing a role in changing the educational architecture of Benedictine England, undermining the viability of an apparatus which had emerged during a period of monastic reform. A collapse in evidence for new copies of the *Excerptiones de arte grammatica anglice* after c.1110 and a decline in evidence for new annotations from the second half of the twelfth century suggests that the school-text ultimately stopped shaping boys' experience of Latin instruction over the course of the twelfth century. With no clear evidence for any other single replacement of that school-text in Anglo-Norman monastic libraries and with no evidence for the emergence of a new grammatical school-text tailored to meet the needs of monastic boys in the twelfth century, change in the elementary curriculum appears to have been marked by a fragmentation. We can understand this fragmentation in terms of a turn to practices of instruction which depended on an assortment of grammatical primers of Late Antiquity not crafted in a monastic context or tailored for the instruction of oblates. Many of these primers, like the *Ars Minor* and *Ars Maior* of Donatus and the *Institutio de nomine* and *Instititiones Grammaticae* of Priscian, seem to have characterised instructional practices at Ramsey Abbey, and the cathedral schools of the European continent, and may have helped to connect England to a process of classicisation in Europe's intellectual landscape which has since become known as the twelfth century 'renaissance'.[111]

---

[111] For more on this fragmentation see Lucia Kornexl, 'From Ælfric to John of Cornwall: Evidence for Vernacular Grammar Teaching in Pre- and Post-Conquest England', in *Bookmarks from the Past: Studies in Early English Language and Literature in Honour of Helmut Gneuss*, ed. Lucia Kornexl and Ursula Lenker (Oxford, 2003), 245-8. Hunt, *Teaching and Learning Latin I*, pp. 166-7. Nine surviving copies of Priscian's *Institutitones Grammaticae* provide material evidence for continued grammatical instruction: Gameson, *Manuscripts of Early Norman England*, nos. 30, 35, 109, 165, 327, 771, 791, 804, 939, pp. 58, 67, 73, 92, 142, 144, 146, 158. For more on the western Latin curriculum during the twelfth century 'renaissance', see Jaakko Tahkokallio, 'The Classicization of the Latin Curriculum and "The Renaissance of the Twelfth Century": A Quantitative Study of the Codicological Evidence', *Viator* 46 (2015), pp. 129-53.

CHAPTER THREE: EDUCATION AND LITERACY

There may be other reasons for why the material base of elementary Latin instruction might have fallen into disuse in England, however. If we return to the autobiographical writings of Orderic Vitalis, first seen in the introduction to this work, and consider in particular a part of his childhood recollection which describes that he had spent five-years in the instruction of a parish priest at Atcham in Shrewsbury, we could consider that changes in instruction in Benedictine monasteries were also connected to changes in the role of the monastery:

> Deinde cum quinque essem annorum apud urbem Scrobesburiam scolae traditus sum, et prima tibi servitia clericatus obtuli in basilica sanctorum Petri et Pauli apostolorum. Illic Siguardus insignis presbiter per quinque annos Carmentis Nichostratae litteris docuit me, ac psalmis et hymnis aliisque necessariis instructionibus mancipavit me.[112]

This passage allows us to consider that Benedictine houses were more likely to receive into their houses oblates who had already received a rudimentary degree of instruction in Latin letters. Monasteries were no longer the main providers of elementary instruction. If this trend continued, and if it coincided at all with contemporary evidence for increases in the recruitment of adult novices into Benedictine houses in a similar period, visible in surviving lists of monastic professions at New Minster in Winchester c.1100x1320, it would not be difficult to connect a decline in evidence for the use of elementary Latin school-texts, with a possible decline in the number of entirely untutored oblate students.[113]

---

112 Orderic Vitalis, *Historia Ecclesiastica*, ed. and trans. Chibnall, VI, bk. 13, pp. 552-3: 'Afterwards when I was five years old I was put to school in the town of Shrewsbury, and performed my first clerical duties for thee in the church of St. Peter and St. Paul the apostles. There, Siward, an illustrious priest, taught me my letters for five years, and instructed me in psalms and hymns and other necessary knowledge'.
113 Increases in the recruitment of adults are widely accepted, but are visible in the *Liber Vitae* of New Minster, Winchester, which lists all new entrants between c.1030 and 1230, see *Liber Vitae of the New Minster and Hyde Abbey, Winchester: British Library Stowe 944: together with leaves from British Library Cotton Vespasian A. VIII and British Library Cotton Titus D. XXVII*, ed. Simon Keynes, Early English Manuscripts in Facsimile 26 (Copenhagen: Rosenkilde and Bagger, 1996). For more on the emergence of the local parish and episcopal school, see Lahaue-Geusen, *Das Opfer der*

Still, this broader perspective does not throw much light onto what education the boys who continued to enter religious houses received in a post-Conquest context. If we can infer that an assortment of established grammatical primers played a part in supporting instruction in grammar, we can perhaps also imagine that the Psalter continued to provide teachers and boys with a basis for improving comprehension of biblical text.[114] William of Malmesbury (c.1080-1143), in his early-twelfth century version of the *Vita Wulfstani* described the boy reading deeply through the contents of the Psalter at Peterborough Abbey, for example, and he appears to have imagined too that Wulfstan (1002-1095) had instituted a similar emphasis after he had been elevated to the office of *custos puerorum* and subsequently to the episcopal see.[115] Also useful to understanding changes in the contents, course, and expectations of a literary education in a Benedictine house after the Norman Conquest is the small collection of *Epistolae* or 'Letters' which survive from the circle of Bishop Herbert of Norwich (fl. 1090-1119), and which describe the educational experiences of boys who were growing up at Norwich cathedral from c.1093.

These letters are significant because they provide us with accounts of the actual experiences of boys who grew up at Norwich cathedral in the very late eleventh and early twelfth century.[116] Although no letters from any students have survived in this collection, Herbert's responses to them reveal his procedures as *magister*, and point towards and occasionally appear to provide quotations or paraphrases of the contents of students' letters too. The *Epistolae* suggest, for example, that Bishop Herbert required boys to engage in a grammatical 'trivium' and had expected them to encounter a form of learning in Latin grammar similar to that of Ramsey a generation earlier, which had come to depend on an assortment

---

Kinder, p. 10.
114 Richard Gameson dated ten Psalter manuscripts to c.1066-1130, of which three retained Old English glosses, Gameson, *Manuscripts of Early Norman England*, nos. 47, 86, 325, 356, 358, 406, 748, 819, 906, 912, at no. 47.
115 William of Malmesbury, *Vita Sancti Wulfstani*, in *Lives of SS. Wulfstan, Dunstan, Patrick, Benignus and Indract*, ed. and trans. Winterbottom and Thomson, p. 21.
116 For all the letters Bishop Herbert addressed to students of Norwich, see Herbert de Losinga, *Epistpolae Herberti*, in *Epistolae Herberti de Losinga Primi Episcopi Norwiciensis, Osberti de Clara et Elmeri, Prioris Cantuariensis*, ed. Robert Anstruther (Brussels, 1846), nos. 9, 22, 24, 28, 30, 32, 39, 41, 42, 47, 49.

of grammatical primers, including works by Donatus and Sergius.[117]

Sadly, the *Epistolae* do not reveal much else of this stage. They fail to account for the sources of doctrinal or monastic learning which might have replaced that provided by pre-Conquest grammars. Nor do they confirm exactly the influence of Norman French as a medium. What they do show are new horizons and associations with Latin study. They point, for example, towards the growing influence of a new corpus of Latin texts, like Aesop's fables and Ovid's poetry. These would have given oblates direct examples of Latin text in a classical style which pre-Conquest teachers like Ælfric had known, but deliberately avoided.[118] The *Epistolae* also indicate that Herbert had instructed two students in particular, Otto (fl. 1100) and William Turbe (d.1174). If we can assume that Herbert's correspondences with these students are representative of boys' access to instruction at Norwich in the late eleventh or early twelfth century, the collection would suggest that access to a literary education might also have become more selective for students who progressed. Since we know that William Turbe later became bishop of Norwich (1147-74), Herbert's *Epistolae* suggest that he may even have intervened as teacher to achieve that precise

---

117 Herbert de Losgina, *Epistolae Herberti*, ed. Anstruther, no. 9, p. 44: 'Reddituri mihi estis corde prius Donatum, declinationes, conjugationes, voces, Serviolam, pedes et omnes grammaticae regulas ... ut praeparatis responsiones vestras futurae ratiocinationi vestri examinis'; trans. Henry Symonds and Edward M. Goulburn, *The Life, Letters and Sermons of Bishop Herbert de Losinga* (Oxford, 1878), I, no. 9, pp. 19-20: 'You are first to repeat to me your Donatus by heart with all the declensions, conjugations, and voices, and also your compendium of Servius with the feet and all the rules of grammar ... get up your answers in readiness for your examination'.

118 Herbert de Losinga, *Epistolae Herberti*, ed. Anstruther, no. 30, p. 62: 'Lege poetas, dicta ex poetis, quoniam et in sterquilinio ille Aesopi gallus invenit margaritam'; trans. Symonds and Goulburn, *Letters of Bishop Herbert*, I, p. 28: 'Read your poets, make your centos out of the poets, since even in a dunghill that cockerel of Aesop's picked up a pearl'. For Ovid see, *Epistpolae Herberti*, ed. Anstruther, no. 39, p. 75: 'Quales infantes tales pueri quales pueri tales adolescentes eisdem vestris sinalimphis et barbarissimis infantiliter inhaeretis non est multum loqui de Ovidio si non discatis loqui ex Ovidio [...] ex Ovidio deinceps meo judicio loquimini quoniam vestris non applaudo pedibus'; trans. Symonds and Goulburn, *Letters of Bishop Herbert*, I, pp. 22-3: 'What ye were when babies that ye were as boys; what ye were as boys, ye are as youths; most childishly ye stick still to your ellisions and barbarisms. To talk about Ovid is of very little value, unless you learn from Ovid how to talk [...] If henceforth, then, you mean to be guided by my judgement, adopt the style of Ovid, since I do not approve of your verses'.

outcome. This would certainly chime with a point made earlier too - that oblates were shaped by the institutional nature of the houses they entered. Monastic sees, like Herbert's, could provide experiences not available in abbeys, and were able to exploit canonical rights to train their own bishops from within the confines of their own schools.

Communities of Religious Women: Infancy

In his *Vita Sancte Wihtburge*, Goscelin imagined that Whitburh's (d.743) nurses and tutors might have instructed the girl from infancy in order to 'charm her mind with the name of Christ' (*animos ad Christi nomen permulcere*).[119] In describing her exposure to the name of Christ (and we are left to imagine whether through the monosyllabic and vernacular *Crist* or the disyllabic and Latin *Christus*), Goscelin disclosed his subscription to the idea that the exposure of infant girls to words of a Christian nature would have an influence on a girl's development. Indeed, Goscelin's *Vita Wihtburge* appears to reveal a contemporary strategy of religious socialisation in infancy which we do not find in relation to boys of a similar age, and an assumption that religious language had potential to shape a girl's emergent vocabulary, her developing patterns of speech, and even her religious inclinations.

Saints' lives also suggest that infant girls were expected to experience some kind of instruction in Latin 'letters', and in a way which intersects with evidence we have seen in chapter one of the sometimes much younger ages of girls who entered religious houses. According to the author of the *Vita Regis Edwardi* (c.1065x1070), for example, Queen Eadgyth of England, (d.1075), who had commissioned the *Vita*, had begun her 'study of letters from her infancy' upon entering Wilton Abbey as a secular pupil in the late 1020s or early 1030s.[120] We find this picture

---

119 Goscelin, *Vita Sancte Wihtburge Virginis*, in *The Hagiography of the Female Saints of Ely*, ed. and trans. Love, pp. 54-5.
120 *Vita Edwardi Regis*, in *The Life of King Edward who rests at Westminster*, ed. and trans. Frank Barlow, OMT (rev. ed., Oxford, 1992), p. 22: 'A tempore infancie [in] studiis literarum in monasterio'. Strictly speaking, the *Collectio Capitularis* forbade monasteries from taking secular/non-oblated pupils, but evidence here from Wilton

of infant 'literacy' again in the twelfth century, in fact, and in the *Gesta Regum*, where William of Malmesbury appears to have thought it credible that Saint Eadburh, daughter of King Eadward the Elder of Wessex and Mercia (899-924), would have acquired some knowledge in Latin letters by the time of her infancy too, and, indeed by the time she had entered Nunnaminster as an oblate, at the age of three.[121]

Girlhood

The *Regula Benedicti,* the *Old English Rule* and the vernacular version of the *Regularis Concordia*, do not appear to expect this dynamic in infancy, but allow us to imagine that girls encountered Latin in their houses shortly after oblation, acquiring a functional degree of knowledge useful to making prayers and engaging in a liturgical round. These prescriptive documents also indicate that girls might have been expected to enter into formal educational structures. While they provide no certainty about girls' own conditions, we have seen in chapter one that saints' lives and letters to religious women suggest that girls' lives were informed by one of two systems. One of these, and based largely upon contemporary writings on Barking Abbey, suggests religious girls experienced a collective system of formal education which conformed closely to organisational forms anticipated by the *Regularis Concordia*. It suggests a context which included dedicated pedagogic offices for women teachers (*magistrae*), and described a 'school' environment (*schola*) of 'little girls' (*puellulae coetanae*).[122] Another, however, and based largely on Goscelin's writings

---

and Ramsey (in the *Enchiridion*) suggests it was accepted in England - possibly in the hope they would stay.

121 William of Malmesbury, *Gesta Regum Anglorum/History of the English Kings*, ed. and trans. Roger A. B. Mynors, Michael Winterbottom, and Rodney M. Thomson, OMT (Oxford, 1998-9), II, c. 126, p. 201; Osbert of Clare, *Vita Sancte Ædburge Virginis*, in *Royal Saints of Anglo-Saxon England*, ed. Ridyard, pp. 264-5: 'Subtractis vero in modico nutricis uberibus, devote Deo femine Edeldrithe committitur, cuius instantia sacris litterarum apicibus informatur/A short while after she was weaned, and was committed to Æðelthryth, a woman devoted to God, she was formed in sacred letters'.
122 Goscelin, *De Translatione vel Elevatione Sanctarum Virginum Ethelburgae, Hildelithae et Wlfhildae*, in 'Texts of Jocelyn of Canterbury', ed. Colker, 453.

relating to the Abbey of Wilton, affords a view of an educational system which centred on the individual girl, on the private 'cell', and on the instruction of internal religious teachers, identified sometimes as abbesses and otherwise as dedicated *magistrae,* and on the instruction of external tutors, identified sometimes as hired scholars and chaplains and otherwise as passing bishops.

Goscelin's *Vita Sancte Edithe Virginis,* which offers us a longitudinal view of the education of Saint Eadgyth, beginning with the moment of her imagined entry into Wilton Abbey as an oblate at the age of two and ending with her death at around the age of thirty, offers a principal source for this second model. This life is useful to us here because Goscelin's narrative raises useful questions about the conditionality of educational experience on age and social status, in ways which may correspond to evidence of how disciplinary conditions might have been affected by infancy and by royal status in chapter one. Eadgyth was a daughter of a king, and so we can consider that Goscelin might also have sought to represent a set of experiences which were elevated, and described conditions which girls of high status may have encountered in particular:

> Auctoritate quoque sancta flagrancie Eadgari, inter sacerdotes Wiltonie qui precedebant arcam federis Domini, ministri dominici tabernaculi, pollebant duo, tam morum quam scientie philosophia venerandi, quorum alter Radbodo Remensis de Sancto Remegio alter memoratur Benna Treverensis canonicus de Sancti Paulini Patrocinio [. . .] Hi condigna reverentia vicissim erudiebant alumnam spiritus sancti; hi portabant pedibus eius lucernam verbi Domini, ut, accensis lampadibus scripturarum, lectis gradibus virtutum, niteretur ad etherei regis solium [. . .] eruditor pudicus a foris *per fenestram docebat* et audiri magis quam videri assueverat, ut sancti pudoris vernulam decebat. Ornabant aures eius margaritis celestibus mater *interius,* magister *exterius.*[123]

---

[123] Goscelin, *Vita Sancte Edithe Virginis,* in 'La légende de ste Èdith', ed. Wilmart, pp. 50-1; trans. Hollis et al., *Writing the Wilton Women,* p. 32: 'Among the priests of Wilton who went in procession before the Ark of the Covenant of the Lord, ministers of the Lord's tabernacle, there were twin instructors who were of special weight by Eadgar's authority, venerable for their wisdom both in life and in scholarship, of whom one is remembered as Radbodo of Rheims, from St. Remegius, the other as

Goscelin accounts for the provision here of several teachers, with an internal teacher in the form of her mother, Abbess Wulfthryth, and at least two external teachers, in the form of two chaplains who had been hired by her father King Eadgar – Radbod, a monk of Rheims, and Benno, a canon of Trier. Goscelin's account of Eadgyth's education gives an impression that her Latin learning at Wilton might not necessarily have been a collective experience. By using the imperfect past tense form of the verb *docere*, Goscelin indicates that her experience of isolated instruction could even have been a normal practice. Goscelin also indicates that much of Eadgyth's education by external male chaplains, its reliance on oral dictation, choreographed behind screens or through windows, might have been determined by her gender and by her emergence into a marriageable age – her learning conditions becoming more restricted as she approached adulthood. If this was the case, it remains unclear whether and how this sort of anticipated enclosure might have also shaped her Latin literacy. Goscelin's account suggests that it might have made for a more difficult context of learning, but his reference to specialist tutors also suggest royal girls had privileged access to some of the most learned scholars available.

Unlike evidence for the differentiation of use of violence on girls of different social status seen in chapter one, however, there are some reasons for supposing that these conditions might have been rather more widely shared by girls of different status at royal foundations like Wilton. Goscelin described very similar conditions in a personal letter to Eafe, for example, a girl of perhaps noble but not royal stock and who had entered Wilton a decade or so before the Norman Conquest.[124] The *Liber Confortatorius* shows that

---

Benno, canon of Trier under the patronage of St. Paulinus [. . .] These men took turns to teach, with worthy reverence, this pupil of the Holy Spirit; these men brought to her feet the light of the word of God, so that by the light of the lamps of the scriptures and by choosing the steps of the virtues, she might advance towards the throne of the eternal king [. . .] The chaste teacher instructed her from outside through a window and accustomed himself to being heard rather than being seen, as was appropriate for the young pupil with her holy modesty. Her mother within and her teacher from outside adorned her ears with heavenly pearls'.

124 Goscelin, *Liber Confortatorius*, ed. Talbot, p. 41: 'Hodie Normanni in angliam Brittanniam in qua te quoque cum anglica gente constat fuisse advenam; sed et patre Dano et matre Lotaringa a claris natalibus filiam emessiste anglicam'; trans. Otter, p. 42: 'Nowadays the Normans [who have come] to England or Britain, where the entire English people were once newcomers – including yourself who, the well-born

Goscelin had acted as personal tutor to her at that house in a similar fashion to Radbod and Benno, and his account of his own teaching practices there in the 1050s and 1060s confirms that divided structures of education, split up between internal and external teachers and between female and male tutors, were important at Wilton in the late eleventh century:

> Continuata quoque silentia tua, sollicita continentia, frequens psalmodia, pia magistre testimonia, magis accenderunt vota mea.[125]

Goscelin's *Liber Confortatorius* does not account for the possibility that he had taught other girls simultaneously, and so it would seem reasonable to consider that he had also been asked to instruct Eafe in a fashion similar to Saint Eadgyth, in person and in relative isolation. Goscelin's *Liber Confortatorius* provides us with a series of recollections of their early encounters in rough chronological sequence, beginning with her 'infancy' (*infantia*) in c.1058 and continuing until her confirmation as a 'virgin' (*virgo*) in c.1065.[126] Unfortunately, Goscelin's account side-steps much of her childhood, and only begins to sketch out a portrait of Eafe as a young woman in 1065, when she already appears to have been able to participate in Latin conversation. His portrait of her capabilities by adulthood can be obtained from Goscelin's description of an occasion when they joined a feast to celebrate the dedication of Wilton's church to St. Mary. On this occasion, Goscelin recalled that he had 'passed [to Eafe] a plate of fish', and had enjoined upon her a spiritual lesson on the mortification of the flesh and the death of Christ with a cleverly arranged Latin pun, *piscis assus Christus passus* (our fish has been roasted, so Christ suffered).[127] In doing so, Goscelin appears to confirm that he had played at least some role in

---

daughter of a Danish father and a Loatharingian mother, turned out English'.
125 Goscelin, *Liber Confortatorius*, ed. Talbot, p. 28; trans. Otter, *Liber Confortatorius*, p. 23: 'And as I continued to witness your silence, your careful continence, your singing of the psalms and the praises of your teacher, my desire was inflamed even more'.
126 Goscelin, *Liber Confortatorius*, ed. Talbot, p. 28.
127 Goscelin, *Liber Confortatorius*, ed. Talbot, p. 28: 'Cumque ex affectu patris interesses epulis cum matre mittens piscem tibi, tali elogyo carnis mortificationem mandavi, *Piscis assus Christus passus*'; trans. Otter, *Liber Confortatorius*, p. 25: 'And when, through the generosity of your father, you and your mother attended the banquet, I passed you a platter of fish and enjoined upon you the mortification of the flesh with these words "*Piscis assus, Christus passus*"'.

supporting Eafe's acquisition of fluency in Latin speaking. Indeed, it may confirm even more than this, and could suggest that Eafe had not only acquired the experience in Latin conversation necessary for understanding Goscelin's ad hoc witticisms, but may have been tutored in the structure of Latin verse, and had learnt to appreciate in this case Goscelin's proficiency in a popular rhetorical device known as 'homeoteleuton', playing on the repetition of inflectional endings.

The *Liber Confortatorius* also suggests that Goscelin had played a role in instructing Eafe on Latin composition. We find evidence of this, for example, in Goscelin's recollection: 'my parchments and letters brought Christ to you'.[128] The passage is clearly poetic. Since parchments could not have undertaken any such action by themselves, it would seem wiser to re-impose Goscelin as the agent of instruction - 'very frequently bringing his own parchments and letters [to Eafe], in order to instruct [her] on matters relating to Christ'. It would also allow us to confirm that external male tutors played a role at Wilton in encouraging girls' closer studies of Latin school-texts. Sadly, Goscelin did not record quite what he meant by 'letters' (*litter[a]e*) – and whether, indeed, he had been responsible for instructing Eafe on grammar, on 'sacred letters' or on the Psalter and other Latin texts of a biblical and liturgical nature, or indeed school-texts of a more classical type.[129] By adding immediately afterwards, that Eafe had composed '[her] own very chaste letters' to him in response (*tue castissimae littere*), Goscelin's *Liber Confortatorius* could perhaps point us in the direction of his role in advancing her literary independence, and it could suggest that Goscelin had even played a role at Wilton analogous to Bishop Herbert at Norwich Cathedral as we have seen previously – providing girls with a similarly intensive form of instruction in Latin, carried out through the mutual exchange of correspondences.

Sadly, this means that we possess little evidence, either in the works

---

128 Goscelin, *Liber Confortatorius*, ed. Talbot, p. 29: 'Afferebant tibi Christum frequentes membrane et schedule nostre, nec tue vacabant castissime littere'; trans. Otter, *Liber Confortatorius*, p. 25: 'My parchments and tablets brought Christ to you, and your very chaste letters were not slow in coming'.
129 Just one copy of a Latin Psalter with a continuous Old English Gloss has been connected to a community of women, at Shaftesbury, *The Salisbury Psalter*, ed. Celia Sisam and Kenneth Sisam, EETS o.s. 242 (Oxford, 1959), p. v.

of Goscelin or elsewhere, to show how girls like Eafe might have first acquired their understanding of Latin. In asking whether any school-text might have supported girls' literary instruction in a pre- or post-Conquest context, it would seem useful to ask whether the manuscript base allows for the transmission to women's houses of school grammars which we know had been tailored for the instruction of Benedictine oblates. In doing so, we could centre our considerations on Ælfric's well-attested *Excerptiones de arte grammatica anglice* for example, and although the text has not often been seriously considered in this light, there are reasons to commend it.

It may be useful to recognise that a large portion of the extant fourteen complete or partial copies of Ælfric's school-text on grammar have never been assigned a provenance to a Benedictine community, male or female.[130] It will be useful to recognise too that the contents and structure of the *Excerptiones de arte grammatica anglice* allow for a wide audience, and fall in line with a contemporary practice visible in prescriptions which gave communities access to glossed or bi-lingual texts, and which possessed an inclusive and gender neutral vocabulary. We can note, for example, that the preface to the *Excerptiones de arte grammatica anglice* was addressed to an audience of students in twinned Latin and Old English versions, and while the Latin described 'little boys' (*pueruli*), the vernacular preface used the neutral *cild* (child) familiar from Old English translations of rules.

Scholars have often considered that the contents of the *Excerptiones de arte grammatica anglice*, and its many internal references to 'boys', indicate that it may have seen use in male houses. But it would also seem reasonable to consider that its internal references sustain an argument for a female audience, and allow us to situate the *Excerptiones de arte grammatica anglice* in view of the instruction of Benedictine girls. This potential acquires some credibility, for example, if we recognise that for each *fraterculus* and *lytel brodor*, Ælfric chose to offer a paradigm for a 'little sister', *sororcula* and *lytel swustor*.[131] For 'boy' and 'boyish', or *puer* and *puerulis*, Ælfric provided a corresponding *puella* (girl), *mægden* (maiden), *puellaris*

---

130 Copies of the EGA have only been confidently located at Exeter, Canterbury, a house in the south-east, and Durham (Gneuss, *Handlist*, nos. 13, 244, and 686), for the rest, see Gneuss, *Handist*, nos. 115, 182, 331, 336, 435, 441, 480, 494, 541, 876.
131 EGA, p. 16.

(girlish), and *mædenlic* (virginal).¹³² In his section on the morphology of feminine pronouns of the third declension, Ælfric demonstrated all forms through a complete declination of *soror* (sister).¹³³ If Ælfric's inclusion of *virgo* (virgin) also prompted a measure of instruction and learning about the concept of chastity, Ælfric's framework of Latin terms and Old English equivalents appears to have associated girls in particular with *virgo*, using the same vernacular term of reference, *mæden*, to provide a translation for both *virgo* (virgin) and *puella* (girl).¹³⁴

As we have seen above, Ælfric added into his *Excerptiones de arte grammatica anglice* features which were not present in his exemplar, the *Excerptiones de Prisciano*. What has less often been appreciated, however, is that some of these additions relate to religious girls and women. These occasions include an example where Ælfric provided his audience with the relatively new-coined Old English term for a monastic woman, *mynecenu*, a term which had gained currency in the tenth century as a direct equivalent for the male *munuc*, and which might have been as useful in the education of religious girls and women as for religious boys and men.¹³⁵ More significant than this, however, are occasions where Ælfric introduced into a list of examples of nouns of the third declension a series of terms which recognised female holders of monastic offices, including *doctrix* (i.e. female teacher) *lectrix* (i.e. female reader) and *cantrix* (i.e. female choirmaster/cantor).¹³⁶ In fact, Ælfric appears to have deliberately introduced into his school-text an apparatus which connected with the occupations of contemporary religious women. We may find two such examples in a section on pronouns, where he introduced into his *Excerptiones de arte grammatica anglice* Latin and Old English terms for 'seamstress' or for women who embroidered or fashioned cloth (*sartix, seamystre*) and where he introduced a paradigmatic phrase describing 'those who spin wool' in order to weave cloth (*illae nent lanam, illarum vestis est/hi spinnað wulle,*

---

132 BT: n. *mægden:* 'a maiden, girl, virgin'.
133 EGA, pp. 24-6, at p. 111.
134 EGA, pp. 16-17, 37, at 17.
135 EGA, p. 151; for more on this vocabulary, see Foot, *Veiled Women I*, p. 100.
136 EGA, p. 48 and again at p. 71; compare with the solitary example of a masculine *doctor doctoris* in the *Excerptiones*, c. 219, p. 118 and compare also c. 272, p. 132.

heora hrægl is).¹³⁷ Indeed, we also find examples where Ælfric described women who gave sermons (*ab istis mulieribus audivimus sermonem*), and where he appears to have introduced into a section on adverbs a paradigmatic sentence relating to Christ as a spiritual 'bridegroom' (*uti sponsus, swaswa brydguma*).¹³⁸

If these examples provide tentative grounds for establishing a connection to religious girls and women, there is much less room to doubt that Ælfric had intended to refer to girl religious in a paradigmatic sentence describing how the 'religious woman watches over her girls when teaching' (*ipsa monialis vigilat docendo puellas, seo mynecene wacað tæcende ðam mædencildum*).¹³⁹ Added to this, however, and perhaps more than any other single addition which could give visibility to communities of religious girls and women in the school-text, we should recognise Ælfric's decision to introduce into a section concerning *gentilia*, or adjectives signifying communities or groups, the example of *wilteniensis vel wiltunisc* - Latin and Old English equivalent adjectives which described those who 'belonged to the town of Wilton'.¹⁴⁰

Ælfric's mention of Wilton is striking, but its significance has perhaps not enjoyed the recognition which it has deserved. It is very likely original to the *Excerptiones de arte grammatica anglice*, it being very unlikely to have come from any continental exemplar. It would also seem to have been included with a particular interest to involve religious girls and women; its presence here, therefore, is surprising for a school-text which scholars have otherwise tended to associate closely, if not exclusively, with the instruction of religious boys. While it could be explained away with a view to that male audience, and understood as part of a desire on Ælfric's part to ensure that boys could identify houses of religious women, its presence in the context of the *Excerptiones de arte grammatica anglice* would also make it one of the most visible examples of recognition of a community

---

137 For *sartor, sartix, seamystre*, see EGA, p. 190; compare *Excerptiones*, c. 119, p. 240. For those who spin wool see also EGA, p. 97 (my translation).
138 EGA, pp. 97-8; compare *Excerptiones*, c. 13, p. 164. For 'as a bridegroom' see EGA, p. 229; compare *Excerptiones*, c. 47-8, p. 264. DOE: n. *brydguma*: 'husband, bridegroom, suitor, mystically, epithet for Christ, in relation to a holy woman as bride, in relation to the Church as bride'.
139 EGA, p. 151 (my translation); compare with *Excerptiones*, pp. 124-5.
140 EGA, p. 13; compare *Excerptiones*, c. 12, p. 64.

of religious girls and women in any school-text on Latin grammar known to have been composed in this period. The connection of this work with religious girls and women who occupied Wilton Abbey is clear. Indeed, as clear as we could expect to find in a contemporary context. By referring to it, Ælfric would seem to have considered that that community would have been of interest to his audience, and this point, taken together with references which add to the visibility of girls and women, contributes to the idea that it served in their houses. These indications only point us tentatively in this direction of course, but these elements do at least allow us to consider that the *Excerptiones de arte grammatica anglice* played a more significant role. Indeed, they allow us to consider that it may even have helped to foster something approaching an historically unprecedented elementary grammatical 'curriculum' in the emerging and increasingly cohesive polity of England, contributing significantly to meeting the declared ideals of uniformity which, as we have seen in the introduction to this book, Bishop Æthelwold of Winchester, key leader in the kingdom-wide reorganisation of religious life known as 'the monastic reform', had articulated in the *Regularis Concordia*.

CHAPTER FOUR: ADOLESCENCE AND ADULTHOOD

This chapter focusses on the formative influences of monastic adolescents and asks how oblates became adults. It assesses the role of rites of profession which allowed children to confirm their oblation, and it explores how children might have become adults in the absence of or in addition to the experience of any single ritual event. In doing so, it leans on the researches of Shannon Lewis-Simpson by considering that adulthood in the early medieval period can be treated as a status which needed to be 'acquired' through multiple factors with various social, chronological, cognitive, emotional, motor, and biological aspects. It is with this in mind, that this chapter therefore also assesses the significance of experiences in adolescence which depended on disciplinary, liturgical, and literary spheres encountered in previous chapters.[1]

This chapter also gives attention to questions relating to monastic and church careers, and asks whether the prospect of a 'future' development might have also had a role in signposting the emergence of religious children into religious adulthood. This multi-focus approach lends itself to producing somewhat unsatisfying conclusions perhaps, and allows us only to gauge the different ways in which contemporary religious children may have entered into adulthood between the tenth and twelfth centuries. But this approach is appropriate to a study which is concerned with understanding an incomplete human life-cycle. It recognises the

---

1 Shannon Lewis-Simpson, 'The Challenges of Quantifying Youth and Age in the Medieval North', in *Northern World: Youth and Age in the Medieval North*, ed. Shannon Lewis-Simpson (Leiden, 2008), p. 4.

multi-directional nature of evidence for children's lives and it represents the uncertainty of future experience. It is partly for these reasons, however, that I provide another anchor to arguments entertained in this chapter, and indeed throughout my work as a whole, by reserving space at the very end of this chapter to consider surviving evidence of children's "Voice".

Anglo-Saxon England: The end(s) of boyhood

We can first ask whether religious boys emerged into adulthood by virtue of experiencing a single ritual event which conferred that status. There are problems with assuming that Anglo-Saxon boys would have *needed* to acquire a full monastic status equivalent to a senior monk of course. As we have seen in the introduction Æthelwold's *Old English Rule* insisted on the use of oaths in order to secure the religious entry of children into late Anglo-Saxon monasteries, and this evidence suggests that he had considered child monks as permanent members of contemporary communities. The opening lines of Ælfric of Eynsham's *Colloquium* disclose this too. Katherine O'Brien O'Keeffe has argued, for example, that the *Colloquium* not only gives us a window onto Ælfric's irrevocable view of oblation but shows that Ælfric had encouraged boys to identify themselves as professed as well:[2]

> Professus sum monachus
> psallam omni die septem sinaxes cum fratribus
> et occupatus sum lectionibus et cantu.[3]

Evidence for continued study of this section by generations of teachers and students in the form of new copies and vernacular glosses indicates

---

[2] For the original scholarship, see Katherine O'Brien O'Keeffe, *Stealing Obedience: Narratives of Agency and Identity in Later Anglo-Saxon England* (Toronto, 2012), chapter 2 'Esto quod es: Ælfric's Colloquy and the Imperatives of Monastic Identity', pp. 94-150. For a more recent discussion see also, Rebecca Stephenson, *The Politics of Language: Byrhtferth, Ælfric, and the Multilingual Identity of the Benedictine Reform* (Toronto, 2015), chapter 5: 'The Politics of Ælfric's Prefaces', pp. 135-8, esp. pp. 153-5.
[3] ÆlfColl, p. 19: 'I am a professed monk. I sing seven times every day with the brothers, and I am kept busy with reading and singing' (my translation).

that Ælfric's position remained current long after he was writing.[4] The evidence of the *Colloquia* of Ælfric Bata also supports this analysis. The *Colloquia* express Bata's position on oblation in very different ways to his teacher, and in ways which depend on the significance of the terminology he used to describe religious children and religious adults. Ælfric Bata allowed the occasional Latin diminutive *fraterculi* to throw light on differences in age between boys and men, for example, but in all other cases he equated boys with seniors, confirming his acceptance of their shared status by describing children and adults through the same fraternal vocabulary (i.e. *frater*).[5]

If Æthelwold's, Ælfric's, and Bata's shared position on the irrevocability of the oblation ritual was upheld for the remainder of the late Anglo-Saxon period, we should be careful not to preclude entirely the possibility that the Anglo-Saxon position on oblation was mixed, and perhaps as mixed as the already inconsistent body of church canons on oblation which we encountered in the introduction to this work, and which the Anglo-Saxons had inherited from Carolingian Europe. It remains a possibility that some Anglo-Saxon religious adopted a ritual mechanism for signposting boys' emergence into adulthood by virtue of observing closely documents which were drawn up shortly after the Council of Aachen in c.817. These documents introduced into England church canons declaring the irrevocability of child oblation rituals while also requiring *pueri* to undergo a ritual to 'confirm' (*confirmare*) their religious commitment at a vaguely defined 'age of understanding' (*in tempore intelligibili*).[6]

In the absence of evidence for the observance of an elevation ritual in

---

4   Joyce Hill identifies three versions of Ælfric of Eynsham's *Colloquium*, one of which acquired an apparatus of Old English glosses in the eleventh century, see Joyce Hill, 'Winchester Pedagogy and the *Colloquy* of Ælfric', *Leeds Studies in English* n. s. 29 (1998), pp. 137-52.
5   E.g. ÆlfBColl, pp. 80, 84, 92, 110, 120, 160-1.
6   *Collectio Capitularis*, CCM I, c. 48, 529. See also de Jong, *In Samuel's Image*, pp. 35, 46-7. A copy of this capitulary can be found in CCCC MS 57, fols. 37r-41v: 'ut puerum pater aut mater tempore oblationis offerant ad altare, et petitionem pro eo coram laicis testibus faciant, quam tempore intelligibili regulam observare promiserit, ipse puer confirmet/that the father or mother in the time of oblation should offer the boy at the altar, and make their petition for him before lay witnesses, which the boy will confirm at the age of reason [and] promise to observe the Rule', (transcription and translation are my own).

later Anglo-Saxon monasteries, we can only turn to consider alternative mechanisms of transition, and ask whether closures in the gaps in the daily round which had set boys apart from seniors might have played a role in children's emergence into adulthood before the Norman Conquest instead. For this, we can return to explore evidence seen in chapter one, concerning monastic discipline and conditions of behavioural learning. As I have explored previously, boy oblates and men living at the Old Minster appear not to have been expected to observe the same daily round. The *Regularis Concordia* points to differences in their conditions of supervision and the ways in which experiences of violent punishment depended on the influence of *magistri*. Indeed, it reveals differences in the ways boys participated in the choir, a *schola*, and in fixed routines for eating, for washing, and for using the toilet. But the *Regularis Concordia* also reveals a vacuum of regulation about the nature of the children's own round, obscuring our view of how boys closed those gaps and emerged into structures with which adults were otherwise associated.

We can perhaps turn to a more useful context of evidence which related to the role of the liturgy, and explore how changes in the areas of experience raised in chapter two, and which concern a gap visible between boys' and seniors' liturgical performances in choir, might have provided a mechanism of elevation into adulthood. As we have already seen in the Latin *Regularis Concordia*, at the section where Æthelwold referred to *Tenebrae* on Maundy Thursday, three groups of boys described as *pueri* were required to sing *Kyrie eleison, Christe eleison* and *Domine miserere nobis* from different parts of the church, one after the other. If the Latin *Regularis Concordia* revealed no expectation that that service should or might have been carried out by boys of significantly different ages, however, the same cannot be said of Old English glosses which were later added to a copy of the *Regularis Concordia* which was available at Canterbury in the eleventh century. This copy reveals instead that some houses expected a distinction between boy-singers, and expected that the two individuals who were to sing *Kyrie eleison*, would be *cnapan*, while the four remaining singers, who performed *Christe eleison*, and *Domine miserere nobis*, should be *cildra* or 'children'.[7]

---

7   RC, p. 36. *Die Regularis Concordia*, ed. Kornexl, p. 75, the word by word gloss appears

The decision of the glossator in this copy to describe the first group as *cnapan* is a surprising one. In every other location in the scribe's apparatus of vernacular glosses to the Latin *puer*, the glossator had chosen to use the form *cild*, the direct cognate of the modern 'child' and, incidentally, Æthelwold's own preferred vernacular equivalent to *infans* in his *Old English Rule*.[8] *Cnapa* is and can be a synonym of sorts for *cild*, and roughly translates as 'boy'. It shares a semantic range with *cild*. But this gloss also resists such a reading here. It is also the case that *cnapa* was not an exact replacement, and possessed a usage in vernacular versions of Latin texts which also translated the Latin *adolescens*, meaning that glossators could differentiate our six singers by age, and give visibility in the liturgy to boys who were either approaching puberty or who were approaching an age and status equivalent to early adulthood.

That *cnapa* could mean adolescent and/or young man should not simply be accepted, of course. It is important to demonstrate not only that this was possible, but that there are in fact many cases in the works of Abbot Ælfric of Eynsham, Bishop Æthelwold of Winchester and in their social circles where contemporaries appear to have used the term *cnapa* to describe post-adolescent youths. We find just such a case, for example, in the homiletic writings of Abbot Æfric of Eynsham, and in homily no. 28 of his first series in particular, where he described *cnapa* as boys who could be up to sixteen years old (*þæra cnapena þe binnon syxtyne geara ylde wæron*).[9] We also find this in the writings of Bishop Æthelwold of Winchester, and, indeed, in chapter 30 of his *Old English Rule*, where he translated the original Latin *adulescentiores ætate* with the phrase *stiðe cnapan*.[10] We also find this in sacred texts, and in a careful Old English

---

    as follows: '*Cnapan** on swyðran dæle chores þa mid geswegre singan stæfne/ Let the two boys/*adolescents** on the left part of the choir sing with a sonorous voice' (my translation).

8 *Die Regularis Concordia*, ed. Kornexl, p. 75; DOE: n. *cild:* 'child', n. *cnapa*: (1) 'male child, boy, youth, young man', (2) 'specifically a son', (3) 'a boy servant – of any childhood age', (4) 'a servant of God – of any age'.

9 ÆCHom I, 28, p. 24, line 412: '. . . of the boys who were within sixteen years of age . . .' (my translation).

10 RSB, c. 30, pp. 114-5; OERB, c. 30, pp. 53-4: 'Þonne geonge cild and stiðe cnapan . . . ðe hwonlice understandan magan hu micel wite is þæt man on amansungunge sie, þa ðyllice þonne hy agultað, him man styre oðþe mid swiðlicum fæstenum oðþe mid teartum singellum . . . /When young boys or manly lads, who hardly ever understand

CHAPTER FOUR: ADOLESCENCE AND ADULTHOOD

translation of Genesis (39:10) now preserved in the *Old English Hexateuch* (an attempt to translate the first six books of the Old Testament into the vernacular, and of which Abbot Ælfric of Eynsham was an important contributor). This text provides several clear occasions which demonstrate a contemporary capacity to translate the Latin *adolescentes* with *cnapan*. Indeed, we find an occasion which demonstrates how *cnapa* related to chronology in the Anglo-Saxon view of a male life-cycle, describing Jospeh as a *geong cnapa* when he was 'sixteen years (winters) old' (*Ða iosep wæs syxtyne wintre*). This passage suggests too that *cnapa* were thought at the time to be sexually mature, and might, like Joseph, have been old enough to have been capable of 'illicit sex' (i.e. *7 þæt wif wearþ wraþ þam geongum cnapan 7 he ascunode unriht hæmed = et mulier molesta erat adolescenti et ille recusabat stuprum*).[11]

This context of use of the word *cnapa* for an older boy, and potentially of boys who were of a post-adolescent age in the documentary record, intersects neatly with the distinction a glossator made to the *Regularis Concordia*. It helps us to understand the wider semantic range of *cnapa*, and allows us to give serious consideration to the visibility of older boys and adolescents in the apparatus of liturgical activities represented by surviving copies of the *Regularis Concordia*. It allows us to recognise that contemporaries may have given distinctive roles to the *cild* and to the *cnapa*, and that liturgical services such as *Tenebrae* on Maundy Thursday played a role in communicating transitions between boyhood, adolescence, and adulthood.

Contributing further to the idea that this gloss for *cnapa* gives visibility to older boys if not 'adolescents', we can also turn to a fragmentary copy of the vernacular *Regularis Concordia* which we have seen previously had required 'two [children] of greater age' (*twegen on maran ylde*) to perform *Domine miserere nobis*, at *Tenebrae* on Maundy Thursday.[12]

---

how great a punishment it is to be excommunicated, let them as such, when they commit an error, be disciplined either with a severe fast or with sharp beatings . . .' (my translation). N.b. *stiðe* 'manly' means 'stiff, hard, strong', but I have considered that its purpose here is to emphasise maturation, see BT: adj. *stiþ*

11   DRV Genesis: 39:10: 'Both the woman was importunate with the young man, and he refused the adultery'. Now in MS London BL Cotton Claudius B IV. See *The Old English illustrated Hexateuch: British Museum Cotton Claudius B. IV*, ed. Charles Reginald Dodwell and Peter Clemoes (Copenhagen, 1974), fol. 57v.

12   Zupitza, 'Ein weiteres Bruchstück', p. 6.

This vernacular fragmentary copy reveals a similar response to the same Latin prescription, showing, and perhaps confirming, an expectation of difference in the ages of participants. If we accept that it points towards the participation of significantly 'older' oblates, and, since it occurs in one of only two known fragmentary copies of the vernacular version of the *Regularis Concordia* which attracted feminine word forms, it may even have potential to connect us to religious girls and women, supporting the idea that at some reformed Benedictine houses the liturgy came to play a role in signalling the transitions of girls and boys into adulthood on a parallel basis.

We can also consider the role which might have been played by Latin instruction in signposting the emergence of religious boys into a status of religious adulthood. Pre-Conquest saints' lives provide evidence for a shift in educational focus, suggesting that religious boys were expected to turn at a stage of adolescence away from a pattern of studying Latin grammar and towards a focus on Christian poetry instead. Although Æthelwold had not been offered to a monastery as an oblate, and had acquired a monastic education, apparently from a relatively rudimentary stage, much later in life, Wulfstan Cantor's (d.996) *Vita Sancti Æthelwoldi* framed the bishop's earliest formal education at Glastonbury in these terms, emphasising a shift from learning the art of Latin grammar, to studying Latin metrics, or poetry, and subsequently to reading 'the best-known Christian writers'.[13] Indeed, Wulfstan's own recollections of oblate schooling at the Old Minster in Winchester under Bishop Æthelwold suggest the bishop had been particularly enthusiastic in encouraging him to study Latin verses and metre in adolescence too.[14] Byrhtferth of Ramsey

---

13 Wulfstan Cantor, *Vita Sancti Æthelwoldi*, in *The Life of Saint Æthelwold*, ed. and trans. Michael Winterbottom and Michael Lapidge, OMT (Oxford, 1991), pp. 14-5: 'Didicit namque inibi liberalem grammaticae artis peritiam atque mellifluam metricae rationis dulcedinem, et morae apis prudentissimae; que solet boni odoris arbores circumvolando requirere et iocundi saporis holeribus incumbere, divinorum carpebat flores voluminum. Catholicos quoque et nominatos studiose legebat auctores/At Glastonbury he learned skill in the liberal art of grammar and the honey-sweet system of metrics; like a provident bee that habitually flits around looking for scented trees and settling on greenery of pleasant taste, he laid toll on the flowers of religious books. He was eager to read the best known Christian writers'.

14 Wulfstan Cantor, *Vita Sancti Æthelwoldi*, ed. and trans. Winterbottom and Lapidge, pp. 46-9: 'Dulce namque erat ei adolescentes et iuvenes semper docere et Latinos libros

(fl. 986-1016), schoolmaster to the adolescents of Ramsey Abbey, tells us in his *Enchiridion*, that his own students scrutinised a body of texts by Latin Christian poets as well.[15] In fact, Byrhtferth's school-text is somewhat more instructive, and named a handful of the school-texts which boys had studied there, including the *Disticha Catonis*, the *Epigrammata* of Prosper of Aquitaine, the verses of Aelius Sedulius' *Carmen Paschale* (or The Easter Song), and Arator's versified *Historia Apostolica*. In terms of their contents, many of these school-texts were relatively short in length and had the sort of repetitive structures and shared vocabulary that might have helped with the task of memorisation of different types of verse. They also offered students opportunities to acquire experience in handling biblical scripture.[16]

If educational manuscripts, including Cambridge University Library Gg.5.25, and the surviving body of didactic glosses added to surviving copies of school-texts present in them, give any indication of the extent of use of school-texts, Abbo of Saint Germain-des-Prés' (d.922) *Descidia Parisiacae Polis* (Wars of the City of Paris) (and more specifically, book three) and Bishop Aldhelm of Sherborne's (d.709/10) twinned works, the verse and prose *De Virginitate* (Song/Prose On Virginity), appear to have informed a particular apex of Latin scholarship and literary ambition in late Anglo-Saxon England.[17] Alistair Campbell and Michael Lapidge

---

Anglice eis solvere et regulas grammaticae artis ac metricae rationis tradere et iocundis alloquiis ad meliora hortari/ It was always sweet to him to teach adolescents and youths, translating Latin texts into English for them, and passing on the rules of the arts of grammar and of metrics'.

15 Byrhtferth, *Enchiridion*, ed. Peter Baker and Michael Lapidge, EETS s.s. 15 (Oxford, 1995), pp. 120-1.

16 For some of the most important studies on our educational corpus, see Alan Rigg and Gernot Wieland, 'A Canterbury Classbook of the Mid-Eleventh Century (the "Cambridge Songs" Manuscript)', *ASE* 4 (1975), pp. 113-30; Gernot Wieland, *The Latin Glosses on Arator and Prudentius in Cambridge, University Library MS Gg.5.35* (Toronto, 1983); Patrizia Lendinara, Lorendana Lazzari, and Maria Amalia D'Aronco (eds.), *Form and Content of Instruction in Anglo-Saxon England in the Light of Contemporary Manuscript Evidence* (Turnhout, 2007).

17 Gernot Wieland, 'The Anglo-Saxon manuscripts of Prudentius' *Psychmoachia*', *ASE* 16 (1987), p. 217. Gneuss, *Handlist*, no. 12, pp. 27-8. For all extant copies of the *Descidia Parisicase Polis* [or *Bella Parisiacae Urbis*], see Gneuss, *Handlist*, nos. 12 (27), 93 (36), 252 (53), 435 (77), 438 (77). For more on the uses of hermeneutic texts, see the entry for 'Glossaries' in *Wiley Blackwell Encyclopedia on Anglo-Saxon England*, ed. Lapidge,

have drawn particular attention to the popularity of these three works in fact, and have argued that contemporaries used them as material bases for cultivating a rhythmic and Greek-filled style of Latin composition called 'hermeneutic'.[18]

Although the school of Æthelwold at the Old Minster in Winchester is particularly well known for the cultivation of this elevated Latin style – indeed, the prologue to the *Regularis Concordia* offers some example, and illustrates the prestige and importance which was already being attached to it at the outset of reform – the surviving documentary record suggests that it was cultivated much more widely. Byrhtferth of Ramsey may not have mentioned any study of the works of Abbo or Aldhelm in his *Enchiridion*, but his choice of title for that work (from the Greek equivalent of 'manual'), his very extensive use of Aldhelm's exotic vocabulary, and his similar use of a characteristic rhythm and poetic phraseology in all of his known Latin compositions – including his *Enchiridion*, which he might have begun compiling in his late teens (988x996), his lives of Saints Oswald and Ecgwine, and also his contributions to the *Historia Regum* (c.997x1002) – demonstrate the significance of this Latin style in his own educational training from boyhood.[19]

Scholars such as Rebecca Stephenson and Jonathan Secord-Davis have gone as far as to suggest that the hermeneutic style of which he and several of his contemporaries, including Ælfric Bata, were proficient, had become an identifying feature of the literary works of Benedictine monks in pre-Conquest England.[20] Their studies have been concerned with

---

Blair, Keynes, and Scragg, p. 212.

[18] Alistair Campbell and Michael Lapidge postulate that the study of Aldhelm might have originated at the school of Glastonbury in the 940s, Alistair Campbell, 'Some Linguistic Features of Early Anglo-Latin Verse and its Use of Classical Models', *Transactions of the Philological Society* 11 (1953), pp. 4-5; Lapidge, 'The Study of Latin Texts in Late Anglo-Saxon England I: The Evidence of Latin Glosses', pp. 99-140.

[19] For Michael Lapidge's study of Byrhtferth's Latin style and grecisms, of which 'many were derived from . . . the writings of Aldhelm', see Byrhtferth, *Lives of St Oswald and St Ecgwine*, ed. and trans. Lapidge, p. xlix. Campbell, 'Features of Early Anglo-Latin Verse', pp. 6-9.

[20] Stephenson, *The Politics of Language*, p. 19; Jonathan Davis-Secord, 'Sequences and Intellectual Identity at Winchester', in *Latinity and Identity in Anglo-Saxon Literature*, ed. Rebecca Stephenson and Emily Thornbury, Toronto Anglo-Saxon Series 22 (Toronto: University Press, 2016), passim.

CHAPTER FOUR: ADOLESCENCE AND ADULTHOOD

understanding the relationship between acquired literary style and expressions of religious identity, and they have argued that the hermeneutic style had acquired the qualities of a private register of the Latin language. Indeed, they have argued that it had come to serve the purpose of allowing monastic students to signal to their peers the nature of their upbringing, signifying their possession of an identity as Benedictine monks, and, perhaps, their worthiness for career progression, at a time when monks could expect to dominate the episcopal bench.[21]

If this was the case at Winchester and Ramsey between c.950 and c.1000, it pays to ask too whether and how far similar educational trajectories might have informed the experiences and literary identities of adolescent monks who grew up at houses which are overlooked by virtue of the fact that they have not left behind evidence of outstanding scholarship. We can turn, for example, to consider a booklist which survives from Peterborough Abbey from shortly after its (re)foundation in c.970 (then known as *Medeshamstede* or *Burh*).[22] This booklist suggests that Peterborough held very few school-texts at an early stage, but insofar as we can observe this lack when compared to evidence of learning at much larger religious houses, the library would still appear to have allowed at that time for a limited study of intermediate versified Latin texts. Indeed, it would seem to have supported the study of Latin poetry through an untitled metrical work on the twelve vices and virtues and a versified version of the *Vita* of Saint Felix. In fact, it would also appear that the library of Peterborough in c.970 was capable of allowing students to study the hermeneutic style, and could support their cultivation in adolescence or early adulthood of a characteristic vocabulary and rhythmic prose through

---

21 Stephenson, *The Politics of Language*, p. 19; Jonathan Davis-Secord, 'Sequences and Intellectual Identity at Winchester', in *Latinity and Identity in Anglo-Saxon Literature*, ed. Rebecca Stephenson and Emily Thornbury (Toronto, 2016), esp. p. 115: [Hermeneutic Latin was the] 'defining feature of Benedictine monasteries in the Anglo-Saxon period [...] Byrhtferth presented knowledge of Latin and mastery of this challenging style as defining features of Benedictine monasteries in Anglo-Saxon England'.

22 See Michael Lapidge, 'Surviving booklists from Anglo-Saxon England', in *Learning and Literature in Anglo-Saxon England, Studies Presented to Peter Clemoes on the Occasion of his Sixty-Fifth Birthday*, ed. Michael Lapidge and Helmut Gneuss (Cambridge, 1985), pp. 52-5.

study of a copy of Abbo of Saint-Germain-des-Prés' *Descidia Parisiacae Polis*.[23] It is worth noting that Abbo's work is a singular representative of this type of study in the Peterborough booklist. The absence of any other supporting school-text, or indeed of any other popular school-text of the late Anglo-Saxon period, is more indicative of poverty in the material base at that foundation. But the presence of this school-text would suggest that Peterborough had co-ordinated to some extent with a set of educational expectations pursued at the largest Benedictine houses of the late tenth century, enabling students to acquire a literary identity which had come to be seen as a signifier of good Latinity in England before the Conquest.

It is possible too that the emergence of a number of boys into senior communities was shaped by mechanisms of promotion to holy orders. The *Regularis Concordia* required brethren to minister at the altars of churches and to support priests who celebrated two daily masses. Indeed, it anticipated that members of religious communities would need to fill positions as priests, deacons, and sub-deacons, serving duties on a rotational basis each week.[24] The *Regularis Concordia* never directly referred to boys in relation to these roles. But there is evidence to suggest that boys were allowed to train for them, and were given opportunities to learn by imitation how to approach holy spaces, hold or clean ritual items, and carry out the complex of rituals which would make a candidate suitable for ordination once they had reached a canonical age.

The evidence base for this is not especially rich. Christopher Jones' study of an erasure of the word *puer* visible in a surviving copy of Ælfric's *Epistula ad monachos* has shown that Abbot Ælfric of Eynsham might, on one occasion, have expected a boy to carry out duties proper to acolytes or sub-deacons, supporting the priest who celebrated the morrow mass on Palm Sunday.[25] But the idea that contemporary houses enabled boys to participate in sacraments and train for ordination depends more on the significance of the evidence of contemporary saints' lives. Byrhtferth of

---

23 Lapidge 'Surviving booklists', pp. 52-5.
24 RC, pp. 40, 47, 64; EME, pp. 124-5.
25 EME, pp. 124-5: 'Interim dum matutinalis missa canitur, agatur a sacerdote cum quodam puero* processio in claustro/While the matutinal mass is being sung, the procession in the cloister shall be carried out by a priest, with a boy as server'; Christopher Jones notes that this mention of a boy* appears to have been later erased from the MS.

Ramsey and Eadmer of Canterbury both framed the acquisition of holy orders in this way in their versions of the *Vita Sancti Oswaldi*, for example, treating ordination as a key watershed in their narratives on Oswald's religious life-cycle. Eadmer in particular went as far as to suggest that Oswald had been promoted to the diaconate while still in his adolescence (*decanus factus adolescens*), and used the moment of describing Oswald's elevation in order to emphasise the shift which it brought about, enabling his emergence from being a student and from being subject to the guidance of seniors, to being a teacher and a model of heavenly discipline for those senior to him in age (*studio disciplinae caelestis*).[26]

Anglo-Norman England: The end(s) of boyhood

If the Carolingian Councils at Aachen in c.817 had led to the fragmentation of a position on the irrevocability of child oblation in England, evidence for the conditionality of oblation and for the emergence of a ritual event which signposted boys' acceptance into an adult religious society only seems to materialise after the Norman Conquest. This evidence emerges in the more detailed prescriptive context of a chapter of the *Constitutiones* of Canterbury, where Lanfranc articulated a Carolingian expectation that boys at Christ Church would need to undergo a ritual of profession upon reaching the age of fifteen:[27]

> Cum vero adulta etate facturus professionem fuerit, fiant ei cetera que superius debere fieri converso iam diximus. Hoc enim quod modo factum est, iterari non oportet.[28]

This adulthood profession appears to have been intended to secure boys

---

26 Byrhtferth, *Vita Sancti Oswaldi*, in *Vita Sancti Oswaldi*, in *Lives of St Oswald and St Ecgwine*, ed. and trans. Michael Lapidge, pp. 50-1. Eadmer, *Vita Sancti Oswaldi*, in *Eadmer of Canterbury: Lives and Miracles of Saints Oda, Dunstan, and Oswald*, ed. and trans. Benjamin J. Muir and Andrew J. Turner, OMT (Oxford, 2006), pp. 224-5.
27 De Jong, *In Samuel's Image*, p. 188.
28 *Constitutiones*, c. 105, pp. 164-5: 'When he has grown up and is to make his profession, all is done as described previously for the case of one coming into the monastery from the world: for the part which has been done already should not be repeated'.

to the religious life, differing in form from both an oblation and the profession of adult novices. Eadmer of Canterbury's (1060-1126) *Vita Sancti Anselmi* confirms the emergence of this ritual of profession for oblates in a near contemporary account of the elevation of Osbern, a boy who appears to have entered the Norman Abbey of Bec under Anselm. Eadmer disclosed that Osbern underwent a ritual which secured his status after oblation (*oblatio*) and which he and his contemporaries at Canterbury appear to have called a 'profession' (*professio*). Indeed, his account suggests that he had considered that this ritual was similar to oblation, and was believed to have had a similar sacramental quality and a purifying efficacy.[29] Insofar as Eadmer describes a ritual which he believed had been observed in Normandy, however, the contemporary manuscript record also preserves evidence for ritual *ordines* which seem to organise rituals of profession used in England, and in a Benedictine context outside of Archbishop Lanfranc's Benedictine Chapter at Canterbury. We find this, for example, in the case of the *Pontifical* of Bishop Samson of Worcester (1096-1112) which was compiled for use at his Benedictine Chapter after the death of Bishop Wulfstan.[30] This *ordo*, which now appears in the unprinted manuscript, Cambridge, Corpus Christi College, MS 146, under a section entitled, 'the blessing of a boy as a monk' (*benedictio pueri in monachum*), initially appears to offer a framework for oblation, but presents us with a formulation which does not appear to be consistent with the form described in the *Regula Benedicti* or indeed, anywhere else in contemporary documentary record:

> Ego frater N[omen] offero hunc puerum illum cum oblatione in manu atque petitione ... Illum abbatis presentia trado coram testibus regulariter permansurum ... promitto cum iureiurando coram

---

[29] Eadmer, *Vita Sancti Anselmi*, in *The Life of St. Anselm, Archbishop of Canterbury*, ed. and trans. Richard William Southern, OMT (rev. ed., Oxford, 1972), c. 10, pp. 18-9: 'Priusquam a parentibus ad servitium Dei in monasterium offerretur commiserate [...] post oblationem parentum ante suam professionem fecerat illum accusavit [...] post professionem ante obitum/[His sins were wiped clean, which he had made] before he was offered by his parents to the service of God in the monastery [...] and the sins he had committed since he made his profession [were wiped clean by his vows] [...] and [those sins he made] after his profession before his death [were wiped clean by his confession]'.

[30] CCCC, MS 146, pp. 56-59.

CHAPTER FOUR: ADOLESCENCE AND ADULTHOOD

> Deo et sancta Maria quod nunquam per suspectam personam nec quolibet modo per rerum mearum facultates aliquando egrediendi ei de monasterio tribuam occasionem.[31]

In some respects, its wording resembles the petition set out in chapter 59 of the *Regula Benedicti*, but the *ordo* opens unexpectedly, revealing discrepancies which indicate that it was intended for a different purpose. It is voiced by a professed monk rather than by a parent (*Ego . . . frater*). It does not require any promise to be given by secular parents or guardians in order to fasten the child to the monastic life. Indeed, it seems to have assumed that the boys who would have been subject to its ritual would also have already been members of that community:

> Adesto domine supplicationibus nostris et hunc famulum n[omen] benedicere dignare cui in sancto tuo nomine habitum sacrae religionis imponimus ut te largiente devotus in ecclesia persistere et vitam percipere mereatur eternam.[32]

This closing intercession, assigned to the abbot (or bishop) and undertaken in the presence of the community, appears to have required boys to promise that they would *stay* in their specific monastic community. It is the presence of the Latin verb *persistere* which suggests this intended purpose, grounding a consideration that the ritual was a 'confirmation' ritual. This ritual could have taken place after a period of time during which boys had been housed and educated, and once they had either reached a sufficient threshold of compliance with monastic norms or attained an 'age of understanding'.

Attitudes to irrevocable oblation were likely to have been mixed too,

---

31 CCCC MS 146, p. 56: 'I brother [name] offer this boy with oblation in my hand and with petition . . . I give this [boy] in perpetuity in accordance with the rule in the presence of the abbot and before witnesses . . . [and] I promise under oath before God and holy Mary [that] never through me nor through any appointed person nor by any means of mine will I give occasion for the boy to leave the monastery', (my transcription and translation).

32 CCCC MS 56, p. 56: 'Attend our prayers O Lord, and deign to bless this [name] on whom we confer the habit of holy religion in your holy name so that having vowed to remain/stay in the church and through your assistance he may deserve to receive eternal life', (my transcription and translation).

however, and evidence for contemporary views on the irrevocability of oblation would suggest that they remained mixed long into the twelfth and thirteenth centuries. First, the documentary base of the twelfth century allows us to identify several houses where an irrevocable line on child oblation might have continued to be upheld.

From c.1030 onwards, generations of authors contributed to a list recording the oblations of some 129 boys (*pueri*) in a document known as the *Liber Vitae* or 'Book of Life' (see cover for prefatory illustrations), compiled at the New Minster (later renamed Hyde Abbey) in Winchester. This list, which gives us a record of all those who became permanent members of the community as monks, offers powerful insight into the irrevocability of oblation practices at that house in the late Anglo-Saxon period and until the late twelfth century, when the record abruptly stops.

Indeed, careful study of the document gives further insight still. For example, by grouping the list of names by phases we can confidently associate with recruitment under different abbots, we can ask and potentially answer important questions about recruitment patterns *before* and *after* the Norman Conquest. The challenge of grouping is greater in the pre-Conquest Anglo-Saxon portions of the list, where all individuals were named at the moment of their entry into the community. But we are helped by the additions of post-Conquest writers. They carefully underlined the precise moments in the list that a new abbacy began, and so which monks he "received" (*ipsos monachos ipse recepit*):

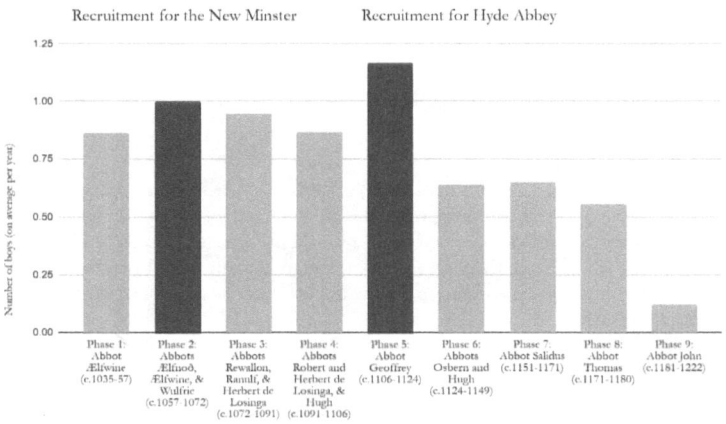

CHAPTER FOUR: ADOLESCENCE AND ADULTHOOD

Assessment of recruitment in these given chronologies reveals previously unexplored but possibly quite significant evidence of increases in oblate recruitment in two distinctive periods, with the first immediately surrounding the Norman Conquest, and the second in the years immediately following the refoundation of the community at Hyde Abbey (c.1109-10). The document therefore not only gives a clear picture of continuity in ideas of irrevocability after the Conquest, continually listing boys (or *pueri*) as permanent members of the monastic community after the Conquest and revealing an all-time hiatus in oblation under the abbacy of Geoffrey, but it potentially reveals how oblations played a vital role in times of extreme stress around the Conquest and of refoundation at Hyde Abbey. Evidence for an uptick in recruitment of oblates around the time of the Conquest should prompt us to entertain the possibility that local Anglo-Saxon landholders, at sudden risk of losing their property to incoming Normans, may have used the irrevocability of oblation as a calculated survival mechanism. We could imagine, for example, landholders offering their children along with a portion of land to monastic houses in order to safeguard the lifestyle of their sons and secure some future influence and status for themselves as benefactors of a powerful religious institution.[33]

---

33 *Liber Vitae of the New Minster and Hyde Abbey, Winchester: British Library Stowe 944: Together with leaves from British Library Cotton Vespasian A. VIII and British Library Cotton Titus D. XXVII*, ed. Simon Keynes (Copenhagen, 1996), fols. 21v-23v: I have organised these groups into "phases" rather than strictly according to abbacy primarily due to the lack of precision in the earliest portion of the list of the beginning and end of each abbacy. To overcome this difficulty, I resolved to include into the first phase of the list all *pueri* who were listed up to Ælfwine II (1064–1066)– who entered New Minster as a boy, later became abbot, and died at the Battle of Hastings. Given he must have entered in childhood, and died an abbot in 1066, we can safely assume he entered the house in the 1030s or 40s, under the abbacy of Ælfwine I (1035–1057). I have made a further assumption, given the same hand which entered Ælfwine *puer* also appears to have written the names of the *pueri* Wulfmaer, Wulfric, Egelric, and Ælfric, that is more likely than not that those four boys entered New Minster at a similar time, and could therefore be included in, and provide a *terminus post quem* for the first phase, associated with Abbot Ælfwine I. The second phase is therefore constructed on the basis of a subsequent change in hand, suggesting a new phase in recruitment, and the addition of "Riwallonus Abbas" (referring to Abbot Riwallon c.1072-1091) which was entered in a later hand, signalling when this abbot took over the community. Trusting in the change of hand, and contemporary perceptions of recruitment, we can therefore

Equally, continuities of irrevocable oblation are visible in the post-Conquest portion of the *Liber Vitae* simply by virtue of the fact it openly recorded hundreds of *pueri* as monks - including one appropriately named *Deodatus*, meaning literally. 'I have been given to God'. This list continued into the abbacy of John Sutcliff c.1178x1222, and only visibly ends somewhere under his rule with a final two entries for *pueri*, whose ages as 'boys' appear to have been retrospectively erased, or hidden, after they had entered – perhaps with a view to masking the persistence of irrevocable positions in a time leading up to the Synod of Oxford c.1222 which forbade rituals from tying boys permanently to a house until they reached at least 15.[34]

Other sources, relating to other Benedictine houses, are of course necessary to confirm that oblations continued across England. Richard of Ely (d.1189), author of the *Liber Eliensis* in the late-twelfth century, still described boys of that house as professed monks at the time he was writing.[35] The twelfth-century *Chronicon Monasterii de Abingdon* categorised 'boys' as 'monks' well into the twelfth century as well, and, in the cases of a knight of Henry I's called Gilbert Basset who had his son Robert made a monk of Abingdon (*Robertum monachum in hac ecclesia fecit*), and of another knight called Norman, who petitioned for his son Eudo to be made a monk at Abingdon under Abbot Vincent (1120-30), the *Chronicon de Abingdon* suggests that boys were being secured irreversibly to the oblate status simply by virtue of having been clothed in the monastic habit.[36]

Where oblations were still considered irrevocable in this way, and where rites of profession might not have provided a significant watershed in boys' religious lives between childhood and adulthood, we can expect that other mechanisms of elevation, including those which depended on the closure of gaps between the routines of boys and seniors on a daily

---

construct a "most likely" picture of recruitment in a second phase from c.1057–1072. This phase remains unhelpfully broad, crossing the period of the Norman Conquest. But it is clear that recruitment levels were elevated in this period, even when calculated on an average-per-year basis. This formed a paper I gave to the IMC at Leeds, 2015.

34 *Liber Vitae*, fols. 22v, 23r, 23v.

35 Richard of Ely accounts for the presence of boy monks during the episcopacy of Nigel of Ely (1133-1169), see *Liber Eliensis*, ed. Blake, bk ii, p. 169, and bk. iii, p. 379.

36 *Chronicon Monasterii de Abingdon*, ed. Joseph Stephenson (London, 1858), II, pp. 145, 169, 170, 207.

CHAPTER FOUR: ADOLESCENCE AND ADULTHOOD

round, might have continued to be significant. In terms which build upon the environmental and disciplinary structures outlined in chapter one for example, the *Constitutiones* allow us to consider the importance of a moment in boys' lives of the role of elevation in a hierarchy of seating in the choir, and of the movement of boys from their own places and conditions of supervision, into spaces and systems of seating which were shared by and which signalled peership with seniors.[37] Lanfranc's consuetudinary reveals this elevation in the choir, for example, in prescriptions relating to the services of Maundy Thursday, where he required boys to observe different arrangements from adults. Here, Lanfranc required youths or *iuvenes* to enter and stand with seniors (*iuvenes vero qui in custodia sunt mixtim sint in ordine seniorum*), and in a way which expected youths to adhere to a form of seating signalling their acquisition of a senior liturgical status.[38]

Lanfranc's *Constitutiones* also provide evidence for an intermediary round which was followed by youths and which may have facilitated a gradual transition into senior routines between boyhood and adulthood. We can see this where the *Constitutiones* required youths to experience different, and indeed potentially more intensive supervisory conditions from boys for example. Lanfranc required youths to be tutored and guarded by different groups of *magistri*, and he anticipated that every two would either continue to be overseen by at least one *magister*, or, if the community were large enough, that each youth would have his own (or more) guardian(s) (*singuli singulos, aut plures, sit anta copia est, custodes habeant*).[39] He expected that each youth would either continue to share a lantern with another youth, or, if resources permitted, that each youth would be given their own lantern. Indeed, in addition to this, Lanfranc required youths to use their own 'ward room' (*locus custodie*), a

---

37 For the role of the seating hierarchy, see *Constitutiones*, c. 107, pp. 168-9.
38 *Constitutiones*, c. 28-31, pp. 42-3: 'In matutinis laudibus, cum incipiunt psalmum *Laudate Dominum de celis*, vadant magistri inter infantes, qui et versi sint ad priores, sicut et ipsi infantes; iuvenes vero, qui in custodia sunt, mixtim sint in ordine seniorum/ At lauds, when the psalm *Laudate Dominum* is begun, the masters shall join the children and face the seniors with them; the young monks under ward shall be mingled with the seniors'.
39 *Constitutiones*, c. 110, pp. 174-5: 'They have each one or more guardians, if this is practicable'.

room which appears to have been set apart from the *schola* and which was governed by its own *magistri*.[40] The *Constitutiones* suggest therefore that youths were to be isolated from both boys and seniors, and were subject to more prescriptive regulations than had their less visible Anglo-Saxon counterparts, and in a way that also marked their transition away from boyhood and towards a status which approached that of adulthood.

Maria Lahaye-Geusen has previously drawn attention to areas of Lanfranc's *Constitutiones* that reveal discrepancies in activities between boys and youths and which also seem likely to have played a role in signposting transitions into adulthood. She has noted in particular, for example, that differences in the duties of boys and youths manifest themselves in the *Constitutiones* in terms which restricted boys – which forbade boys from attending to the dying during Divine Offices and from preparing dead bodies for burial – but which lifted restrictions for all older groups; expecting youths to take up psychologically more challenging tasks, like having to wash the deceased bodies of former brethren.[41] We find more evidence suggesting that the daily round played a role in integrating youths into a senior round in relation to prescriptions which concerned their diet, for example. Indeed, Lanfranc appears not to have permitted youths to enjoy privileges which we have seen were allowed to boys, such as an earlier

---

40 *Constitutiones*, c. 110, pp. 174-5: 'Singuli singulas laternas in nocte ferant/each one carries a lantern by night' and 'Extra locum custodie sue sine custode nusquam procedant /They shall go nowhere outside their ward room without one of their guardians and also 'Preter abbatem, priorem, magistrosque eorum, nulli liberum sit in loco custodie eorum deputato sedere/Save for abbot, prior, and their masters no one may sit in the place set aside as their ward-room'.

41 See the chapter on 'Kinderkrankeiten' in Maria Lahaye Geusen, *Das Opfer der Kinder*, pp. 320-4. For this evidence of difference in the rounds of boys and youths in relation to the provision of Last Rites and to the washing of the corpse of a dead brother, see *Constitutiones*, c. 112, pp. 180-3: 'Remanentibus in choro infantibus cum magistris suis et aliquibus fratribus quibus iussum fuerit, reliqui omnes ad egrum currant/ If someone is dying during mass or an office, the children and masters stay in choir to maintain the daily offices while all the rest go to the bedside of the dying brother', and also c.112, pp. 182-3: 'Portetur corpus ad lavandum ab iis de quorum ordine fuit id est sacerdos a sacerdotibus, diaoncus a diaconis et sic in reliquis ordinibus, conversus a conversis; infans tamen non ab infantibus sed a conversis/The corpse shall be taken for washing by those of the same order as the dead man, that is, priests for a priest, deacons for a deacon, and so forth converses for converses. A boy's corpse shall, however, not be washed by children but by converses'.

CHAPTER FOUR: ADOLESCENCE AND ADULTHOOD

meal before Vespers on Holy Saturday, or, indeed, an automatic entitlement to a breakfast or interval meal called the *mixtum*.[42] We find evidence of change in boys' rounds in Lanfranc's section on shaving or tonsuring as well.[43] Here, Lanfranc required 'oblate youths' (*iuvenes nutriti*) to be separated from one another and to adhere to procedures which differentiated them from both younger boys (*pueri*) and seniors (*seniores*). Lanfranc expected that youths would know how to shave but required that they should not shave one another, and would only be permitted to shave their own dedicated custodians in turn.[44] Allowing youths to shave masters allowed for a far greater level of responsibility to youths than he had given to boys of younger age, but in addition to this, Lanfranc also allowed that youths could be shaved by another trustworthy senior monk if their own guardians were unable. In doing so, Lanfranc reveals too that the practice of shaving had a role in allowing youths to leave behind routines of boyhood, and indeed, the *Constitutiones* suggest that shaving – and we could postulate further perhaps that the shaving of beards, a contemporary signifier of maturity, might have become important – played a role in allowing youths to step much more closely into the social orbit of adults too.

Evidence of the integration of youths into the senior liturgical round takes a form more familiar to us from the *Regularis Concordia*, and in a

---

42 To remind readers of this allowance, see *Constitutiones*, c. 46-9, pp. 70-1: 'Fiat oratio vespertina, qua facta vadant *infantes* in refectorium, si aliqui adeo parvi sunt ut usque post Vesperas expectare non possint'.
43 *Constitutuones*, c. 94, pp. 136-9, esp. pp. 138-9: 'Iuvenes qui sunt in custodia custodes suos radant, et custodes ipsos iuvenes. Quod si custos nequiverit, aut nescierit radere, roget aliquem maturum fratrem, ut eum radat, ipse tamen custodiens ipsum iuxta eum sedeat. Iuvenes quoque, sive nutriti, sive de seculo venientes, utrique tamen extra huiusmodi custodiam existentes, non presumant ut alter alterum radat, sed seniores ab illis, et illi a senioribus radantur/The juniors under ward shall shave their guardians, and the guardians shall shave their juniors. If a guardian knows not how, or is physically unable to shave, he shall ask a brother of mature age to shave his junior for him, but he himself shall sit by meanwhile. The juniors no longer under ward, whether alumni of the house or those who have come from the world shall not presume to shave one another, but shall shave, and be shaved by, senior monks', and for the sake of comparison, on boys 'Magistri pueros radant, et ipsi a pueris radantur, si tamen huiusmodi scientiam habent/ The masters shall shave their children and they shall be shaved by them, if they know how to do it'.
44 *Constitutuones*, c. 94, pp. 136-9.

way that depends upon a similar vacuum of evidence. To be clear, the invisibility of youths is not absolute. Lanfranc does in fact provide a single context in chapter no. 73 where he expected *iuvenes* to play a specific role in singing the antiphons at Vespers on feast days of the third rank, suggesting that the liturgy at Canterbury played a role in signposting an individual's emergence into 'youth'. But the rest of Lanfranc's prescriptive context makes it difficult to say and understand much more.[45] We can perhaps consider that Lanfranc's silence on the participation of youths was deliberate, and stemmed from a desire to ensure that boys merged seamlessly into duties associated with *seniores*. If this was the case, however, we cannot confirm it. We can only consider that the liturgy might have played a function in signposting a radical shift in boys' performances as they matured, requiring them not only to abandon conditions of supervision encountered in earlier chapters and with which they had associated since their oblation, but to participate in the choir in ways which depended upon a corporate liturgical identity and on prescriptions otherwise directed as seniors.

Our picture of educational transitions after the Norman Conquest is complicated by the fact that a large number of saints' lives composed in this period took as their subjects saintly men and women who had been educated within an Anglo-Saxon monastic culture. In cases where no pre-Conquest life for a saint survives, our sources make it difficult to distinguish records as being representative of earlier Anglo-Saxon or early Anglo-Norman monastic practice. There are some post-Conquest lives which appear to show practices that might even have bridged pre-Conquest and post-Conquest experiences. We may find one such case in William of Malmesbury's *Vita Sancti Wulfstani*. This saint's life allows us to consider that students' emergence into religious adulthood might have been signposted by the movement of students from one house to another. While describing at first the pre-Conquest movement of the young Wulfstan and his departure from Evesham Abbey for training at the larger Abbey at Peterborough on the cusp of adolescence, William of

---

45 *Constitutiones*, c.73, pp. 98-9: 'Antiphonas super psalmos ad Vesperas imponant iuvenes, quibus cantor precepit. Cetera agantur, sicut ad Vesperas precedentis diei/ At Vespers those of the young monks who are so directed by the cantor shall begin the antiphons'. These feasts are listed on pp. 98-9.

CHAPTER FOUR: ADOLESCENCE AND ADULTHOOD

Malmesbury also added that Wulfstan's own student, Nicholas, had gone to Canterbury in c.1080 as well, playing a role in transmitting knowledge of Lanfranc's customs to Worcester in the years before he was promoted to the post of prior at Worcester (1116-1124). In doing so, William reveals to us that such movements might have had a secondary function in marking the lives of adolescents, and might have done so before and after the Norman Conquest as well.[46]

Most saints' lives present a picture of educational experience suggesting that Latin instruction continued to shape adolescents in ways which depended on a shift in the focus of boys' Latin studies. Eadmer of Canterbury introduced a division into his version of the *Vita Sancti Oswaldi*, for example, separating the earliest period of his education on 'the knowledge of secular books' (*scientia librorum saecularium*), from a later period of 'reading the pages of biblical scripture' (*pagines divinarum litterarum*).[47] Some lives express a trajectory of Latin instruction which differs slightly from this model, and William of Malmesbury's recollection of his own education serves to remind us that Latin instruction might have played a subtly different role in the lives of capable Latin students who did not obtain a promotion to higher monastic or church office. William's recollections of his 'early manhood' (*iuventus*), for example, suggest that his adolescence was not only marked by his experience of study of an emerging corpus of pagan texts popular after the Conquest such as Lucan's (d.65) poem *De Bello Civili* (On Civil War), but by a continuation of his studies into areas of a scientific quadrivium.[48] William's experience of Latin instruction appears in fact to have allowed him to continue his Latin reading without obvious terminus, allowing him to range widely, and to 'give an ear to instruction on logic' (*logicam solo auditu libavi*), as well as medicine (*physicam pressius concepi*), and ethics.[49]

---

46 William of Malmesbury, *Vita Sancti Wulfstani*, in *Lives of SS. Wulfstan, Dunstan, Patrick, Benignus and Indract*, ed. and trans. Winterbottom and Thomson, pp. 132-3.
47 Eadmer, *Vita Sancti Oswaldi*, in *Lives and Miracles*, ed. and trans. Muir and Turner, pp. 222-4.
48 William of Malmesbury, *Gesta Regum/History of the English Kings*, ed. and trans. Mynors, Winterbottom, and Thomson, I, pp. 150-2.
49 William of Malmesbury, *Gest Regum/History of the English Kings*, ed. and trans. Mynors, Winterbottom, and Thomson, I, pp. 150-2.

Boys also appear to have been encouraged to acquire and express a different style of Latin literacy after the Norman Conquest. The *Versus allegorici* (or 'Allegorical Verses') composed by Bishop Patrick of Dublin after the Norman Conquest (1074-1084), belonged to a tradition characterised by a hermeneutic vocabulary and rhythm considered in the section above.[50] But Patrick was also among only very few monks, including Osbern of Canterbury and Osbert of Westminster (d.1158), who we know wrote in this style between c.1070 and 1150.[51] Surviving manuscripts and catalogues of school libraries shed light on changes in Latin instruction, and indicate that the period which followed the Conquest in England saw an expansion in the scope of metrical and quadrivial study in Benedictine houses as well as a shift towards the study of school-texts which were valued for a plainer, classical Latin style.[52] Only a small number of manuscripts compiled at particularly conservative houses between the late-eleventh and early-twelfth century give witness to a continued preoccupation with texts popular in pre-Conquest libraries. An un-localised and unprinted manuscript of the second quarter of the twelfth century, now London, British Library MS Harley 4092, preserves copies of Prudentius' *Psychomachia* and Sedulius' *Carmen Paschale* and other hymns, testifying to a degree of continued interest in established authors.[53] A collection from Æthelwold's foundation at Thorney Abbey c.1100, now preserved in Edinburgh, National Library of Scotland MS advocates 18.6.12 and 18.7.8, indicates too that 'hermeneutic' school-texts, such as Abbo of St-Germain's *Descidia Parisiacae Polis*, continued to be influential into the twelfth century.[54] But even in this very conservative compilation, there were classical Latin school-texts, including works by Horace (*Epistulae*),

---

50 Patrick of Dublin, *Versus allegorici,* ed. and trans. Aubrey Gwynn, *Writings of Bishop Patrick of Dublin, 1074-1084* (Dublin, 1955), pp. 89-91, 97.
51 Rodney Thomson, 'Two Versions of a Saint's Life from St Edmund's Abbey: Changing Currents in Twelfth-Century Monastic Style', *Revue Bénédictine* 84 (1974), p. 383.
52 For more on this expansion c.1066 and 1130, see Gameson, *Manuscripts of Early Norman England*, pp. 13, 25-9; Suzanne Reynolds, 'Glossing Horace: Using the Classics in the Medieval Classroom', in *Medieval Manuscripts of the Latin Classics: Production and Use,* ed. Claudine A. Chavannes-Mazel and Margaret Smith (London, 1996), pp. 103-17; Antonia Gransden, 'Traditionalism and Continuity during the Last Century of Anglo-Saxon Monasticism', *Journal of Ecclesiastical History* 40 (1989), p. 202.
53 Gameson, *Manuscripts of Early Norman England,* no. 453, p. 108.
54 Gameson, *Manuscripts of Early Norman England,* nos. 290, 291, p. 88.

CHAPTER FOUR: ADOLESCENCE AND ADULTHOOD

Cicero (*Orationes*), and Sallust (*Invectiva*) which appear on the basis of surviving manuscript evidence to have been relatively unknown to Anglo-Saxon libraries, and which represent the emergence in England's Benedictine houses of a programme of reading connected with continental trends in education and ensuring that students adopted a style valued by a much wider European community.[55]

As we have seen in chapter three, the *Epistolae* or 'Letters' of Bishop Herbert of Norwich (1096-1119) provide direct evidence for the education of oblates, and this remains the case at a more advanced stage of the Latin curriculum too. On one occasion, these *Epistolae* suggest that boys studied classical poetry, advancing later still into the study of Aristotle's *Topics* and *Categories*.[56] But they also suggest that boys read Sedulius' *Carmen Paschale* with some enthusiasm, indicating that Christian poets continued to provide a base of study of the gospels, Latin hexameters, and modes of biblical exegesis.[57] At the same time, the *Epistolae* reveal that Herbert strongly disapproved of students' reading of Christian poets,

---

55 For more on the twelfth century 'renaissance', see Rodney Thomson, *Books and Learning in Twelfth Century England: The Ending of the "Alter Orbis"* (Walkern Herts, 2006), pp. 5-10; Rodney Thomson, 'Where were the Latin Classics in Twelfth-Century England?', *English Manuscript Studies 1100-1700*, 7 (1997), 25-40; Rodney Thomson, 'Books and Learning at Gloucester Abbey in the Twelfth and Thirteenth Centuries', in *Books and Collectors c.1200-1700, essays presented to Andrew Watson*, ed. James P. Carley and Colin G. C. Tite (London, 1997), pp. 4, 12-3.

56 Herbert de Losinga, *Epistolae Herberti*, ed. Anstruther, no. 49, pp. 86-7: 'Labora terminare Topicas differentias et digilienter accipe praedicamenta Aristotelis antequam veniam domum. Non attendas tui college delicias cui sufficit nosse nomina librorum quos legit et suae lectionis nominare folia [...] tuo desiderio trivium commendo et quadrivium, septem videlicet liberales artes'; trans. Symonds and Goulburn, *Letters of Bishop Herbert*, I, no. 49, pp. 35-6: 'Strive to finish the different kinds of Topics and take up diligently the Categories of Aristotle before I get back home. Do not copy your associate (Otto) who thinks it sufficient to know the names of books and to assert the number of pages he has read [...] I commend to your ardent pursuit the study of the Trivium and the Quadrivium, that is, of the seven liberal arts'. Herbert says that they were 'preadolescent boys', *Epistolae Herberti*, ed. Anstruther, no. 30, p. 62: 'Item in versu xi, te numquam vocavi 'iuvenem' quia *adhuc impuber es*'; trans. Symonds and Goulburn, *Letters of Bishop Herbert*, I, no. 30, p. 28: 'Also in line 11, take note that I have never called you a 'youth', because *you are still under age*'.

57 Herbert directly refers to the boys as adolescents, see Herbert de Losinga, *Epistolae Herberti*, ed. Anstruther, nos. 22, 30, pp. 41, 62; trans. Symonds and Goulburn, *Letters of Bishop Herbert*, I, nos. 22, 30, pp. 28, 37.

and on the occasion of one letter he both demanded to know 'how long [students] intended to loiter in the study of Sedulius?' and asked them to 'break off what [they were] reading'.[58] Herbert's justifications for this break in study show that his disapproval stemmed from a concern about the potential impact on boys' Latinity and biblical learning of a Late Antique text and versified Gospel.[59] They disclose too that Herbert did not believe that the study of these formerly popular versions of the Gospels was appropriate to adolescents either. Indeed, his *Epistolae* suggest that Herbert had thought that Holy Scripture should not be studied through an intermediary, but should be postponed until students had 'reached a maturity' of age suitable to a more direct type of study of the 'more excellent style' of the Gospels themselves, suggesting that adolescents should initially focus on the study and imitation of classical Latin texts instead.[60]

Elevation to holy orders likely continued to play an important role in signalling a religious individual's emergence into adulthood. We have already seen in the introduction, and in chapter three, that Orderic Vitalis, a boy monk who had been born in England, at Atcham near Shrewsbury, and who had been sent by his father to an abbey in Normandy at the age of around ten, had measured the space of his own religious childhood in these terms, emphasising the moment he became a sub-deacon at the age of sixteen:

---

58 Herbert de Losinga, *Epistolae Herberti*, ed. Anstruther, I, no. 9, p. 13; trans. Symonds and Goulburn, *Letters of Bishop Herbert*, I, no. 9, p. 19.
59 Herbert de Losinga, *Epistolae Herberti*, ed. Anstruther, I, no. 9, pp. 43-4: 'Quousque in Sedulis delitescitis? Magna quidem sunt sacramenta Sedulii, sed ea Matthaeus et Marcus, Lucas et Joannes luculentiori exsequuntur stilo. Solidus cibus est evangelicus sermo et perfectis mentibus conservandus. Aetas tenera lacteis adoletur alimentis, et inter lascivientes fabellas tenerae puerorum mentes urbanas dictiones et subtilium orationum compositione sinseparabiliter imbibunt'; trans. Symonds and Goulburn, *Letters of Bishop Herbert*, I, no. 9, pp. 19-20: 'How long do you mean to skulk in your Sedulius? Great, no doubt, are the mysteries of Sedulius, but Matthew and Mark, Luke and John methinks, relate those mysteries in a more excellent style. The Gospel story and doctrine are strong meat, to be retained and digested only by those whose minds have reached maturity. A tender age is nourished with a diet of milk and amidst playful little pieces of fiction, the tender minds of boys gradually but surely imbibe polished diction and the method of tasteful composition'.
60 Herbert de Losinga, *Epistolae Herberti*, ed. Anstruther, I, no. 9, pp. 43-4.

CHAPTER FOUR: ADOLESCENCE AND ADULTHOOD

Undecimaque kalendas octobris dominico clericali ritu tonsoratus sum [...] idus Martii cum xvi essem annorum, iussu Serlonis electi Gislebertus Luxoviensis presul ordinavit me subdiaconum.[61]

Orderic served the altars of a Norman Benedictine abbey, but there are grounds for considering that he described a practice which was also current in Anglo-Norman England. Goscelin's post-Conquest *Vita Sancti Wulsini*, or 'Life of Saint Wulfsige' (1002) framed the boy's elevation to holy orders in this same way, for example, as a kind of watershed moment in religious life, allowing Wulfsige to 'leave behind his ... boyhood' (*excussa ... pueritia*) and enter into an entirely new adult-centric pattern of advancement 'through the holy grades of the [priestly] offices' (*conscendit per sacros gradus officiorum ... iam maturo evo*).[62] Eadmer of Canterbury's version of the *Vita Sancti Dunstani* framed promotion into minor ecclesiastic grades in this way too. He presented ordination as an opportunity for boys to 'flee childish pastimes' and 'the pleasures of the world', allowing boys to enter into routines which signalled a coequality of status with adult men. Eadmer's work tells us that ordination allowed boys to share in environments which were otherwise monopolised by men, allowing boys to go to the oratory more freely, to light candles, to pour water on the hands of priests and deacons, to enjoy opportunities to serve water and wine in the Eucharist, and to train further for promotion in the grades of clerical orders.[63]

---

61 Orderic Vitalis, *Historia Ecclesiastica*, ed. and trans. Chibnall, VI, bk. 13, pp. 552-5: 'I was given a clerical tonsure on Sunday the twenty-first of September 1085 [...] [and] on the fifteenth of March 1091, when I was just sixteen years old, Gilbert, Bishop of Lisieux, ordained me as sub-deacon'.
62 Goscelin, *Vita Sancti Wulfinsi*, in 'The Life of Wulfsin of Sherborne by Goscelin', ed. Charles H. Talbot, *Revue Bénédictine*, 69 (1959), p. 75; trans. Love, 'The Life of St. Wulfsige of Sherborne by Goscelin of Saint-Bertin: A New Translation with Introduction, Appendix and Notes', in *St. Wulfsige and Sherborne: Essays to Celebrate the Millennium of the Benedictine Abbey 998-1998*, ed. Katherine Barker, David. A. Hinton, and Alan Hunt (Oxford: 2005), p. 105.
63 Eadmer, *Vita Sancti Dunstani*, in *Lives and Miracles*, ed. and trans. Muir and Turner, pp. 56-7: 'Ut liberius oratorium frequentare, luminaria accendere, manibus sacerdotum ac levitarum aquam fundere, vinum et aquam in eucharistiam corporis Christi sumministrare, legere atque cantare diei ac noctis posset, minores gradus suscepit/He took minor orders so that he could frequent the oratory more easily, light candles, pour water on the hands of the priests and deacons, serve the water and wine in the Eucharist of the

Communities of Religious Women: The end(s) of girlhood

> Ubi vero inter quattuordecim virgines, coruscantibus cereis tanguam syderibus et lampadibus supernis, ad dominicas nuptias trepida et penultima accessisti ac, populosa caterva sollemniter expectante, pignus fidei divine cum sacrata veste induisti, ille humilis habitus, ille tremebundus accessus, ille suffusus vultus, tamquam ab igneo throno Dei sedentis super cherubim, sapienter metuentis, altius viscera me percussere cum hoc epithalamico carmine admirabilis gratie: "Ipsi sum desponsata, cui angeli serviunt, et annulo suo subarravit me". Tacitus sum rore celesti et fervore irriguo flevi. Continuata quoque silentia tua, sollicita continentia, frequens psalmodia, pia magistre testimonia, magis accenderunt vota mea.[64]

Goscelin's account of the childhood of Eafe (fl.1058-1125) ended with a ritual marking her reception into a professed adult community at Wilton Abbey in c.1065. The precise nature of this ritual, its significance in her religious life, and her age at the time it took place have all been subject to debate in recent years but scholars now generally agree that Goscelin did not witness an oblation ceremony.[65] Aside from the fact that the account does not conform well to any record of an insular or continental

---

body of Christ, and read and sing in both the day and night offices'.
64 Goscelin, *Liber Confortatorius*, ed. Talbot, p. 28; trans. Otter, *Liber Confortatorius*, p. 23: 'But when you walked up to the Lord's wedding, with trepidation, the penultimate of fourteen virgins, with glittering candles like the stars and constellations above; when, before a large crowd waiting in solemn silence, you put on the sacred vestment, it was as if from the fiery throne of God sitting above his cherubim, I was struck to the quick with this wonderously beautiful epithalamium: "I am given in marriage to him whom the angels serve, and he has wedded me with his ring". I was touched by the heavenly dew and wept in tearful fervor (sic). And as I continued to witness your silence, your careful continence, your singing of the psalms and the praises of your teacher, my desire was inflamed even more'.
65 Daphne Stroud has argued that Goscelin became Eafe's teacher when she was about twelve years old, see Daphne Stroud, 'Eve of Wilton and Goscelin of St Bertin at Old Sarum ca 1070-1080', *Wiltshire Archaeological and Natural History Magazine* 99 (2006), p. 205. Katherine O'Brien O'Keeffe on the other hand has argued that she was neither a young child nor an oblate when Goscelin first knew her but an adult who was consecrated as a nun after a period of education as a secular girl, see Katherine O'Brien O Keeffe, 'Goscelin and the Consecration of Eve', *ASE* 35 (2006), pp. 251-70.

oblation, Goscelin's remembrance of Eafe singing psalms and holding her silence indicates that she was older than seven and had developed a monastic disposition. This has led some scholars, including Katherine O'Brien O'Keeffe, to argue that Goscelin witnessed an adult consecration instead. But insofar as Goscelin implied Eafe's maturity, his account of her experience also resists this categorisation. For one, it ignores her condition in childhood, subject to the strictures of a religious life. It also fails to explain gaps in what we might expect from an adult consecration ritual; Goscelin referred to her sacred habit, but he did not mark clearly her reception of the veil, and made no reference at all to her offering of sacred vows.[66] Scholars have forwarded no settled and satisfying answer to these discrepancies, and it may remain the case that we will never identify the ritual elevation which Eafe experienced. But it is possible that Goscelin witnessed something in between, a contemporary response to the emergence of confirmation rituals in houses of religious men. This possibility has been overlooked until now, and perhaps by virtue of the fact that there have been no studies on religious girlhood in England, but it would explain many of the unusual features present here, and it would allow us to suppose Eafe's experience recognised her oblate status while also securing her future as a religious woman.

Whatever the case may be, we can still consider the significance of the ritual which Goscelin described for Eafe of Wilton and ask why it appears not only to have marked her emergence into adulthood, but into a sexual status as a 'virgin', and, indeed, into a privileged relationship with the divine, partaking of the language of betrothal:

---

66 For a contemporary account of an adult consecration, see *Vita Sancte Sexburge Regine*, ed. and trans. Love, pp. 170-1: 'Prima diei terminata, usu regulari capitulum complet. Inde profecta virago insignis flammeo Christi consecrates accersit. Hortatur religioni insistere, et bonis attentius operibus insudare, victrices mundi fieri ut victorie premiis remunerentur, estus libidinis vincere, et sacre virginitatis victricia signa palmamque portare. Manusque apprehendens singularum super altare ordinatas instruxit/ When the first hour of the day had been completed, as is the custom of the rule she completed chapter. Setting out from there the noble heroine summoned those who had been consecrated to the bridal veil of Christ. She exhorted them to pursue piety, and more carefully to labour at good works, to become victorious over the world so that they might be rewarded with the prizes of victory, to vanquish the heat of lust, and to bear the victorious emblems and palm of holy virginity. So taking the hand of each one in order she placed it on the altar'.

> Altius viscera me percussere cum hoc epithalamico carmine admirabilis gratie: Ipsi sum desponsata, cui angeli servient, et annulo suo subarravit me.[67]

Goscelin's letter suggests that the timing of this ceremony may have coincided with Eafe's acquisition of biological maturity, and that her confirmation into religion served to confirm her emergence into a status of sexual integrity as *virgo* or 'virgin', allowing him to consider her as bound in marriage to Christ. In fact, Goscelin's narrative choices in the sections of the *Liber Confortatorius* which followed add further to this understanding, and demonstrate that Goscelin expected Eafe to adopt this view of herself as she emerged into adulthood. Indeed, Goscelin's letter to Eafe encouraged her to project onto Christ concepts of marital desire, encouraging her to consider the reception of Christ's body in the Eucharist in terms which approximated the act of consummation in marriage, and allowing her to 'become one with Christ's body', and in the same way that 'two are made one flesh' in sexual copulation, but without presenting a risk to her status as *virgo*.[68]

If religious girls did not emerge into adulthood by means of a single ritual, we can consider that girls' emergence into religious adulthood might have been shaped by these associations and closures in gaps of routine which separated them from religious women. Sadly, and apart from returning to specific evidence for girl's own routines, such as their attendance of a school of Barking Abbey, it is not quite as possible as it has been in relation to boys to ask what role such changes may have played. Indeed, we can say little more about the potential role of changes in girls' participation in the liturgical community either, or at least, we can say little more than what

---

[67] Talbot, *Liber Confortatorius*, p. 28; trans. Otter, *Liber Confortatorius*, p. 23: 'I was struck to the quick with this wondrously beautiful epithalamium, "I am betrothed to him whom the angels serve, and he has wedded me with His ring"'.

[68] Goscelin, *Liber Confortatorius*, ed. Talbot, p. 114; trans. Otter, *Liber Confortatorius*, p. 110. I owe this idea to Stephanie Hollis, whose studies articulate and argue for the significance of Goscelin's use of marriage imagery in women's religious identities, see Stephanie Hollis, 'Edith as Contemplative and Bride of Christ' in *Writing the Wilton Women: Goscelin's Legend of Edith and Liber Confortatorius*, ed. and trans. Stephanie Hollis, W. R. Barnes, Rebecca Hayward, Kathleen Loncar, and Michael Wright (Turnhout, 2004), pp. 281-306.

we have already considered in relation to evidence preserved in vernacular copies of the *Regularis Concordia* – that *Tenebrae* on Maundy Thursday might have played a role in signposting the emergence of girls into a status 'of greater age' (*on maran ylde*) in parallel to older boys or *cnapan*.

Of the three areas of experience which we have encountered so far, we are perhaps only in a position to consider how the experience of Latin instruction might have shaped girls' emergence into a mature literary identity. In his *Vita Sancte Edithe Virginis*, Goscelin suggests that adolescence might have been an important watershed when girls were required either to continue in their studies or to move away from an occupation with Latin school-texts and enter into a more contemplative pattern of life followed by senior religious women. We find an example of this division for instance in the context of Goscelin's *Vita* of Saint Eadgyth of Wilton, where he imagined that the young girl had chosen to devote so much of her attention to her spiritual development as she approached adulthood that 'the sweetness of the Lord ... and the light of His countenance supplanted her former great enthusiasm as an academic student'.[69]

If this shift represents the experience of some, however, there is evidence to suggest that girls who were able to advance were allowed to continue in their Latin studies at Wilton, and might even have been encouraged to undertake a course of instruction in Latin texts which parallelled the experiences of adolescents in contemporary male houses. There is only slight evidence in the documentary record which allows us to identify the form and material basis of this prolonged type of Latin instruction, however. We find some evidence, for example, in Eadmer of Canterbury's *Vita Dunstani*, where he interpolated a choir of female religious into a passage not present in earlier versions of the *Vita*, describing a group of young girls (*chorus virginum ... duae puellae de choro*) singing the verses of Sedulius' *Carmen Paschale*.[70] The event is likely to be invented, since the first *Vita* of Saint Dunstan mentioned no such

---

69 Goscelin, *Vita sancta Edithe Virginis*, in 'La légende de ste Édith', ed. Wilmart, c. 7, pp. 51-2: 'Magnum etiam fervorem scolaris gymnasii maior supplantebat pregustata dulcedo domini et illuminatio vultus sui'; trans. Hollis et al., *Writing the Wilton Women*, p. 33.
70 Eadmer, *Vita Sancti Dunstani*, in *Lives and Miracles*, ed. and trans. Muir and Turner, pp. 132-3.

girl-choir, but it is significant that Eadmer had chosen to add the detail, and had thought it credible that a[n] [arch]bishop on visitation might have encountered religious girls in a Benedictine context who had studied a popular Latin school-text. Scholars have also pointed to several surviving death-bills which circulated in houses of religious women in England following the death of Abbess Mathilde of the Abbey of Ste Trinité, Caen (d.1113), and which preserve verses composed by a religious woman of Shaftesbury who had studied Virgil's *Ecloga*.[71] Others have isolated letters written by the monk Osbert of Westminster to Abbess Adelidis of Barking in particular, arguing that they may be indicative of the Abbess' familiarity with the Latin texts which he cited, throwing light onto her knowledge of Aldhelm's *Prosa* and *Carmen de Virginitate*, as well as more classical authors such as Seneca, Virgil, and Ovid.[72]

Goscelin's *Liber Confortatorius* to Eafe indicates a similar context of education in houses of women religious. In the passage set out below, for example, Goscelin appears to list the Wisdom books of Solomon, along with a larger corpus of non-scriptural patristic and poetic Latin texts, among the works he expected Eafe to encounter. Goscelin's words, 'as you know', locate the Wisdom books in Eafe's own education at Wilton before the moment he wrote, and, what is more, they explain the effect he expected them to have on Eafe's views on discipline, sexual integrity, and the divine:

> Nosti, ipse est sapientissimus Salomon [. . .] tres libros edidit: Parabolam, Ecclesiastes, et Cantica Canticorum; primus disciplinam timoris domini et recte vivendi regulam point, secundus in concione diversorum desideriorum vanitati omnia subicit, ut ad tertium gradum in cantica canticorum eternitatis, appetitu nos rapiat ubi a servitute varitatis libera, in pace conditoris mens contemplativa pertendat.[73]

---

71 Stephanie Hollis, 'Barking's Monastic School, Late Seventh to Twelfth Century: History, Saint-Making and Literary Culture', in *Barking Abbey and Medieval Literary Culture: Authorship and authority in a Female Community*, ed. Jennifer N. Brown and Donna Bussell (Woodbridge, 2012), p. 53; *Rouleaux des Morts*, ed. Delisle, no. 18, p. 190.
72 Morton and Wogan-Browne, *Guidance for Women*, pp. 17, 21.
73 Goscelin, *Liber Confortatorius*, ed. Talbot, p. 39; trans. Otter, *Liber Confortatorius*,

These, and a wider body citations of Latin works present in Goscelin's letter to Eafe, indicate that Eafe's education was a very contemporary one; indebted to both a late Anglo-Saxon literary culture, and to an emerging expansion in the scope of Latin instruction generally connected to the twelfth century 'renaissance'.[74] Goscelin added citations from biblical scripture, most notably including the Psalter and Gospels, but he referred to poetic school-texts, such as Prudentius' *Psychomachia* and *Cathemerinon*, and Aldhelm's *Prosa De Virginitate* and *De Laudibus Virginitatis*. He also referred to works on logic and philosophy, including Boethius' *De Consolatione Philosophiae*. The chance survival of a copy of that work, which appears on the grounds of *ex-libris* marks to have been offered by an 'Ælfgyth of Barking' to Horton Abbey in the mid-eleventh century, also confirms that it had been available to religious women at a similar time.[75] Alongside these, Goscelin's *Liber Confortatorius* suggests that Eafe might have encountered a corpus of poetic works by authors who were more popular on the continent, such as Horace's *Satires* and *Epistulae*, and Virgil's *Aeneid*, *Ecloga*, and *Georgicae*.[76]

The poverty of surviving copies of didactic manuscripts from houses of religious women means that it is incredibly difficult to assess whether

---

p. 39: 'As you know, he is Solomon the wise man himself [...] He wrote three books, Proverbs, Ecclesiastes, and the Song of Songs. The first sets down the discipline of fearing God and the rule for right living; the second preaches that all things are subject to the vanity of our various desires, in order to ravish us to the third stage: the eternal Song of Songs, where, freed from the servitude to vanity, the contemplative mind may rush towards the peace of its maker'.

74 Sharon Elkins argues that the *Liber Confortatorius* represents Eafe's and Goscelin's 'shared learning', Sharon K. Elkins, *Holy Women of Twelfth-Century England* (Chapel Hills NC, 1988), p. 11. Stephanie Hollis also argues that her education was touched by changing taste for the classical, Stephanie Hollis, 'Wilton as a Centre of Learning', in *Writing the Wilton Women: Goscelin's Legens of Edith and Liber Confortatorius*, ed. and trans. Stephanie Hollis, W. R. Barnes, Rebecca Hayward, Kathleen Loncar, and Michael Wright (Turnhout, 2004), p. 338.

75 Goscelin, *Liber Confortatorius*, ed. Talbot, pp. 48, 81: 'Boetius noster... fabulam proponens/Our Boethius... relates a story' and 'respice... Boetium de Consolatione Philosophie/Look back... at Boethius on the Consolation of Philosophy'. For more on the copy of Boethius' *Consolatio Philosophiae* in Madrid, El Escorial, Real Biblioteca MS e.II.1, see Hollis, 'Wilton as a Centre of Learning', p. 312.

76 Goscelin, *Liber Confortatorius*, ed. Talbot, passim; David Bell, 'What Nuns Read: State of the Question', in *The Culture of Medieval English Monasticism*, ed. James C. Clark (Woodbridge, 2007), pp. 113-33.

this aspect of Goscelin's *Liber Confortarius* reflects Eafe's actual education or just Goscelin's aspirations and, even if the former, whether her education might have been representative of other girls at Wilton or just Eafe's particularly close relationship with a very learned tutor. It is perhaps only possible to read significance into these lists insofar as we can see that Goscelin had sought to instruct Eafe on these works. Eafe remains a silent figure in the historical record. We will never know for certain, therefore, whether her adolescence was marked by the study of classical Latin poetry. But even so, the balance of evidence afforded to us, and the nature of the evidence which we obtain from Goscelin, who, we should remind ourselves, had acted in the office of a teacher to Eafe, would seem to point us in a positive direction.

Goscelin's *Vita Sancte Edithe Virginis* also suggests that promotion to high office might have provided another mechanism of elevation in the lives of some girls, serving to mark a transition between girlhood and adulthood and from being subject to monastic prescriptions to being enforcers of religious government. Goscelin framed Eadgyth's early adulthood in this way, as an emergence from a stage of life in which she had been a student and subject to the rule of others, to a moment, at the age of just fifteen, when her father, King Eadgar, recommended that she should be elevated to the status of an abbess, and given the extraordinarily weighty responsibility of governing three Benedictine abbeys, of which Goscelin named only two – Nunnaminster and Barking:

> Vix ergo quindecennis processerat palmula in Christo dotalis Editha, iam paternis affectus Eadgari magis ecclesie quam regni propaginem propsens[a] in filia hanc super tria sanctimonialium, Deo dispendatnte dispendat monasteria.[77]

If Eadgyth's age at just fifteen at the time of her supposed elevation seems rather too incredible to believe, it may be important to note that

---

77 Goscelin, 'La légende de ste Édith', ed. Wilmart, p. 76; trans. Hollis, *Writing the Wilton Women*, p. 47: 'Scarcely had Edith, whose dowry in Christ was her own hand, progressed for fifteen years when the paternal affection of Eadgar, intending his daughter for the increase of the church than of his kingdom, placed her over three monasteries of nuns with God's dispensation'.

CHAPTER FOUR: ADOLESCENCE AND ADULTHOOD

this account has another parallel, in Goscelin's historical account of the appointment of his contemporary, Ælfgifu, an oblate girl who had entered Barking as an infant and who was raised to the office of Abbess at the age of fifteen in 1065.[78] It is possible that her appointment at that age was also unusual. It seems to have occurred in the very exceptional circumstances of King Eadward's (1042-1066) growing illness without a settled heir, and his appointment of Ælfgifu might have been intended to secure Barking Abbey as a place of safety for royal women for the duration of a period which ultimately led to the Norman Conquest. In any case, her acquisition of that office demonstrates that contemporary circumstances allowed girls to accede to high religious offices at much younger ages than is found anywhere for boys. Ælfgifu's accession would seem likely to have marked a very significant watershed in her religious life too. Indeed, even if we imagine that other senior religious women might have supported her in the capacity of abbess, in the same way that Goscelin described of Abbess Wulfthryth of Wilton on behalf of Saint Eadgyth, it would seem likely to have dramatically altered any conditions under which she might have previously lived. Promotion to a high monastic office at that age would perhaps also allow us to consider the possibility that girls of a similar age might have aspired to obtaining other and less senior offices, and that mechanisms of promotion could have played a role in marking the emergence of adolescent girls into patterns of life followed by their seniors too.[79]

---

78 Goscelin, *De Aelfgiva Abbatissa*, in 'Texts of Joycelin of Canterbury', ed. Colker, p. 437: 'Adolescebat in monasterio infantula Deo decreta, mente et forma ut adhuc vernat gratiosa, vigili intelligentia, perfusa omni benivolentia [...] Monasterialem curam favente sacra revelatione suscepit per regem Eadwardum quindecennis puella/ The little girl, ordained to God, grew up in the monastery and sprang gracious in mind and body, with an intelligence at vigil and perfuse with all kindness [...] The fifteen year old girl took up the charge of the monastery with the favour of holy revelation and the support of King Edward' (my translation). For more on Ælfgifu's elevation, see Slocum, Kay, 'Goscelin of Saint Bertin and the Translation Ceremony of Saints Ethelburg, Hildelith, and Wulfhild', in *Barking Abbey and Medieval Literary Culture*, ed. Jennifer N. Brown, and Donna Bussell (Woodbridge, 2012), p. 83.
79 Slocum, 'Goscelin of Saint-Bertin and the Translation Ceremony for Saints Ethelburh, Hildelith and Wulfhild', p. 83.

EVIDENCE OF CHILDREN'S "VOICES"

It will now be clear that the arguments we can reach with respect to considering the significance of a confirmation ritual, and with respect to the potentially more significant and many different ways in which contemporary categories of religious boys and girls may have emerged from their own discrete forms of religious childhood, provide for very open-ended conclusions about the nature of religious boyhood and girlhood in Anglo-Saxon and Anglo-Norman England. While these directions are useful, and seem likely to reflect the nature of children's religious experiences and the various ways in which they could signpost their acquisition of a status as religious adults, they fail to provide the sort of confirmation for the actual transitions of boys and girls which would allow us to reach a more settled view of these formative experiences.

It is useful therefore to consider the nature of surviving evidence of children's "Voice" in the written record. If there are not many locations in the documentary base today where we could hope to find evidence of children's own writings, there are occasions in the prescriptive record which suggest that boys and youths once had many opportunities to compose in Latin. We see this in Lanfranc of Canterbury's *Constitutiones*, for example, where he required that 'death bills shall be given . . . to the master of the children' so that the boys could write out their own messages in memory of deceased brethren.[1] If boys at Canterbury did indeed have opportuni-

---

[1] *Constitutiones*, c. 90, pp. 130-1: 'Breves pro defunctis per manum illius magistro infantum dari, vel in capitulum deferri debent/Death-bills shall be given by him to the master of the children, or brought by him into chapter'. No Anglo-Saxon customary appears to have connected this activity with children, see RC, p. 66: 'Mittitur et episticula ad vicina quaeque monasteria/Moreover, a breve shall be sent to neighbouring monasteries'. EME, pp. 142-3: 'Mittatur et epistola ad vinica quaeque monasteria/ And a letter shall be sent to all the neighbouring monasteries'.

ties to compose letters in memory of religious who had recently deceased, however, none, sadly, appear to have survived to testify to the skills, knowledge-base, grammatical ability, conceptual or spiritual beliefs, or gender and religious identities of the boys who grew up at Christ Church after the Conquest.

We do, however, possess evidence for this activity in the form of a string of Latin verses attached to a cycle of death-bills which arrived at Norwich Priory after the death of Abbess Mathilde of Caen, d.1113:

Versus iuvenis Ottonis

Scribere disposui tantae praeconia laudis;
sed mihi verborum copia pauca fuit.
Primitias Domino dum libat virginitatis,
Perpetua meruit virginitate frui.
Virgo dicata Deo, rebus subtracta caducis,
Percepit merito praemia digna suo.
In laudes gemitus redeant, in gaudia fletus:
Nil dignum lacrimis vita perennis habet.
Transiit ad vitam felix et plena dierum,
et meruit sponsi regna videre sui.[2]

The preceding title, *Versus iuvenis Ottonis*, or 'the verses of the youth Otto' identifies the author of these few verses as Otto, one of only two adolescent students at Norwich who are known to have received personal instruction in Latin under Bishop Herbert and whose educational trajectories can be retrieved in part through the bishop's surviving *Epistolae*. This poem is

---

2 *Les Rouleaux des Morts du IXe au XVe siècle*, ed. Léopold V. DeLisle (Paris, 1866), no. 40, pp. 195-6:
I have decided to compose praises of her [Abbess Matilda of Caen, d.1113] very great glory;
But I have only a small number of words.
While she offers (sic) the first-fruits of her virginity to the Lord,
She deserved (sic) to rejoice in perpetual virginity.
This virgin, dedicated to God, has been taken away from her inalienable house,
And she has secured the worthy prize with its own reward
Let them turn sighs into praises, crying into joys,
[she] has nothing worthy of tears in an eternal life.
Happy and full of days, she has crossed over to life,
And has merited to see the kingdoms (sic) of her bridegroom', (my translation).

highly significant, and gives us direct access to his "Voice". We see this most clearly where Otto declares his role in writing it, and where he employed the first person, 'I decided to write' (*scribere disposui*), to explain his reasons for entering the historical record. His poem therefore provides us with a unique window of opportunity to consider the nature of Otto's own disciplinary, liturgical, and educational formation at Norwich.

An immediate, if obvious, point to take from the poem is that it is in Latin. It demonstrates a foundation in Latin grammar, a degree of confidence in writing, and a familiarity with a common stock of tropes and Latin vocabulary. The poem suggests that the author's learning might have been confined in some ways. Otto appears to have preferred to stick with the indicative active voice in Latin verbal forms. It suggests too that the author was also relatively confined in or preferred to confine himself to two tenses, to the present and perfect indicative. He shows too that he could make use of perfect passive participles if he wished (i.e. *dicata deo*, or 'she was consecrated to God'), and could correctly use a deponent verb (*frui*) requiring its object to be in the ablative case. The author appears to have sought to display his awareness of all Latin noun types and with the Latin case system, using nouns belonging to each of the first (i.e. *primitia/vita*), second (*praeconium/dominus/regnum*), third (*laus/ virginitas/ felix*), fourth (*gemitus*) and fifth declensions (*dies*).

What is also significant about this poem, however, is that Otto's work contains several elements which contemporaries might have considered odd or erroneous. For one, Otto appears to have had some difficulty arranging his tenses. His Latin verbs turn between the present active indicative and past active indicative tenses within the space of a single verse, meaning that we are told that Matilda 'offers' (*libat*) her virginity in one moment but had already 'deserved' (*meruit*) to enjoy eternal virginity in another. These difficulties are minor, and we can still understand Otto's causal chain here. But there are places which suggest he had difficulty in using pronouns too. In fact, he avoided these throughout. We might explain some of these as an accident of genre, and as a result of a need to ensure that his lines conformed to metrical rules, but his failure to provide them does confuse verses where they would have been useful, where there is no obvious agent, and where, for example, Otto referred to someone, probably Matilda, whom he thought 'had nothing meriting tears' (*nil dignum lacrimis... habet*).

It is worth noting that Otto does seem to be aware of his powers of self-expression, and recognised in his opening verses that 'I could not produce a large number of words' (*mihi verborum copia pauca fuit*). It is the case that statements of insufficient learning were also a very common trope of composition in poetry, hagiography, and in letters of an encomiastic nature. While Otto's statement here would not appear to constitute false humility, and would seem to convey something of his concerns about his capacity to eulogise Abbess Matilda, we should perhaps consider that Otto's claims of inadequacy reflect his awareness of that literary tradition too.

It is worth recognising that his composition discloses his acquisition of several conceptually-heavy images belonging to contemporary religious thought-systems. We can see, for example, that Otto had considered that Matilda had been 'dedicated to God' (*dicata Deo*). His language here demonstrates that Otto had interiorised a view of oblation and consecration as religious acts which bound individuals like Matilda, and himself, to the religious life. We can also see that Otto placed a positive value on religious behaviours which were fundamental to the monastic liturgy, and we find this, for example, where he described the need to give out 'praises' for Matilda on two separate occasions (*laudes*). Indeed, his very poem could be seen as a manifestation of Otto's acceptance of the efficacy of intercession.

He also adopted the idea of heaven, describing it in terms which reflect the evidence of pre-Conquest glosses to Psalter copies, and understanding it symbolically, as a 'kingdom' (*regna sponsi*). In relating to heaven, and to Matilda's reward after death, Otto also discloses his personal awareness of the idea of travelling on to 'an afterlife' (*transit ad vitam*). Otto's poem shows great awareness of mortality in fact. He notes that Matilda had been of an advanced age when she died, that she was 'full of days' (*plena dierum*), and he appears to have sought to describe life as a kind of preparation stage and part of a divine reward system which judged the sacrifices individuals made before death. Indeed, Otto's poem appears to be heavily concerned with the idea that religious should be carefully judged before they were found worthy of obtaining an eternal life. Of all the verbs present in his poem, Otto only ever used *meruit* (she merited/ was found worthy) more than once, and indeed he added the second declension nouns *meritum* (reward) and *dignum* (appropriate/deserving) in order to add to this imagery of worthiness further still.

The performance of virginity appears to have been at the centre of Otto's idea of worthiness, and four references to Matilda's acquisition of virginity (*virginitas*), her acquired status as a virgin (*virgo*), and her reward of eternal virginity (*perpetua virginitate*) and 'enjoyment' of that virginity even (*virginitate . . . frui*) provided Otto with his most important source of praise. Indeed, it provides his only qualification for salvation. We should be careful not to give credit to the idea that virginity was Matilda's only claim to religious celebrity, however, and we should probably view Otto's insistence about her virginity here in terms which recognise that he probably knew very little about her. But his praises and emphasis tell us a great deal about his own projected assumptions, and demonstrate that he had attached great importance to the status of virginity over the course of his own religious upbringing.

Otto also used the phrase *sponsi sui*, describing Christ as Matilda's 'own bridegroom'. This phrase is more gender-specific, and was commonly used to describe a relationship between religious women and Christ in terms which equated the religious profession with the vow of marriage. We have seen it before, in the context of chapter three and in Ælfric's school-text on grammar, and, indeed, immediately above, in Goscelin's writings about religious girls and women at Wilton Abbey, but its presence here confirms that adolescent students in male houses would also be familiar with this imagery. Indeed, it suggests that boys were encouraged to imagine how religious women would use it in order to relate to the divine. In using it, Otto recognises that Matilda was different from him, that she partook of experiences and forms of personal and religious development and in an identifying vocabulary which were different to boys and men, and his poem demonstrates that he had learnt to recognise the needs of his wider religious audience and of the need to employ phrases which would signify her religious status too.

His Latin also discloses a great deal about the stylistic preferences which had been influential in the social environment where he grew up. His poem indicates that Otto's education involved the study of vocabulary with a biblical origin for example. A very cursory survey of Otto's terminology illustrates that the vast majority of his word choices can be found in sacred texts, including the Psalter, Proverbs, Ecclesiastes, Wisdom, and the Song of Songs.³ There are some word forms which are more difficult to explain, including Otto's access to the verbs *libare* (to pour in offering) and *frui* (to enjoy) and indeed his entire phrase *subtracta caducis*. There are other moments in his phraseology which we might locate with specific Latin texts, however. One of these, *transiit ad vitam*, which Otto used to describe Matilda's passing from death to eternal life, has a clear parallel in the phrases, *transisse ad vitam*, and, *translati sumus de morte ad vitam* – occurring in 2 Maccabees (6:24) and in 1 John (3:14) respectively. Otto's phrase *plena dierum* was also a common turn of expression which occurs in several places in Genesis (i.e. 25:8 and 35:29). Otto's phrase *tantae praeconia laudis* finds an origin in the funerary eulogy known as the *Panegyricus Messallae*, traditionally attributed to Albius Tibullus (i.e. *non ego sum satis ad tantae praeconia laudis*).⁴ Otto's use of the phrase *virginitatis frui* finds a parallel in Ovid's *Metamorphoses*,⁵ and the phrase *virgo dicata deo* (incidentlly exemplifying homeoteleuton) occurs in Aldhelm of Sherborne's *Carmen de Virginitate* as well as in the slightly earlier Christian poetry of Venantius Fortunatus which enjoyed a wide popularity throughout Europe from the seventh to the twelfth century.⁶ We cannot know for certain how Otto obtained his Latin vocabulary,

---

3 To give example, the exact forms, *disposui, laudis, verborum, fuit, primitias, dum, domino, merito, gemitus, gaudia, habet, vitam, plena,* and *regna* are all in the *Psalter*. The exact forms for *pauca, perpetua, rebus, digna, transiit, felix,* and *sponsi* occur in the remaining books of Proverbs, Wisdom, Ecclesiastes, and the Song of Songs. *Scribere, tantae, copia, virginitas/atis, virgo, percepit,* and *praemia* occur throughout.
4 This phrase could have been obtained from an elegy traditionally attributed to Tibullus, see *Panegyricus Messallae*, in *Catullus, Tibullus, Pervigilium Veneris*, ed. Francis Warre Cornish, John Percival Postgate, John William Mackail, revised and translated by George P. Goold (rev. ed., Cambridge MA, 2014), bk. iii, pp. 320-1, line 177: 'Non ego sum satis ad tantae praeconia laudis/I am not strong enough to advertise such glory'.
5 Ovid, *Metamorphoses*, ed. and trans. George P. Gould and Frank Justus Miller (rev. ed., Cambridge MA, 2014), bk. i, pp. 36-7, lines 485-6: '"Da mihi perpetua, genitor carissime", dixit "virginitate frui! Dedit hoc pater ante Dianae!/O father, dearest, grant me to enjoy perpetual virginity. Her father has already granted this to Diana"'.
6 Aldhelm, *Carmen de Virginitate*, ed. Rudolf Ehwald, MGH, Scriptores, Auct. ant. xv, p. 434, line 1975; Andy Orchard demonstrates that this phrase belonged to Aldhelm's *Carmen* and to Venantius Fortunatus, see Andy Orchard, *The Poetic Art of Aldhelm* (Cambridge, 1994), p. 194: 'Virgo dicata Deo, florebat tempore prisco'. R. W. Hunt, 'Manuscript Evidence for Knowledge of the Poems of Venantius Fortunatus in Late Anglo-Saxon England', *ASE* 8 (1979), pp. 279-95.

and whether his turns of phrase owe an origin to these precise sources or other intermediaries. But this breakdown of the content of his poem is perhaps sufficient to show that he was acquainted with several Latin texts and literary devices. Even if we cannot say that his Latin knowledge and style depended on study of parts of the Latin Vulgate, on the Psalter, on the Gospels, and on a handful of poetic school-texts, we can still see that his literary formation at Norwich was wrapped up with contemporary changes in education on the European continent and with shifts in literary taste which increasingly viewed plain Latin as a signifier of literary competence.

When it comes to asking whether the contemporary source base allows us access to the "Voices" of religious girls and young women, it is possible that we possess a small number of verses written by Eadgyth of Wilton. The authorship of the verses cannot be easily settled, however, and their significance depends on the very uncertain ascription of Goscelin of Saint Bertin who claimed in his *Vita Sancte Edithe Virginis* to have found verses in 'a manual of her devotions, [being kept] as a token of her memory . . . [and] written in her virginal hands':[7]

[a]
Domine,
Pater et dominator vitae meae,
ne derelinquas me in cogitatu maligno
extollentiam oculorum meorum ne dederis michi,
et desiderium malignum, adverte a me
Domine.[8]

---

7 Goscelin, *Vita Sancte Edithe Virginis*, in 'La légende de ste Édith', ed. Wilmart, c. 8, p. 55: 'Colitur in monasterio orationalis eius pugil, memorabili pignore . . . virginea eius manu cum subscriptis, orati unculis depictae'.
8 Goscelin, *Vita Sancte Edithe Virginis*, in 'La légende de ste Édith', ed. Wilmart, c. 8, p. 56 ; trans. Hollis et al., *Writing the Wilton Women*, p. 34:
'O lord,
father and ruler of my life,
do not leave me in evil thoughts,
do not give me pride of the eyes,
and turn away evil desire from me,
O lord'.

[b]
Omnipotens mitissime, Domine
qui sitienti populo fontem
viventis aquae de petra produxisti,
educ de cordis mei duritia compunctionis.⁹

If these verses had indeed been penned by Eadgyth of Wilton, and were written into a Wilton manual at some point in her early adulthood, they might have provided a significant parallel to Otto's verses and might have revealed something about the disciplinary, liturgical, and educational activities the author had encountered beforehand. Unfortunately for us, however, neither of these verses are what we might call 'original' compositions. The first verse [a] appears to have been borrowed almost entirely from the Bible, or to be more specific, from Ecclesiastes (23:4-5), and the second verse [b] appears to have been lifted from the services of the Roman Missal, or to be more specific, from collects which were meant to be used by ordained priests as part of the liturgical framework of Confession.

This means that we cannot treat these verses in quite the same way as we have the *Versus iuvenis Ottonis*. We know that, even if Eadgyth penned them, she did not construct them herself. We know that much of the content and style presented by these two verses cannot be seen as demonstrative of her own acquisition of skills in Latin composition and we should therefore dismiss the verses as evidence of a religious woman's own 'Voice'. If these conditions appear to limit what these verses allow us to ask and understand about the individual who wrote them down, however, there is still a case for considering that the verses are significant in more inductive ways. They may be significant, for example, in the sense that contemporaries thought them consistent with the Latinity of a contemporary religious woman, and they may be useful too to the degree that

---

9 Goscelin, *Vita Sancte Edithe Virginis,* in 'La légende de ste Édith', ed. Wilmart, c. 8, p. 56; trans. Hollis et al., *Writing the Wilton Women,* p. 34:
'Almighty and most merciful Lord,
who brought forth for your thirsty people a spring
of living water from the rock,
bring forth from the hardness of my heart tears of contrition'.

they represent literary choices, and are suggestive of a mind which had invested in biblical study and the liturgy.[10]

These verses present us with an individual who had probably also understood the contents of the Latin texts they penned. The two poems suggest that the scribe related to Christian virtues and disciplined behaviours. They ask for control of the senses, and display an anxiety about vices such as pride, and, in requests that the lord enable her to 'bring forth tears of contrition' (*educ... compunctionis lacrimas*), they imply the author's interest in an index of religious gestures. The presence of nouns in the vocative case, framed with a view to allowing the reader to call out to 'the Lord' (*Domine*), also fits neatly with an intercessory view of the liturgy. In terms of education, these verses not only imply literacy, but suggest that the writer subscribed to a Christian religious belief system, and chose to understand God as the 'ruler of her life' (*dominator vitae meae*), providing a parallel to the autobiographical recollections of Orderic Vitalis, and suggesting that the scribe might have come to interiorise a view of their own life as part of a 'Divine Plan'.

In addition to these lines, however, we can also return to evidence of an alb seen in chapter two and consider how this might allow us to reach for a more settled assessment of experiences which shaped the lives of religious girls in Anglo-Saxon and Anglo-Norman England:

> Circa pedes aureas apostolorum ymagines Dominum circumstantes [...] se vice suplicis Mariae affusam, dominica vestigia exosculantem.[11]

In addition to giving witness to the place and role of girls' instruction in craft at houses of women religious, Goscelin's description suggests the alb was crafted by an individual who had learnt to subsume herself into religious narratives and into a familial relationship with the figure of Christ,

---

10 See for example a reference to *Ecclesiastes* 1:1 in dialogue no. 4, ÆlfBColl, pp. 86-7: 'Omnis sapientia a Domino est'.
11 Goscelin, *Vita Sancte Edithe Virginis*, in 'La légende de ste Èdith', ed. Wilmart, 79; trans. Hollis et al., *Writing the Wilton Women*, p. 48: 'Around the feet, the golden images of the Apostles surrounding the Lord [...] and Edith herself prostrated in the place of Mary the supplicant, kissing the Lord's footprints'.

replacing the Virgin Mary (*vice Mariae*). Similar to evidence seen in chapter one, of feminine pronouns added into copies of the *Regula Benedicti*, and similar also to evidence of feminisation of biblical passages in a vernacular version of the *Regularis Concordia*, so too Eadgyth's alb suggests that religious adolescents were allowed to imagine themselves as agents of Latin and Old English texts. Indeed, Eadgyth's alb indicates more than this. It suggests that, once girls emerged into adulthood, they were not only encouraged to relate to a learnt or *aquired* status of virginity and to the Divine on a personal level, but were expected to express that status and affinity through the proxies of their crafted liturgical items too.

CONCLUSIONS

In the introduction to this study, I set out how we might improve our understanding of monastic childhood in late Anglo-Saxon and Anglo-Norman England. I first drew attention to an account of oblation by the Norman historian, Orderic Vitalis, and pointed to the ways in which research connected to church history and childhood history have handled this and similar portraits of oblation in the past. I argued here that attempts to situate the experience of oblation through single portraits and in terms which confine our view of oblates to a single moment of recruitment, or construct them as victims of adult intentions, do not allow us to understand children's experiences after they entered religious houses. Arguably, a child-centric approach has proven useful to challenging some of these perspectives. It has allowed this study to focus in each chapter on evidence for the acquisition of experience, and to recognise how religious children engaged with their monastic communities through different lenses to seniors. This perspective has been useful to understanding and representing children's development in a more realistic way, exploring how their world-views may have been informed by encounters with various kinds of religious knowledge which were tied up with disciplinary, liturgical, and literary spheres.

Since there are many gaps in our understanding of how children's lives connected with the surviving material corpus, I have explored both prescriptive and documentary sources that are indicative of children's conditions and asked how far they contribute to our understanding of childhood realities. My decision to focus on prescriptive sources first has been particularly useful with respect to handling an ideal of uniformity articulated by Anglo-Saxon monastic reformers: that all religious should be of one mind when it came to religious custom and practice. This ideal suggested that contemporaries worked to reduce variation in boys' and girls' experiences, and we have seen that the *Old English Rule* and

Regularis Concordia did indeed shape the conditions and experiences of children across England, but we have also seen that the primary source base allowed for evolution of practice, albeit building upon a shared framework, and allowed for the emergence of difference in observance and interpretation depending on local conditions. We have also considered in each chapter whether and how far the *Constitutiones* of Canterbury marked a break from expectations of uniformity which had shaped the lives of boys and girls before the Conquest. This has been especially useful in contributing to our understanding of how boys' formative experiences might have become more dependent on prescriptive regulations, and, potentially, how boys' formative experiences in discipline, and in liturgical drama, might have come to focus more heavily on the formal meeting of a boyhood Chapter, and on the elaboration of ritual processions.

In handling these prescriptions, and in exploring the significance of childhood development represented within them, we have also assessed the significance of age-related terminology used by contemporaries. It has been useful to examine and recognise, for example, evidence for the relative interchangeability of Latin and vernacular terms relating to 'infants', 'boys', and, indeed, 'children' in the cases of the *Old English Rule,* the *Regularis Concordia*, and the *Constitutiones*. This has been important to gauging how far contemporary prescriptions tell us about conditions imposed upon children of different age groups, and the nature of their 'development' as they grew up, for example. It has also been useful to recognising where terminology relating to age is most surprising, or most clear, as we consider in the case of 'adolescents' or 'youths' before and after the Norman Conquest. Indeed, it has also meant that we have been able to rest arguments about development and experience on a more clear-sighted understanding of how evidence of children's conditions and activities likely intersected with pre- and post-adolescent age groups.

My central chapters aimed to show how contemporary sources provide evidence for the discrete experiences of both boys and girls in a comparative framework, asking how disciplinary, liturgical, and literary experiences enabled children to integrate into religious communities after their oblation. In chapter one, on discipline, I drew attention to a vacuum of disciplinary prescriptions in Anglo-Saxon regulatory documents, and I suggested that Anglo-Saxon systems of discipline were more dependent on the figure of the teacher rather than on a clear prescriptive framework.

While I have considered that prescriptive sources are not always useful to understanding children's disciplinary experience before the Conquest, I have suggested that we can use pre-Conquest school-texts composed for boys as an alternative source of evidence. Ælfric of Eynsham and Ælfric Bata likely knew one another in the capacity of teacher and student, and their works testify to the similarity of their disciplinary principles and to Bata's own learning of those attitudes from Ælfric. We have considered therefore that their works are capable of revealing how systems of discipline in boys' houses were connected to systems of education, and how teachers and school-texts likely played a role in transferring monastic knowledge from one generation to another.

Chapter two has explored how the liturgy enabled children to integrate into their monastic communities. It has asked what the contemporary prescriptive record tells us about children's earliest visible entry into liturgical communities in Anglo-Saxon and Anglo-Norman England, and it has asked what contemporaries demanded of children as they grew up. In doing so, this book has given attention to evidence contained in prescriptive records of expectations of learning and performance which might have had a role in reinforcing a communal monastic identity, and idiosyncratic liturgical identities as well. With respect to the liturgy in women's houses, I have also drawn attention to how far women's use of craft-work might have been an area of experience that was important to religious girls' development. This skill-set has not often been connected with religious girlhood or contributed to an understanding of how girls might have encountered a monastic liturgy, but it has allowed us to consider how craft might have been important to girls' lives in later chapters too.

In chapter three, I explored questions relating to becoming 'literate' and asked what purpose Latin school-texts might have served in monastic education beyond the confines of providing a basic understanding of Latin grammar. In this chapter, I approached surviving school-texts composed for the benefit of religious children in order to ask whether they might also be capable of expressing the role of monastic education in shaping students' behaviours and Christian identities as comprehension of Latin improved. A key aim has been to challenge optimal views of educational attainment in a monastic context, and so I asked too whether and how far the surviving source base can disclose another reality of educational variation. This aim has, I think, proven useful. It has enabled us to explore evidence for the emergence of intellectual hierarchies in boys' schools. Realisation and recognition of relative failures seem to have prompted teachers like Ælfric Bata to describe students who assigned to one another comparative levels of ignorance and inability. This study explored whether the source base can sustain a similar exploration of the educations of girls. While lacking similar material, it has been possible to show that saints' lives tell us that girls' experience of Latin education might have depended on one of two systems, centred on a cell, or a collective 'school'.

Infancy

The diachronic and synchronic structures which I have used in this work not only allow a mechanism for reading by life-stage through infancy, childhood, and adolescence, but mean that my conclusion can draw together arguments entertained for each age-group too. This has enabled us to ask, for example, whether infancy for children of both sexes was an important space for religious socialisation, exploring the ways in which children's earliest experiences might have been informed by the monastic structures they first encountered. I have considered that neither Anglo-Saxon nor Anglo-Norman religious communities appear to have expected much from infants, either boys or girls. For infant boy oblates who might have entered religious communities after a period of monastic reform from c.950, I supposed that a first experience of monastic routines might have begun with the oblation ritual described in chapter 59 of the *Regula*. That being so, however, I have also recognised that neither the *Regula* nor Æthelwold's contemporary translation, the *Old English Rule*, gives us access to his expectations of infants after that ritual. I have drawn attention, for example, to how Æthelwold removed rules relating to *infantes* from his own translation, and his use of *geonge men* in chapter 45 in particular has potential to point us away from infants in a choir structure at Winchester. But I have suggested that the nature of this terminology does not allow us to be confident of Æthelwold's intentions. We have turned to the *Regularis Concordia* in order to ask whether this prescriptive context provides a view of monastic 'infants' instead, but, again, we have argued that this source is not helpful, since it confines us to just a single reference which either confuses the activities of *infantes* and *pueri* or reveals the interchangeability of those age-related terms in that period.

A study of the *Constitutiones* has made it possible to explore some of the activities expected of the youngest monastic children who performed in the liturgy after the Conquest. The single youngest oblates of Christ Church, Canterbury, were assigned their own duty to say out loud, *Benedicite,* in order to signal the end of an office, for example. I have argued that this duty suggests that Lanfranc had expected the liturgy to particularise the experiences of the youngest boys, and that selection might have been important to boys' religious identities from a much earlier point in the life-cycle than can be seen in the prescriptive record of Anglo-Saxon England. Indeed, this use of *Benedicite* may even have served to mark transitions between infancy and boyhood at Canterbury. If we can assume contemporaries upheld these rules closely, loss of responsibility over this sequence and replacement by other younger boys would seem likely to have marked their accession into 'boyhood', signalling their integration into an ordinary liturgical community.

Not all houses of women may have accepted infant girls into their communities, but I have recognised evidence which suggests that girls were sometimes given by their parents to religious foundations at much younger ages than we find of boys, and indeed, shortly after they were weaned. They might even have begun their monastic lives at a stage when they were dependent on the personal care of a religious nurse. What is more, saints' lives, including those of Saint Eadgyth of Wilton and Saint Eadburh of Nunnaminster, which describe infant girls in religious houses, suggest that their communities excluded infants from many ordinary rules, and imposed few prescriptive demands on their behaviour.

Childhood

The central chapters of this work have considered how primary materials describe children's conditions, and indicate how their experiences on a monastic round and in the choir or school might have shaped them before adulthood. Throughout these chapters I have endeavoured to cross-reference evidence for children's experiences in different spaces to illustrate the interdependence of their training, with the choir supporting their learning in behaviour, liturgical recitation, and in Latin, and the school, Chapter, cell, and daily round, providing similarly vital support to their development in each of those respects too. A degree of similarity in the experiences of children at women's and men's houses from the mid-tenth to the late-eleventh century has been grounded on the basis of shared observance of the same index of regulations. I have shown that both Anglo-Saxon and Anglo-Norman prescriptive sources assumed that children would follow an aspired daily round which was different to a round followed by adults, and which was signposted in the monastic soundscape by the ringing of bells or the striking of other kinds of *signa*. They suggest children entered into choirs and schools that mirrored the communal organisation of seniors, offering a proxy community for their training under dedicated guardians and teachers.

Sadly, pre-Conquest prescriptive records are less detailed on the nature of the school than their post-Conquest successors. For late Anglo-Saxon England, only monastic school-texts allow us to consider the role of teachers in shaping experiences within them. School-texts not only confirm the importance of dynamics explored in a prescriptive context – such as entering a liturgical community, participating in a daily round coordinated by bells and learning of ritual gestures – but they show that teachers encouraged boys to develop a degree of behavioural self-awareness and reveal teachers were particularly concerned about boys' behaviours in the sacred spaces of the church and choir. These materials also suggest that some teachers preferred verbal warnings and threats of violence when boys misbehaved. Others indicate that boys experienced corporal punishment, and, indeed, and along with post-Conquest saints' lives, indicate that teachers might have imposed violence on boys in order to reinforce the gravity of offences such as theft, as well as to remind boys of the efficacy of prayers to saintly intercessors.

While I have considered that teachers played an important role in Anglo-Saxon Winchester, filling a vacuum of prescriptive authority, I have considered that they may not have enjoyed as much autonomy at Canterbury after the Norman Conquest. Lanfranc's *Constitutiones* were more detailed, and outlined his expectations of teachers as well as boys. Lanfranc appears to have borrowed disciplinary principles directly from the *Regula Benedicti*, and used a model belonging to the cellarer in order to set down qualities he expected teachers to espouse. Lanfranc also introduced more regulation for boys' supervisory experiences; teachers were to maintain more precise standards of behaviour, requiring boys to be kept apart at lessons and insisting that they should never be allowed to make signs or distract one another. At the same time, the *Constitutiones* also suggest that boys' experiences of corporal violence may have shifted away from the teacher and the context of the *schola* and towards a formal meeting of a boyhood Chapter, bringing boys' disciplinary conditions into close alignment with those of their seniors. I have recognised that the *Constitutiones* also limit what we can infer about boys' experiences of Chapter, however. While I have approached rules which suggest that boys ought to be whipped in their Chapter 'in the same way' that seniors were in theirs, and while I have taken this to mean that boys' behaviours might have been measured according to the same framework of 'light' or 'grave' errors and punishments, I accept that we cannot determine how far boys shared these conditions with seniors.

I have asked whether prescriptive materials give us access to the conditions of girls, and suggested that we might approach terminology relating to *pueri* in Latin customaries and *cild* in the *Old English Rule* in terms which suppose that girls participated in an apparatus designed for the 'child'. This has meant that I have taken a more uncertain line in some respects, assuming that girls' conditions might have paralleled those of boys in fundamental ways. I have also highlighted evidence of feminine adjustments to surviving prescriptive sources, and argued that they support this line too. They suggest that girls were governed by disciplinary guidelines present in chapter 45 of the *Regula Benedicti,* for example, but in the place of prescriptive evidence, I also turned to saints' lives written in this period, such as the *Vita Sancte Edithe Virginis*, in order to ascertain whether they describe experiences corresponding to those outlined in more prescriptive contexts. Goscelin's writings on the women of Barking Abbey, for example, indicate that girls there sang from the two sides of a choir which surrounded the tombs of their saintly protectors, and they tell us that girls entered a communally orientated 'school' under a dedicated 'teacher' or *magistra* as well. Goscelin's writings provide a window onto his disciplinary methods too, and confirm that contemporaries used verbal forms of correction against religious girls. In questioning whether these sources provide a representative picture of the role of physical punishment, however, I have drawn attention to post-Conquest sources which suggest that the experience of violence was also important. While they show that female disciplinarians could impose forms of corporal punishment on a reactive basis, I have also suggested that they indicate that the experience of violence depended on social status, and that royal girls in particular may not ordinarily have been subject to physical correction.

While we can suppose that all religious children entered the choir at some stage, the *Regularis Concordia* and *Constitutiones* suggest that the timing of children's entrance into this structure was contingent on reaching a certain enabling age, and was subject to a minimum level of training in reciting liturgical Latin texts. Sadly, the *Regularis Concordia* does not allow us to consider how they contributed to the Divine Offices in general, so we have only been able to consider their participation in liturgical duties like the *Trina Oratio* in particular. The imprecision of terminology relating to age in the *Regularis Concordia* has, again, made it difficult to consider how Æthelwold of Winchester expected children of different ages (and, indeed, sexes) to learn the component skills and texts necessary for undertaking the *Trina Oratio* too. I have therefore only considered in detail how and why how the *Regularis Concordia* expected them to perform the *Trina Oratio* as a distinctive community, without the support of their seniors. In addition to this, I have also examined how the *Regularis Concordia* allowed *pueri* to make solo performances, such as at the close of a dramatic sequence known as *Quem Queritis*, and I argued that this evidence, along with school-texts like the *Colloquia*, reveals dynamics of competition, and suggests that teachers encouraged boys to measure their performances according to metrics of 'correctness' (*rectius*) and 'beauty' (*pulchrius*) in singing.

Both Anglo-Saxon and Anglo-Norman prescriptions suggest that boys' awareness of major festivals was enabled by participation in memorable liturgical dramas; both required children to take part in elaborate sequences on Palm Sunday and Maundy Thursday. But I have also drawn attention to the fact the *Constitutiones* did not allow the boys of Canterbury to replicate the liturgical emphases of boys of the Old Minster in Winchester. Lanfranc no longer associated boys with the antiphons animating the voices of the Hebraic boys on Palm Sunday, as these were to be sung by dedicated cantors. Lanfranc did not require boys to sing in divided couplets at *Tenebrae* in Holy Week as had been the case at the Old Minster either. Instead, Lanfranc only appears to have given boys a particular role in *Tenebrae* in an indirect way, by requiring them to hold lanterns shortly after *Tenebrae* had been observed. I have shown how this requirement intersected with boys' disciplinary conditions – Lanfranc used lamps in order to help guardians watch over their charges. But I have argued here that these lamps allowed boys to acquire a higher degree of visibility in the context of a liturgical drama, and in a way which may have reinforced boys' sense of collective identity. Although we cannot know how far Æthelwold's and Lanfranc's customaries represent the full extent of boys' engagement in either liturgical context, I have highlighted that Lanfranc's customary also made greater use of the procession, and I have therefore entertained the idea that the procession played a bigger role in boys' experiences of the liturgy at Canterbury after the Conquest. What is more, I have considered that processions may even have had a role in informing boys about their status, drawing attention to privileges which divided them from seniors, including duties in bearing holy texts and vessels.

Contemporary canon law forbade girls and women from engaging directly with sacramental aspects of liturgical activity centred on altars and ordained clergy. While I have therefore supposed in this section that girls might have focussed on activities centred on the regular hours in the choir, surviving evidence has not allowed direct comparison of their conditions with those of boys. Because of this, I explored in more detail an idea first raised by Maureen Miller in *Clothing the Clergy*, that girls engaged with the liturgy by crafting the vestments and fabrics which adorned their churches and officiating ministers. I have suggested that we might even find evidence for this kind of opportunity in a contemporary prescriptive record. I show that a fragmentary vernacular copy of the *Regularis Concordia* provided readers with a feminine form of a gospel reading, *Partit[a]e vestimenta mea*, which was said when deacons 'parted' a tacked piece of cloth. It is not entirely clear what this instance of a feminine adjustment expresses about the use and users of this text, and whether its significance should be confined to an unintentional scribal error, or represents something more intentional. While I suggest here that it may have encouraged a lesson which introduced a female agency into the liturgy, allowing girls and women to imagine themselves parting the garbs instead of the required deacons, I recognise that it does not confirm it. Even if it does not connect us to girls in this precise instance, however,

I suggest that the nexus of evidence presented in this section is indicative of the role of sewing in the liturgy, and this context, along with evidence for girls' crafting of albs in Goscelin's *Vita Sancte Edithe Virginis*, allows us to think about how sewing might have been important to religious girls' formations in corresponding ways.

In my chapter on education and Latin literacy, I argued that little research has contributed to our understanding of how instruction in Latin grammar connected with boys' education in systems of religious thought. Since Ælfric's *Excerptiones de arte grammatica anglice* is the best attested work of its type, I have argued that it provides the most useful basis for exploring these learning outcomes before the Conquest. By undertaking a line by line comparison of Ælfric's school-text with his most important exemplar, the *Excerptiones de Prisciano,* I have been able to reinforce past scholarship by Jeanine Bender-Davis and David Porter and show that he had crafted this text in order to ensure it would function in a contemporary pedagogic context. I also suggested, however, that Ælfric's content encouraged boys' awareness of their monastic status, identity, and progress, that it enabled boys to describe paraphernalia used in liturgical processions and ritual services, and that it nudged boys into viewing documents like the *Regula Benedicti* and the *Regularis Concordia* as sources of personal and collective regulation. Ælfric's additions also suggest that he intended lessons on grammar to play a role in shaping boys' basic understanding of Christian faith, their understanding of 'heaven' and 'hell', of sexual status and ritual 'purity', and their understanding of and relationship with biblical scripture. It also introduced boys to the idea of Christ's sacrifice, the idea that prayer was a means of interceding with God on behalf of society, and the concept of a Final Judgement.

For a small number of boys who advanced beyond lessons in elementary grammar in late childhood, I have also suggested that the Psalter could have provided a familiar bridge to a more demanding level of active reading of poetic Latin texts. I have built upon earlier scholarship on the role of the Psalter which has suggested students were encouraged to adopt a form of reading by relating to Latin word forms for blushing by interpreting them as signifiers of shame. I have argued that Psalter copies also demonstrate that readers were encouraged to learn a form of biblical exegesis, and were expected to learn how to read a wider body of terms relating to kingdoms, inheritances, and worldly princes by interpreting them as relating to 'heaven', 'the reward of salvation', and 'religious seniors' instead. At the end of this chapter, I argued that the picture these two sources create, of a kind of uncomplicated inertia in educational development, from learning Latin grammar to reading sacred texts, is not entirely credible. I therefore explored how far the contemporary source base also gives us access to experiences of learning failure. I argued here that Bata's *Colloquia* are particularly capable of connecting us to these outcomes, revealing that boys sometimes compared one another's Latin comprehension and identified peers in terms of their inability too.

The *Constitutiones* give us a clearer view of how Lanfranc expected boys to attend a school, and what he expected them to learn inside it. Indeed, I argue that the 'school' may have acquired a physical location at Canterbury. But our view of the shape of grammatical education in the late-eleventh and early-twelfth centuries continues to rely on the group of school-texts composed in England between 950 and 1010. Glosses added to these materials reveal the growing influence of French speakers, whose different linguistic abilities and needs began to have a visible impact on the material culture of instruction. But I point out that these materials may have fallen out of use by the mid-twelfth century. Attempting to explain this decline and to locate the materials which took their place, I argued that changes in education after the Conquest might have undermined the role of monastic houses as centres of Latin instruction to oblate boys, and Orderic Vitalis provides further evidence to suggest there was a decline in the number of boys who entered schools without any literary experience. A pattern for a secular education in letters may have become more common, and meant that literary training played a smaller role in boys' monastic formations. For the rest of the twelfth century, I have considered that our evidence also corresponds with an area of scholarship relating to the twelfth century 'renaissance', which suggests that the material basis of instruction in Latin grammar gradually became less monastic in origin and more dependent on the primers of Late Antiquity which rather served clerics across Latin Europe.

Where I have only been able to speculate about the nature of elementary education after the Norman Conquest, I have suggested that the *Epistolae* or letters of Bishop Herbert of Norwich confirm changes in the material base of instruction, revealing a preference in the twelfth century for an assortment of grammatical primers popular on the European continent. I have also suggested that these letters connect us to another aspect of experience, however, and suggest that boys who entered episcopal sees enjoyed opportunities to participate in a more selective system of tutoring as their Latin comprehension improved. This tutoring took place through the exchange of correspondences as well as in person, but I highlighted in particular the role of the bishop in teaching, and argued that boys' access to these figures might have given them wider horizons than boys who entered smaller abbeys or priories. Considering evidence for the accession of one of Bishop Herbert's students, William Turbe, to the episcopal see of Norwich in the mid-twelfth century, I have suggested that these opportunities may even have placed boys who grew up in cathedrals in a much stronger position for promotion to higher church office.

Contemporary sources are less capable of showing whether and how girls might have obtained the same enabling grammatical knowledge. We have speculated that girls may have had access to grammatical primers which were important to conditions of instruction in male houses and in the lives of some boys. But I have only been able to demonstrate that primary sources reveal differences in educational structures and forms of learning support between communities of women. Writings commissioned by Abbess Ælfgifu of Barking Abbey provide an example in a woman's house for a large school of girls who shared their experiences of religious instruction under the guidance of dedicated teachers. At other nunneries, however, structures for education in behaviour and literacy seem to have centred on individual girls, and may have occurred in cell. Evidence of teaching practices at Wilton suggests that privileged religious girls also had access to private tutors, part supplied through windows by literate chaplains and part by the personal instruction of the abbess. I have argued that this system, exemplified by Goscelin's *Vita Sancte Edithe Virginis* and *Liber Confortatorius* to Eafe, might have connected with anxieties about girls' adolescence, and imply that the experience of instruction under chaplains became progressively more isolating as they grew up.

Adolescence

In chapter four I asked how monastic children became monastic adults. In doing so, I built upon earlier scholarship which understands adulthood as an acquired status, and asked rather how children adopted signifiers of adulthood, and how boys' and girls' experience in areas of discipline, liturgical training, and literary training might have played a role in signposting that adult status. I first drew attention to the role of a confirmation ritual. Arguing that we have no means of knowing whether Anglo-Saxons observed a ritual first advocated by Carolingian church canons, I suggested that evidence for an elevation first occurs after the Norman Conquest, at Canterbury in the *Constitutiones* of Lanfranc, and at Worcester in an *ordo* on the 'blessing of a boy as a monk'. I have made a similar argument in the case of a ritual which Goscelin of Saint Bertin described in his *Liber Confortatorius* to Eafe of Wilton. The nature of this ritual and Eafe's age at the time it took place have been subject to debate in recent years, but I suggest here it could represent a contemporary response in a community of religious women to the emergence of evidence for rituals of profession in houses of religious men. I argued that this ritual might have taken place once girls reached marriageable age, and that it was intended to mark the time when they could be considered 'virgins' and 'brides of Christ'.

This study has argued that changes in boys' and girls' daily routines could have played a similar role in marking adulthood. This section depends upon and supports evidence for children's daily rounds explored in chapter one, suggesting that oblates observed a different routine to adults. I argue that transitions into adulthood depended on children closing the gaps between their own routines and those of their seniors. I understand that loss of access to extra food, in the form known as the *mixtum*, arrangements of supervision and seating in the choir and refectory, training in a school or cell, choir, and Chapter, and procedures of shaving in the case of boys in particular might have signposted children's elevations in this way. I have suggested that boys' literary activities may have played a similar role too. In late Anglo-Saxon monastic houses, the most capable boys progressed into a stage of close reading of school-texts useful to cultivating an elevated Latin style that would mark them out as members of a Benedictine elite and worthy of promotion to church office at a time when monks could expect to dominate the episcopal bench. I have followed established scholarship by arguing that the structure and purpose of a literary education in male houses did not change immediately after the Norman Conquest. But I have argued that gradual changes to the material base of instruction also affected experiences of instruction at an advanced level, bringing adolescents into contact with classical Latin poetry, and ensuring that they acquired a style valued by a much wider European community as well.

Goscelin's Life of Saint Eadgyth of Wilton suggests that girls may have been expected either to focus more heavily on their spiritual development, or continue along a course of Latin instruction once they approached adolescence. There is evidence from Goscelin's Letter to Eafe of Wilton to suggest that some girls were able to undertake a course of instruction similar to boys, but this only survives in the form of a single letter produced by Goscelin of Saint Bertin. The singularity of this evidence makes it difficult to interpret, and so I understand that very few girls might have benefitted from this type of instruction; Eafe may only have acquired her experiences by virtue of attracting the support of a particularly invested and learned tutor. While it is not clear whether this course of instruction was characteristic of most girls' experiences, however, I consider that they confirm the importance of literary identities in some girls' lives, and indicate that they could parallel those of contemporary boys.

Extending from the example of Orderic Vitalis, whose testimony we encountered at the very beginning of this study, I have argued that promotion to the lowest grades of holy orders, like the sub-diaconate, likely played a role in conferring an adult status too. Progress into the sub-diaconate may not have required much formal training, boys could obtain the necessary skills through observation of their seniors and so this elevation could have marked the elevation of many adolescents. Girls could not enter holy orders, however, and so promotion through church offices would not have marked an end-point to religious girlhoods. Despite this, I argue that girls could acquire promotion to monastic offices, and sometimes became abbess at much younger ages than we have seen of boys as abbots. I have also entertained the idea that girls might therefore have aspired to less weighty offices too, and considered that girls might have emerged into adulthood by virtue of acquiring one of a larger number of offices as *circatores, cantrices, lectrices, nutrices*, if not also as *magistrae*.

It has only been possible to give space at the end of this book to examine evidence for children's own writings and explore what remains of the "Voices" and "Agencies" of religious students themselves. The verses of Otto of Norwich have been particularly useful because they give us an unusually direct connection to an individual who disappeared from the historical record shortly after he completed his composition. In this sense, his words are significant beyond the confines of his composition. They are emblematic of experiences which can no longer be retrieved, and connect us to the interests and capabilities of a much broader demographic of religious boys than is usually the case. The *Versus iuvenis Ottonis* confirm that several of the dynamics explored in the chapters above shaped Otto's religious boyhood. For one, these verses demonstrate that he was instructed in Latin grammar, displaying his awareness of passive and active forms, and of Latin noun-types from all five declensions. But they also show that he had been instructed in a common stock of literary tropes. They disclose his acquisition of several concepts important to religious profession, including ideas which we have encountered in the context of the oblation ritual and in the autobiographical writings of Orderic Vitalis, of being dedicated to God. He referred to heaven as a kingdom, and in doing so confirms that boys were encouraged to understand and represent heaven in ways which we have encountered in the context of Psalter glosses in chapter three. His poem also confirms that boys encountered the concept of virginity, and were encouraged to view and express virginity as an important qualification for personal salvation. In addition to these aspects, his verses also seem to confirm ideas raised in chapter four, on changes in stylistic preferences between the eleventh and twelfth centuries. The majority of his word forms can be traced to biblical scripture, including many of those which scholars suspect served as school-texts in the grammatical curriculum, and these suggest that the study of sacred text remained important when he was writing. But I have suggested that his word choices also reveal the impact of his study of more advanced works of poetry. These may have included school-texts by Aldhelm of Sherborne and Venantius Fortunatus, which had been popular in late Anglo-Saxon England, but his verses also indicate that his experiences of Latin instruction had extended into the study of Ovid and Albius Tibullus, whose works were more characteristic of library and school-text collections after the Norman Conquest.

There are no parallels, sadly, when it comes to asking what girls and women thought themselves. Verses attributed to Saint Eadgyth do not give us access to her own voice in quite the same way, and since they are not original compositions, they may only, and at most, allow us a view of her editorial choices and liturgical interests. They may be significant, for example, in the sense that contemporaries thought them consistent with the Latinity of a contemporary religious woman, and they may be useful too to the degree that they represent literary choices, and are suggestive of a mind which had invested in biblical study and the liturgy, and related to Christian virtues and disciplined behaviours. But the primary source base cannot confirm, one way or another, whether the dynamics of discipline, liturgical training, and literary formation which we have set out rather tentatively in preceding chapters, informed the experiences of this particular religious too.

The attribution to Eadgyth of Wilton of a decorated alb may not be sufficient to make any firm conclusions about the lives of young women in contemporary Benedictine houses either, but I have suggested that it provides a better anchor for this study. This alb indicates what contemporaries expected girls to learn and how contemporaries expected girls to express their learning in a religious context. I suggest that references to Eadgyth's embellishment of this alb remind us of the significance of skills in sewing which have left little trace today but which might have been important to girls' monastic development, and I consider that this activity might have been important to girls' sense of religious identity as they approached adulthood too. This alb is significant because it represents the development of an individual who had learnt to subsume herself into religious narratives and into a familial relationship with the figure of Christ, replacing the Virgin Mary (*vice Mariae*). It is significant too because it presents us with evidence similar to that which we encountered in chapter one, of feminine pronouns added into copies of the *Regula Benedicti*, and, indeed, in chapter two, of a feminisation of a biblical passage in a vernacular version of the *Regularis Concordia*, both of which suggest that religious women observed a practice of imagining themselves into biblical texts and dramatic liturgies, casting themselves as agents of religious narratives. Although we can hardly push conclusions any further, it is certainly tempting to consider how this evidence might be understood in even broader terms, and when examined in the light of evidence for the activities of contemporary boys and men. It would be tempting to speculate, for example, that craft might have provided religious girls and women with a means to develop and acquire a specific reputation, providing them with an arena in which women's religious houses could foster the kinds of idiosyncratic religious identities, selective engagement with the liturgy, and dynamics of competition in craft which we have previously only been able to consider in the light of boys' performance in the liturgy and on the basis of the Latin *Regularis Concordia* and contemporary school-texts.

One could perhaps question the wisdom of assuming that craft skills were exclusively or predominantly connected to the experiences of religious girls. We should therefore perhaps be careful not to preclude entirely the possibility that boys were expected to engage in a similar area of development, allowing the possibility that boys and girls were not as differentiated by these skills as sources imply. We can, after all, find accounts which associate religious boys and men with other kinds of craft, including all contemporary versions of the life of Saint Dunstan, which attributed to him skill in the design of religious garments and in iron-working.[1] But even so, and as far as I know, no records surviving from this period connect a skill in needlework with the religious experience of boys or men, and so it would seem reasonable to consider that needlework was more or less particular to girls, marking out their lives from boys.

Over the course of the preceding chapters we have drawn attention to different emphases of childhood development which may have informed and also resulted from differences in the trajectories of the careers to which boys and girls could aspire. We have considered that, while girls could not aspire to priestly offices, religious girls and women responded to limitations in their access to the liturgy by engaging with religious life from different angles, by adjusting rules to allow girls to adopt a proxy, and by allowing girls to work on crafts that were likely to have a function in a sacramental context. We have suggested that the presence of feminine

---

1 Eadmer, *Vita Sancti Dunstani,* in *Lives and Miracles,* ed. and trans. Muir and Turner, see pp. 60-1: 'Haec inter opera eius rogatur a quadam matrona, religiosa quidem et stadium habente placendi Deo, domum suam venire, et orarium sibi, quod ad ornatum et ministerium aecclesiae Dei inaurare volebat, artificiosa quam in auri opera imitaretur arte praepingere/ Among the things he did, he was asked by a certain matron, who was indeed religious and possessed by a desire to please God, that he come to her house and design a stole for her with his craftsman's skill which she could copy in golden thread; she wished to cover this stole with gold for the embellishment of the church of God and its service' and also 66-7 'Quadam igitur vice, cum vir ipse, iam die advesperascente, fabrili intenderet operi, astitit, fenestrae ipsius demon unus humana effigie tectus, rogans sibi nescio quid operis ab homine fieri/ Therefore on a certain occasion, as day was advancing towards evening and Dunstan was engaged in smith's work, a demon appeared at his window clothed in human likeness and asked him to do some task or other for him'.

word forms in a dramatic ritual described in a surviving fragment of the *Regularis Concordia* provides this sort of evidence, and, indeed, if we can allow ourselves to push the limits of these conclusions slightly, we might be tempted to consider they provide evidence of how girls and women may even have acted out this ritual, and developed their own traditions in the liturgy, allowing deacons to narrate their dramas. Such a degree of participation cannot be ascertained with any certainty, but, if accurate, it would mean that girls participated in dramatic rituals in far closer parallel to boys than has often been entertained; and it would also provide an origin to the abundance of evidence we possess for religious women who participated in and organised dramatic rituals in later medieval centuries too.[2]

One could press our evidence in other ways, by exploring the limits of girls' participation in the sacramental liturgy and the extent to which it provided an important axis of difference with the experience of boyhood. It is clear of course that religious boys had access to the altar space by helping priests and deacons, that they enjoyed privileged access to a later career in the priestly orders, and, if they had entered a cathedral see in particular, where they encountered bishops, enjoyed access to and might aspire to a career on the episcopal bench too. Girls did not share in these future trajectories, and their formative years could not, therefore, have been shaped by the possibility of obtaining in later adulthood positions of responsibility, aside from, that is, as office holders within the confines of the monastic enclosure.

But there may have been other areas of activity that were open to girls, such as the cleaning and handling of holy vessels and other objects associated with and centred on services that took place at the altar, which we have

---

2 For more on this, and for a discussion of the emergence of one of the earliest sources of evidence for liturgical dramas in the houses of religious women, coincidentally at the Benedictine houses of Wilton and Barking, see Alison Findlay, *Playing Spaces in Early Women's Drama* (Cambridge, 2006), p. 148: 'Dunbar Ogden has identified twenty-three music dramas performed by nuns from across Europe, from the twelfth century to 1600, which answer a need for dramatic expression by women and for the education of women [...] In the Wilton and Barking scripts for the *Visitatio Sepulcri* (a dramatisation of the three Maries' visit to Christ's tomb), the Maries were personated by nuns'. See also, Dunbar Ogden, *The Staging of Drama in the Medieval Church* (Newark DE, 2001).

not covered in these chapters but which we might also have approached in this work and which would seem very likely to provide fruitful ground for further investigation. Evidence for girls' cleaning of holy vessels would not remove an important distinction between the career trajectories open to religious women and men, but these activities would allow scholars to explore the significance of engaging with the sacraments in religious childhood. Evidence of girls cleaning the objects which served a function on the altar, and which held the Eucharistic offerings, could provide ground useful to better understanding the nature of divisions between the childhoods of girls and boys, and could throw light onto where and how far childhood provided a space which allowed girls to engage with their communities in ways that may not have been far removed from boys, providing them with a similar opportunities to invest themselves in the religious activities of reformed Benedictine houses of late Anglo-Saxon or Anglo-Norman England c.950-1200.

BIBLIOGRAPHY

Manuscript and archival resources

Cambridge,
  Corpus Christi College, MS 57.
  Corpus Christi College, MS 146.
  Corpus Christi College, MS 201.
  Corpus Christi College, MS 473.
  University Library, MS Hh.1.10.
London, British Library,
  Additional MS 49598.
  Cotton Julius MS A. ii.
  Harley MS 3271.
  Stowe MS 944.
Oxford,
  Bodleian Library, Bodley MS 579.
  Bodleian Library, Hatton MS 48.
  St. John's College, MS 154.

Printed primary sources

Abbo of Fleury, *Questiones Grammaticales*, ed. Anita Guerreau-Jalabert., *Abbo Floriacenis: Questiones Grammaticales*, Auteurs Latins du Moyen Âge (Paris: Belles Lettres, 1982).

Abbo of Saint-Germain-des-Prés, *Bella Parisiacae Urbis*, ed. Anton Pauels., *Bella Parisiacae Urbis. Buch I: Lateinischer Text, Deutsche Übersetzung und Sprachliche Bemerkungen*, Lateinische Sprache und Literatur des Mittelalters (Frankfurt: Frankfurt a.M, 1984); ed. and trans. Anthony Adams and Alan G. Rigg, 'A Verse Translation of Abbo of St. Germain's *Bella Parisiacae Urbis*', *Journal of Medieval Latin* 14 (2004), pp. 1-68.

Abbots, *Lives of the Abbots of Wearmouth and Jarrow*, ed. and trans. Christopher Grocock, and Ian N. Wood., *The Abbots of Wearmouth and Jarrow* (Oxford: Clarendon Press, 2013).

Ælfric Bata, *Colloquia [et Colloquia Difficiliora]*, ed. and trans. Scott Gwara, and David Porter, *Anglo-Saxon Conversations: The Colloquies of Ælfric Bata* (Woodbridge: Boydell Press, 1997).

Ælfric of Eynsham, *Colloquium*, ed. George N. Garmonsway., *Ælfric's Colloquy* (London: Methuen, 1939), rev. ed. Exeter: University Press, 1991.

— *Epistula ad monachos Egneshamnenses directa*, ed. Hadrianus Nocent, with Candida Elvert and Kassius Hallinger, in *Consuetudinum Saeculi x/xi/xii Monumenta Non-Cluniacensia*, ed. Kassius Hallinger, 7.3 (Siegburg: Franz Schmitt, 1984), pp. 155-85; ed. and trans. Christopher Jones, *Ælfric's Letter to the Monks of Eynsham*, Cambridge Studies in Anglo-Saxon England 24 (Cambridge: University Press, 1998).

— *Excerptiones de arte grammatica anglice*, ed. Julius Zupitza., *Ælfrics Grammatik und Glossar: I Text und Varienten*, Sammlung Englischer Denkmäler in Kritischen Ausgaben (Berlin: Weidmann, 1880); also ed. Tony Hunt, *Teaching and Learning Latin in Thirteenth Century England* (Cambridge: D. S. Brewer, 1991), 3 vols.

— *Prefaces*, ed. and trans. Jonathan Wilcox, Durham Medieval Texts 9 (Durham, 1994).

Aelred of Rievaulx, *De Sanctimoniali de Wattun*, ed. Jacques-Paul Migne, PL 195, 789-96.

Æthelwold of Winchester, *Old English Rule of Benedict*, ed. Arnold Schröer, *Die Angelsächsischen Prosabearbeitungen der Benediktinerregel*, Bibliothek der Angelsächsiechen Prosa II (Kassel: G.H. Wigand, 1885-88), 2 vols; rev. ed. with supplement by Helmut Gneuss, Darmstadt: Wissenschaftliche Buchgesellschaft, 1964.

— *Regularis Concordia Anglicae Nationis Monachorum Sanctimonialiumque*, ed. and trans. Thomas Symons, *Regularis Concordia Anglicae Nationis Monachorum Sanctimonialiumque. The Monastic Agreement of the Monks and Nuns of the English Nation*, Medieval Classics (New York: Oxford University Press, 1953). ed. Lucia Kornexl, *Die Regularis Concordia und ihre Altenglische Interlinearversion mit Einleitung und Kommentar*, Münchener Universitätsschriften. Philosophische Fakultät. Texte und Untersuchungen zur Englischen Philologie 17 (Munich: Fink, 1993).

Aldhelm of Sherborne, *Carmen de Virginitate*, ed. Rudolf Ehwald, MGH, Scriptores, Auct. ant. xv.

Apophthegmata Patrum: *The Sayings of the Desert Fathers*, ed. Benedicta Ward (London: Mowbrays, 1975); rev. ed., 1981.

Anselm of Canterbury, *Epistolae*, ed. and trans. Walter Fröhlich, *Letters of Saint Anselm of Canterbury*, Cistercian studies series, 96-7, 142 (Kalamazoo, Mich: Cistercian Publications, 1990-4), 3 vols.

Asser of Sherborne, *de Rebus Gestis Aelfredi*, ed. William H. Stevenson, *Asser's Life of King Alfred: Together with the Annals of Saint Neots Erroneously Ascribed to Asser* (Oxford: Clarendon Press, 1904); rev. ed. Dorothy Whitelock, Oxford 1959; trans. Simon Keynes and Michael Lapidge, *Alfred the Great: Asser's Life of King Alfred and Other Contemporary Sources* (London: Penguin Books, 1983).

Aurelian of Arles, *Regula ad monachos/A Rule for Monks*, ed. Jacques-Paul Migne, PL 68, 385-398.

'B'., *Vita Sancti Dunstani*, ed. William Stubbs., *Memorials of Saint Dunstan Archbishop of Canterbury*, Rerum Britannicarum Medii Aevi Scriptores 63 (London: Longman, 1874), 3-52; ed. and trans. Michael Winterbottom and Michael Lapidge, *Early Lives of Saint Dunstan*, OMT (Oxford: Clarendon Press, 2012), pp. 1-109.

Basil of Caesarea, *Asketikon*, ed. Jacques-Paul Migne, 'eiusdem regulae fusius tractatae', PG 31, cols. 890-1050; Rufinus of Aquileia, *Regula Basili*, ed. Klaus Zelzer., *Basili Regula*, Corpus Scriptorium Ecclesiasticorum Latinorum 86 (Vienna: Hölder-Pichler-Tempsky, 1986); ed. and trans. Anna M. Silvas, *The Rule of St Basil in Latin and English: A Revised Critical Edition* (Collegeville Minn: Liturgical Press, 2013).

— *Epistolae Basilii*, ed. and trans. Roy J. Deferrari., *Saint Basil: The Letters*, Loeb Classical Library (London: Heinemann, 1962), 4 vols.; repr. Cambridge, MA: Harvard University Press, 2014.

Bede, *Historia Ecclesiastica*, ed. and trans. Bertram Colgrave and Roger A. B. Mynors, *Ecclesiastical History of the English People*, Oxford Medieval Texts (Oxford: Clarendon Press, 1969).

Benedict of Aniane, *Collectio Capitularis*, ed. Josef, Semmler, 'Regula Sancti Benedicti Anianensis sive Collectio Capitularis: Legislatio Aquisgranensis', in *Corpus Consuetudinum Monasticarum* I, ed. Kassius Hallinger (Siegburg: Fanciscum Schmitt, 1963), pp. 502-536.

Benedict of Monte Cassino, *Regula Sancti Benedicti*, ed. and trans. Bruce Venarde, *The Rule of Benedict*, Dumbarton Oaks Medieval Library 6 (Cambridge, Mass: Harvard University Press, 2011); ed. and trans. Henri Logeman, *The Rule of St. Benet: Latin and Anglo-Saxon Interlinear Version*, Early English Text Society Original Series 90 (London: N. Trübner, 1888).

Boniface, *Epistolae*, ed. Michael Tangl, MGH Epist. 1; trans. Ephraim Emerton, *The Letters of Saint Boniface*, Records of Western Civilization (New York: Columbia University Press, 2000).

— *Vitae Sancti Bonifatii Archiepiscopi Moguntini*, ed. Wilhelm Levison, Scriptores Rerum Germanicarum in Usum Scholarum ex Monomentis Germaniae Historicis Recusi 57 (Hanover: Impensis Bibliopolii Hahniani, 1905).

Breviary of Hyde Abbey, ed. John B. L. Tolhurst., *The Monastic Breviary of Hyde Abbey, Winchester*, Henry Bradshaw Society, vols. 69-71, 76, 78, 80 (London: Boydell Press, 1932-42).

Byrhtferth of Ramsey, *Enchiridion*, ed. and trans. Peter Baker and Michael Lapidge, EETS s.s. 15 (Oxford: University Press, 1995).

— *Vita Sancti Oswaldi*, in *Byrhtferth of Ramsey: Lives of St Oswald and St Ecgwine*, ed. and trans. Michael Lapidge, OMT (Oxford: Clarendon Press, 2009), pp. 2-203.

Caesarius of Arles, *Regula ad virgines*, ed. Jacques-Paul Migne, PL 67, 399-404; trans. Maria C. McCarthy, *The Rule for Nuns of Saint Caesarius of Arles:*

A Translation with Critical Introduction (Washington: Catholic University of America Press, 1960).

Capitula Neustrica, in MGH Capit. Episc. I & III.

Cartularium Saxonicum, ed. Walter de Grey Birch, *Cartularium Saxnicum: A Collection of Charters Relating to Anglo-Saxon History* (London: Whiting, 1885-93), 3 vols; ed. and trans. Peter H. Sawyer, *Anglo-Saxon Charters*, Royal Historical Society: Guides and Handbooks 8 (London: Royal Historical Society, 1968).

Chronicon Abbatiae Rameseiensis: A Saeculo x. Usque ad Anum Circiter 1200, ed. William D. Macray, Rerum Britannicarum Medii Aevi Scriptores 83 (London: Longman, 1886).

Chronicon Monasterii de Abingdon, ed. Joseph Stephenson, Rerum Britannicarum Medii Aevi Scriptores (London: Longman, 1858), 2 vols.

Concilia Africae, ed. Charles Munier, *Corpus Christianorum*, Series Latina 149 (Turnhout: Brepols, 1974).

Concilia Galliae, ed. Charles Munier and Charles De Clerque., *Corpus Christianorum*, Series Latina, 148 (Turnhout: Brepols, 1963).

Concilios Visigoticos, ed. José Vives, Marín Martínez, and Gonzalo M. Díez., *Concilios Visigóticos e Hispano-Romanos*, España Cristiana 1 (Barcelona: Consejo Superior de Investigaciones Cientificas, 1963).

'Concordia episcoporum (a. 813)', MGH Conc. I, 12, 298-9.

Donatus, Aelius, *Ars minor*, ed. Louis Holtz, *Donat et la Tradition de L'Enseignement Grammatical: Étude sur l'Ars Donati et sa Diffusion (IVe-IXe siècle) et Édition Critique, 585-602* (Paris: Centre Nationale de la Recherche Scientifique, 1981).

'Duplex legationis edictum (a. 789)', MGH Capit. 1, 63.

Eadmer of Canterbury, *Epistola ad Glastonienses*, in *Memorials of Saint Dunstan*, ed. William Stubbs, Rerum Britannicarum Medii Aevi Scriptores (London: Longman, 1874), pp. 412-22; ed. and trans. Richard Sharpe, 'Eadmer's Letter to the Monks of Glastonbury', in *The Archaeology and History of Glastonbury Abbey: Essay in Honour of the Ninetieth Birthday of C. A. Raleigh Radford*, ed. Lesley Abrams, James P. Carley, and Courtenay A. R. Radford (Woodbridge: Boydell, 1991), pp. 205-216.

— *Historia Novorum*, ed. Martin Rule., *Eadmeri Historia Novorum in Anglia et Opuscula Duo de Vita Sancti Anselmi et Quibusdam Miraculis Eius*, Rerum Britannicarum Medii Aevi Scriptores 81 (London: Longman, 1884); trans. Richard W. Southern., *Eadmer's History of Recent Events in England/Historia Novorum in Anglia* (London: Cresset Press, 1964).

— *Miracula Sancti Dunstani*, in *Memorials of Saint Dunstan: Archbishop of Canterbury*, ed. William Stubbs, Great Britain. Public Record Office (London: Longman & Co., 1874), pp. 223-250; ed. and trans. Benjamin Muir and Andrew Turner, *Eadmer of Canterbury: Lives and Miracles of Saints Oda, Dunstan, and Oswald*, OMT (Oxford: Clarendon Press, 2006), pp. 44-159.

— *De Reliquiis Sancti Audoeni*, ed. Arnold Wilmart, 'De Reliquiis Sancti Audoeni et Quorundam Aliorum Sanctorum quae Cantuariae in Aecclesia

Domini Salvatoris Habentur', *Revue des Sciences Religieuses* 15 (1935), pp. 362-70.
— *Vita Sancti Anselmi*, ed. and trans. Richard W. Southern, *Life of Anselm, Archbishop of Canterbury* Oxford Medieval Texts (London: Thomas Nelson, 1962); rev. ed., Oxford: Clarendon, 1972.
— *Vita Sancti Dunstani*, ed. and trans. Benjamin J. Muir, and Andrew J. Turner, *Lives of Saints Oda, Dunstan, and Oswald*, Oxford Medieval Texts (Oxford: Clarendon Press, 2006), pp. 44-159.
— *Vita Sancti Oswaldi*, ed. and trans. Benjamin J. Muir and Andrew J. Turner, *Lives of Saints Oda, Dunstan, and Oswald*, Oxford Medieval Texts (Oxford: Clarendon Press, 2006), pp. 217-89.
Evagrius of Antioch, *Vita Beati Antonii Abbatis*, ed. Jacques-Paul Migne, PL 73, 127-194.
Excerptiones de Prisciano, ed. and trans. David Porter, *The Source for Ælfric's Latin-Old English Grammar*, Anglo-Saxon Texts 4 (Cambridge: D.S. Brewer, 2002).
Faricius of Arezzo, *Vita Sancti Aldhelmi*, ed. Michael Winterbottom, 'An Edition of Faricius, Vita S. Aldhelmi', *Journal of Medieval Latin* 15 (2005), pp. 93-147.
Fredegaud of Winchester, *Breviloquium Vitae Beati Wilfredi*, ed. Alistair Campbell., *Frithegodi Monachi Breviloquium Vitae Beati Wilfredi et Wulstani Cantoris Narratio Metrica de Sancti Swithuno*, Thesauri Mundi: Bibliotheca Scriptorium Latinorum Mediae et Recentioris Aetatis (Zürich: In Aedibus Thesauri Mundi, 1950).
Goscelin of Saint Bertin, *Lectiones in Festivitate Sancte Sexburge*, in *The Hagiography of the Female Saints of Ely*, ed. and trans. Rosalind Love, OMT (Oxford: Clarendon Press, 2004), pp. 1-10.
— *Lectiones in Natale Sancte Eormenhilde*, in *Goscelin of Saint Bertin: The Hagiography of the Female Saints of Ely*, ed. and trans. Rosalind Love, OMT (Oxford: Clarendon Press, 2004), pp. 11-23.
— *Liber Confortatorius*, ed. Charles H. Talbot, 'The *Liber Confortatorius* of Goscelin of Saint Bertin', *Analecta Monastica* 37 (1955), 1-117; trans. Moniker Otter, *Goscelin of St Bertin: The Book of Encouragement and Consolation [Liber Confortatorius]*, Library of Medieval Women (Cambridge: D.S. Brewer, 2004).
— *De Translatione vel Elevatione Sanctarum Virginum Ethelburgae, Hildelithae et Wlfhildae*, ed. Marvin Colker, 'The Texts of Jocelyn of Canterbury which Relate to the History of Barking Abbey', *Studia Monastica* 7 (1965), pp. 383-460.
— *Translatio Sancte Edithe Virginis*, in 'La légende de ste Édith en Prose et Vers par le Moine Goscelin', ed. Arnold Wilmart, *Analecta Bollandiana* 56 (1938), pp. 265-307.
— *Translatio Sancte Wulfhilde*, ed. Marvin Colker, 'The Texts of Jocelyn of Canterbury which Relate to the History of Barking Abbey', *Studia Monastica* 7 (1965), pp. 431-434.
— *Visio Abbatisse* Ælfgive, ed. Marvin Colker, 'The Texts of Jocelyn of Canterbury which Relate to the History of Barking Abbey', *Studia Monastica* 7 (1965), pp. 452-454.

— *Vita Sancte Edithe Virginis*, ed. Arnold, Wilmart, 'La légende de Ste Édith en Prose et Vers par le Moine Goscelin', *Analecta Bollandiana* 56 (1938), pp. 5-101; trans. Michael Wright and Kathleen Loncar, 'Goscelin's Legend of Edith', in *Writing the Wilton Women: Goscelin's Legend of Edith and Liber Confortatorius*, ed. Stephanie Hollis, W. R. Barnes, Rebecca Hayward, Kathleen Loncar, and Michael Wright, Medieval Women: Texts and Contexts 9 (Turnhout: Brepols, 2004), pp. 17-67.

— *Vita Sancte Wihtburge Virginis*, in *The Hagiography of the Female Saints of Ely*, ed. and trans. Rosalind Love, OMT (Oxford: Clarendon Press, 2004), pp. 53-93.

— *Vita Sancte Wulfhilde*, ed. Mario Esposito, 'La Vie de Sainte Vulfhilde par Goscelin de Cantorbery', *Analecta Bollandiana* 32 (1913), pp. 10-26.

— *Vita Sancti Wulfsini*, ed. Charles Talbot, 'The Life of Wulfsin of Sherborne by Goscelin', *Revue Bénédictine* 69 (1959), pp. 68-85; trans. Rosalind Love, 'The Life of St Wulfsige of Sherborne by Goscelin of St. Bertin: A New Translation with Introduction, Appendix and Notes', in *St Wulfsige and Sherborne: Essays to Celebrate the Millennium of the Benedictine Abbey, 998-1998*, ed. Katherine Barker, David Hinton, and Alan Hunt, Bournemouth University School of Conservation Sciences: Occasional Paper 9 (Oxford: Oxbow, 2005), pp. 98-123.

Herbert of Losinga, *Epistolae*, ed. Robert Anstruther., *Epistolae Herberti de Losinga, Primi Episcopi Norwiciensis, Osberti de Clara et Elmeri, Prioris Cantuariensis*, Caxton Société (Brussels: A. Vandale, 1846); trans. Henri Symonds and Edward M. Goulburn., *The Life, Letters, and Sermons of Bishop Herbert de Losinga* (Oxford: James Parker, 1878), 2 vols.

Hexateuch, ed. Samuel J. Crawford., *The Old English Heptateuch: Ælfric's Treatise on the Old and New Testament and his Preface to Genesis*, EETS o.s. 160 (London: Oxford University Press, 1922); ed. Charles R. Dodwell and Peter Clemoes., *The Old English Illustrated Hexateuch: British Museum Cotton Claudius B.IV*, Early English Manuscripts in Facsimile 18 (Copenhagen: Rosenkilde and Bagger, 1974); ed. Richard Marsden., *The Old English Heptateuch and Ælfric's Libellus de Veteri Testamento et Novo*, EETS s.s. 330 (Oxford: University Press, 2008).

Hugh Candidus, *The Chronicle of Peterborough*, ed. and trans. Charles Mellows and William T. Mellows., *The Peterborough Chronicle of Hugh Candidus* (Peterborough: Natural History, Scientific and Archaeological Society, 1941); rev. ed. Peterborough: Museum Society, 1966.

Isidore of Seville, *Etymologiae sive Originum*, ed. Jacques-Paul Migne, PL 82, pp. 73-728; trans. Stephen Barney, J. A. Beach and Oliver Berghof., *The Etymologies of Isidore of Seville* (Cambridge: University Press, 2006).

John Cassian, *Collationes*, ed. and trans. Boniface Ramsey, *The Conferences*, Ancient Christian Writers 57 (New York: Newman Press, 1997).

— *Institutiones*, ed. and trans. Boniface Ramsey, *The Institutes*, Ancient Christian Writers 58 (New York: Newman Press, 2000).

Lanfranc of Canterbury, *Constitutiones*, ed. and trans. David Knowles., *The Monastic Constitutions of Lanfranc/Decreta Lanfranci Monachis Cantuariensibus Transmissa*,

Medieval Classics (London: Nelson, 1951); rev. ed. Christopher N. L. Brooke, Oxford Medieval Texts (Oxford: Clarendon Press, 2002).
— *Epistolae*, ed. and trans. Helen V. Clover and Margaret T. Gibson, *Letters of Lanfranc, Archbishop of Canterbury*, Oxford Medieval Texts (Oxford: University Press, 1979).
Liber Eliensis, ed. Eearnest O. Blake, Royal Historical Society: Camden Third Series 92 (London: Offices of the Royal Historical Society, 1962); trans. Janet Fairweather., *Liber Eliensis: A History of the Isle of Ely from the Seventh to the Twelfth Century* (Woodbridge: Boydell, 2005).
Liber Vitae, ed. Simon Keynes, *The Liber Vitae of the New Minster and Hyde Abbey, Winchester: British Library Stowe 944: Together with Leaves from British Library Cotton Vespasian A. VIII and British Library Cotton Titus D. XXVII*, Early English Manuscripts in Facsimile 26 (Copenhagen: Rosenkilde and Bagger, 1996).
Miracula Sancti Erkenwaldi, in *The Saint of London: The Life and Miracles of St. Erkenwald*, ed. Gordon, E. Whatley, Medieval and Renaissance Texts & Studies Series 58 (Binghampton, NY: Medieval and Renaissance Texts and Studies, 1989), pp. 86-97.
Monasteriales Indicia: The Anglo-Saxon Monastic Sign Language, ed. and trans. Debbie Banham (Pinner, Middlesex: Anglo-Saxon Books, 1991).
Orderic Vitalis, *Historia Ecclesiastica*, ed. and trans. Marjorie Chibnall, *The Ecclesiastial History of Orderic Vitalis*, Oxford Medieval Texts (Oxford: Clarendon Press, 1968-1980), 6 vols.
Ordinale and Customary of the Benedictine Nuns of Barking Abbey: Oxford University College, MS 169, ed. Joseph B. L. Tolhurst, HBS 2 vols. (London, 1926); repr. Woodbridge: Boydell, 2010.
Osbern of Canterbury, *Miracula Sancti Dunstani*, in *Memorials of Saint Dunstan: Archbishop of Canterbury*, ed. William Stubbs, Great Britain. Public Record Office (London: Longman & Co., 1874), pp. 129-161.
— *Vita Sancti Alphegi*, ed. Henry Wharton, 'Vita S. Alphegi Archiepiscopi Cantuariensis Auctore Osberno', *Anglia Sacra* 2 (1691); trans. Francis Shaw, *Osbern's Life of Alfege* (London: St. Paul's, 1999).
Osbert of Clare, *Vita Sancte Ædburge Virginis*, in *Royal Saints of Anglo-Saxon England: A Study of West Saxon and East Anglian Cults*, ed. Susan Ridyard, Cambridge Studies in Medieval Life and Thought: 4th series., 9 (Cambridge: University Press, 1988), pp. 253-308.
Ovid, *Metamorphoses*, ed. and trans. George P. Gould and Frank Justus Miller, Loeb Classical Library, 42 & 43 (London: Heinemann, 1921), rev. ed., George P. Goold, Cambridge MA: Harvard University Press, 2014, 2 vols.
Patrick of Dublin, *Versus allegorici*, ed. and trans. Aubrey Gwynn, *The Writings of Bishop Patrick of Dublin, 1074-1084*, Scriptores Latini Hiberniae I (Dublin: Institute for Advanced Studies, 1955).
Patrologia Latina, ed. Jaques-Paul Migne, 221 vols. (Paris, 1844-64).

Pope Gregory IX, *Decretales*, ed. Emil Friedberg and Aemilius L. Richter., *Corpus Juris Canonici: Decretalium Collectiones: Decretales Gregorii P. IX* (Lepzig: Tauchnitz, 1879-1881), 2 vols.

Priscian, *Institutiones Grammaticae*, ed. Heinrich Keil, *Grammatici Latini*, II (Leipzig: B.G. Teubneri, 1857-1880), 8 vols.

Prudentius, *Opera*, ed. Henry John Thomson, Loeb Classical Library 387, 398 (London: W. Heinemann, 1949-1953); repr. Cambridge MA: Harvard University Press, 2014.

Psalter, ed. Phillip Pulsiano., *Old English Glossed Psalters: Psalms 1-50*, Toronto Old English Series 11 (Toronto: University Press, 2001); *Salisbury Psalter*, ed. Celia Sisam and Kenneth Sisam., EETS o.s. 242 (Oxford: University Press, 1959).

Rankin, Susan (ed.), *The Winchester Troper: Facsimile Edition and Introduction*, Early English Church Music 50 (London: Stainer & Bell, 2007).

De Raris Fabulis Retractata, ed. William H. Stevenson, *Early Scholastic Colloquies*, Anecdota Oxoniensia: Mediaeval and Modern Series (Oxford: Clarendon Press, 1929).

Regula Magistri/ La Régle du Maître, ed. and trans. Adalbert De Vogüé, Sources Chrétiennes. Série des Textes Monastiques d'Occident (Paris : Editions du Cerf, 1964-5); trans. Adalbert De Vogüé, and Luke Eberle., *The Rule of the Master*, Cistercians Studies Series 6 (Kalamazoo Mich: Cistercian Publications, 1977).

Remigius of Auxerre, *In Artem Maiorem Donati Commentum*, ed. Heinrich Keil, GL vol. 8.

Robert of Arbrissel, *Versus on Eva*, ed. Therese Latzke, 'Robert von Arbissel: Ermengard und Eva', *Mittellateinisches Jahrbuch* 19 (1984), pp. 116-154.

Robert of Flamborough, *Liber Poenitentialis*, ed. J. J. F. Firth., *Liber Poenitentialis*, Studies and Texts 18 (Toronto: Pontifical Institute of Mediaeval Studies, 1971).

Rouleaux des Morts du IXe au XVe Siècle, ed. Léopold V. DeLisle., Société de L'Histoire de France 135 (Paris: Mme. Ve. J. Renouard, 1866).

Rufinus of Aquileia, *Asketikon*, ed. Klaus Zelzer., *Basili Regula*, CSEL 86 (Vienna: Hölder-Pichler-Tempsky, 1986); trans. Anna M. Silva, *The Rule of St Basil in Latin and English: A Revised Critical Edition* (Collegeville Minn: Liturgical Press, 2013).

Schröer, Arnold, 'De Consuetudine Monachorum', *Englische Studien: Organ für Englische Philologie* 9 (1886), pp. 290-6.

Smaragdus of Saint-Mihiel, *Expositio in Regulam Sancti Benedicti*, ed. and trans. David Barry and Jean Leclerqc., *Smaragdus of Saint-Mihiel: Commentary on the Rule of Saint Benedict* (Kalamazoo Mich: Cistercian Publications, 2007).

Statuta Ordinis Cisterciensis, ed. Joseph M. Canivez, *Statuta Capitulorum Generalium Ordinis Cisterciensis ab Anno 1116 ad Annum 1786*, I, Bibliothèque de la Revue d'Histoire Ecclésiatique (Louvain: Bureaux de la Revue, 1933-41), 8 vols.

Stephen of Ripon, *Vita Sancti Wilfridi*, ed. and trans. Bertram Colgrave, *Life of Bishop Wilfrid* (Cambridge: University Press, 1927), rev. ed. Cambridge, 1985.

Stubbs, William and Arthur W. Haddan (eds. and trans.), *Councils and Ecclesiastical*

Documents Relating to Great Britain and Ireland (Oxford: Clarendon Press, 1869-78), 3 vols; repr. Oxford, 1964.

Theodore of Canterbury, *Canones Theodori Cantuariensis*, ed. Paul Finsterwalder., *Die Canones Theodori Cantuariensis und ihre Überlieferungsformen*, Untersuchungen zu den Bussbüchern des 7., 8. und 9. Jahrhunderts 1 (Weimar: H. Böhlaus, 1929).

Thomas of Elmham, *Historia Monasterii Sancti Augustini Cantuariensis*, ed. Charles Hardwick, Rerum Britannicarum Medii Aevi Scriptores: Chronologia Augustinensis 8 (London: Longman, 1858).

Tibullus, *Panegyricus Messallae*, ed. Francis Warre Cornish, John Percival Postgate, John William Mackail, *Catullus, Tibullus, and Pervigilium Veneris*, Loeb Classical Library 6, (Cambridge MA: Harvard University Press, 1913), rev. ed. George P. Goold, Cambridge MA: Harvard University Press, 2014, pp. 306-23.

Turgot of Durham, *Vita Sancte Margarete*, ed. and trans. William Forbes-Leith, *Life of St. Margaret, Queen of Scotland* (Dunfermline: St. Margaret's Catholic Church Press, 1880), rev. ed. Edinburgh, 1884.

Vita Beate Sexburge Regine, in *Hagiography of the Female Saints of Ely*, ed. and trans. Rosalind Love, OMT (Oxford: Clarendon Press, 2004), pp. 133-89.

Vita Edwardi Regis, ed. and trans. Frank Barlow., *Vita Aedwardi Regis qui apud Westmonasterium Requiescit/ The Life of King Edward Who Rests at Westminster*, [Later Oxford] Medieval Texts (London: Thomas Nelson, 1962); rev. ed. Oxford: Clarendon Press, 1992.

William of Malmesbury, *Gesta Pontificum Anglorum/The History of the English Bishops*, ed. and trans. Michael Winterbottom and Rodney M. Thomson, Oxford Medieval Texts (Oxford: Clarendon Press, 2007), 2 vols.

— *Gesta Regum Anglorum/The History of the English Kings*, ed. and trans. Roger A. B. Mynors, Michael Winterbottom and Rodney Thomson, Oxford Medieval Texts (Oxford: Clarendon Press, 1998-9), 2 vols.

— *Vita Sancti Wulfstani*, in *Lives of SS. Wulfstan, Dunstan, Patrick, Benignus and Indract*, ed. and trans. Michael Winterbottom and Rodney M. Thomson, Oxford Medieval Texts (Oxford: University Press, 2002), pp. 9-155.

Willibald of Eichstätt, 'Vita Willibaldi Episcopi Eichastetensis', MGH Script. supp. tom. pars III, no. VII, 86-106.

Whitelock, Dorothy, and Harold D. Hazeltine (ed.), *Anglo-Saxon Wills*, Cambridge Studies in English Legal History (Cambridge: University Press, 1930).

Whitelock, Dorothy, M. Brett, and Christopher N. L. Brooke (eds. and trans.), *Councils and Synods, with Other Documents Relating to the English Church AD. 871-1204* (Oxford: Clarendon Press, 1981), 2 vols. [A continuation of Arthur W. Hadden and William Stubbs (eds.) above].

Whitelock, Dorothy, *English Historical Documents I, c. 500-1042*, English Historical Documents I (London: Eyre & Spottiswoode, 1955), rev. edn., London: Routledge 1996.

Wulfstan Cantor, *Narratio Metrica de Sancto Swithuno*, ed. Alistair Campbell., *Frithegodi Monachi Breviloquium Vitae Beati Wilfredi et Wulfstani Cantoris*

Narratio Metrica de Sancto Swithuno, Thesauri Mundi: Bibliotheca Scriptorium Latinorum Mediae et Recentioris Aetatis (Zürich: In Aedibus Thesauri Mundi, 1950); trans. Alexander. R. Rumble, Martin Biddle, Birthe Kjølbye-Biddle and Michael Lapidge, *The Anglo-Saxon Minsters of Winchester*, Winchester Studies (Oxford: Clarendon Press, 2002), 3 vols.

— *Vita Sancti Æthelwoldi*, ed. and trans. Michael Winterbottom and Michael Lapidge, *The Life of Saint Æthelwold*, Oxford Medieval Texts (Oxford: Clarendon Press, 1991).

Wulfstan of York, *Collectio Wigorniensis*, ed. and trans. James E. Cross and Andrew Hamer., *Wulfstan's Canon Law Collection*, Anglo-Saxon Texts I (Cambridge: D.S. Brewer, 1999).

Zupitza, Julius, 'Ein weiteres Bruchstück der *Regularis Concordia* in Altenglischer Sprache', *Archiv für das Studium der neueren Sprachen und Literaturen* 84 (1890), 1-24.

Printed secondary works

Alldred, Pam, 'Ethnography and Discourse Analysis: Dilemmas in the Representation of the Voices of Children', in *Feminist Dilemmas in Qualitative Research: Public Knowledge and Private Lives*, ed. Jane Ribbens McCarthy, and Rosalind Edwards, SAGE Research Methods (Thousand Oaks, Calif: SAGE, 1998), pp. 147-170.

Amos, Ashley, 'Old English Words for Old', in *Aging and the Aged in Medieval Europe: Selected Papers from the Annual Conference of the Centre for Medieval Studies, University of Toronto, Held 25-26 February and 11-12 November 1983*, ed. Michael M. M. Sheehan, Toronto: Pontifical Institute of Mediaeval Studies (Toronto: Pontifical Institute of Mediaeval Studies, 1990), pp. 95-106.

Ariès, Philippe., *L'Enfant et la Vie Familiale sous l'Ancien Régime* (Paris: Plon, 1960); trans. Robert Baldick., *Centuries of Childhood* (London: J. Cape, 1962).

Asad, Talal, 'On Ritual and Discipline in Medieval Christian Monasticism', *Economy and Society* 12 (1983), pp. 287-327.

Bailey, Derrick Sherman, *Homosexuality and the Western Christian Tradition* (London: Longmans, 1955).

Bailey, Merridee, *Socialising the Child in Late Medieval England, c.1400-1600* (Woodbridge: York Medieval Press, 2012)

Baker, Derek (ed.), *Medieval Women*, Studies in Church History 1 (Oxford: B. Blackwell, 1978).

Baroutsis, Aspa, Glenda Mcgregor, and Martin Mills, 'Pedagogic Voice: Student Voice in Teaching and Engagement Pedagogies', *Pedagogy, Culture & Society* 24 (2016), pp. 123-140.

Barratt, Alexandra, 'Books for Nuns: Cambridge University Library MS Additional 3042', *Notes and Queries* 242:3 (1997), pp. 310-9.

— 'Small Latin? Post-Conquest Learning of English Religious Women', in *Anglo-Latin and its Heritage: Essays in Honour of A. G. Rigg on his 64th Birthday*, ed. Siân Echard and Gernot R. Wieland, Publications of the Journal of Medieval Latin 4 (Turnhout: Brepols, 2001), pp. 51-65.

Barrow, Julia S, 'The Chronology of the Benedictine Reform', in *Edgar, King of the English, 959-975: New Interpretations*, ed. Donald Scragg, Publications of the Manchester Centre for Anglo-Saxon Studies 8 (Woodbridge: Boydell Press, 2008), pp. 211-23.

— *The Clergy in the Medieval World: Secular Clerics, Their Families and Careers in North-Western Europe, c.800-1200* (Cambridge: University Press, 2015).

Bartlett, Robert, *England under the Norman and Angevin Kings 1075-1225*, New Oxford History of England (Oxford: Clarendon Press, 2000).

Baumeister, R. F., *Identity: Cultural Change and the Struggle for Self* (Oxford: University Press, 1986).

Bayless, Martha, 'Beatus Quid Est and the Study of Grammar in Late Anglo-Saxon England', in *History of Linguistic Thought in the Early Middle Ages*, ed. Vivien Law, Amsterdam Studies in the Theory and History of Linguistic Science. Series III: Studies in the History of the Language Sciences 71 (Amsterdam: John Benjamins, 1993), pp. 67-110.

Berend, Nora, 'La Subversion Invisible: La Disparition de l'Oblation Irrévocable des Enfants dans le Droit Canons', *Médiévales* 13 (1994), pp. 123-136.

Berlière, Ursmer., *Le Recrutement dans les Monastères Bénédictins aux XIIIe et XIVe siècles*, Mémoires de la Classe des lettres 18 (Brussels : M. Lamertin, 1924).

Berry, Mary, 'What the Saxon Monks Sang: Music in Winchester in the Late Tenth Century', in *Bishop Æthelwold: His Career and Influence*, ed. Barbara Yorke (Woodbridge: Boydell Press, 1988), pp. 149-60; repr. Woodbridge, 1997.

Bell, David N., *What Nuns Read: Books and Libraries in Medieval English Nunneries*, Cistercian studies series 158 (Kalamazoo Mich: Cistercian Publications, 1995).

— 'What Nuns Read: The State of the Question', in *The Culture of Medieval English Monasticism*, ed. James C. Clark, Studies in the History of Medieval Religion 30 (Woodbridge: Boydell Press, 2007), pp. 113-33.

Billett, Jesse., *The Divine Office in Anglo-Saxon England, 597-c.1000*, Henry Bradshaw Society. Subsidia 7 (London: Boydell Press, 2014).

Blair, John., *The Church in Anglo-Saxon Society* (Oxford: University Press, 2005).

Boswell, John, *The Kindness of Strangers: The Abandonment of Children in Western Europe from Late Antiquity to the Renaissance* (New York: Pantheon Books, 1988).

Boyes, Michael, and Chandler, Michael, 'Cognitive Development, Epistemic Doubt, and Identity Formation in Adolescence', *Journal of Youth and Adolescence* 21 (1992), pp. 277-304.

Boynton, Susan, and Eric Rice (eds.), *Young Choristers c.650-1700*, Studies in Medieval Renaissance Music (Woodbridge: Boydell Press, 2008).

Brooks, Nicholas, *The Early History of the Church of Canterbury: Christ Church from 597 to 1066*, Studies in the Early History of Britain (Leicester: University Press, 1984).

— 'The Anglo-Saxon Cathedral Community, 597-1070', in *A History of Canterbury Cathedral*, ed. Patrick Collingson, Nigel Ramsey, and Margaret Sparks (Oxford: University Press, 1995), pp. 1-37.

Brown, George Hardin, 'The Psalms as the Foundation of Anglo-Saxon Learning', in *The Place of the Psalms in the Intellectual Culture of the Middle Ages*, ed. Nancy Van Deusen, SUNY Series in Medieval Studies (New York: University Press, 1999), pp. 1-24.

— 'The Dynamics of Literacy in Anglo-Saxon England', in *Textual and Material Culture in Anglo-Saxon England: Thomas Northcote Toller and the Toller Memorial Lectures*, ed. Donald Scragg (Cambridge: D.S. Brewer, 2003), pp. 109-42.

Brown, Peter, 'The Notion of Virginity in the Early Church', in *Christian Spirituality: Origins to the Twelfth Century*, ed. Bernard McGinn and John Meyendorff, World Spirituality 16 (London: Routledge & Kegan Paul, 1985), pp. 427-43.

Bullough, Donald, 'The Educational Tradition from Alfred to Ælfric: Teaching *Utrius Linguae*', *Settimane di Studio del Centro Italiano di Studi sull'Alto Medioevo* 19 (Spoleto, 1972), pp. 453-94.

— 'The Continental Background of the Reform', in *Tenth Century Studies: Studies in Commemoration of the Millennium of the Council of Winchester and Regularis Concordia*, ed. David Parsons (London: Phillimore, 1975), pp. 20-36.

Bullough, Vern L., 'The Sin against Nature and Homosexuality', in *Sexual Practices and the Medieval Church*, ed. Vern L. Bullough and James Brundage (Buffalo, New York: Prometheus Books, 1982), pp. 55-71.

Burnbaum, Tahlia, 'Naming Shame: Translating Emotion in the Old English Psalter Glosses', in *Anglo-Saxon Emotions: Reading the Heart in Old English Language, Literature and Culture*, ed. Alice Jorgensen, Frances McCormack, Jonathan Wilcox, Studies in Early Medieval Britain and Ireland (Farnham: Ashgate, 2015), pp. 109-26.

Burrow, John A., *The Ages of Man: A Study in Medieval Writing and Thought* (Oxford: University Press, 1988).

Burton, Janet., *Monastic and Religious Orders in Britain 1000-1300*, Cambridge Medieval Textbooks (Cambridge: University Press, 1994).

Burton, Janet and Julie Kerr (eds.), *The Cistercians in the Middle Ages* (Woodbridge: Boydell Press, 2011).

Butler, Ian, 'Children and the Sociology of Childhood', in *A Case of Neglect? Children's Experiences and the Sociology of Childhood*, ed. Ian Butler, and Ian Shaw, Cardiff Papers in Qualitative Research (Aldershot: Avebury, 1996), pp. 1-18.

Campbell, Alistair, 'Some Linguistic Features of Early Anglo-Latin Verse and its Use of Classical Models', *Transactions of the Philological Society* 11 (1953), pp. 1-20.

Carruthers, Mary, 'Reading with Attitude: Remembering the Book', in *The Book and the Body*, ed. Dolores W. Frese, and Katherine O'Brien O'Keeffe, Ward-Phillips Lectures in English Language and Literature 14 (London: University of Notre Dame Press, 1997), pp. 1-33.

— *The Book of Memory: A Study of Memory in Medieval Culture*, Cambridge Studies in Medieval Literature 70 (Cambridge: University Press, 1990); rev. ed. Cambridge, 2008.

Catalano, Richard, and David J. Hawkins, 'The Social Development Model: A Theory of Anti-Social Behaviour', in *Delinquency and Crime: Current Theories*, ed. David J. Hawkins (Cambridge: University Press, 1996), pp. 149-97.

Chambers, Edmund K., *The Medieval Stage* (Oxford: Clarendon Press, 1903), 2 vols.; repr. in 1 volume, New York: Dover Press, 1996.

Chapman, Don, 'Uterque lingua/ Ægðer gereord: Ælfric's Grammatical Vocabulary and the Winchester Tradition', *Journal of English and Germanic Philology* 109 (2010), pp. 421-45.

Clanchy, Michael T., *From Memory to Written Record 1066-1307* (London: Edward Arnold, 1979); rev. ed. Oxford: B. Blackwell, 1993.

Clark, Ann L, 'Why All the Fuss about the Mind? A Medievalist's Perspective on Cognitive Theory', in *History in the Comic Mode: Medieval Communities and the Matter of Person*, ed. Rachel Fulton Brown and Bruce Holsinger (New York: Columbia University Press, 2007), pp. 170-81.

Clemoes, Peter, 'The Chronology of Ælfric's Works', in *The Anglo-Saxons: Studies in Some Aspects of Their History and Culture Presented to Bruce Dickens*, ed. Peter Clemoes (London: Bowes & Bowes, 1959), pp. 212-47.

Cochelin, Isabelle, 'Besides the Book: Using the Body to Mould the Mind, Cluny in the Tenth and Eleventh Centuries', in *Medieval Monastic Education*, ed. George Ferzoco, and Carolyn Muessig (London: Leicester University Press, 2000), pp. 21-34.

— 'Introduction: Pre-Thirteenth-Century Definitions of the Life Cycle', in *Medieval Life Cycles: Continuity and Change*, ed. Isabelle Cochelin and Karen Smyth, International Medieval Research 18 (Turnhout: Brepols, 2013), pp. 1-54.

Cochelin, Isabelle, and Susan Boynton, 'The Sociomusical Role of Child Oblates at the Abbey of Cluny in the Eleventh Century', in *Musical Childhoods and the Cultures of Youth*, ed. Susan Boynton and Roe-Min Kok (Middleton, CT: Wesleyan University Press, 2006), pp. 3-24.

Constable, Giles, 'Ailred of Rievaulx and the Nun of Wattun', in *Medieval Women*, ed. Derek Baker, Studies in Church History: Subsidia I (Oxford: B. Blackwell, 1978), pp. 205-26.

Contreni, John, J, 'Carolingian Biblical Studies', in *Carolingian Essays*, ed. Uta-Renate Blumenthal (Washington, DC: Catholic University of America Press, 1983), pp. 71-98.

— 'The Carolingian School: Letters from the Classroom', in *Carolingian Learning, Masters, and Manuscripts*, ed. John Contreni (Aldershot: Variorum, 1992), pp. 84-111.

Cooke, Kathleen, 'Donors and Daughters: Shaftesbury Abbey's Benefactors, Endowments and Nuns c.1086-1130', *Anglo-Norman Studies* 12 (1989), pp. 29-45.

Corsaro, William A., *The Sociology of Childhood*, Sociology for a New Century Series (Thousand Oaks, Calif: Pine Forge, 1997); 4th ed. Thousand Oaks Calif: SAGE, 2014.

Coupland, Simon, 'The Vikings in Francia and Anglo-Saxon England to 911', *New Cambridge Medieval History* II, ed. in Rosamond McKitterick (Cambridge: University Press, 1995-8), pp. 90-201. 7 vols.

Cownie, Emma, *Religious Patronage in Anglo-Norman England, 1066-1135* (Woodbridge: Boydell Press, 1998).

Cox, Robert, 'The Old English Dicts of Cato', *Anglia* 90 (1972), pp. 1-42.

Crawford, Sally., *Childhood in Anglo-Saxon England* (Stroud: Sutton, 1999).

— 'Gomol is Snoterost: Growing Old in Anglo-Saxon England', in *Collectanea Antiqua: Essays in Memory of Sonia Chadwick Hawkes*, ed. Martin Henig and Tyler J. Smith, BAR International Series (Oxford: Archaeopress, 2007), pp. 53-9.

Crick, Julia, 'The Wealth, Patronage, and Connections of Women's Houses in Late Anglo-Saxon England', *Revue Bénédictine* 109 (1999), pp. 154-85.

Croakley, John, *Women, Men and Spiritual Power: Female Saints and Their Male Collaborators* (New York: Columbia University Press, 2006).

Cubitt, Catherine, *Anglo-Saxon Church Councils c.650-c.850*, Studies in the Early History of Britain (London: Leicester University Press, 1995).

— 'The Tenth Century Benedictine Reform in England', *Early Medieval Europe* 6 (1997), pp. 77-94.

— 'Virginity and Misogyny in Tenth- and Eleventh-Century England', *Gender & History* 12:1 (2000), pp. 1-32.

Cunningham, Hugh, *Children and Childhood in Western Society Since 1500*, Studies in Modern History: Children & Childhood in Western Society Since 1500 (London: Longman, 1995).

Dalkilic, Maryam, and Jennifer A. Vadeboncœur, 'Education and Discipline: Regulating the Child in Early Childhood Education: The Paradox of Inclusion', *Global Studies of Childhood* 6 (2016), pp. 17-30.

Davis-Secord, Jonathan, 'Sequences and Intellectual Identity at Winchester', in *Latinity and Identity in Anglo-Saxon Literature*, ed. Rebecca Stephenson and Emily Thornbury, Toronto Anglo-Saxon Series 22 (Toronto: University Press, 2016), pp. 93-117.

DeMause, Lloyd, *The History of Childhood* (London: Psychohistory Press, 1974).

Deroux, M. P., *Les Origines de l'Oblature Bénédictine: Étude Historique* (Vienne: Abbaye Sainte-Martin de Ligugé, 1927).

Diem, Albrecht, 'Inventing the Holy Rule: Some Observations on the History of Monastic Normative Observance in the Early Medieval West', in *Western Monasticism Ante Litteram. The Spaces of Monastic Observance in Late Antiquity and the Early Middle Ages*, ed. Hendrik Dey, and Elizabeth Fentress, Disciplina Monastica 7 (Turnhout: Brepols, 2011), pp. 53-84.

Donaldson, Margaret, *Children's Minds* (London: Croom Helm Press, 1978).

Doran, John, 'Oblation or Obligation? A Canonical Ambiguity', in *The Church and*

Childhood: Papers Read at the 1993 Summer Meeting and the Winter Meeting of the Ecclesiastical History Society, ed. Diana Wood, Studies in Church History 31 (Oxford: Blackwell, 1994), pp. 127-41.

Douglas, Mary, *Purity and Danger: An Analysis of Concepts of Pollution and Taboo* (London: Routledge & Kegan, 1966); 3rd ed. London: Routledge, 2003.

Duke, John, *The Columban Church* (London: Oxford University Press, 1932).

Dumitrescu, Irina A., 'The Grammar of Pain in Ælfric Bata's Colloquies', *Forum for Modern Language Studies* 45 (2009), pp. 239-253.

Dumville, David, *Wessex and England from Alfred to Edgar: Six Essays on Political, Cultural, and Ecclesiastical Revival*, Studies in Anglo-Saxon History 3 (Woodbridge: Boydell Press, 1992).

Duncan, Edwin, 'Fears of the Apocalypse: the Anglo-Saxons and the Coming of the Millennium', *Religion & Literature* 31 (1999), pp. 15-23.

Dunn, Marilynn, 'Mastering Benedict: Monastic Rules and their Authors in the Early Medieval West', *English Historian Review* 105 (1990), pp. 567-94.

— 'The Master and Benedict, A Rejoinder', *English Historical Review* 107 (1992), pp. 104-11.

— *The Emergence of Monasticism: From the Desert Fathers to the Early Middle Ages* (Oxford: Blackwell, 2000).

Eales, Richard G. and Richard Sharpe (eds.), *Canterbury and the Norman Conquest: Churches, Saints and Scholars, 1066-1109* (London: Hambledon, 1995).

Echard, Siân and Gernot Wieland (eds.), *Anglo-Latin and its Heritage: Essays in Honour of A. G. Rigg on his 64th Birthday*, Publications of the Journal of Medieval Latin 4 (Turnhout: Brepols, 2001).

Elkins, Sharon K. (ed.), *Holy Women of Twelfth-Century England*, Studies in Religion (Chapel Hills, University of North Carolina Press, 1988).

Ennew, Judith, 'Time for Children or Time for Adults?', in *Childhood Matters: Social Theory, Practice and Politics*, ed. Jens Qvortrup, Giovani Sgritta, and Helmut Wintersberger, European Centre for Social Welfare Policy and Research: Public Policy and Social Welfare 14 (Aldershot: Avebury, 1994), pp. 125-43.

Farmer, David, 'The Progress of the Monastic Revival', in *Tenth Century Studies: Essays in Commemoration of the Millennium of the Council of Winchester and Regularis Concordia*, ed. David Parsons (London: Phillimore, 1975), pp. 10-9.

Fass, Paula, 'The World is at Our Door: Why Historians of Children and Childhood Should Open Up', *Journal of the History of Childhood and Youth* 1 (2008), pp. 11-31.

Fell, Christina, Cecily Clark, and Elizabeth Williams (eds.), *Women in Anglo-Saxon England and the Impact of 1066* (London: British Museum, 1984); repr. New York: B. Blackwell, 1987.

Ferrante, Joan, *To the Glory of her Sex: Women's Roles in the Composition of Medieval Texts*, Women of letters (Bloomington, IN: University Press, 1997).

Findlay, Alison, *Playing Spaces in Early Women's Drama* (Cambridge: University Press, 2006).

Finocchiaro, Mary and Christopher Brumfit., *The Functional-Notional Approach: From Theory to Practice* (Oxford: University Press, 1983).

Flint, Valerie I. J., 'Space and Discipline in Early Medieval Europe', in *Medieval Practices of Space*, ed. Barbara A. Hanawalt and Michal Kobialka, Medieval Cultures 23 (Minneapolis: University Press, 2000), pp. 149-65.

Foot, Sarah, 'Anglo-Saxon Minsters: A Review of Terminology', in *Pastoral care before the Parish*, ed. John Blair and Richard Sharpe, Studies in the Early History of Britain (Leicester: University Press, 1992), pp. 212-25.

— 'Language and Method: the Dictionary of Old English and the Historian', in *Dictionary of Old English: Retrospects and Prospects*, ed. M. J. Toswell and Antonette di Paolo Healey, Old English Newsletter. Subsidia 26 (Kalamazoo, Mich: Medieval Institute, 1998), pp. 73-87.

— *Veiled Women I: The Disappearance of Nuns from Anglo-Saxon England, 871-1066*, Studies in Early Medieval Britain (Aldershot: Ashgate, 2000).

— *Veiled Women II: Female Religious Communities in England, 871-1066*, Studies in Early Medieval Britain (Aldershot: Ashgate, 2000).

— *Monastic Life in Anglo-Saxon England c.600-900* (Cambridge: University Press, 2006).

— *Æthelstan: The First King of England* (New Haven: Yale University Press, 2011).

Fox, Michael, and Manish Sharma (eds.), *Old English Literature and the Old Testament*, Toronto Anglo-Saxon Series 10 (Toronto: University Press, 2012).

Gardner, Elizabeth, 'The English Nobility and Monastic Education c. 1100-1500', in *The Cloister and the World: Essays in Medieval History in Honour of Barbara Harvey*, ed. Barbara Harvey, John Blair, and Brian Golding (Oxford: Clarendon, 1996), pp. 80-94.

Gameson, Richard, 'St Wulfstan, the Library of Worcester and the Spirituality of the Medieval Book', in *St Wulfstan and His World*, ed. Julia S. Barrow and Nicholas. P. Brooks (Aldershot: Ashgate, 2005), pp. 59-104.

— *The Manuscripts of Early Norman England (c. 1066-1130)*, British Academy Post-doctoral Fellowship Monograph (Oxford: University Press, 1999).

Gayley, Charles M., *Plays of Our Forefathers: And Some of the Traditions Upon Which They Were Founded* (London: London & Co, 1908), repr. New York: Biblio and Tannen, 1968.

Gibson, Margaret T., *Lanfranc of Bec* (Oxford: Clarendon Press, 1978).

Gittos, Helen and Martin B. Bedingfield (eds.), *The Liturgy of the Late Anglo-Saxon Church*, Henry Bradshaw Society. Subsidia 5 (London: Boydell Press, 2005).

Gittos, Helen, *Liturgy, Architecture, and Sacred Places in Anglo-Saxon England* (Oxford: University Press, 2013).

Gneuss, Helmut, 'Die Benediktinerregel in England und ihre Altenglische Übersetzung', in *Die Angelsächsischen Prosabearbeitungen der Benedikinerregel*, ed. Arnold Schröer, Bibliothek der Angelsächsischen Prosa II (Darmstadt, 1885-8), rev. ed. with supplement by Helmut Gneuss, Darmstadt: Wissenschaftliche Buchgesellschaft, 1964, pp. 263-84. 2 vols.

— 'The Study of Language in Anglo-Saxon England', *Bulletin of the John Rylands Library* 72 (1990), pp. 3-32.

— *Handlist of Anglo-Saxon Manuscripts: A list of Manuscripts and Manuscript Fragments Written or Owned in England up to 1100*, Medieval & Renaissance Texts & Studies 241 (Tempe Ariz: Centre for Medieval and Renaissance Studies, 2001).

Godden, Malcom, 'Apocalypse and Invasion in Late Anglo-Saxon England', in *From Anglo-Saxon to Early Middle English: Studies presented to E. G. Stanley*, ed. Malcom Godden, Douglas Gray, and Terry Hoad (Oxford: Clarendon Press, 1994), pp. 130-62.

Golding, Brian., *Gilbert of Sempringham and the Gilbertine Order c. 1130-c.1300* (Oxford: Clarendon Press, 1995).

Goldberg, J. P., and Felicity Riddy (eds.), *Youth in the Middle Ages* (Woodbridge: York Medieval Press, 2004).

Goodich, Michael E., Goodich, Michael., *The Unmentionable Vice: Homosexuality in the Later Medieval Period* (Santa Barbara, Calif: ABC-Clio, 1979).

— *From Birth to Old Age: The Human Life-Cycle in Medieval Thought, 1250-1350* (Lanham, MD: University Press of America, 1989).

Gransden, Antonia, 'Traditionalism and Continuity during the Last Century of Anglo-Saxon Monasticism', *Journal of Ecclesiastical History* 40 (1989), pp. 159-207.

Greatrex, Joan, 'The Almonry School of Norwich Cathedral Priory in the Thirteenth and Fourteenth Centuries', *Studies in Church History* 31 (1994), pp. 169-81.

Green, Roger, *Latin Epics of the New Testament: Juvencus, Sedulius, Arator* (Oxford: University Press, 2006).

Greenberg, David, and Marcia Bystryn, 'Christian Intolerance of Homosexuality', *American Journal of Sociology* 88 (1982), pp. 515-48.

Greene Sheila, and Diane Hogan (eds.), *Researching children's experience: methods and approaches* (London: SAGE publications, 2005).

Greene Sheila, and Malcom Hill, 'Researching Children's Experience: Methods and Methodological Issues', in *Researching Children's Experience: Methods and Approaches*, ed. Sheila Greene and Diane Hogan (London: SAGE publications, 2005), pp. 1-21.

Greene, Sheila, *The Psychological Development of Girls and Women: Rethinking Change in Time*, Women and Psychology (London: Routledge, 2003); rev. ed. London, 2015.

Gretsch, Mechthild, *Die Regula Sancti Benedicti in England und ihre Altenglische Übersetzung*, Texte und Untersuchungen zur Englischen Philologie 2 (Munich: Fink, 1973).

— 'Æthelwold's Translation of the *Regula Sancti Benedicti* and its Latin Exemplar', *Anglo-Saxon England* 3 (1974), pp. 125-151.

— 'The Roman Psalter: Its Old English Glosses and the English Benedictine Reform', in *Liturgy and Ecclesiastical History of Late Anglo-Saxon England*, ed. David Dumville (Woodbridge: Boydell Press, 1992), pp. 13-28.

— 'The Benedictine Rule in Old English: a Document of a Bishop Æthelwold's Reform Politics', in *Words, Texts and Manuscripts: Studies in Anglo-Saxon Culture Presented to Helmut Gneuss on the Occasion of his Sixty-Fifth Birthday*, ed. Michael Korhammer, Karl Reichl, and Hans Sauer (Cambridge: D. S. Brewer, 1992), pp. 131-58.

— *The Intellectual Foundations of the English Benedictine Reform*, Cambridge Studies in Anglo-Saxon England 25 (Cambridge: University Press, 1999).

Guijarro, Susana, 'The Monastic Ideal of Discipline and the Making of Clerical Rules in Late Medieval Castille', *Journal of Medieval Monastic Studies* 2 (2013), pp. 131-50.

Hadley, Dawn, *Medieval Childhood: Archaeological Approaches* (Oxford: Oxbow Books, 2014).

Halpin, Patricia, 'Women Religious in Late Anglo-Saxon England', *Haskins Society Journal* 6 (1994), pp. 97-110.

Hanawalt, Barbara, *Growing up in Medieval London: The Experience of Childhood in History* (New York: Oxford University Press, 1993).

Harbus, Antonia, 'Affective Poetics: The Cognitive Basis of Emotion in Old English Poetry', in *Anglo-Saxon Emotions: Reading the Heart in Old English Language, Literature and Culture*, ed. Alice Jorgensen, Frances McCormack, and Jonathan Wilcox, Studies in Early Medieval Britain and Ireland (Farnham: Ashgate, 2015), pp. 19-35.

Harmless, William, *Desert Christians: An Introduction to the Literature of Early Monasticism* (Oxford: University Press, 2004).

Harris, Stephen J, 'Happiness and the Psalms', in *Old English Literature and the Old Testament*, ed. Michael Fox and Manish Sharma, Toronto Anglo-Saxon Series 10 (Toronto: University Press, 2012), pp. 292-314.

Hawkins, David, and Richard F. Catalano, 'The Social Development Model: A Theory of Anti-Social Behaviour', in *Delinquency and Crime: Current Theories*, ed. David J. Hawkins (Cambridge: University Press, 1996), pp. 149-97.

Herlihy, David, 'Medieval Children', in *Essays on Medieval Civilization: The Walter Prescott Webb Memorial Lectures*, ed. Richard E. Sullivan, Bede K. Lackner, and Kenneth R. Philip, Walter Prescott Webb Memorial Lectures (Austin, Tex: University Press, 1978), pp. 109-41.

— *Opera Muliebra: Women and Work in Medieval Europe*, New Perspectives on European History (New York: McGraw-Hill, 1990).

Heywood, Christopher., *A History of Childhood: Children and Childhood in the West from Medieval to Modern Times*, Themes in History (Cambridge: Polity Press, 2001).

Hiley, David, *Western Plainchant: A Handbook* (Oxford: Clarendon Press, 1993).

Hill, Joyce, 'The *Regularis Concordia* and its Latin and Old English Reflexes', *Revue Bénédictine* 101 (1991), pp. 299-315.

— 'Winchester Pedagogy and the *Colloquy* of Ælfric', *Leeds Studies in English* n. s. 29 (1998), pp. 137-52.

— 'The Benedictine Reform and Beyond', in *A Companion to Anglo-Saxon Literature*, ed. Philip Pulsiano and Elaine Treharne, Blackwell Companions to Literature and Culture 11 (Oxford: Blackwell, 2001), pp. 151-69.

— 'Lexical choices for Holy Week: Studies in Old English Ecclesiastical Vocabulary' in *Lexis and Texts in Early English: Studies Presented to Jane Roberts*, ed. Christian J. Kay and Louise M. Sylvester, Costerus New Series 133 (Amsterdam: Rodopi, 2001), pp. 117-128.

— 'Learning Latin in Anglo-Saxon England: Traditions, Texts and Techniques', in *Learning and Literacy in Medieval England and Abroad*, ed. Sarah Rees Jones, Utrecht Studies in Medieval Literacy 3 (Turnhout: Brepols, 2003), pp. 7-29.

— 'Rending the Garment and Reading by the Rood: *Regularis Concordia* Rituals for Men and Women', in *The Liturgy of the Late Anglo-Saxon Church*, ed. Helen Gittos, and Marvin B. Bedingfield, Henry Bradshaw Society. Subsidia 5 (London: Boydell Press, 2005), pp. 53-64.

— 'Ælfric's *Colloquy*: The Antwerp/London Version', in *Latin Learning and English Lore: Studies in Anglo-Saxon Literature for Michael Lapidge*, ed. Katherine O'Brien O'Keeffe, Andy Orchard, and Michael Lapidge, Toronto Old English series (Toronto: University Press, 2005), pp. 331-48.

— 'Ælfric's Grammatical Triad', in *Form and Content of Instruction in Anglo-Saxon England in the Light of Contemporary Manuscript Evidence*, ed. Patrizia Lendinara, Lorendana Lazzari, and Maria Amalia D'Aronco, Textes et Études du Moyen Âge 39 (Turnhout: Brepols, 2007), pp. 285-307.

— 'Ælfric: His Life and Works', in *A Companion to Ælfric*, ed. Hugh Magennis and Mary Swan, Brill's Companions to the Christian Tradition 19 (Leiden: Brill, 2009), pp. 35-65.

— 'Childhood in the Lives of Anglo-Saxon Saints', in *Childhood and Adolescence in Anglo-Saxon Literary Culture*, ed. Susan Irvine and Winfried Rudolf, Toronto Anglo-Saxon Series 28 (Toronto: University Press, 2018), pp. 139-61.

Hofstetter, Walter, 'Winchester and the Standardization of Old English Vocabulary', *Anglo-Saxon England* 17 (1988), pp. 139-61.

Hollis, Stephanie., W. R. Barnes, Rebecca Hayward, Kathleen Loncar, and M. Wright (eds.), *Writing the Wilton Women: Goscelin's Legend of Edith and Liber Confortatorius*, Medieval Women: Texts and Contexts 9 (Turnhout: Brepols, 2004).

Hollis, Stephanie, *Anglo-Saxon Women and the Church: Sharing a Common Fate* (Woodbridge: Boydell Press, 1992).

— 'Edith as Contemplative and Bride of Christ' in *Writing the Wilton Women: Goscelin's Legend of Edith and Liber Confortatorius*, ed. and trans. Stephanie Hollis, W. R. Barnes, Rebecca Hayward, Kathleen Loncar, and Michael Wright, Medieval Women: Texts and Contexts 9 (Turnhout: Brepols, 2004), pp. 281-306.

— 'Wilton as a Centre of Learning', in *Writing the Wilton Women: Goscelin's Legend of Edith and Liber Confortatorius*, ed. and trans. Stephanie Hollis, W. R. Barnes, Rebecca Hayward, Kathleen Loncar, and Michael Wright, Medieval Women: Texts and Contexts 9 (Turnhout: Brepols, 2004), pp. 307-38.

— 'Barking's Monastic School, Late Seventh to Twelfth Century: History, Saint-Making and Literary Culture', in *Barking Abbey and Medieval Literary Culture: Authorship and Authority in a Female Community*, ed. Jennifer N. Brown, and Donna Bussell (Woodbridge: York Medieval Press, 2012), pp. 33-55.

Huneycutt, Lois, 'The Life of St Margaret in the Reign of Matilda II (1100-1118)', *Anglo-Norman Studies* 12 (1989), pp. 81-97.

Hunt, Richard William, 'Manuscript Evidence for Knowledge of the Poems of Venantius Fortunatus in Late Anglo-Saxon England', Anglo-Saxon England 8 (1979), pp. 279-95.

Hunt, Tony (ed.), *Teaching and Learning Latin in Thirteenth Century England* (Cambridge: D. S. Brewer, 1991), 3 vols.

Irvine Susan, and Winfried Rudolf (eds.), *Childhood and Adolescence in Anglo-Saxon Literary Culture*, Toronto Anglo-Saxon Series 28 (Toronto: University Press, 2018),

Jaeger, Stephen C., *The Envy of Angels: Cathedral Schools and Social Ideals in Medieval Europe, 950-1200*, Middle Ages (Philadelphia: University Press, 1994).

James, Allison and Alan Prout, (eds.), *Constructing and Reconstructing Childhood: Contemporary Issues in the Sociological Study of Childhood* (London: Falmer Press, 1990), rev. ed., Washington DC, 1998.

James, William, *The Principles of Psychology* (New York: Henry Holt, 1890); rev. ed. London: Encyclopaedia Britannica Press, 1990.

Jamieson, Anne, 'Theory and Practice in Social Gerontology', in *Researching Aging and Later Life: the practice of social gerontology*, ed. Anne Jamieson and Christina R. Victor (Buckingham: Open University Press, 2002), pp. 7-20.

Jayatilaka, Rohini, 'The Old English Benedictine Rule: Writing for Women and Men', *Anglo-Saxon England* 32 (2003), pp. 147-87.

Jenks, Christopher, *The Sociology of Childhood: Essential Readings* (London: Batsford Academic and Educational Press, 1982).

Jenson, Jeffrey, 'Advances in Preventing Childhood and Adolescent Problem Behaviour', *Research on Social Work Practice* 20 (2010), pp. 701-13.

Jeudy, Colette, 'A Glossed Manuscript of Priscian's *Institutio*, Vatican MS Reg. Lat. 1578', in Lesley J. Smith (ed.), *Intellectual Life in the Middle Ages: Essays Presented to Margaret Gibson* (London: Hambledon, 1992), pp. 61-70.

John, Eric, 'The King and the Monks in the Tenth-Century Reformation', *Bulletin of the John Rylands Library* 42 (1959), pp. 61-87.

Jones, Christopher, 'The Irregular Life in Ælfric Bata's Colloquies', *Leeds Studies in English* 37 (2006), pp. 241-60.

— 'Ælfric and the Limits of "Benedictine Reform"', in *A Companion to Ælfric*, ed. Hugh Magennis and Mary Swan (Leiden: Brill, 2008), pp. 67-108.

— '*Meatim Sed et Rustica*: Ælfric of Eynsham as a Medieval Latin Author', *Journal of Medieval Latin* 8 (1998), pp. 1-57.

De Jong, Mayke, *Kind en Klooster in de Vroege Middeleeuwen: Aspecten van de Schenking van Kinderen aan Kloosters in het Frankische Rijk (500-900),*

Amsterdamse Historische Reeks 8 (Amsterdam: Historisch Seminarium van de Universiteit, 1986).

— *In Samuel's Image: Child Oblation in the Early Medieval West*, Brill's Studies in Intellectual History 12 (Leiden: Brill, 1996).

— 'Carolingian Monasticism: The Power of Prayer', in *The New Cambridge Medieval History II: c.700-c.900*, ed. Rosamond McKitterick (Cambridge: University Press, 1995-9), pp. 622-53. 7 vols.

— 'Imitatio morum. The Cloister and Clerical Purity in the Carolingian world', in *Medieval Purity and Piety: Essays on Medieval Clerical Celibacy and Religious Reform*, ed. Michael Frassetto, Medieval Casebooks 19 (New York: Garland Press, 1998), pp. 49-56.

Jorgensen, Alice, 'Learning about Emotion from Old English Prose Psalms of the Paris Psalter', in *Anglo-Saxon Emotions: Reading the Heart in Old English Language, Literature and Culture*, ed. Alice Jorgensen, Frances McCormack, and Jonathan Wilcox, Studies in Early Medieval Britain and Ireland (Farnham: Ashgate, 2015), pp. 127-42.

Karras, Ruth, *From Boys to Men: Formation of Masculinity in Late Medieval Europe*, Middle Ages (Philadelphia: University Press, 2002).

Keenan, Hugh, 'Children's Literature in Old English', *Children's Literature* 1 (1972), pp. 16-20.

Kerr, Julie, *Monastic Hospitality: The Benedictines in England, c.1070-c.1250*, Studies in the History of Medieval Religion 32 (Woodbridge: Boydell Press, 2007).

Kirby, David P, 'Bede, Eddius Stephanus and the Life of Wilfred', *English Historical Review* 98 (1983), pp. 101-14.

Knowles, D., *The Monastic Order in England: A History of its Development from the Times of St. Dunstan to the Fourth Lateran Council, 940-1216* (Cambridge: University Press, 1940); rev. ed. Cambridge, 1963.

Kobialka, Michael, 'Staging Place/Space in the Eleventh-Century Monastic Practices', in *Medieval Practices of Space*, ed. Barbara A. Hanawalt and Michal Kobialka, Medieval Cultures 23 (Minneapolis: University Press, 2000), pp. 128-148.

Kornexl, Lucia, 'The *Regularis Concordia* and its Old English Gloss', Anglo-Saxon England 24 (1995), pp. 95-130.

— 'From Ælfric to John of Cornwall: Evidence for Vernacular Grammar Teaching in Pre- and Post-Conquest England', in *Bookmarks from the Past: Studies in Early English Language and Literature in Honour of Helmut Gneuss*, ed. Lucia Kornexl, Ursula Lenker, and Helmut Gneuss, Texte und Untersuchungen zur englischen Philologie 30 (Oxford: Peter Lang, 2003), pp. 229-60.

Kuefler, Matthew, '"A Wryed Existence": Attitudes toward Children in Anglo-Saxon England', *Journal of Social History* 24 (1991), pp. 823-34.

Labouvie-Vief Gisela, Grühn Daniel, Manfred Diehl, and Mark Lumley, 'Developmental Trajectories for Ego-Development across the Adult Life-Span: Evidence from a 12-year Longitudinal Study', *International Journal of Psychology* 43 (2008), p. 392.

Laes, Christian and Katariina Mustakallio (eds.), *The Dark Side of Childhood in Late*

Antiquity and the Middle Ages: Unwanted, Disabled, and Lost, Childhood in the Past: Monograph Series 2 (Oxford: Oxbow, 2011).

Lahaye-Geusen, Maria, *Das Opfer der Kinder: ein Beitrag zur Liturgie- und Sozialgeschichte des Mönchtums im Hohen Mittelalter*, Münsteraner Theologische Abhandlungen 13 (Altenberge: Oros verlag, 1991).

Lansford Jennifer, Michael M. Criss, Robert D. Laird, Daniel. S. Shaw, Gregory Pettit, John E. Bates, and Kenneth A. Dodge, 'Reciprocal Relations Between Parents: Physical Discipline and Children's Externalizing Behaviour During Middle Childhood and Adolescence', *Development and Psychopathology* 23 (2011), pp. 225-38.

Lapidge, Michael, 'Three Latin Poems from Æthelwold's School in Winchester', Anglo-Saxon England 1 (1972), pp. 85-137.

— 'The Hermeneutic Style in Tenth-Century Anglo-Latin Literature', *Anglo-Saxon England* 4 (1975), pp. 67-111.

— 'The Study of Latin Texts in Late Anglo-Saxon England, I: The Evidence of Latin Glosses', in *Latin and the Vernacular Languages in Early Medieval Britain*, ed. Nicholas Brooks, Studies in the Early History of Britain (Leicester: University Press, 1982), pp. 99-140.

— 'Surviving Booklists from Anglo-Saxon England', in *Learning and Literature in Anglo-Saxon England, Studies Presented to Peter Clemoes on the Occasion of His Sixty-Fifth Birthday*, ed. Michael Lapidge, and Helmut Gneuss (Cambridge: University Press, 1985), pp. 33-89.

— 'Æthelwold as Scholar and Teacher', in *Bishop Æthelwold: His Career and Influence*, ed. Barbara Yorke (Woodbridge: Boydell, 1988), pp. 89-117; repr. in his, *Anglo-Latin Literature II* [see below], pp. 183-211.

— *Anglo-Latin Literature II: 900-1066* (London: Hambledon Press, 1993).

— *Anglo-Latin Literature I: 600-899* (London: Hambledon Press, 1996).

— *The Anglo-Saxon Library* (Oxford: University Press, 2006).

Lapidge Michael, John Blair, Simon Keynes, and Donald Scragg (eds.), *The Wiley Blackwell Encyclopaedia of Anglo-Saxon England* (Oxford: Blackwell, 1999); repr. Chichester: Wiley & Sons, 2014.

Larington, Carolyne, 'Awkward Adolescents: Male Maturation in Norse Literature', in *Youth and Age in the Medieval North*, ed. Shannon Lewis-Simpson, The Northern World 42 (Leiden: Brill, 2008), pp. 151-66.

Law, Vivien., *The Insular Latin Grammarians* (Woodbridge: Boydell Press, 1982).

— 'Anglo-Saxon England: Ælfric's *Excerptiones de arte grammatica anglice*', *Histoire Épistémologie Langage* 9 (1987), 47-71.

— 'The Study of Grammar', in *Carolingian Culture: Emulation and Innovation*, ed. Rosamond McKitterick (Cambridge: University Press, 1994), pp. 88-110.

— *Grammar and Grammarians in the Early Middle Ages*, Longman Linguistics Library I (London: Longman, 1997).

Leach, Arthur, 'The Schoolboys' Feast', *Fortnightly Review* 59 (1896), p. 128.

— *The Schools of Medieval England* (London: Methuen, 1915).

Leclercq, Jean, 'Pédagogie et Formation Spirituelle du VI au IX siècle', *La Scuola nell'Occidente Latino dell'Alto Medioevo* (1972), pp. 255-90.

— *L'Amour des Lettres et le Désir de Dieu: Initiation aux Auteurs Monastiques du Moyen Âge* (Paris: Éditions du Cerf, 1957); trans. Catherine Misrahi, *The Love of Learning and the Desire for God: A Study of Monastic Culture*, Mentor-Omega Book (New York: Fordham University Press, 1961); 3rd ed. New York, 1982.

Lee, Christina, 'Forever Young: Child Burial in Anglo-Saxon England', in *Youth and Age in the Medieval North*, ed. Shannon Lewis-Simpson, Northern World 42 (Leiden: Brill, 2008), pp. 17-36.

Lendinara, Patrizia, "Il Colloquio di Ælfric e Il Colloquio di Ælfric Bata', in *Feor ond Neah: Scritti de Filogia Germanica in Memoria di Augusto Scaffidi Abbate*, ed. Patrizia Lendinara and Lucio Melazzo Palermo, Annali della Facoltà di Lettere e Filosofia dell'Università di Palermo. Studi e Ricerche 3 (Palermo: Università di Palermo, 1983), pp. 173-249.

— 'The Third Book of the *Bella Parisiacae Urbis* by Abbo of Saint-Germain-des-Prés and its Old English Gloss', *Anglo-Saxon England* 15 (1986), pp. 73-89.

— 'The World of Anglo-Saxon Learning', in *The Cambridge Companion to Old English Literature*, ed. Malcom Godden, and Michael Lapidge (Cambridge: University Press, 1991), pp. 295-312.

— 'The Colloquy of Ælfric', in *Anglo-Saxon Glosses and Glossaries*, ed. Patrizia Lendinara, Collected Studies 622 (Aldershot: Ashgate, 1999), pp. 207-87.

— 'Instructional Manuscripts in England: The Tenth and Eleventh-Century Codices and the Early Norman Ones', in *Form and Content of Instruction in Anglo-Saxon England in the Light of Contemporary Manuscript Evidence: papers presented at the International Conference, Udine, 6-8 April 2006*, ed. Patricia Lendinara, Loredana Lazzari, and Maria A. D'Aronco, Textes et Études du Moyen Âge 39 (Turnhout: Brepols, 2007), pp. 59-113.

Lendinara, Patrizia, Lorendana Lazzari, and Maria Amalia D'Aronco (eds.), *Form and Content of Instruction in Anglo-Saxon England in the Light of Contemporary Manuscript Evidence*, Textes et Études du Moyen Âge 39 (Turnhout: Brepols, 2007).

Lett, Didier, and Danièle Alexandre-Bidon (eds.), *Les Enfants au Moyen Âge, Ve-XVe Siècles* (Paris: Hachette, 1997); trans. Jody Gladding, *Children in the Middle Ages: Fifth-Fifteenth Centuries* (Notre Dame, Ind: University Press, 1999).

Leyser, Conrad and Lesley Smith (eds.), *Motherhood, Religion, and Society in Medieval Europe, 400-1400: Essays Presented to Henrietta Leyser*, Church, Faith, and Culture in the Medieval West (Farnham: Ashgate, 2011).

Lewis-Simpson, Shannon (ed.), *Northern World: Youth and Age in the Medieval North*, Northern World 42 (Leiden: Brill, 2008).

— 'The Challenges of Quantifying Youth and Age in the Medieval North', in *Northern World: Youth and Age in the Medieval North*, ed. Shannon Lewis-Simpson, Northern World 42 (Leiden: Brill, 2008), pp. 1-17.

Lockett, Leslie, *Anglo-Saxon Psychologies in the Vernacular and Latin Traditions* (Toronto: University Press, 2011).

Lorain, Prosper, *Histoire de l'Abbaye de Cluny : Depuis da Fondation jusqu'à sa Destruction à l'Époque de la Révolution Française* (Paris: Sagnier & Bray, 1845).

Loyn, Henry R., *The English Church, 940-1154*, Medieval World (Harlow: Longman, 2000).

Lynch, Joseph, *Simoniacal Entry into Religious Life from 1000-1260: A Social, Economic, and Legal Study* (Columbus Ohio: University Press, 1976).

Mabry, Patricia, 'Developmental Systems Science: Exploring the Application of Systems Science Methods to Developmental Science Questions', *Research in Human Development* 8 (2011), pp. 1-25.

Mackenzie, Neil, *The Medieval Boy Bishops* (Leicester: Matador Press, 2012).

MacLehose, William F., *"A Tender Age": Cultural Anxieties over the Child in the Twelfth and Thirteenth Centuries* (New York: Columbia University Press, 2008).

MacNaughton, Glenda, Kylie Smith and Heather Lawrence (eds.), *Hearing Young Children's Voices*, Centre for Equity and Innovation in Early Childhood (Melbourne: University Press, 2003).

Marsden, Richard, 'Wisdom books in Non-Biblical Manuscripts', in *The Text of the Old Testament in Anglo-Saxon England*, ed. Richard Marsden, Cambridge Studies in Anglo-Saxon England 15 (Cambridge: University Press, 1995), pp. 307-21.

Matthews, Sarah H., 'A Window on the 'New' Sociology of Childhood', *Sociology Compass* 1 (2007), pp. 322-34.

McCreesh, Bernadine, 'The Birth, Childhood and Adolescence of the Early Icelandic Bishops', in *Youth and Age in the Medieval North*, ed. Shannon Lewis-Simpson, The Northern World 42 (Leiden: Brill, 2008), pp. 87-102.

McKitterick, Rosamond., *The Frankish Church and the Carolingian Reforms, 789-895*, Royal Historical Society Studies in History (Cambridge: University Press, 1977).

— 'England and the Continent', in *The New Cambridge History II: c.700-c.900*, ed. Rosamond McKitterick (Cambridge: University Press, 1995), pp. 64-84.

Menzer, Melinder J., 'Ælfric's Grammar: Solving the Problem of the English-Language Text', *Neophilologus* 83 (1999), pp. 637-52.

— 'Ælfric's English Grammar', *Journal of English and Germanic Philology* 103 (2004), pp. 106-24.

Miller, Maureen C., *Clothing the Clergy: Virtue and Power in Medieval Europe* c.800-1200 (New York: Cornell University Press, 2014).

Miller, Timothy M., *The Orphans of Byzantium: Child Welfare in the Christian Empire* (Washington DC: Catholic University of America Press, 2003).

Miller, Patricia, *Toward a Feminist Developmental Psychology* (New York: Routledge, 2000).

Mooney, Catherine (ed.), *Gendered Voices: Medieval Saints and Their Interpreters*, Middle Ages (Philadelphia: University Press, 1999).

— 'Voice, Gender, and the Portrayal of Sanctity', in her *Gendered Voices: Medieval Saints and Their Interpreters*, Middle Ages (Philadelphia: University Press, 1999), pp. 1-15.

Morison, Earnest F., *St Basil and his Rule: A Study in Early Monasticism* (Oxford: University Press, 1912).
Morton, Vera and Jocelyn Wogan-Browne (eds.), *Guidance for Women in Twelfth-Century Convents*, Library of Medieval Women (Woodbridge: D. S. Brewer, 2003).
Mukherji, Penny and Deborah Albon, *Research Methods in Early Childhood* (London: SAGE, 2009).
O'Brien O'Keeffe, Katherine., *Stealing Obedience: Narratives of Agency and Identity in Later Anglo-Saxon England*, Toronto Anglo-Saxon Series 11 (Toronto: University Press, 2012).
— 'Goscelin and the Consecration of Eve', *Anglo-Saxon England* 35 (2006), pp. 251-70.
— 'Leaving Wilton: Gunhild and the Phantoms of Agency', *Journal of English and Germanic Philology* 106 (2007), pp. 203-23.
O'Brien O'Keeffe, K. and A. Orchard (eds.), *Latin Learning and English Lore: Studies in Anglo-Saxon Literature for Michael Lapidge* (Toronto: University Press, 2005), 2 vols.
Ogden, Dunbar, *The Staging of Drama in the Medieval Church* (Newark DE: University of Delaware Press, 2001).
O'Neill, Patrick, 'Latin Learning at Winchester in the Early-Eleventh Century: The Evidence of the Lambeth Psalter', *Anglo-Saxon England* 20 (1991), pp. 143-66.
Orme, Nicholas, *English Schools in the Middle Ages* (London: Methuen, 1973).
— 'Children and the Church in Medieval England', *Journal of Ecclesiastical History* 45 (1994), pp. 563-87.
— *Medieval Children* (New Haven: Yale University Press, 2001).
— *Medieval Schools: From Roman Britain to Renaissance England* (New Haven: Yale University Press, 2006).
— *Fleas, Flies, and Friars: Children's Poetry from the Middle Ages* (Exeter: Impress Books, 2011).
— *English School Exercises, 1420-1530*, Studies and Texts: Pontifical Institute of Medieval Studies 181 (Toronto: Pontifical Institute of Mediaeval Studies, 2013).
Orchard, Andy, *The Poetic Art of Aldhelm*, Cambridge Studies in Anglo-Saxon England 8 (Cambridge, University Press, 1994).
Orlandis, José, 'La Oblación de Niños en la España Visigótica', in *Estudios sobre Instituciones Monásticas Medievales*, ed. José Orlandis (Pamplona: Universidad de Navarra, 1971), pp. 54-67.
Page, Raymond Ian, 'More Old English Scratched Glosses', *Anglia* 97 (1979), pp. 27-45.
— 'The Study of Latin Texts in Late Anglo-Saxon England II: The Evidence of English Glosses', in *Latin and the Vernacular Languages of Medieval Britain*, ed. Nicholas Brooks, Studies in the Early History of Britain (Leicester: University Press, 1982), pp. 141-65.
Papaconstantinou, Arietta. and Alice Talbot (eds.), *Becoming Byzantine: Children and Childhood in Byzantium*, Dumbarton Oaks Byzantine Symposia and Colloquia (Washington, DC: Dumbarton Oaks, 2009).

Peters, Greg, 'Offering Sons to God in the Monastery: Child Oblation, Monastic Benevolence, and the Cistercian Order in the Middle Ages', *Cistercian Studies Quarterly* 38 (2003), pp. 285-95.

Pfaff, Richard, *The Liturgy in Medieval England: A History* (Cambridge: University Press, 2009).

Pinker, Steven, *The Blank Slate: The Modern Denial of Human Nature* (New York: Viking, 2002).

Piper, Alan, 'The Durham Cantor's Book', in *Anglo-Norman Durham, 1093-1193*, ed. David Rollason, Margaret Harvey, and Michael Prestwich (Woodbridge: Boydell Press, 1994), pp. 79-92.

Pollock, Linda A., *Forgotten Children: Parent-Child relations from 1500 to 1900* (Cambridge: University Press, 1983).

Ponesse, Matthew, 'Smaragdus of St. Mihiel and the Carolingian Monastic Reform', *Revue Bénédictine* 116 (2006), pp. 367-92.

Porter, David, 'The Latin Syllabus in Anglo-Saxon Monastic Schools', *Neophilologus* 78 (1994), pp. 463-82.

— 'The Hypocorism Bata – Old English or Latin?', *Neuphilologische Mitteilungen* 96:4 (1995), pp. 345-49.

— 'Ælfric›s Colloquy and Ælfric Bata', *Neophilologus* 80 (1996), pp. 636-60.

Prout, Alan, 'Researching Children as Social Actors: An Introduction to the Children 5-16 Programme', *Children and Society* 16 (2002), pp. 67-76.

Quinn, Patricia, *Better than the Sons of Kings: Boys and Monks in the Early Middle Ages*, Studies in History and Culture 2 (New York: Peter Lang, 1989).

Rankin, Susan (ed.), *The Winchester Troper: Facsimile edition and introduction*, Early English Church Music 50 (London: Stainer & Bell, 2007).

Reinharz, Shulamit, 'Who Am I, The Need for a Variety of Selves in the Field', in *Reflexivity and Voice*, ed. Rosanna Hertz (London: SAGE, 1997), pp. 3-21.

Reynolds, Suzanne, 'Glossing Horace: Using the Classics in the Medieval Classroom', in *Medieval Manuscripts of the Latin Classics: Production and Use*, ed. Claudine A. Chavannes-Mazel and Margaret Smith (London: Red Gull Press, 1996), pp. 103-17.

Riché, Pierre, 'La Vie Quotidienne dans les Écoles Monastiques d'après les Colloques Scolaires', *Sous la Règle de Saint Benoit: Structures Monastiques et Sociétés en France du Moyen Âge à l'Époque Moderne*. Hautes Études Médiévales et Modernes 47 (Paris, 1982), pp. 417-26.

— *Écoles et Enseignement dans le Haut Moyen Âge: Fin du Ve Siècle – Milieu du XIe Siècle* (Paris : Picard, 1989).

Ridyard, Susan (ed.), *The Royal Saints of Anglo-Saxon England: A Study of West Saxon and East Anglian Cults*, Cambridge Studies in Medieval Life and Thought. 4th ser., 9 (Cambridge: University Press, 1988).

Rigg, Alan and Gernot Wieland, 'A Canterbury Classbook of the Mid-Eleventh Century (The "Cambridge Songs" Manuscript)', *Anglo-Saxon England* 4 (1975), pp. 113-30.

Rigg, Alan, *A History of Anglo-Latin Literature 1066-1422* (Cambridge: University Press, 1992).
Rimbault, Edward, 'The Festival of the Boy Bishop in England', *Camden Miscellany* 7 (1875), pp. 1-34.
Ristuccia, Nathan, 'Ideology and Corporal Punishment in Anglo-Saxon Monastic Education', *American Benedictine Review* 61 (2010), pp. 373-86.
Robertson, Nicola, 'The Benedictine Reform: Current and Future Scholarship', *Literature Compass* 3:3 (2006), pp. 282-99.
— 'Dunstan and Monastic Reform: Tenth-Century Fact or Twelfth-Century Fiction?', in *Anglo-Norman Studies XXVIII: Proceedings of the Battle Conference 2005*, ed. Christopher P. Lewis (Woodbridge: Boydell Press, 2006), pp. 153-67.
Robinson, Armitage J., 'A Sketch of Osbert's Career', in *The Letters of Osbert of Clare*, ed. Edward W. Williamson (London: Oxford University Press, 1929), pp. 1-20.
Robinson, Fred, C., 'Syntactical Glosses in Latin Manuscripts of Anglo-Saxon Provenance', *Speculum* 48 (1973), pp. 443-75.
Robinson, Pamela, 'Self-Contained Units in Composite Manuscripts of the Anglo-Saxon Period', *Anglo-Saxon England* 7 (1978), pp. 231-38.
— 'A Twelfth-Century *Scriptrix* from Nunnaminster', in *Of the Making of Books: Medieval Manuscripts, Their Scribes and Readers: essays presented to M. B. Parkes*, ed. Pamela R. Robinson and Rivkah Zim (Aldershot: Scolar Press (sic), 1997), pp. 73-93.
Ruff, Carin, 'The Place of Metrics in Anglo-Saxon Latin Education: Aldhelm and Bede', *Journal of English and Germanic Philology* 104 (2005), pp. 149-70.
Rushton, Neil, 'Spatial Aspects of the Almonry Site and the Changing Priorities of Poor Relief at Westminster Abbey c.1290-1540', *Architectural History* 45 (2002), pp. 66-91.
Sánchez-Martí, Jordi, 'Age Matters in Old English Literature', in *Youth and Age in the Medieval North*, ed. Shannon Lewis-Simpson, The Northern World 42 (Leiden: Brill, 2008), pp. 205-26.
Sawyer, Robert, 'Music and Conversation', in *Musical Communication*, ed. Dorothy Miell, Raymond MacDonald and David J. Hargreaves (Oxford: University Press, 2005), pp. 45-60.
Sayer, Duncan, and Sam Dickinson, 'Reconsidering obstetric death and female fertility in Anglo-Saxon England', *World Archaeology* 45 (2013), pp. 85-97.
Schroeder, Henry J. (ed.), *Disciplinary Decrees of the General Councils: Text, Translation and Commentary* (London: B. Herder, 1937).
Scragg, Donald (ed.), *Edgar, King of the English, 959-975: New Interpretations*, Publications of the Manchester Centre for Anglo-Saxon Studies 8 (Woodbridge: Boydell Press, 2008); repr. Woodbridge, 2014.
Searle, Eleanor, 'Women and the Legitimisation of Succession at the Norman Conquest', in *Proceedings of the Battle Conference on Anglo-Norman Studies III 1980*, ed. Reginald A. Brown (Woodbridge: Boydelll Press, 1981), pp. 159-87.

Semper, Philippa, 'Byð se Ealda Mann Ceald ond Snoflig. Stereotypes and Subversions of the Last Stages of the Life Cycle in Old English Texts and Anglo-Saxon Contexts', in *Medieval Life Cycles: Continuity and Change*, ed. Isabelle Cochelin and Karen Smyth, International Medieval Research 18 (Turnhout: Brepols, 2013), pp. 287-318.

Sennis, Antonio, 'Narrating Places: Memory and Space in Medieval Monasteries', in *People and Space in the Middle Ages, 300-1300*, ed. Wendy Davies, Guy Halsall and Andrew Reynolds, Studies in the Early Middle Ages 15 (Turnhout: Brepols, 2006), pp. 275-94.

Shahar, Shulamith., *Childhood in the Middle Ages* (London: Routledge, 1990).

Sharpe, Richard, 'Words and Music by Goscelin of Canterbury', *Early Music* 19 (1991), pp. 95-7.

Shultz, James, *The Knowledge of Childhood in the German Middle Ages, 1100-1350*, Middle Ages (Philadelphia: University Press, 1995).

Slocum, Kay, 'Goscelin of Saint Bertin and the Translation Ceremony of Saints Ethelburg, Hildelith, and Wulfhild', in *Barking Abbey and Medieval Literary Culture*, ed. Jennifer N. Brown, and Donna Bussell (Woodbridge: York Medieval Press, 2012), pp. 73-93.

Smalley, Beryl, *The Study of the Bible in the Middle Ages* (Notre Dame, IN: University Press, 1964); 3rd ed. Oxford, 1983.

Smith, Julia A., *Ordering Women's Lives: Penitentials and Nunnery Rules in the Early Medieval West* (Aldershot: Ashgate, 2001).

Smith, Mary F., Robin Fleming, and Patricia Halpin, 'Court and Piety in Late-Anglo-Saxon England', *The Catholic Historical Review* 87 (2001), pp. 569-602.

Soper, Harriet, 'Eald Aefenscop: Poetic Composition and the Authority of the Aged in Old English verse', *Questio Insularis: Selected Proceedings of the Cambridge Colloquium in Anglo-Saxon, Norse and Celtic* 17 (2016), pp. 74-101.

Southern, Richard W., *The Making of the Middle Ages* (New Haven: Yale University Press, 1953); repr. with revisions, London: Hutchinson, 1967.

Springer, Carl (ed.), *The Gospel as Epic in Late Antiquity: The Paschale Carmen of Sedulius*, Supplements to Vigiliae Christianae II (Leiden: Brill, 1988).

Stancliffe, Clare, 'Dating Wilfred's Death and Stephen's Life', in *Wilfrid: Abbot, Bishop, Saint. Papers from the 1300th Anniversary Conferences*, ed. N. J. Higham (Donington, Lincs: Shaun Tyas, 2013), pp. 17-26.

Standing, Kay, 'Writing the Voices of the Less Powerful: Research on Lone Mothers', in *Feminist Dilemmas in Qualitative Research: Public Knowledge and Private Lives*, ed. Jane Ribbens and Rosalind Edwards (London: SAGE, 1998), pp. 186-202.

Stephenson, Rebecca, 'Ælfric of Eynsham and Hermeneutic Latin: *Meatim Sed et Rustica* Reconsidered', *Journal of Medieval Latin* 16 (2006), pp. 111-41.

— *The Politics of Language: Byrhtferth, Ælfric, and the Multilingual Identity of the Benedictine Reform*, Toronto Anglo-Saxon series 18 (Toronto: University Press, 2015).

Stevenson, Jane, *Women Latin Poets: Language, Gender, and Authority from Antiquity to the Eighteenth Century* (Oxford: University Press, 2005).
Stock, Brian, *The Implications of Literacy: Written Language and Models of Interpretation in the Eleventh and Twelfth centuries* (Princeton, NJ: University Press, 1983).
Stroud, Daphne, 'Eve of Wilton and Goscelin of St Bertin at Old Sarum ca 1070-1080', *Wiltshire Archaeological and Natural History Magazine* 99 (2006), pp. 204-12.
Summit, Jennifer, 'Women and Authorship', in *The Cambridge Companion to Medieval Women's Writing*, ed. Carolyn Dinshaw and David Wallace, Cambridge Companions to Literature (Cambridge: University Press, 2003).
Swan, Mary, 'Imagining a Readership for Post-Conquest Old English Manuscripts', in *Imagining the Book*, ed. Susan Kelly and John J. Thomson, Medieval texts and cultures of Northern Europe 7 (Turnhout: Brepols, 2005), pp. 145-57.
Symons, Thomas, 'A Note on the Trina Oratio', *Dominican Review* 42 (1924), pp. 67-83.
— 'Sources of the Regularis Concordia', *Downside Review* 59 (1941), pp. 14-36, 143-70, and 264-89.
Tahkokallio, Jaakko, 'The Classicization of the Latin Curriculum and "The Renaissance of the Twelfth Century": A Quantitative Study of the Codicological Evidence', *Viator* 46 (2015), pp. 129-53.
Thomas, Hugh M., *The Norman Conquest: England after William the Conqueror*, Critical Issues in History (Lanham, Md: Rowman & Littlefield, 2008).
Thompson, Evan, *Mind in Life: Biology, Phenomenology, and the Sciences of the Mind* (Cambridge Mass: Harvard University Press, 2007).
Thompson, Sally, *Women Religious: The Founding of English Monasteries after the Norman Conquest* (Oxford: Clarendon Press, 1991).
Thomson, Rodney, 'Two Versions of a Saint's Life from St Edmund's Abbey: Changing Currents in Twelfth-Century Monastic Style', *Revue Bénédictine* 84 (1974), pp. 383-408.
— 'The Norman Conquest and English Libraries', in *The Role of the Book in Medieval Culture*, ed. Peter Ganz, Bibliologia 3 (Turnhout: Brepols, 1986), pp. 27-40.
— 'Books and Learning at Gloucester Abbey in the Twelfth and Thirteenth Centuries', in *Books and Collectors c.1200-1700: Essays Presented to Andrew Watson*, ed. James P. Carley and Colin G. C. Tite, British Library Studies in the History of the Book (London: British Library, 1997), pp. 3-26.
— 'Where were the Latin Classics in Twelfth-Century England?', *English Manuscript Studies 1100-1700*, 7 (1997), pp. 25-40.
— *Books and Learning in Twelfth Century England: The Ending of the "Alter Orbis": the Lyell lectures 2000-2001* (Walkern Herts: Red Gull Press, 2006).
Tilliette, Jean-Yves, 'Le Vocabulaire des Écoles Monastiques d'après les Prescriptions des Consuetudines (XI-XII siècles)', in *Le Vocabulaire des Écoles et des Méthodes d'Enseignement au Moyen Âge*, ed. Olga Weijers (Turnhout: Brepols, 1992), pp. 60-72.

Torrance Nancy and David Olson (eds.), *The Handbook of Education and Human Development: New Models of Learning, Teaching and Schooling* (Malden, Mass: Blackwell, 1998).

Valentine, Kylie, 'Investment, Risk, and Other Ways of Thinking about Children', in *Critical Childhood Studies and the Practice of Interdisciplinarity: Disciplining the Child*, ed. Faulkner J, and Żółkoś M, *Children and Youth in Popular Culture* (Lanham: Lexington Books, 2016), pp. 127-44.

Vanderputten, Steven, *Monastic Reform as Process: Realities and Representations in Medieval Flanders 900-1100* (Ithaca, NY: Cornell University Press, 2013).

van Houts, Elizabeth, *Memory and Gender in Medieval Europe 900-1200*, Explorations in Medieval Culture and Society (Basingstoke: Macmillan, 1999).

De Vogüé, Adalbert., *Les Règles Monastiques Anciennes (400-700)*, Typologie des Sources du Moyen Âge Occidental 46 (Turnhout : Brepols, 1985).

— 'Debate: the Master and St Benedict: A Reply to Marilyn Dunn', *English Historical Review* 107 (1992), pp. 95-111.

Webber, Teresa, 'Script and Manuscript Production at Christ Church, Canterbury, After the Norman Conquest', in *Canterbury and the Norman Conquest: Churches, Saints and Scholars, 1066-1109*, ed. Richard Eales and Richard Sharpe (London: Hambledon, 1995), pp. 145-58.

Weber, Max, and Shmuel Noah Eisenstadt (ed.), *Max Weber on Charisma and Institution Building: Selected Papers*, Heritage of Sociology (Chicago: University Press, 1968).

Whalen, Georges, 'Patronage Engendered: How Goscelin Allayed the Concerns of Nuns' Discriminatory Public', in *Women, the Book and the Godly: Selected Proceedings of the St Hilda's Conference*, ed. Lesley Smith and Jane H.M. Taylor (Cambridge: D.S. Brewer, 1995), pp. 123-35.

White, Caroline Lousia, *Ælfric: A New Study of his Life and Writings*, Yale studies in English 2 (Boston: Lamson, Wolffe & Co, 1898).

Whitelock, Dorothy, 'The Authorship of the Account of King Edgar's Establishment of Monasteries', in *Philological Essays: Studies in Old and Middle English Language and Literature in Honour of Herbert Dean Meritt*, ed. James L. Rosier, Ianua linguarum. Series Maior 37 (The Hague: Mouton, 1970), pp. 125-36.

Wieland, Gernot, *The Latin Glosses on Arator and Prudentius in Cambridge, University Library MS Gg.5.35*, Studies and Texts 61 (Toronto: Pontifical Institute of Medieval Studies, 1983).

— 'The Glossed Manuscript: Classbook or Library Book?', Anglo-Saxon England 14 (1985), pp. 153-73.

— 'The Anglo-Saxon Manuscripts of Prudentius' *Psychomachia*', *Anglo-Saxon England* 16 (1987), pp. 213-31.

Wilcox, Jonathan, 'An Embarrassment of Clues: Interpreting Anglo-Saxon Blushes', in *Anglo-Saxon Emotions: Reading the Heart in Old English Language, Literature and Culture*, ed. Alice Jorgensen, Frances McCormack, and Jonathan Wilcox, Studies in Early Medieval Britain and Ireland (Farnham: Ashgate, 2015), pp. 91-108.

Wilkins, David A, 'Grammatical, Situational and Notional Syllabuses', in *The Communicative Approach to Language Teaching*, ed. Christopher J. Brumfit and Keith Johnson (Oxford: University Press, 1979); rev. ed. Oxford, 1986.

Williams, Anne, *The English and the Norman Conquest* (Woodbridge: Boydell Press, 1995).

Willoughby, James, 'The Transmission and Circulation of Classical Literature', in *The Oxford History of Classical Reception in English Literature, 800-1558*, ed. Rita Copeland, Patrick Cheney, Philip Hardie, I (Oxford: University Press, 2012-16), 95-120. 5 vols.

Wogan-Browne, Jocelyn, 'Powers of Record, Powers of Example: Hagiography and Women's History', in *Gendering the Master Narrative: Women and Power in the Middle Ages*, ed. Mary C. Erler and Maryanne Kowaleski (Ithaca, NY: Cornell University Press, 2003), pp. 71-93.

Wood, Diana (ed.), *The Church and Childhood: Papers Read at the 1993 Summer Meeting and the 1994 Winter Meeting of the Ecclesiastical History Society*, Studies in Church History 31 (Oxford: Blackwell, 1994).

Wormald, Patrick, 'How Do We Know So Much about Anglo-Saxon Deerhurst?', in *The Times of Bede: Studies in Early English Christian Society and its Historian*, ed. Patrick Wormald and Stephen Baxter (Oxford: Blackwell, 2006), pp. 229-48.

Yardley, Anne, B, 'The Musical Education of Young Girls in Medieval English Nunneries', in *Young Choristers: 650-1700*, ed. Susan Boynton and Eric Rice, Studies in Medieval and Renaissance Music (Woodbridge: Boydell Press, 2008), pp. 49-67.

Yorke, Barbara (ed.), *Bishop Æthelwold: His Career and Influence* (Woodbridge: Boydell Press, 1988); repr. Woodbridge, 1997.

— *Nunneries and Anglo-Saxon Royal Houses*, Women, Power and Politics (London: Continuum, 2003).

Unpublished theses

Bender-Davis, Jeannine M., 'Ælfric's Techniques of Translation and Adaptation as Seen in the Composition of his Old English Latin Grammar', *Ph.D. Dissertation, Pennsylvania State University* (1985).

Cheatham, Karen., 'They Hasten toward Perfection: Virginal and Chaste Monks in the High Middle Ages', *Ph.D. Dissertation, University of Toronto* (2006).

Elliot, Michael., 'Canon Law Collections in England ca 600-1066: The Manuscript Evidence', *Ph.D Dissertation, University of Toronto* (2013).

Jayatilaka, Rohini, 'The Regula Sancti Benedicti in Late Anglo-Saxon England: the Manuscripts and their Readers', *D.Phil Dissertation, University of Oxford* (1996).

Laing, Gregory L., 'Bound by Words: The Motif of Oath-taking and Oath-Breaking in Medieval Iceland and Anglo-Saxon England', *Ph.D Dissertation, Western Michigan University* (2014).

Porck, Matthijs H., 'Growing Old Among the Anglo-Saxons: The Cultural Conceptualisation of Old Age in Early Medieval England', *Ph.D Dissertation, University of Leiden* (2016).

Stephenson, Rebecca L., 'Deliberate Obfuscation: The Purpose of Hard Words and Difficult Syntax in the Literature of Anglo-Saxon England', *Ph.D Dissertation, University of Notre Dame IN* (2004).

Web resources

Anglo-Saxon Penitentials: A Cultural Database: http://www.anglo-saxon.net/penance/TCTH8558_151b.html.

Bible [The Vulgate], Douay-Rheims Latin Vulgate: http://www.drbo.org/lvb.

BT: *Bosworth-Toller Anglo-Saxon Dictionary*: http://www.bosworthtoller.com/. Last updated c. 2013.

DML: *Dictionary of Medieval Latin from British Sources Online*: http://clt.brepolis.net/dmlbs/Default.aspx.

DOE: *Dictionary of Old English: A to H online*, eds., Angus Cameron, Ashley Crandel Amos, Antonette diPaolo Healy et al (Toronto, 2016): http://tapor.library.utoronto.ca/doe/.

DOEWC: *Dictionary of Old English Web Corpus*, eds., Antonette diPaolo Healey with John Price Wilkin and Xin Xiang (Toronto, 2009): http://tapor.library.utoronto.ca/doecorpus/.

Domesday Book Online Database: http://opendomesday.org/.

MGH: *Monumenta Germaniae Historica*: http://www.dmgh.de/.

ODNB: *Oxford Dictionary of National Biography:* http://www.oxforddnb.com/view/article/2082.

INDEX

Æ

Ælfric of Eynsham 27, 30, 38, 54, 56, 58-65, 68, 82, 106, 117-118, 125-126, 142-143, 151-166, 170-171, 175-176, 181, 188-197, 202, 230, 238, 245
  Colloquium 59, 60-63, 67-68, 117-118, 166, 193
  Epistula ad Monachos 30, 54, 58, 125-126, 142, 151, 202
  Excerptiones de Arte Grammatica Anglice 64-65, 153-166, 170-171, 175-178, 188-190
  Ideals of purity 161, 245
  Doctrinal learning 159, 166, 181
  Paradigmatic models 159, 163, 164, 165, 177, 188, 189
  Removal of classical text 161-162, 181
Ælfthryth, Queen of England 114
Æthelhelm of Jumieges 32
Æthelstan, King of England 14, 66fn
Æthelwold of Winchester 14, 25-30, 35, 44-49, 51, 54-59, 63-64, 78, 108, 112-125, 132, 135, 138-142, 150, 154, 157, 191-200, 214, 239, 243-244
  Old English Rule 25, 27, 28, 35, 44, 46, 47, 48, 49, 63, 68, 96, 110, 139, 150, 183, 193, 196, 236, 237, 239, 242
  Regularis Concordia 28-35, 48-63, 68, 71-83, 97-103, 113-151, 159, 173, 183, 191, 195-202, 211, 221, 235, 237, 239, 243-245, 251-253

A

Abbey of Abingdon 14, 15, 32, 70, 173, 208
Abbey of Barking 12, 33, 94, 102, 143, 183, 220, 222-225, 242, 247
Abbey of Benet St. Holme 33, 117fn
Abbey of Bury St. Edmunds 32-34, 117
Abbey of Cluny 29, 42
Abbey of Glastonbury 3, 14, 152, 198
Abbey of Horton 223
Abbey of Hyde 206, 207
Abbey of Nunnaminster 109-110, 183, 224, 240
Abbey of Peterborough 3, 32, 70, 180, 201, 202, 212
Abbey of Ramsey 198-201, 203
Abbey of Saint Bertin 40, 87, 143
Abbey of Thorney 214
Abbey of Wilton 92-95, 100-101, 104, 106, 108, 144, 182-187, 190, 218-219, 221-225, 230, 232-233, 240, 247-249, 251
Abbo of Saint Germain-des-Prés
  Descidia Parisiacae Polis 199, 202, 214
Acolytes 202
Adelidis of Barking 222
Admonitio Generalis 10
Adolescence
  lifecycle 45
  male 192-217
  female 217-225
Aelred of Rievalx 103, 106-108
Age of Understanding (*Tempus Intelligibilis*) 11, 194, 205
Aldhelm of Sherborne 222, 230-231, 250
  Prosa (and *Carmen*) *de Virginitate*

199, 222, 223, 230-231
Aldwin, Abbot of Ramsey 33
Alfwyn of New Minster 32
Alstrita, Abbess of Wherwell 33
Anselm, Archbishop of Canterbury
  89-91, 204
Ariès, Philippe 4-6, 11
Aristotle
  Topics and Categories 215
Ars Minor and *Ars Major*, Donatus 153,
  155, 178

B
Baldwin, Abbot of Bury St. Edmunds,
  King's Physician 33
Barking (See Abbey of)
Basset, Gilbert and Robert 208
Bata, Ælfric 38, 50, 61-65, 68, 108,
  118, 171, 194, 200, 238, 239
  Colloquia 34-36, 56-61, 95, 104, 106,
  110-112, 153, 157-158, 180, 230-233
Battle of Hastings 32, 204
Behaton 26
Benet St. Holme (See Abbey of)
Bender-Davis, Jeanine 157, 159, 245
Beorhtric, Abbot of Burton 33
Berend, Nora 15
Berlière, Dom Ursmer 6
Biblical Exegesis 166, 169, 215, 245
Birth 2, 43, 47fn, 69, 92fn, 92, 110
Boethius
  De Consolatione Philosophiae 223
Boswell, John 6, 11
Boyhood (*Pueritia*) 49-67, 71-90, 113-
  126, 127-137, 150-18
  Lifecycle 45
Brand of Peterborough 32
Burnbaum Tahlia 153-154
Bury St. Edmunds (See Abbey of)
Byrhtferth of Ramsey 124, 153, 198-200,
  202
  Enchiridion 153, 199, 200
  Historia Regum 200

Lives of Saints Oswald and Ecgwine
  200
Bullying 172

C
Campbell, Alistair 199
Canons of Archbishop Theodore of
  Tarsus 43
Careers 22, 33, 72, 192, 202, 213, 217,
  224, 225, 247-249
Carolingian (Empire) 9-10, 13-14, 28,
  155, 159, 194, 203, 248
Cell 95, 100
Charles the Great (Charlemagne)10
Child Voice2, 23-24, 64, 104, 118, 120,
  154, 193, 205, 226, 228, 232, 233,
  243, 249, 250
Chronicon Monasterii de Abingdon 208
Cicero
  Orationes 214
Cild 47, 96, 98-99, 139-141, 154, 188,
  190, 195-197, 242
Cnapa 195, 196, 192, 221
Cnut, King of England, Norway &
  Denmark 117
Coenwald of Worcester 14
Collectio Capitularis 10
Collectio Wigorniensis 43
Confirmation Ritual 11, 104, 186, 192,
  194, 204, 205, 219, 220, 226, 248
Confraternity 34
Constitutiones (See Lanfranc)
Corporal Punishment
  Bundle of fine rods 85
  Expulsion 86
  Flog / Flail 51, 63, 64, 84, 159
  Stout rods 85
Council of Aachen 10, 194, 203
Cowl 87
Crawford, Sally 8

D
Death 210, 222, 226-227, 229, 231

INDEX

De Jong, Mayke 9-11, 18
DeMause, Lloyd 4-5
Deodatus 268
Deroux, M.P. 6
Disciplinary groups (*Ordo seniorum/ Servientum/Infantum*) 83
Disticha Catonis 199
Doran, John 15
Dramatic Liturgy 21, 32, 119-122, 135-136, 140-141, 145-147, 237, 243, 244, 251, 253
Dumitrescu, Irina 64, 66
Dunstan, Archbishop of Canterbury 14, 25, 87-88, 152, 157, 217, 221, 252

E

Eadgyth, Queen of England 182
Eadgyth of Wilton 92-95, 100-101, 106, 108, 144-145, 182, 184-186, 221, 224-225, 232-235, 240, 249, 250-251
Eadmer of Canterbury 3, 43, 87-91, 203-204, 213, 217, 221-222
Eafe of Wilton 103-104, 185-187, 218-224, 247-249
Early Adulthood (Iuvenis) 8, 45-46, 196, 201, 215, 223-224, 233, 247-24-9
Eadgar, King of England 29, 114, 157, 184, 185, 224
Eadward, King of England 225
Eadward of Ramsey 33
Eadward The Elder, King of England 183
Elevation to Holy Orders 203, 216-217, 249
Emotion 4, 121, 166-169, 192
Excerptiones de Prisciano 155-157, 160-162, 181, 243
Expositio in Regulam (See Smaragdus)

F

Fæstnung 26
Faricius of Malmesbury 173-174
Fortunatus, Venantius 231, 280

French (language) 176, 177, 181, 246

G

Gallican Psalter 152, 167
Gefæstnian 26-27
Geoffrey of St. Evroult 33
Geoffrian 26
Gestural learning 54-56, 60, 62, 76, 78, 85, 99, 103-104, 133, 159
Gewrit / Petitio 26-27, 38, 204, 205, 208
Gilbertine Priory of Watton 103, 106, 108
Girlhood 96-110, 140-147, 183-191
Glastonbury (See Abbey of)
Goscelin of Saint Bertin 40, 87-88, 92-96, 100-108, 143-147, 182-187, 217-225, 230, 232, 242, 247-249
Greek 9, 43, 156, 158, 174, 200
Greene, Sheila 16
Gwara, Scott 37, 38

H

Habit 69, 108, 205, 208, 218-219
Harbus, Antonia 167
Hebraic Boys of Jerusalem 120, 132, 140, 141, 174, 243
Henry VIII, King of England 13
Herbert of Losinga 33, 34, 180-182, 187, 215-216, 227, 246-247
Herlihy, David 5
Hermeneutic Latin 200, 201, 214
Hill, Joyce 31, 40, 52, 145, 146
Holy Innocents 120
Horace
   Epistolae 214, 223
Horton (See Abbey of)
Hyde (See Abbey of)
Hugh Candidus of Peterborough 3, 70

I

Idealtyp 11
Identity 6, 8, 21-22, 30, 40, 49, 51-52, 54, 104, 110, 115, 120, 121-123, 129,

138, 140-143, 161, 170, 172, 176, 183-184, 190, 193, 200-202, 212, 221, 227, 230, 240, 244-246, 249, 251
   Corporate 51, 129, 138, 212
   Individual 122, 125, 136, 138, 142, 145, 194, 234, 238, 251
Illiteracy 36, 149, 171, 172
Infancy (*Infantia*) 43-48, 68-70, 91-95, 112, 123, 138-139, 182
   Lifecycle 45
Ingulf, Abbot of Crowland 33
Intercession 88-89, 111, 114, 138, 159, 165, 205, 229, 234, 241, 245
Irvine, Susan 8
Isidore of Seville
   Etymologiae 180-1, 215-216, 227, 246

J
James, Allison 7
Jayatilaka, Rohini 96
John Sutlciff, Abbot of Hyde 208
Jones, Christopher 202

K
Knowles, David 15, 75

L
Lambeth Psalter 167, 169
Lamps 74, 136, 244
Lanfranc, Archbishop of Canterbury
   Constitutiones 34-36, 68-86, 102-103, 127-138, 173, 203, 209-211, 226-227, 240-243, 246, 248
Lapidge, Michael 37, 148-149
Layahe-Geusen, Maria 11-12, 18, 24, 210
Law, Vivien 155, 157
Leofric of Peterborough 32
Liber Confortatorius 103-104, 143, 185-186-187, 220, 222, 247-248
Liber Eliensis (See Richard of Ely)
Liber Vitae 206, 208
Libraries 22, 35, 97, 175, 178, 201, 214, 215, 250
Liturgy
   Difference between genders 21, 145-147
   Feminine adaptation 31, 97, 99, 108, 145-146, 156, 164, 188, 198, 235, 251
   Selectivity 122, 125, 137, 141, 181, 247, 151
   Tenebrae 121, 123, 125, 134-136, 141, 195, 197, 221, 243, 244
   Transitions into adulthood 197-198, 210, 248
   Trina Oratio 48, 113-119, 128-129, 140, 151, 243
   Quem Queritis 122, 123, 243
Lockett, Leslie 159-160
Louis The Pious, Emperor 10
Logeman, Henry 47
Lucan
   De Bello Civili 213
Lynch, Joseph 6

M
Magistra 102-104, 107, 183fn, 183-184, 242, 249
Mason, Emma 34
Mathilde of Ste Trinité, Caen 222, 227
Medicine 213
Miller, Maureen 21, 244
Misbehaviours (examples of) 11, 40, 61, 62, 78, 82, 84, 85, 86, 87, 90, 104, 109
Mistakes (examples of) 46, 62, 97, 112, 116, 150
Mixtum 75
Monasteriales Indicia 56
Monastic Offices 3, 18, 74, 112, 116-119, 124, 128, 129, 131, 138 140, 216, 243

N
Nicholaus (oblate) of Abingdon 70
Norman Conquest 3, 23, 31, 40, 68, 88,

INDEX

102, 149, 154, 178, 180, 185, 195, 203, 206, 207, 212, 213, 214, 225, 237, 241, 246, 248, 250
Norman of Abingdon (knight) 208
Nunnaminster Abbey (See Abbey of)

O

Oblation Ritual 5-6, 9-11, 26, 28, 35, 44, 94
Oda, Archbishop of Canterbury 14
O'Keeffe, Katherine O'Brien 193, 219
Old English Hexateuch 197
O'Neill, Patrick 167
Orme, Nicholas 8
Osbern of Canterbury 87-88, 204, 214
Osbert of Westminster 109-110, 214, 222
Oswald, Archbishop of York 124, 203, 213
Oswald (oblate) of Bury St. Edmunds
Ovid
  Metamorphosis 181, 231

P

Patrick, Bishop of Dublin 214
Penda, King of Mercia 157
Penitential Psalms (Seven) 114, 116, 128
Peterborough (See Abbey of)
Playtime 50-51
Pollock, Linda 5
Porter, David 37, 157, 245
Priest 11, 21, 179, 202, 217, 235, 252, 253
Procession 56, 77, 99, 120, 131-134, 158, 237
Prout, Alan 7
Prudentius
Psychomachia & Cathemerinon 137, 186

Q

Quinn, Patricia 18

R

Radbod of Rheims, 102fn, 184, 185
Ramsey (See Abbey of)
Regula Sancti Benedicti 9-10, 14, 19, 25-28, 44-46, 48, 62, 68, 70, 81, 96-97, 107-108, 111, 117, 139, 159, 183, 204-205, 235, 241, 242, 245, 251
Richard of Ely 70, 86
  Liber Eliensis 56, 208
Ristuccia, Nathan 25, 62-63
Roman Psalter 152
Routines 3, 20, 24, 42, 44, 48-52, 55, 60-61, 71, 84, 95-97, 99, 112, 125, 127, 136, 145 195, 208-209, 211, 217, 220, 239, 248
Rudolf, Winfried 8

S

Sacral Monarchy 114-115
Safeguarding 12, 58, 74, 78-79, 185, 210
Saint Basil
  Ἀσκητικῶν (Asketikon) 9
Saint Eadburh 109-110, 183, 240
Saint Ecgwine 200
Saint Eormenhild 87-89
Saint Wulfhild 92, 143
Sallust
  Invectiva 214
Samson of Worcester
  Pontifical 204
Schola 50, 56, 57-61, 73, 78, 80-81, 96, 103, 119, 126, 151, 154, 155, 173, 183, 195, 209, 242
Secord-Davis, Jonathan 200
Sedulius
  Carmen Paschale 214-215, 221
Seneca 222
Signa (soundscapes)
  of Canterbury 73-74
  of Winchester 51-54
Standardisation of Old English 13, 154
Stephenson, Rebecca 200-201
Sub-deacon 202, 216

Symons, Thomas 29, 51-52

T
Thorney (See Abbey of)
Tibullus, Albius
   Panegyricus Messallae 231, 250
Tonsure 69, 211
Trina Oratio (See Liturgy)

U
Ulfcytel, Abbot of Crowland 33
Urbanisation 13-14

V
Veil 93, 219
Virgil
   Ecloga, Aeneid, Georgica 174, 222-223
Vita Beate Sexburge Regine 104-105
Vitalis, Orderic 1-4, 11, 31, 179, 216-217, 234, 236, 246, 249-250
Vita Sancti Felicis 201
Vita Regis Edwardi 182
Vita Sancte Ædburge Virginis 109
Vita Sancte Edithe Virginis 92, 94, 100, 106, 108, 144, 147, 184, 221, 224, 232, 242, 245, 247
Vita Sancte Wihtburge 182
Vita Sancti Dunstani 217, 221
Vita Sancti Oswaldi 203, 213
Vows 27fn, 219, 230

W
Waltheof, Abbot of Crowland 33
Watton Priory (See Gilbertine)
Weaned 69, 92, 95, 174fn, 183fn, 240
William of Malmesbury 35, 180, 183, 212-213
Wilton (See Abbey of)
Winchester Troper 120
Witnian 63
Women's choir space 143
Wulfric (oblate) of Bury St. Edmunds 27

Wulfric of New Minster 32
Wulfstan, Archbishop of York 43
Wulfstan, Bishop of Worcester 33, 35, 43, 180, 204, 212
Wulfstan, Cantor of Winchester 120, 152, 198
Wulfthryth, Abbess of Wilton 95, 101, 185, 225
Wulfruna, *Magistra* of Barking 102

Steven George Hodgson holds a doctorate specialising in Early Medieval History from the University of Oxford.

www.ingramcontent.com/pod-product-compliance
Lightning Source LLC
Chambersburg PA
CBHW030544080526
44585CB00012B/257